Home Truths

Fictions of the South Asian Diaspora in Britain

W0007718

Home Truths

Fictions of the South Asian Diaspora in Britain

Susheila Nasta

palgrave

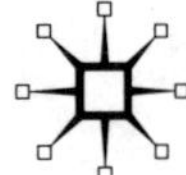

© Susheila Nasta 2002

All rights reserved. No reproduction, copy or transmission of this publication may be made without written permission.

No paragraph of this publication may be reproduced, copied or transmitted save with written permission or in accordance with the provisions of the Copyright, Designs and Patents Act 1988, or under the terms of any licence permitting limited copying issued by the Copyright Licensing Agency, 90 Tottenham Court Road, London W1T 4LP.

Any person who does any unauthorised act in relation to this publication may be liable to criminal prosecution and civil claims for damages.

The author has asserted her right to be identified as the author of this work in accordance with the Copyright, Designs and Patents Act 1988.

First published 2002 by
PALGRAVE
Houndmills, Basingstoke, Hampshire RG21 6XS and
175 Fifth Avenue, New York, N.Y. 10010
Companies and representatives throughout the world

PALGRAVE is the new global academic imprint of
St. Martin's Pres LLC Scholarly and Reference Division and
Palgrave Publishers Ltd (formerly Macmillan Press Ltd).

ISBN 0–333–67005–1 hardback
ISBN 0–333–67006-X paperback

This book is printed on paper suitable for recycling and made from fully managed and sustained forest sources.

A catalogue record for this book is available from the British Library.

Library of Congress Cataloging-in-Publication Data

Nasta, Susheila.
Home truths: fictions of the South Asian diaspora in Britain/by Susheila Nasta.
p. cm.
Includes bibliographical references and index.
ISBN 0-333-67005-1
1. Great Britain—Social life and customs—20th century—Fiction. 2. South Asians—Great Britain—Fiction. I. Title.

PR6114.A88 H66 2001
823¢.910895—dc21 2001133053

10 9 8 7 6 5 4 3 2 1
11 10 09 08 07 06 05 03 02 01

Printed in China

To

a chance meeting between Kanayalal Kalumal Nasta
and Winifred Milnthorpe on Lake Balaton in 1936

and to

Maya and Alexander
my branch of the large tribe that followed

Contents

Illustrations

The two illustrations of Sake Dean Mahomet as Brighton 'Shampooing Surgeon' come from the *Images of Brighton Collection*, in Brighton Local Studies Library. Mahomet's first book was published in Cork in 1794 and entitled *The Travels of Dean Mahomet*. In his second, *Shampooing*, he uses the name S. D. Mahomed. This was also the name of his famous baths in Brighton, which were known as 'Mahomed's Baths'. See bibliography.

Acknowledgements

This book results not only from my individual research and the experience of teaching postcolonial literatures at University level for a number of years, but also from interviews with a number of writers, pedagogical debates in postgraduate seminars and, most important, the encouragement, support and advice of a number of colleagues and friends. It began life as a postgraduate course taught at Queen Mary & Westfield College as part of the Literature, Culture and Modernity MA. I am grateful to have been given the opportunity to develop some of those early ideas by speaking at a number of international conferences. My thanks for this go to the University of Sri Lanka in Colombo and the ATCLALS conference, the MLA conference in Toronto in 1997, the University of Mumbai, where I taught for three weeks, the British Council who invited me to Mauritius in 1998 and Spain in 2000, the Museum of London and the Voice Box, Festival Hall, London, as well as the Inter-University Postcolonial Studies Seminar organized jointly by the Institute of English Studies, University of London and the Open University.

The research for this book has been supported by a number of institutions. I am grateful for a study leave awarded me by the School of English, Queen Mary & Westfield College, University of London, as well as a grant from the British Academy Arts and Humanities Research Board from 1997–8. The project, however, was only able to reach final completion by some more sustained writing time which has generously been provided by the Literature Department of the Open University where I was appointed as a Research Lecturer in 1999. As a member of that department I have not only benefited by gaining the mental space to actually finish the book, but I have also been stimulated by a number of colleagues, particularly Robert Fraser (who put me on to the 1942 BBC Eastern Service Photo and has always listened), Dennis Walder, and Richard Allen.

Many colleagues past and present have offered their friendship and support. Lyn Innes, my onetime supervisor and academic mother, has never failed to be on the end of a phone for advice and moral support at critical moments. Alastair Niven, along with Louis James, has always advised and encouraged. Jacqueline Rose has read early versions of chapters and has given me confidence in times of self-doubt. My thanks also go to Bryan Cheyette and Romesh Gunesekera for an exchange of views which took place in numerous telephone conversations at crucial points in the writing process. I am indebted to Bart Moore-Gilbert for bibliographical material on Hanif Kureishi, to Shirley Chew for her generosity with her time and meticulous critical reading in the final stages, to Homi Bhabha for our discussions on *Nightwaves* and to Rozina Visram for her knowledge of the history of Asians in Britain, her photographs, as well as her friendship as another lonely writer in Greenwich.

Three people in particular, however, have been especially helpful in seeing this manuscript through to publication. I am grateful to them not only for their loyalty and encouragement, but also for their meticulous help with all stages of the book. Elizabeth Maslen and Aamer Hussein have read and commented on all the chapters, continuing the conversations we used to have as colleagues teaching the 'new' and 'postcolonial' literatures on Mondays at *QMW*, and Glenda Pattenden (who works with me on *Wasafiri*, the journal I edit), has patiently copy-edited much of the text wiping out my many computer errors. In fact, all of the staff at *Wasafiri* have been magnificent in allowing me the time to complete: Richard Dyer in relieving me of many of my editorial duties; Hayley Daniels; and Paola Marchionni, once one of my MA students, who has read large sections of the manuscript.

Sections of Chapters 2 and 6 of this book incorporate material revised from previously published pieces: 'Setting Up Home in a City of Words: Sam Selvon's London Novels', in *Other Britains: Essays in Contemporary Fiction*, ed. R. Lee (London: Pluto, 1995), pp. 48–69; reprinted by permission of Pluto Press, Ltd; and 'Homes Without Walls': South Asian Writing in Britain', in *Shifting Continents: Colliding Cultures*, ed. R. Crane and Radikha Mohanran (Amsterdam: Rodopi, 2000), pp. 83–103.

Permission to reproduce illustrations of Sake Dean Mahomet have been provided by the Brighton Local Studies Library and the BBC Picture Archive Library has given me the copyright permission to reproduce the photograph from the 1942 Eastern Service Radio Programme, *Voice*.

This book is dedicated to the meeting of my father and mother on Lake Balaton, Hungary, in 1936, a meeting which began many other diasporic stories. However, its completion was inspired by the love and support of my immediate family, who have allowed me the time and energy to trace my own relationship to my past both through my academic life and through several trips to India. My deepest thanks therefore go to Conrad, my husband, who has long suffered the trials and tribulations of living with this book day and night, Susanna, and my two youngest children, Maya and Alexander. Without the constant plea, 'When will you finish your book and be able to read Harry Potter, Mummy?', as well as numerous cards and words of encouragement, the project would never have left the house.

Preface

This book began its academic life as an MA course which I taught at Queen Mary and Westfield College, University of London. However, like most books, it has its personal roots elsewhere and ghosts another story between its lines. As a child of mixed race growing up in Britain in the late 1960s, I inevitably came into contact in the provincial town in Suffolk, where I was then living with a series of both racist and parochial attitudes regarding my half Indian-half English identity. Not of course being conscious at the time of much more than their absurdity and their irrelevance to the realities of my past, I nevertheless had to live their effects through the patronizing voices of some teachers at school and some of the parents of my friends. I began to find ways of disguising or highlighting the true source of my background. Should I be English? Indian? Pakistani? Southern European? Latin American? The busman's daughter or an oriental princess? Later, as an undergraduate at University, the questions came back again from those keen, because of my gender, to orientalize my exotic past, this time lusting after a received version of the spirituality of the mysterious East.

However, it was in studying what in those days was regionally defined as 'African, Caribbean or Asian' literature that I first began to identify with literary representations of displacement and diaspora – not so much for their therapeutic value – but for the aesthetic valorization of the inscription of realities other than those familiar to a Western worldview. For in my childhood I had travelled widely. Not only had I spent several years of my childhood in Delhi, but I had also lived in Europe, encountering different languages in different countries. When I first attended secondary school in England, I was shocked by the narrow parochialism that constantly reduced my father to the status of an 'immigrant'. We, his children, with our mixed background and largely Western education, could 'pass', as they say, though it was easier for some of us than others. Like many educated Indians of his generation, my father had become familiar with Britain in the 1930s when, as a university student, he lived in London for several years. Later, as an Indian civil servant, he had moved between the two countries and elsewhere. My father's rich history, which involved living through

Partition, moving from Karachi to Bombay, marrying an English woman, having a family together in India, slowly began to be swallowed up by the racist climate he encountered in Britain in the 1960s. Yet his past, like many of the writers I have selected for discussion in this book, extended well beyond the confines of a reductive nationalism, whether of East or West. And whilst, like many others of his generation, he felt passionate about the injustices suffered by his family during Partition, he did not condemn individuals on the basis either of their skin colour or their prejudices.

He was not a literary man, but one of his closest friends, Sankaran Menon Marath, author of three novels set in Kerala, was. They shared accommodation in the early days as students in London and later, when my father worked at India House as a government official, he crossed paths with many figures present in this book, including Krishna Menon, one of the founding editors of Pelican Books, and Sam Selvon, who worked for a time in my father's office as a clerk to support his writing. My father was never aware at the time either of these connections or of the significances they were later to present to me, his youngest daughter.

This book, which derives from an academic career teaching postcolonial literatures to several generations of students in a variety of British universities, seeks in a small way to return to my personal history. It also intends to open up for future generations of readers some of the *home truths* which I myself have imbibed from my readings of these literatures over the past 20 years.

S.N.

Prologue: Some Home Truths?

Home always means England; nobody calls India home
'Letters from Madras 1836–1839'[1]

It is . . . truly when he looks into the eyes of Asia that the Englishman comes face to face with those who would dispute with him the possession of his native land
Enoch Powell[2]

These are strange people, he [Tariq] thought
an Empire, and all this washing,
the underwear, the Englishman's garden
Moniza Alvi[3]

Home, it has been said, is not necessarily where one *belongs* but the place where one *starts* from. As a way therefore of opening this book on the fictions of the South Asian diaspora in Britain, I should outline some questions which have provided the background to its inception. A great deal of critical attention has recently been given to the theoretical remapping of literature and the consequent questioning of the traditional English canon. Cultural and literary theorists have frequently raised the question of how cultures and literary representations of those cultures are to be located in an inherently fluid and transnational global world. Moreover, in the now established field of postcolonial literary studies, the question of 'home' has increasingly come to be a vexed terrain. This is not surprising. For the notion of 'home', with all the political, ideological and symbolic baggage that it still implies, was one which formed an integral part of the naturalized rhetoric of Britain as Empire and has lingered on in the nationalistic grammar of Britain as post-imperial nation.

The seductive power of 'home', both as a force for authority *over* and as a continuing domestic metaphor for maintaining a means of authority *within*, figures most forcefully perhaps in the widely held image of England as colonial 'motherland', an illusory haven which both beckoned and betrayed many of Britain's imperial subjects before and after Independence. The maternal embrace promised by that image was never, of course, forthcoming. Moreover, the challenge of living out the intimacies of a relationship once established, so to speak, at a safe distance in the *Little Englands* set up in the colonies became far less comfortable when it was replayed on home ground. For Britain's contemporary black and Asian diasporic populations, a diverse population that has emerged out of an imperial history dating back at least as far as the early trading activities of the East India company in the early seventeenth century has frequently been seen as the repressed and dark side of the nation's unconscious, an eruption figured through successive waves of 'coloured' immigrant invasions. Moreover, the more visible presence of a substantial black and Asian population in Britain during the years following the Second World War has not only challenged embedded conceptions of 'Englishness', an imagined homeland built on ideas of purity, rootedness and cultural dominance, but also brought into closer view some of the less palatable realities underlying the ancient myth of England as a green and pleasant land.

It is now well known that Britain has had a black and Asian population for well over 400 years, at least as long, that is, as the history of the Empire abroad. It is thus worth noting that Britain was as much the *home* of the colonial encounter as were the colonies themselves, normally situated *abroad* in the so-called peripheries. Hence, as many historians such as Antoinette Burton, Peter Fryer, and Rozina Visram have persuasively argued, the arrival in Britain of several generations of black and Asian 'immigrants' in the period following decolonization and Independence was not simply the residue of the end of Empire, it was the culmination of a long but often hidden relationship, a relationship that has persistently been written out of the nation's political, cultural and literary histories.[4]

It is not the place here to debate why this has been the case. Nor am I attempting to propose a study concerned solely with an act of resistance mediated as cultural reclamation. Many cultural critics and postcolonial scholars have already exposed the extent to which the myth of a homogenous and white British nation, an 'imagined community', was part not only of the agenda of Empire, but of an insular Eurocentric modernity which has consistently failed to acknowledge the true colours of its immigrant past. For although heterogeneity has always been the norm, an indisputable part of the crucible of cultural and racial 'mixtures' that has historically constructed British life, the nationalist myth of purity has nevertheless long endured. As Matthew Arnold, a liberal Victorian poet and critic, tells us in his influential nineteenth-century work, *Culture and Anarchy* (1869), home suggests order, cohesion, the stability of culture, whereas a state of 'homelessness' is its inevitable opposite, a negative and disenfranchised space where anarchy will persist and disrupt the security of tradition and State. And if we follow the questionable logic of this kind of position which continues well into the twentieth century, Britain will inevitably become a polarized cultural territory, an embattled space where difference signified by race, colour or ethnicity is forced into makeshift 'ghettos' on the edges of the nation. Moreover, the 'homes' of those living in such spaces necessarily become temporal and temporary in the xenophobic imaginary of the white population, no-go areas on derelict estates, which contrast with the supposedly 'fixed' landscapes of Anglo-English settlement in the suburban Home Counties. As Caryl Phillips notes in *Extravagant Strangers: A Literature of Belonging* (1997), 'the once great colonial power that is Britain has always sought to define her people, and by extension the nation itself, by identifying those who don't belong'.[5] Thus, he argues, many black or Asian immigrants and their descendants in the postwar period who did not conform to the predominant image of white cultural acceptability felt they had no 'place' or 'space' to express their relationship to the dominant narratives of British life. Metaphors and images suggestive of these kinds of divisions abound whether in the rhetoric of politicians or in the language of cultural critics whatever their political leanings. For although the literary representations of Britain's contemporary diasporic populations attest in one sense to the rich cultural cartography of Britain's recent imperial past, at the same time, they also threaten. For in a post-imperial nation that, by the end of the twentieth century, was fast losing its grip on any sense of a coherent national identity, the presence of these *others within* exposed the underside not only of the faltering myth of Empire and its waning fantasy of an invented 'Englishness', but also complicated the apparently seamless history of Western modernity itself.[6]

There is little point in elaborating at this stage on the numerous debates that have been going on in the fields of cultural studies and postcolonial theory regarding questions of national and cultural identity.[7] However, if we view the presence of Britain's black and Asian communities as organic to, rather than separate from, the body of the nation, as part of the architecture of what is after all an 'invented tradition', the fixity of such boundaries necessarily comes under scrutiny. For the walls of Britain as 'island nation' have consistently been eroded and reconfigured by the uncovering of a more permeable and diasporic geography, a geography which both contradicts and complicates the comfortable nationalist binaries of home and abroad, and provides an alternative reading of the ways in which the bases of modernity have most frequently been conceptualized. Moreover, the *voyages in* of Britain's postcolonial subjects during the period following the Second World War have consistently drawn the attention of cultural critics to the liberatory, transgressive and shape-shifting elements of being 'unhoused', redefining the terms and opening up the reductive prescriptions of essentialist ideologies, whatever their racial or cultural derivations. As a result, the narrow agenda of Britain's domestic policy of cultural containment has been progressively deconstructed. As Edward Said suggests in his wide-ranging study, *Culture and Imperialism*, there was a shift during this period from the 'settled' or 'established' elements of culture

> to its . . . decentred and exilic energies, energies whose incarnation today is the migrant, and whose consciousness is that of the artist and intellectual figure in exile, the political figure between domains, between forms, between homes and between languages.[8]

Of course, Said is speaking here primarily of intellectual movements, of a liberation enjoyed by a select few, a largely elite im/migrant intelligentsia. And he is rightly keen to make the disclaimer that he is not referring to the violent mutilations, the refugeed casualties of twentieth-century migrations who have suffered enforced histories of exile and dislocation.

My concern in this study is likewise with artists and intellectuals, writers of South Asian origin and their descendants who, for the most part, migrated to Britain from the Asian subcontinent and the Caribbean in the latter part of the twentieth century. However, the predominant focus in contemporary postcolonial criticism on the celebratory elements of exile and displacement, the *heroic* potential of migrancy as a metaphor for a 'new' form of aesthetic freedom, does have a number of significant limitations which often dehistoricize and elide important questions of class, gender and cultural difference. It has become increasingly apparent that such issues need to be addressed within specific contexts and in relation to particular histories of migration and/or settlement, in order to chart the complex realities underlying individual historical moments, a process that should not be dismissed when examining the difficulties of survival which many writers have endured over time.

I do not wish to add my voice to the cacophony of criticism surrounding the politics of postcolonial literary studies and its discontents.[9] My argument in this study has in many ways benefited directly from the interventions that many contemporary theorists have made in shifting the 'margins' to the supposed 'centre' and reconfiguring the polarized politics of ethnicity and cultural identity in Britain. Yet as a teacher of postcolonial literatures situated within the academy, but also as the founding editor of *Wasafiri*, a British literary journal which has given space to the voices of African, Caribbean and Asian writers, many of whom have traditionally remained 'unhoused', I have been disturbed by the ways in which the institutional acceptance of the radical politics of postmodernist and postcolonial theory has tended to inadvertently restage some of the very political and cultural inequalities it claims to be addressing. This is not to set up or repeat what is clearly an unworkable opposition between those writers who are 'in' and those who are 'out', the 'mainstream' or the 'ghetto', the complicit or the resistant, but to examine some unresolved questions still evident within the walls of the critical discourses by which many of these writers have been, and still continue to be, framed.

The title of this book may at first glance be misleading. The voicing of *home truths* initially suggests an oppositional process, a means of writing a counter-narrative to the dominant or a process of cultural retrieval, or reclamation. Yet often, home truths are also those 'truths' which are the most painful to accept because they come from within, from a knowledge gained by a great degree of intimacy, not necessarily as stranger but as friend. In addition, they are frequently seen to be articulated from a perspective which makes alien that which was once acceptable, that refurnishes and reconfigures the rooms, so to speak, of the master's house and enacts a symbolic territorialization that is a way of moving forward rather than looking back. My aim here is not simply one of making visible 'what has been rendered absent' (Kobena Mercer's phrase), though that is without doubt a necessary task. Nor am I attempting to replace one 'tradition' with another by the substitution of an alternative form of cultural omnipotence or authority which makes the negative of the frame positive, and replaces an 'anxiety of influence' with a 'politics of narcissism'.[10] Instead, it is my aim to situate the fictions of the South Asian diaspora in Britain as a series of cross-cultural literary interventions which both exist within and outside the borders of a colonial and postcolonial genealogy, forming alliances and interconnections which complicate and reconfigure the critical geographies by which they have most commonly been defined and which exist in excess of such affiliations. In so doing, the specific diasporic histories and backgrounds of individual writers selected for discussion will be viewed from within the particular contexts and diverse cultural histories from which they have emerged.

My focus on the fictions of one supposed 'group', writers of the South Asian diaspora in Britain, has been motivated by a number of factors. In the first place, little critical attention has been paid to the existence of a substantial and influential body of literary work which has been published over the last century by writers of Asian descent resident in Britain. No study as yet exists of the historical, cultural and literary background to the evolution of this branch of writing. There have, however, been individual monographs on the well known. This fact in itself raises significant questions in terms of publishing practices and cultural politics. For whilst the unencumbered figure of the 'migrant' has clearly become a fashionable trope in metropolitan postmodern and postcolonial literary studies – a cultural traveller who can easily access and traverse across the national, political and ethnic boundaries of the new millenium – not all literary migrants are in the same boat. In addition, little serious consideration has been devoted to the ways in which the evolution of this late modern 'Everyman' figure, had its genesis as much in colonial and immigrant histories as the already familiar discourse of 'exile' established by the epistemologies of a Western modernity. Frequently divorced, therefore, from a relationship to a diverse continuum of South Asian writing in Britain, well-known male writers such as V. S. Naipaul, Salman Rushdie, and more recently Hanif Kureishi, have tended most often to be incorporated by a Western readership as 'exoticized' representatives of 'otherness' and readily assimilated into the 'mainstream'. My intention here, therefore, is to attempt to re-angle and open out the discursive territory surrounding the literary locations of a number of these writers. For when such writers are read alongside a number of less immediately visible, but nevertheless highly influential figures crucial to the construction of an aesthetic framework for the genesis of the South Asian literary diaspora, the discursive territory forming the background to the trope of the 'migrant' in contemporary literary studies takes on a different shape.

Like 'home', the term 'South Asian' is, of course, an invented one. Introduced in Britain in the 1970s as another 'ethnic' label to divide and rule, yet another physical signifier of racial difference which developed a political purchase following the expulsion of the Ugandan Asians under Idi Amin, it has its own difficulties. Often used in government censuses as a means of distinguishing Britain's black and Asian populations, it inevitably flattens a diverse range of backgrounds which stem from complex religious, linguistic and regional histories. In addition, the use of 'South Asian' only seems to make sense when viewed from within a context such as Britain, an environment in which ethnicity has frequently been falsely homogenized. The label 'South Asian' is thus used with some caution in this study, as a *starting point* to enter into a dialogue which attempts as much to complicate and differentiate as to force literary links between a number of different literary voices who have shared a diasporic history and colonial relationship to Britain. As such, the varied perspectives of the writers inevitably challenge, extend and reconceptualize this initial frame. Such an approach is not attempting to be exhaustive, nor am I suggesting that the varied range of fictions published during the post-1945 period can be bonded together into a tightly woven 'genre' or 'style'. For the continuities which emerge between them are not necessarily based only on a shared literary or cultural heritage, but have grown out of the ways in which they have been *read* both within and outside the literary environment in which they were originally produced. Yet it is clear that through these writers' individual attempts to construct new fictional locations, a series of important literary journeys have been, and are being made, journeys which figure and frame a new architecture for the im/migrant imagination, an architecture built around the poetics of displacement and the poetics of home. Much of the discussion in this book therefore will also be suggestive as far as readings of other diasporic and im/migrant literatures in Britain are concerned.[11]

It might be said that concepts such as 'immigrant' and 'migrant', 'home' and 'diaspora' sit uncomfortably when placed next to each other. Indeed, some have argued that diaspora as a theoretical model has become yet another 'catch all' phrase in contemporary literary studies, dehistoricizing and catching all those, that is, who don't quite fit, the return of old racisms in a new guise. Diaspora, of course, stems originally from the Greek 'to scatter' and 'to sow', thus suggesting both dispersal and settlement. It has most frequently been employed in the twentieth century in the context of the experience of enforced expulsions, whether of the Jews or the Armenians. Thus whilst it might appear in some respects to be an inappropriate means of describing patterns of Asian migration, which have, of course, varied widely over time in their historical and economic determinants, its association with a sense of exile, displacement or a 'teleology of return'[12] combined with a symbolic longing to create imaginary homelands has made it a suggestive semantic vehicle to describe and analyse the preoccupations of writers who have migrated to the metropole (in this case Britain) from the former colonies. This is not to suggest for one moment that the gaze of such diasporic populations is always directed towards the once imperial centre, or that internal diasporas have not always existed as part of the history of the Asian subcontinent. But rather to propose that living in a diasporic space enables the growth of 'new identities and subjectivities',[13] new alliances which exist 'outside what has been called the national time/space in order to live inside, with a difference'.[14] Importantly, the question of home becomes reconfigured within this space. For diaspora, does not only create an unrequited desire for a lost homeland but also a 'homing desire', a desire to reinvent and rewrite home as much as a desire to come to terms with an exile from it. Diaspora is therefore as much about settlement as displacement and exists on a shifting axes of differently articulated positionalities, which may be linked to specific histories of recent migration but can also, in later generations, depart from them. As one critic has persuasively argued, specific diasporic communities grow out of a 'confluence of narratives', creating the sense of a shared, if heterogeneous, history. As such, the conceptual parameters of a 'diaspora space' is lived not only by migrants or their descendants, but 'equally by those who are constructed and represented as indigenous'.[15]

* * *

The book is divided into three parts. The first, 'Passages to England', echoes the title of Nirad Chaudhuri's famous autobiographical work *A Passage to England* (1959). In the first chapter, 'Points of Departure', I have adopted a reading strategy which extends the gaze backwards in imperial and colonial history towards early representations of Britain which are suggestive and illuminating in terms of contemporary theoretical paradigms. It is clear, for instance from the examples of Sake Dean Mahomet in the eighteenth century and J. M. Malabari in the nineteenth, that 'Asians' have long been put into a position of either playing on exotic stereotypes or finding strategies to reinvent their cultural identities. Thus while Sake Dean Mahomet's (see plate illustrations, pp. 18–19) various constructions of himself as 'East Indian', 'Oriental' or English 'Shampooing Surgeon' of Brighton may have been in keeping in one sense with other comparable literary experimentations of his day, they can also be seen to act as the ghostly precursors of an orientalist pattern that Hanif Kureishi ironically exploits in the creation of his 'Buddha of Suburbia' in mid-1970s Chislehurst. Focusing in detail on the twentieth-century writings of Mulk Raj Anand, Aubrey Menen, Attia Hosain and G. V. Desani, the first chapter provides a context for reviewing modernity through Asian eyes. Moreover 'modernity', as such, not only came with these writers in a variety of indigenous configurations, but had already transformed itself before arrival into a 'critical force' which could challenge the supposed *roots* of its 'established premises'.[16]

The second chapter 'Crossing Over and Shifting the Shapes' develops the influence of such interconnections by examining the work of the Indo-Caribbean writer Sam Selvon and his writing of working-class 'black' London in the period 1950–75. A Trinidadian contemporary of V. S. Naipaul, Selvon's comic deconstruction of any stable signifiers surrounding race and/or national identity both signals from an early stage what

Stuart Hall has described as the heterogeneity of 'blackness' and makes his creolized city of London the diasporic space for a new epic as a result. Yet Selvon's mythic creation of a 'black' city of words never fails to highlight the realities of survival many black and Asian immigrants had to face in being accommodated in Britain. Selvon's work not only anticipated a whole wave of writing that was to follow, but also deftly illustrates the extent to which the construction of restrictive stereotypes (whether determined by cultural politics or the rhetoric of race) have long been a subject for transgression and serious literary scrutiny.

The second part takes up the now popular theme of 'Imaginary Homelands'. Although the idea was originally coined by Salman Rushdie in the 1980s as a powerful metaphor to describe the fragmented vision of the migrant abroad, it reflects a preoccupation with 'Indias' and 'Englands of the mind' which also frequently manifests itself in the work of his predecessor, V. S. Naipaul, as well as many others. For in these works, 'home' is not necessarily a real place but a mythical construct built on the discontinuous fragments of memory and reconceived in the imagination. My reading in Chapter 3, of V. S. Naipaul's colonial anxieties, his fear as a colonial immigrant of being forever unhoused both by history and the traditional house of 'English' letters, is juxtaposed with a similar sense of equivocation in Rushdie's more celebratory migrant stance in Chapter 4. For as we see in Rushdie's postcolonial version of im/migrant London in *The Satanic Verses*, the business is still unfinished. In fact Naipaul's less popular and exilic version of a sense of disorder in the aftermath of Empire sits, surprisingly easily, next to Rushdie's migrant embrace of a hybrid and mongrelized identity. And whilst Rushdie has frequently critiqued V. S. Naipaul for a lack of passion in his fiction, an absence of love, it is clear from an analysis which compares the artistic preoccupations of *The Enigma of Arrival* and *The Satanic Verses* (two ostensibly very different 1980s novels) that not only is there a buried Oedipal relationship between them, but that both writers are unable to release themselves from the diasporic umbilicus of continually 'writing home'.

Entitled 'Homes without Walls', the third part examines a younger generation of writers who came to prominence in the late 1980s and 1990s and charted a new experience in 'Asian-Britain'. 'Homing In' focuses on living in the present and making a home in the hybrid in two first novels by Hanif Kureishi and Ravinder Randhawa. Hanif Kureishi has been heralded by sympathetic metropolitan critics as the creator of a new kind of Englishman, an Englishman of mixed race whose journey is as much from his lower middle-class suburban origins to the city, as it is with issues of race and ethnicity. Ravinder Randhawa, on the other hand, is most frequently placed as a Women's Press 'feminist' whose groundbreaking novel *A Wicked Old Woman* belongs firmly in the margins. Yet when these two writers are examined as the co-inhabitants of a similar space, the boundary lines are far from clear. Moreover, the supposed circumscriptions of the urban 'ghetto', as Ravinder Randhawa is keen to show us, can drive you equally as mad as the pursuit of a hedonist life in the postmodernist metropole. Although boundaries of race, class and sexuality are transgressed in both *The Buddha of Suburbia* and *A Wicked Old Woman,* it is the power of narrative and storytelling which redeems rather than its explicit political agenda. Significantly too, like Attia Hosain in Chapter 1, Randhawa complicates issues of gender as they are often traditionally perceived in relation to questions of women, race and nationalism. She thus reconfigures 'home' as a site not only for nationalism, but as a space for female action, pointing the way forward for a large number of British-born Asian women writers that followed.

The final chapter, 'Birds of Passage', moves the debate away from an analysis of the ethnic straitjackets operating in Asian Britain to a consideration of three writers who have focused their attentions primarily on using memory and language to create fictional homes within the text itself. A British location is therefore less significant than in Kureishi or Randhawa and the subject-matter of these texts shifts seamlessly across a broad spectrum of diasporic experience whether at 'home' or 'abroad'. In the works of Sunetra Gupta, Romesh Gunesekera and Aamer Hussein, it is no longer possible to create imaginary homelands of the kind inhabited by Rushdie or V. S. Naipaul. For the present is not a foreign country and the panoramic sweep of the narrative of reclamation common in Rushdie has shifted in emphasis to focus on the personal, where such reclamations can no longer represent potential acts of fidelity. Much of Romesh Gunesekera's work is set in his two homelands, Sri Lanka and Britain. Yet, the primary concern of his novel *The Sandglass* is less with a reconstruction of a past lost, replaying the possibility of an imaginative or physical return, than with discovering a form by which to make the narrative of memory the conduit of an ever shifting present. Similarly (though employing very different literary devices), Gupta and Hussein highlight the literary bi-culturalism of the mirrored spaces which memory creates for those living in the multiple interstices of diaspora, and question how to shift the gaze away from the seemingly narrow and repetitive thematic prescriptions for the migrant of loss, absence or displacement.

This book seeks to address a number of still unresolved questions concerning the location of South Asian writing in Britain. Have the boundaries of 'home' actually been shifted by the construction of new homes in the imagination? Will 'home' continue to figure, even in the new twenty-first century, as a repetitive surrogate for old models of nationality built on displacement and unbelonging? Are all postcolonial writers forever consigned to either being irresponsible migrants, divorced from any real sense of historical contingency or, alternatively, the representatives of a seemingly unpalatable doctrine of identity politics? Do we consistently have to retreat back to worn-out categories, whatever their apparent theoretical or political guise, taking up the voices of some who fit into the comfortable niches of fashionable orthodoxies but leaving out others? If the dominant canonical tradition has really begun to be redefined by the presence of a large community of diasporic artists in Britain, the creation of what has been called a 'third space', do we have much evidence of this in mainstream reviewing practices, or, any convincing indicators as to whether modernity is genuinely ready to display another face?

The fictional texts selected for discussion here are not of course intended to define in any comprehensive way the enormous output of the South Asian literary diaspora in Britain.[17] Nor are they illustrative of the often varied elements of a particular writer's oeuvre. Exemplary works have been chosen to both highlight certain significant moments in the history of im/migrant writing in Britain as well as to enable a manageable discussion which extends the critical boundaries of how such writing has most commonly been contained. I am not attempting to propose an alternative theoretical paradigm or to impose a tight chronology which forces some kind of neat *telos* or resolution. I would, however, concur with those who have stressed a need for us to replenish our critical grammars by a return in the postcolonial field to the 'conditions of possibility' generated by the creative text itself.[18] For many of the writers and fictions examined in this book have not only anticipated a number of theoretical dialogues now common in the reading of postcolonial fictions, but have also dramatized and made 'real' the emotional and historical realities of surviving within that space, a role that they will no doubt continue to play in defining and analysing the political terrain of our imagined futures. As Salman Rushdie once put it, citing the words of the film director, Luis Bunuel, ' "I would give my life for a man [or woman] who is looking for the truth. But I would gladly kill a man who thinks he has found the truth" '.[19]

Part 1
Passages to England

1

Points of Departure: Early Visions of 'Home' and 'Abroad'

Only connect
E. M. Forster[1]

My India I carry with me wheresoever I go
Raja Rao[2]

I have a soul which . . . far from being dead is three times livelier than most people's for I have no less than three native lands which I can call my own
Aubrey Menen[3]

Where does one culture begin and another end when they are housed in the same person?
Nayantara Sahgal[4]

The narrative of 'modernity' has never been a straightforward one; nor have its multiple origins ever been contained solely within the European body. In seeking to uncover some points of departure for this study of the fictions of the South Asian diaspora in Britain, it is important to recognize from the outset that diasporic histories are often by their very nature discontinuous and frequently involve a doubling of vision, a 'form of accountability to more than one location', more than one tradition.[5] Furthermore, the spaces opened up by the dominant narrative of a Western modernity have always derived from a process of filtration built on a series of cross-cultural encounters and interconnections, whether staged at 'home' or 'abroad'. For whilst the historic experience of Empire was clearly significant in creating a climate for cultural reconfigurations, the encounter with European philosophical and epistemological systems was only *one* of many other parallel and indigenous processes influencing the translation and genesis of new literary forms and genres. In the case of the

Asian subcontinent, as Nayantara Sahgal implies in the epigraph above, it is difficult to define where 'one culture begin[s] and another end[s] when they are housed in the same body'. For, if we view the 'colonial' as the 'new *Anno Domini* from which events are to be everlastingly measured', we will unfortunately, she says, limit the range of our vision and only ever see one side of the picture. As she goes on to say:

> My own awareness as a writer reaches back to x-thousand B.C., at the very end of which measureless time the British came, and stayed, and left. And now they're gone . . . their residue is simply one more layer added to the layer upon layer of Indian consciousness. Just one more.[6]

Sahgal is of course highlighting the fact here that whilst writers in the subcontinent were undoubtedly profoundly affected by the experience of colonialism – in the most recent case, the encounter with the British – they were not necessarily primarily 'preoccupied with their erstwhile contact with Europe'.[7] Their experience of modernity was one, therefore, which both paralleled and existed in excess of its colonial affiliations. Moreover, the locations of such cultural and political encounters, the 'contact zones', as Mary Louise Pratt describes them in her influential work *Imperial Eyes: Travel Writing and Transculturation* (1992), were not only situated *abroad* in the supposed colonial peripheries, or only determined by the logic and dictums of the imperial project conducted *outside* Britain's shores. For as many historians have demonstrated, Asians had been voyaging in to Britain at least since the formation of the East India company in 1599 and even before.[8] In addition, the effects of the Asian presence within the social spaces of British domestic culture, within the so-called boundaries of the 'sceptred isle' that came to be called 'home' in imperialist discourse, had always been one of accretion, translation, and cultural and linguistic transformation rather than simply one either of Western appropriation or Asian ventriloquism.[9]

This chapter seeks to make visible a series of connections, often subtly hidden and difficult to define, between a number of Asian writers who were writing their own visions of 'home' and 'abroad' in Britain prior to and immediately following the Second World War. In order, however, to understand the environment in which many of these writers were working, as well as the diversity of their own backgrounds, it is worth extending the gaze backwards in imperial and colonial history towards pre-twentieth-century representations of Britain by im/migrant writers and travellers which existed well before contemporary contextualizations. We may be less familiar today with the refiguration of colonial Britain through the voices of her Asian subjects than with the writing of India through 'imperial eyes', but there are, in fact, several such literary examples dating back as early as Sake Dean Mahomet's *The Travels of Dean Mahomet*,[10] published in Ireland in 1794 and arguably one of Britain's first works by an Indian in English. There are also a number of travelogues and diaries penned by figures such as J. M. Malabari, perhaps one of the most significant commentators amongst the large number of nineteenth-century Indian travellers to Britain. The presence of these figures, as Antoinette Burton has shown, as well as their finely nuanced representations of Britain during this period, challenges the logic of those imperialist and nationalist myths which repeatedly locate Britain's non-white citizens as 'simply the [twentieth-century] fallout from Empire'.[11] In addition, as Rozina Visram's invaluable research demonstrates in *Ayahs, Lascars and Princes: The History of Indians in Britain 1700–1947,* it is clear that Indians have been part of the British population for several hundreds of years, a presence which long pre-dates the formal beginning of Empire in India. As she says:

> it is often forgotten that Britain had an Indian community long before the Second World War and that the recent arrival of Asian people in Britain is part of the long history of contact between Britain and India. The arrival of Asians [post-1945] has taken place precisely because of these long established connections.[12]

As has already been indicated in the Prologue, the strategies for survival in Britain employed even by an eighteenth-century writer such as Sake Dean Mahomet, in his negotiation of a number of different cultural and racial roles – whether assimilative, subversive or simply exploitative of the populist economy of orientalism (see Plates 1 and 2), as 'native' of India or 'brown Englishman' – were self-consciously manipulative of the prevailing attitudes of the society he lived in; similarly, whilst drawing on the familiar epistolary genre of the European travel narratives of his time, he managed both in *The Travels of Dean Mahomet* and in *Shampooing*[13] to construct himself within a range of differently inflected positions. He thus avoided marking out an insupportable territory of conflict between East and West, colonizers and colonized, or the need to take up a distinctive cultural identity or political position. Instead, as Michael Fisher has argued, he negotiated his duality by presenting to his readers the 'virtues and flaws' of both his English and Indian worlds.[14]

PLATE 1 Sake Dean Mahomed, Shampooing Surgeon. Drawn on stone from life by T. M. Baynes, Brighton. *Circa* 1825. From the *Images of Brighton Collection*, by courtesy of the librarian of Brighton Local Studies Library.

PLATE 2 Mahomet, Shampooing Baths, Brighton. *Circa* 1822. From the *Images of Brighton Collection* by courtesy of the librarian of Brighton Local Studies Library. This illustration first appeared in the 1822 edition of *Shampooing* by S. D. Mahomed.

Comparably perhaps, J. M. Malabari, the main figure for more detailed consideration here, visited Victorian Britain regularly between 1870 and 1890. Already an established Parsi journalist and Gujarati poet in Bombay before his arrival in Britain, he wrote one of the most significant ethnographic studies of London during this period. Like many other travellers, Malabari emphasized the question of spectacle and gaze in his *The Indian Eye on English Life* (1893), and it was a theme he developed in some detail as he adopted the 'difficult role of a nineteenth-century "Indian" flanneur' coasting the city, a city which presented itself to him as an 'imperial theatre', where the drama of the ambivalent location of the 'colonial citizen-subject was played out for the benefit of rulers and ruled alike'.[15] Malabari's travelogue is significant not only for its obvious creation of a counter-narrative to the terms by which the 'spectacle of Empire' was produced in the late Victorian metropolis (in fact, it was written around the time of a self-indulgent imperialist exhibition on India which opened in South Kensington in 1886, and it critiqued the exhibition in many ways), but also for the ways in which it demonstrated that Britain was as much the home of the colonial encounter as were the colonies themselves. By writing the metropolis through Indian eyes, he was both able to confront his initial Anglophilia as a Bombay Parsi, being seduced like many others who followed him by the imagined attractions of the English 'mother-land', whilst at the same time deconstructing its image, as a journey to an illusion. Malabari carefully maps the social geography of London for his Indian readers, but he also seriously criticizes the contradictory realities of the heart of darkness within the Britain that he encounters. 'Poor as India is', he says at one point:

> I thank God she knows not much of the poverty to which parts of Britain have become accustomed – take the East End of London for instance [where there are] men and women living in a chronic state of emaciation, till they can hardly be recognised as human.[16]

And although Malabari as a skilled journalist did not tone down his sensationalist descriptions of the poor in English society, his surprise at the poverty at home in imperial society clearly acted as a critique of the frequently 'vaunted discourse of human progress to which [he] as a colonial was particularly subject'.[17] Similarly, he constantly draws the reader's attention to the differences between himself (in terms of his own class and education) and the backgrounds of his working-class English landladies, the owners of the lodging houses where many of these Indian travellers stayed and which were located in a colony of Bayswater, coming to be nicknamed 'Asia Minor'.[18] Furthermore, in reconfiguring London for his own purposes, Malabari was keen, like many other Indian travellers to Britain during this period, to highlight his own urbanity and cosmopolitanism – the breadth of his own modernity – and thus reduce and provincialize Britain's stature on the imperial map.

Malabari's travelogue therefore does not simply portray the arrival of a colonial from 'abroad' who is appropriated and exoticized in the large metropolis, but attempts repeatedly to show that the so-called imperial centre was only one centre amongst many others on a much larger geopolitical map. Indeed, as the subjective narrations of so many of these nineteenth-century travel diaries make clear – one person's centre is often someone else's periphery, so that, as one other traveller, T. N. Mukharji, summed it up in a *A Visit to Europe* (1899), 'the European will learn to see himself as others see him'.[19] It is not possible here to go into any detail about how Malabari's inscriptions of imperial London prefigure the *imaginary homelands* constructed by Britain's later twentieth-century and contemporary postcolonial writers. For 'History', as a character in Romesh Gunesekera's novel *Reef* (1994) once perceptively put it, 'is always the story of somebody's diaspora'. It is, however, important to note that, like Sake Dean Mahomet, and the early twentieth-century generation of Asian writers resident in Britain who followed, Malabari was keen both to display the ease with which he could move within the conventions and literary genres of Victorian culture whilst, at the same time, making Britain itself the object of 'surveillance and critique'.[20] London as a site of imperial display was therefore challenged and appropriated from within, becoming open to what the Jamaican poet Louise Bennett was later to call in the 1950s, a process of colonization in reverse. And Malabari's natural bilingualism in narrating and translating the city through the medium of the English language – his sophisticated possession of English as only another Indian language – is always implicitly and confidently assumed.

My aim in this chapter has not solely been determined by the need for historic retrieval, to set in motion a process of literary archaeology that is without doubt a necessary task. Nor am I attempting to engage in an act of pluralization demonstrating that it is necessary to make visible a 'new critical geography' of cultures of movement and difference, diaspora and migrancy in order to understand the invisible 'others' who have always made up the racial admixture of Britain's long 'immigrant' history.[21] I am concerned, however, to suggest that the ambivalent conflation of images of 'home' and 'abroad' inscribed by some of these writers in their individual creations of an alternative cartography of Britain's literary past, as well as their reconfiguration and radical critiques of the imperial metropolis from within, cast an interesting light on how we read the contemporary literatures of the Asian diaspora in Britain today. For the perceptions of many of these early figures, and the strategies they employed in shifting the angle of the gaze, directly anticipated and rehearsed the difficulties confronting a number of later postcolonial writers in their more recent attempts to break out of narrowly conceived visions of 'home' and 'abroad'. Moreover, these early representations clearly predicted trends that have now become identifiable as the bases for some of the fashionable orthodoxies normally attributed to the radical insights of contemporary postcolonial theory, a discourse which has aimed repeatedly in recent years to break down the grand narratives of European enlightenment, a modernity only seen through Western eyes. Unfortunately, however, the contemporary pursuit of academic orthodoxies, however politically urgent their concerns, has often led to a repetitive myopia in reading practices, a disinclination to see or read the significance of these texts either as literary precursors or as notable representations of a tradition of Asian writing in English which had significant foundations in Britain prior to the now familiar *postcolonial* versions in the post-Independence era following the Second World War.

There is little point in attempting to make a special case for individual writers who have by and large remained invisible until recently in terms of the contribution they have made to the evolution of a poetics of migrant writing in Britain. Literary history and the formation of the canon have done much to exclude such voices, placing them in categories for convenience which do more to distort than clarify. Thus whilst it is well known, for example, that writers such as Mulk Raj Anand and Raja Rao spent many formative years in Britain and France during the period prior to Indian Independence in 1947, they have most commonly been described as the fathers of 'Indo-Anglian writing'[22] and slotted comfortably therefore into a tradition of Indian nationalist writing separate from the later postwar Asian group of so-called 'immigrant', 'expatriate' or 'diasporic' writers. This kind of critical labelling has served both the interests of some Indian critics, keen to preserve an uncomplicated nationalist narrative of resistance, as well as those metropolitan Western reviewers who were unable to read the innovative cross-cultural experimentations of such writers from outside the narrow confines of a Eurocentric gaze. Not surprisingly, then, figures such as Aubrey Menen, who was born in Britain in 1912 of an Irish mother and Indian father and who, like Hanif Kureishi much later in the 1980s, writes England, India and Ireland from a mixed-race perspective, are barely known. And a writer such as Attia Hosain, who lived in London for most of her adult life (arriving just prior to Independence and Partition in 1947), is usually noted, like Sankharan Menon Marath, for her 'nostalgic' and so-called 'exilic' portrayal of a traditional world lost, an inability to move beyond the boundaries of her upper-class Muslim heritage in pre-Partition Oudh.[23]

In contrast, G. V. Desani's novel *All About H. Hatterr* (1948) has had more notice in recent critical coverage, but most frequently because of Salman Rushdie's acknowledged debts to him as a literary model and from whom, as Rushdie has said, he 'learned a trick or two'.[24] Yet, prior to contemporary interest in the writing of fragmented realities in modes either explicitly hybrid or self-consciously fabulist and determined partly by the orthodoxies of pluralist postmodernist techniques, the innovatory significance of Desani's impressive work had, as Anthony Burgess makes plain in his 1970 introduction to the second edition of the novel, all but disappeared. Yet, interestingly, Desani's work was very well received in 1948. Far from being, says Burgess, a 'dweller' 'on a cultural fringe who did remarkably well when one considered his disadvantages', he was a writer who was 'squarely set in the great linguistic mainstream'.[25] Like many other so-called *meteques* (a derogatory term coined by F. W. Bateson and often used at this time for writers with a non-English linguistic, racial or political background) who, of course, could include, as Burgess ironically notes, Poles like Joseph Conrad and Irishmen like James Joyce, Desani was a spirited stylist, a linguistic innovator who, perhaps because of his tripartite vision – created by both a Nairobi and Sindi Indian childhood – could see that the 'English and [their] grammar were in need of a drastic overhaul'.[26] T. S. Eliot and others of the Bloomsbury group were amongst the first to applaud the linguistic pyrotechnics of the book, although Desani's impact as a *modernist* was seldom, if ever, acknowledged in any literary histories. As one of Desani's contemporaries aptly predicted, it was to be 'the next generation' who would come to 'understand' the literary significance of his creolized style as well as the subversive iconoclastic insights of his mixed-race anti-hero, the first im/migrant prophet and 'Everyman' of the twentieth century, the eponymous, H. Hatterr.[27]

Unlike the later generation of economic immigrants from the subcontinent, who were invited into Britain in the 1950s and 1960s to help relieve the labour shortage after the Second World War, many of these writers came as individuals, often as students already familiar through long-established historical, familial and educational links with the world they were entering. Yet in contrast to the better known group of writers from the

Caribbean who migrated to London in the 1950s, these writers were not linked by any immediately discernible connections. The links, such as they were, were fluid ones, tying them together after arrival in subtle ways and, with the advantage of hindsight, also to a future. It is now beyond doubt that the presence of these figures has made a significant impact on the literary history of Britain, but they were, inevitably:

> writers at the crossroads [who] without exception . . . faced . . . the possibly *unexpected* [my italics] task of having to define themselves. These writers fitted no known categories: they had sensibilities that had – because of their histories – become global ones. For the puzzled West, one answer for this phenomenon was to invent new pigeon holes. The writers themselves regarded the labels with scant enthusiasm.[28]

As the editors of *Voices of the Crossing* have demonstrated, their voices stemmed from a range of different histories and often straddled a number of different cultural systems, languages and epistemological traditions. In addition, the acts of translation, which many of their early writings presented, were much broader than a 'matter [of] words alone'. For their journeys were not simply from one country or continent to another – the crossings of geographical space or political boundaries – but translations of sensibility between and across languages, cultures and histories, which were both partial and whole, fragmented and transformative. Moreover, their fictional representations of 'home' and/or 'abroad' are concerned less with the writing of a referential and static version of a past which has been lost than with discovering a number of different literary strategies to explore a sensibility which exists on the cusp of several interconnecting worlds – a revolving axis which stretches beyond notions of 'here' and/or 'there', home and/or abroad – which is the metaphorical and imaginative 'home' of many of these artists. This is not to say that many of these works are not precisely located, referential or realist in terms of their subject-matter or concerns. It is only to stress, as Zulfikar Ghose once put it, that perception is often ambiguous and 'reality' is frequently 'composed of absent things', enabling the 'unseen [to] blaze . . . in our minds with a shocking vividness'.[29]

These early texts, as will be demonstrated later, open up a series of useful questions regarding the background to a diverse range of diasporic writing in Britain which had its origins prior to contemporary agendas. Moreover, their insights both critiqued from within and offered different perspectives on some of the assumptions of a largely exclusionary Western modernist tradition. As F. D. Karaka (first Indian President of the Oxford Union) already noted in 1935, in a vehement essay entitled 'The Barbarian is Born', one of the central paradoxes of Western modernity is that whilst it seems to open up new discursive spaces for some, it simultaneously writes over and closes doors for others.[30] And although today we might agree with the editors of *Modernism and Empire,* that 'no account of contemporary poetry and fiction' should leave out the postcolonial or international literatures in English, 'modernist writing' in the early part of the twentieth century is nevertheless still seen as an 'exclusively European and American phenomenon'. As they argue, this is a false legacy which clearly 'needs overturning'.[31]

These comments rightly draw our attention to a significant absence in most twentieth-century accounts of the history of 'modernist writing'. Such histories have consistently failed to engage with either the historical realities of Empire and the subsequent creation of new fictional 'homes', or the existence of alternatively constituted 'modernisms' in modernity's literary genealogy. This absence in breadth of vision is surprisingly repeated – given that we now supposedly inhabit a postcolonial era – even in a new millennium essay published in the *Times Literary Supplement* (September, 2000), entitled 'How the Critic came to be King', which reviews the new Modernist volume of the *Cambridge History of Literary Criticism.* Ironically, given the exclusively Euro-American subject-matter of the review, an interesting photograph is reproduced in the article from the 1942 BBC Eastern Service monthly radio magazine programme, *Voice*. There are in fact over ten writers and critics in this historic photograph (see Plate 3) They include Una Marson (Caribbean poet), Venu Chitale (assistant producer of the programme), J. M. Tambimuttu (a major poet and editor of *Poetry London* for many years), Mulk Raj Anand (novelist and critic), Narayana Menon (writer and broadcaster), as well as T. S. Eliot, William Empson, Nancy Barratt and George Orwell. However in the recent *TLS* essay, no reference is made to any of the Caribbean or Asian literary figures, who were often featured together on this BBC Radio programme with writers and critics such as Orwell and Eliot. More importantly, these writers were all influential literary presences in 1940s London. The caption beneath the *TLS* reproduction simply reads: 'among others – T. S. Eliot, George Orwell and William Empson'.[32]

How are we to read this caption in 2001? Clearly, the use of 'others' may simply signal a predictable repetition by an influential and international literary magazine to recognize the crosscultural bases hidden within the familiar face of an institutionalized 'Euro-American' modernity. It also,

PLATE 3 From 'Voice' 1942, the BBC monthly radio magazine programme for the Eastern Service: (left to right, sitting) Venu Chitale (assistant producer); J. M. Tambimuttu (poet from Ceylon and editor of Poetry London); T. S. Eliot (poet and critic); Una Marson (Caribbean poet and organizer of BBC West Indian Programme); Mulk Raj Anand (Indian novelist and critic); Christopher Pemberton (member of BBC staff); Narayana Menon (Indian writer); (standing) George Orwell (author and producer of the programme); Nancy Barratt (secretary to George Orwell); William Empson (poet and critic).

however, draws our attention to a further slippage, which suggests that the black and Asian figures present in the picture can perhaps be safely relegated to the ' colonial' or 'postcolonial' and thus excluded from the mainstream history of modernity yet again. By placing such major writers outside the dominant in categories such as 'other', alongside familiar modernist voices such as T. S. Eliot or William Empson, they are neatly divorced from a relationship to modernity in 1940s Britain, a cosmopolitan literary landscape, which as the photograph itself suggests, they were influential in constructing.[33]

It is perhaps worth remembering in this context that Mulk Raj Anand's accounts of his *Conversations in Bloomsbury* during the 1920s and 1930s frequently pointed to similar absences as did the critical essays of several other black and Asian writers resident in Britain at this time.[34] In one notable recollection, where Anand and an Indian friend are in conversation with T. S. Eliot, Edith Sitwell and D. H. Lawrence at a literary party, Anand confesses to having 'dangerous thoughts'. This signalling of a sense of frustration was driven by his desire to shift the focus of the intellectual banter away from the comfortable 'Indian' subject of Rudyard Kipling to the sources of a 'humanism' which was 'integral to the Indian tradition in which [he] grew up', and which represented a differently articulated vision of modernity.[35] Like Salman Rushdie much later in *Imaginary Homelands* (1991), who frequently stresses the eclectic range of his literary influences and the 'stereoscopic' nature of his fragmented cultural vision, Anand was well versed in many literatures (whether English, Indian or European) and included the Russian writers Tolstoy and Chekhov amongst his major influences. Bored with the seemingly inevitable return to the worn-out subject of Lahore, the British Raj, and Kipling's well-known inscriptions of India in his novel *Kim*, he says:

> I felt I must communicate to these intellectuals that I had learnt to love the life of the imagination from Iqbal and that, against such a poet, Kipling's writings seemed fantastic but small-minded.[36]

Anand's reference here to the modernities of the Urdu poet, Dr Muhammad Iqbal, was not simply a means of counteracting the humiliation he felt during many of these social encounters, the sense of always 'being inferior', which 'seared like a wound in my soul' and was to later add fire, along of course with the Gandhian freedom movement in India, to the political fervour of the writing of his first novel, *Untouchable* (1935), as well as the novels that followed. For whilst Anand admired the 'literary skills' of what he calls here, these 'English' writers, and, indeed, as many commentators have pointed out, was initially strongly influenced by Western modernist techniques (most notably, in fact, by the 'Irish' writer, James Joyce), he was passionately committed to giving voice and consciousness to those ordinary, unlettered characters who had been the substance of his Punjabi childhood but had always been written out of previous literary representations in English. In addition, like many other Indian writers resident in Britain during this period, Anand was less concerned to accommodate himself to the prevailing temper of an exclusionary 'Englishness', which he often critiqued, than to attempt to shift the angle of the gaze. He seeks to present a history, as he shows us in *Across the Black Waters* (1940), which not only exposes Britain's exploitative enlisting of Indian *sepoys* to cross to *Vilayet* [England] as 'cannon-fodder' during the First World War, but also shows how so-called 'barbarism', was generated as much from within as without, the inevitable product of a Western modernity that had led to global atrocities worldwide.[37] As one of his contemporaries, Cedric Dover, the Eurasian author of the novel *Half-Caste*, put it in 1937 when writing on the parochial attitude of the English to cultural admixture:

> There is a natural tendency . . . to regard the results of recent mixture between white and coloured peoples as a series of special and highly localised problems, and not a *world* [my italics] issue created by Western protestantism and capitalist 'democracy'[38]

And Anand himself, in 'Prolegomena to a New Humanism' (dedicated to E. M. Forster) stresses that if his childhood world – where he grew up as the son of a peasant mother and coppersmith in the Punjab – was indeed 'going through a process of disintegration and anarchy' so, too, 'were the various countries of Europe'. Nothing, he says, 'seemed more certain in this wasteland than that the towers of London, Vienna and Paris were about to fall'.[39] Moreover, like Dover, who dedicates one of his critical works, *Feathers in the Arrow: An Approach for Coloured Writers and Readers* (1947), to W. E. B. Du Bois and the 'Negro' cause in the USA, Anand was keen to establish a dialogue amongst a community of writers worldwide who might see beyond the pitfalls of either a simplistic patriotism or an essentialist racial or national politics.

It is not possible here to go in depth into Mulk Raj Anand's relationship with E. M. Forster who, like Anand and others, attended the first European Writers Conference against Fascism in 1935. In fact, it was Forster who managed, by writing a preface, to get Anand's first novel *Untouchable* published after 19 rejections from British publishers who felt that the subject-matter too was 'unclean', and did not meet the 'exotic' expectations of a metropolitan reading public. However, what is significant here is that Anand and many of his Asian contemporaries, such as Aubrey Menen, D. F. Karaka and Krishna Menon, as well as those who later came to form part of the influential *Progressive Writers Association* and the *India League*,[40] were deeply committed to the need to question and to revision the West's image of itself. To find a means (as Anand once put it in a discussion with E. M. Forster on his character Aziz in *A Passage to India)* to overcome the difficulty of expressing the truly 'revolutionary potential' of Caliban's desire for revenge.[41]

Like many other intellectuals, including figures such as the Trinidadian writer and critic, C. L. R. James, Anand was initially attracted in the prewar period, to 1930s Marxism as a means of breaking away from the shackles of his position as a British colonial subject, seeing Communism as a possible alternative to imperialism.[42] And as with George Lamming's *The Pleasures of Exile* (1960), which, as we shall see in Chapter 2, similarly takes up the figure of Caliban in Shakespeare's *The Tempest* as a literary trope, a figure of colonial subversion for the Caribbean writer in London in the period immediately following the Second World War, Mulk Raj Anand was clearly conscious from an early stage of both the attractions and the pitfalls of such anti-colonial resistance; the limitations, as one critic has suggested, of forever holding up a mirror between East and West as 'fixed opposites', universally in conflict, rather than as 'mutual deformations' and creative reformations of each other.[43]

As suggested earlier, Anand and his contemporary Raja Rao, author of the groundbreaking *Kanthapura* (1938), have most frequently been *located* as figures who initiated the Indian novel in English, a tradition that Meenakshi Mukherjee has famously called *The Twice-Born Fiction*. Both writers were clearly centrally influenced, in very different ways, by the Gandhian freedom movement and the fervent desire to write *India*, like Forster's Aziz, at least partially into being.[44] In fact, Raja Rao's famous Foreword to *Kanthapura* is oft-quoted as the first international articulation of a distinctively national literary consciousness, and is now seen as an early catechism for all Indian writers in English. As Rao put it in 1938:

> The telling has not been easy. One has to convey in a language that is not one's own the spirit that is one's own . . . We cannot write like the English. We should not.[45]

Interestingly, Rao's understanding of the need for 'translation' in the Indian novel in English, a translation not simply from one language to another – the negotiation between his native Indian language (Kannada) and the effects of an assimilated colonial English – but also a shift in ways of feeling and being across the non-linear trajectories of memory, space and time, predates Salman Rushdie's now well-known vision of a bifurcated migrant sensibility in *Imaginary Homelands* (1991) by at least 50 years. In addition, many of these writers' lives also exemplify what Harish Trivedi has called 'an acute instance of what in post-colonial discourse is [now] variously termed . . . exile, diaspora, migrancy and hybridity'.[46] Rao wrote most of *Kanthapura* between 1929 and 1933 in a thirteenth-century castle in the French Alps belonging, as he has said, to the 'Dauphins of France', whereas Mulk Raj Anand's first published novel,[47] *Untouchable* (1935), was partially fired by his ultimate disregard for the 'art for art's sake' ethos of the London literary circle amidst which the novel initially took shape. Whilst Anand substantially simplified the form and language of the novel as a result of his six month period living with Gandhi in 1927, his use of the sweeper-boy Bakha, from amongst the lowest of Hindu castes, as the main protagonist was also a symbolic and political response to his own sense of frustration with the locked prejudices of the Bloomsbury circle in London.[48] This was a world where, as Edward Sackville-West, remarking on Anand's use of an outcaste as the central protagonist of *Untouchable*, once said: 'you can't do a novel about that kind of person! . . . one only laughs at cockneys, like Dickens does'.[49] Moreover, as Cyril Connolly, one of the first metropolitan reviewers of the novel pertinently observed, the 'untouchable' of the title was perhaps simultaneously a vehicle to represent Anand's sense, not of 'exile' as an Indian writer living in the imperial metropolis, but of alienation in a fundamentally racist climate where all 'WOGS' (Western Oriental Gentlemen as Anand later describes them in *The Bubble*), whatever their intellectual credentials, were still seen as 'untouchables' themselves.[50]

Although critical grammars which attempt to place the doublings of a bifurcated sensibility have varied over time, the notion of the writer in 'exile' or of the 'émigré' is a familiar one both in terms of early twentieth-century modernist discourse and in more recent postcolonial variations on the same theme. Most commonly, as is intimated by Cyril Connolly's review above, the *exile* is seen as suffering from some sense of loss and dislocation whether cultural, racial or historical, and is therefore forever journeying whether literally or metaphorically in search of a new homeland. Such narratives, whether of quest or return, are of course not new: the

Christian story of the Fall, Satan's banishment from 'Heaven' or the ancient Hindu legend of Rama and Sita are ancient examples of similar 'exiles'. However, in modern versions, and particularly those institutionalized in Western literary criticism (as, for example, in Terry Eagleton's *Exiles and Emigres* (1970)), whilst the figure of the exile is centrally placed as a Euro-American theme or metaphor for the fragmentations of Europe following the First World War, the political realities or cultural transformations effected by the presence of the colonial or postcolonial im/migrant are seldom discussed or even acknowledged. If they are discussed, they become located within the 'larger theoretical framework of what is a predominantly Western cultural production', where the usefully disruptive and heterogeneous elements of 'other' cultures are incorporated, assimilated and ultimately institutionalized.[51]

The limitations of this kind of reading are apparent in Andrew Gurr's influential study *Writing in Exile: The Identity of Home in Modern Literature* (1981). Whilst it does deal with a broad range of writers from 'colonial' and 'postcolonial' backgrounds, it becomes caught up in a repetitive 'economy of loss and belonging' where the process of writing is inexorably tied to a search for identity and place.[52] In Gurr's terms, the colonial writer is 'forced to go into exile in the metropolis as a means of compensating for [a] sense of cultural subservience'.[53] Moreover, once 'abroad', such writers are only preoccupied with creating fictional versions of 'home' in order to secure their fragile identities and return to the 'unalterable circumstances' of a childhood lost. Although Gurr is sensitive to the inherent dualities involved in *writing home* from *abroad*, he remains caught in the notion of an overdetermined and simplified version of the realities of diasporic experience, which is not necessarily a literal *exile* but a *migration from choice*, a passage not so much predetermined by the grammar of Western modernity – a discourse of migration – as by the cross-fertilizations enabled by the migration of many discourses. In addition, as Aamer Hussein has argued, such migrations do not necessarily only involve a 'split' (a perennial yearning for a past that can never be restored or, on the other hand, the passionate need, as it were, to write a new 'nation' into existence), but instead create a 'doubling', a 'mobility of mind if not always of matter',[54] that may privilege the workings of the partial and non-linear nature of memory and time over and above the apparently seamless course of dominant versions of received history. This is a falsely imposed temporal and geographical division in which *East* and *West*, as the evidence of the Meridian line in Greenwich Park, South London, still reminds us even in the new millennium, once arbitrarily divided the world.

As subsequent chapters will illustrate, many critics have now shifted the terms of the discussion beyond the reductive binaries of home and abroad, metropolitan centres and colonial peripheries. They highlight the fact that, as Rosemary Marangoly George suggests in *The Politics of Home*, 'home . . . runs along several axes' and is not necessarily 'fixed, rooted, stable', so arguing that the process of voyaging is as much a 'cultural practice' as the desire to find a 'dwelling' place.[55] Yet many of these discussions still return to the idea that the need to come to terms with a politics of location is still a preoccupation that particularly afflicts colonial or postcolonial writers – the implication being therefore that the writer who is not from a colonial background not only already possesses this ability, but is also not caught in what Homi Bhabha and other postcolonial critics have defined as the hybrid spaces in between, still moving from the outside in or from here to there on an ever-moving pendulum.

If, then, as Raymond Williams has persuasively argued, one of the difficulties of discussing modernity is to find a means of moving outside the grammar which it constantly resurrects in defining itself, it would also appear, as he suggests, sensible to think beyond the notion of the Western metropolis as the only cultural mecca. Yet even Williams's analysis, sensitive as it is, still ends up repeating certain now familiar clichés:

> the key cultural factor of the modernist shift is the character of the metropolis . . . The most important general element of the innovations in form is the fact of immigration to the metropolis, and it cannot too often be emphasised how many of the major innovators were in this precise sense, immigrants.[56]

Here, as has recently been noted, modernism is still being viewed as a Western phenomenon produced *in* the metropolis rather than being stimulated by those 'immigrant intellectuals' (not necessarily white or Euro-American), who arrived, driven perhaps by a different experience of a modernity already established *elsewhere*. Thus whilst, as Edward Said has suggested, the grand narratives of nineteenth-century Western realism were challenged by the 'disturbing appearance in Europe of various Others, whose provenance was the imperial domain' and whose presence challenged and 'resist[ed] settled metropolitan histories, modes, forms of thought',[57] it is also important to remember that modernity, however dislocating and disempowering some of its appropriative effects on the colonial psyche, could also be a self-determined force for liberation. For as Kumkum Sangari has noted, it is ironic that the revolutionary possibilities of an 'international' and 'oppositional' modernism came into being for many 'early twentieth century "Third World" writers and artists . . . at a time when [Western] modernism was itself recuperating the cultural products of non-western countries largely within an aesthetic of the fragment'. Sangari's reference here to the notion of 'an aesthetic of the fragment' is, as Patrick Williams rightly suggests, an interesting one. This obviously echoes T. S. Eliot's famous lines in his influential poem *The Waste Land* ('These fragments I have shored against my ruins'), suggesting, like Anand earlier, the idea of the disintegration of Western culture in the aftermath of the First World War. But it can also be read, as we shall see in Attia Hosain's first novel, *Sunlight on a Broken Column* (1961) – which takes its title from T. S. Eliot's 'The Hollow Men' – as an image not only of *Western* fracture and metropolitan dislocation, but as a formal means to knit together the disjunctures and temporal discontinuities of a colonial country and feudal community in transition at a specific moment in history, the time of Independence and Partition in Lucknow, a moment which witnessed the uneasy alliances, juxtapositions and discontinuities of both old and new, tradition(s) and modernity(ies). Thus it creates an imaginative space where memory, however partial, is able to fill and transform the dualistic fault-lines of received versions of history, and language becomes the subversive vehicle of translation itself.

II

In the discussion which follows, the focus will be on selected works by Attia Hosain, G. V. Desani and Aubrey Menen. A series of further departure points will be highlighted as ways of *reading* the past as well as providing an often forgotten historical backcloth to the generation of a diverse poetics of diasporic writing by artists of Asian origin who were resident in Britain during the 1940s and 1950s. There is little point in attempting to set up rigid critical paradigms as a means to identify literary strategies which these writers share, for their individual cultural backgrounds and fictional approaches differ markedly. Yet, as has already been intimated, these works anticipated and mapped out the ground of an affiliated body of fiction that was to follow later in the century; consolidating a series of connections which were already in place. The Asian presence was long established in Britain and, as is well documented in political histories, Britain was also the radical soil of the Indian Nationalist Movement led by Mahatma Gandhi and, later, Jawaharlah Nehru, who were students in

London and Cambridge respectively, though at different times – Gandhi in the 1880s and Nehru in the 1930s.

Attia Hosain, for example, came from an aristocratic Muslim background which had long connections both culturally and politically with Britain. A close friend of Motilal Nehru (Nehru's father), her father, like many other Indians of his class, had many contacts in England and studied to be a lawyer at Cambridge in the nineteenth century. Moreover, it was the example of Sarojini Naidu (Indian poet/politician and contemporary in Britain of the nineteenth-century traveller J. M. Malabari, and whose poetry was *exoticized* by the unconscious orientalism of well-meaning critics such as Edmund Gosse), who presented an 'ideal of womanhood' to the young Hosain that inspired her to overcome her shyness and report on the All India Women's Conference in Calcutta in 1933.[58] As an activist who was committed to making visible the role of women within the evolution of nationalist histories, Naidu's influence as one of the first female members of the Congress Party was later to become evident in Hosain's understated, but powerful rendering of a young woman's interpretation of the story of the nation's tumultuous birth in her novel *Sunlight on a Broken Column* (1961). The first novel of its kind by a Muslim woman to be brought to the attention of an English readership, it unsettles the seamless and often patriarchal tellings of the history of Independence.[59] Yet Hosain was reluctant to take on the dogmas of any political labels or partisan positions; always seeing power and the corruptions of power to be as much the disease of the East as the West, of men as of women, of Hindus and Muslims. Moreover, she was as much influenced in her traditional Muslim home by her classical education in the Koran, in Urdu and Persian, as by the revolutionary politics of the Left and the 'internationality' of the *Progressive Writers Movement* led by family friends – Mulk Raj Anand and Sajjaad Zaheer.[60] As she puts it in an unfinished essay which was published after her death in 1998:

> My mother came from a family of scholars, not from the feudal *taluqdars* of my father's family. One side of our home was my mother's domain, wholly part of an Indian culture, where we studied Persian and Arabic and Urdu poetry. Through a door and a hall was the Western side, my father's . . . His English friends came to our home . . . not the condescending 'imperialist' breed . . . There was no *division* [my italics] between the two elements in my home . . . We lived in many centuries, it seemed, moving across them in moments.[61]

Interestingly, the *division* Attia Hosain experienced most acutely was not a conflict between the meeting of cultures which was part and parcel anyway of the ancient history of Indian civilization, or the difficulties of growing up schooled in both Urdu and English but rather, an inability to come to terms with the 'cracking of India', as Bapsi Sidwha describes it in her powerful Partition novel, into two arbitrary countries. It was a split that resulted in Attia Hosain's decision to continue living in Britain despite Partition in 1947, and which formed the creative inspiration behind her collection of short stories *Phoenix Fled* (1953) as well as her semi-autobiographical novel *Sunlight on a Broken Column*. Both works address a moment in history when, as she has said: 'together with the raising of flags and [Independence] celebrations came the enforced migrations of more millions than ever before, of massacres and infinite loss'. Living in London did not lessen the anguish, but it avoided the difficult choice of national affiliation: 'everyone from the . . . subcontinent had British passports', at that time 'we had a legal right to be British citizens'.[62] More importantly, her decision to *stay on* represented the possibility of inhabiting, albeit briefly, an alternative mental geography, a 'room in the proverbial attic' as she has called it, a 'neutral area where I could still meet those from whom we were now divided by borders of nationality and an artificially nurtured hostility'.[63] This sense of a literary and imaginative refuge was soon to change, as she has commented elsewhere, particularly after the Immigration Acts in 1962 and 1968, the xenophobic rhetoric of Enoch Powell, and the creation of the new and divisive 'ethnic' tag for Asian immigrants in British government parlance, which heralded the subsequent coming to birth of yet another misguided stereotype, the 'Asian woman'.

Most frequently, Attia Hosain's writing has been described in terms of nostalgia and loss, nostalgia for an aristocratic and upper-class Muslim Indian past to which she cannot return, combined with the pain of a self-imposed 'exile' in Britain. Yet when one examines the subjects of her collected short stories in *Phoenix Fled* (1953), or the complexity of her analysis and critique of the breakdown of the ancient feudal world which surrounds the orphaned protagonist Laila of *Sunlight on a Broken Column* (1961), it soon becomes apparent that although Hosain is concerned, at one level, with a delicate and miniaturist painting of the intimate details of a world that is fast disappearing following the social and political upheavals caused by British rule, she is more centrally preoccupied in a chronicle of the unresolved spaces of memory and with those other minoritarian histories of movement and displacement situated outside the often restrictive parameters of the colonial encounter, and the subsequent move for political

Independence. Her work exposes, in short, the poignant and often contradictory realities of a world lived within the secluded *zenana* (women's quarters), behind the doors of tradition in which she grew up: 'half in and half out of purdah'.[64] Whether obliquely in stories such as 'The Daughter-in-Law' and 'Street of the Moon', or more explicitly in 'First Party' and 'Time is Unredeemable', Hosain examines the sometimes arbitrary and hypocritical perpetuation of traditions (whether of East or West), and displays the political manipulations embedded in all relationships of power, concentrating as much on the intimate bonds between servants and their mistresses as on broader questions lived through familial conflicts as well as nations. Such conflicts painfully evoke specific and epiphanic moments within particular individuals's lives but are also emblematic, like fables, of a timeless space in the imagination beyond the boundaries of institutionalized history or its discontents. 'Has it ever happened that anyone has given up power easily?' asks one of her characters suggestively in an observation which sums up one of the primary preoccupations in Hosain's fiction: 'Not even one's parents, who tell one all day how much they sacrifice for one.'[65] Whilst Hosain concentrates on a wide range of different subject positions (whether rural or urban, cosmopolitan or feudal), it is the voices of her characters in *Phoenix Fled* rather than their social contexts that continue to resonate across the boundaries of time and space, as she painstakingly dramatizes the specific effect of the birth and death of a country on human lives, a country broken as much by the torturous passing away of the old feudal order as by fratricide and civil war.[66]

The force of Hosain's self-consciously elliptical style, which conveys as much by its silences as by the partiality of the fragmentary narration, is evident in several stories in the collection. However, the title story 'Phoenix Fled', which enacts the symbolic resurrection of the phoenix from the ashes of history, is particularly suggestive in its evocation both of the atrocities of a violent past and the redeeming nature of the imagination (the process of storytelling) as a means to liberate and transcend buried memories of incomprehensible violence. Yet, as in many of the other stories, the details of time and place are not explicitly drawn. In the memory of the old woman who is the subject of 'Phoenix Fled', the present-day realities of Partition blend seamlessly with the horrors of the 'red-faced . . . monkeys in red coats', the British soldiers of the so-called 'mutiny' of 1857, in an impressionistic yet epic narration which deliberately avoids precise time–space connections and is suggestive of the timeless and communal voice of the village. As we are told early on:

> Everyone who lived in the village and the hamlets nearby knew her. In their minds they associated her deathless years with the existence of their village. Both were facts accepted without question since the birth of consciousness.
>
> ('Phoenix Fled', p. 9)

As the story unfolds, Hosain characteristically dwells less on any notion of plot or narrative progression than on the metonymic function of objects and spaces in the old woman's consciousness, a technique which interweaves the blurred historical spectres of past horrors – the rapes and lootings of the Mutiny – within the same emotional time frame as the religious antagonisms underlying the current Civil War. She lives, as do a number of Hosain's other characters, behind walls. In this case it is the fragile sanctity of her mud house which protects her, shielding her from the 'world outside' by its 'arches, . . . thatch, the courtyard, the doll's house' (pp. 9–10). And it is only when her grandchildren come to visit, to listen to her stories – 'her buried treasure' – that this woman, who lives as much in the past as in the present, can break out of her silence. For it is the 'doll's house', a tiny house standing in the courtyard, which provides a 'visible bond' between the woman and the children, enabling her to 'escape' into a world of fantasy and fable and to be happy to be with them because she lived 'in their time'.

The impact of the story is conveyed by Hosain's juxtaposition of the bald honesty and innocence of the old woman's legendary oral tales with the realities of the children's as yet unstated fears, as they search to find words for why 'violence' in their world ' had changed its face, why they feared the departure of the soldiers as once she had feared their arrival' (p. 13). We are left, as the story closes, with a terrifying image of the burning of the old woman's thatched hut as the ghosts of the past return to haunt the present. The living memory of past atrocities – her refusal to flee during the Mutiny – throws light in the end on her final act of resistance and courage in the face of death. Having fallen asleep inside, the creaking of a door wakes her. The soldiers enter: 'she could not see' in the shadows 'who came, how many'. The story is left open-ended and it is clear that it does not matter, in one sense, who the soldiers are or what actually happens to the woman, for their purpose to loot and kill is the same whatever their colour or creed. More significant are the images and symbols which remain in the imagination as testaments to the stories of her life. Remaining dignified, even when enveloped by her worst fears, she warns enigmatically: 'Mind . . . mind you do not step on the doll's house' (p. 15).

As in 'After the Storm', which is similarly poetic in its rendering of a young child's uncomprehending displacement following the ravages of Civil War, the omniscient narrative voice of 'Phoenix Fled' is an unbiased one putting forward its perspective through the point of view of the character described rather than relying on any explicit moral or political agenda. And even in stories which, on the surface, seem to directly address oppositional subject matter, judgement is withheld as the complexities of the choices confronting her characters are unravelled. In 'The First Party' and 'Time is Unredeemable', the ostensible focus is on conflicts engendered by the meeting of East and West, as experienced through the lives of two young wives who are caught between their sense of duty and honour as traditional Muslim women and a fear of the 'otherness' of a world that has made their husbands strangers. Yet Hosain's story is not concerned with a neat exploration of the divisive effects of modernity as it mingles with and unsettles traditional orthodoxies, but instead with the pain of the human dilemmas that these two characters face, caught as they are on the cusp between these worlds. As the title indicates, 'The First Party' suggests an initiation into an unknown world, a world outside a young bride's experience and one which threatens the securities, however tenuous, of the sanctities of her 'walled home from which marriage had promised an adventurous escape' (p. 22). As the girl (who is not named) stumbles over the threshold of change and into the 'bewildering brightness' of a Western-style party, the characters within (men as well as women) take on surrealistic features. A woman's painted nails appear like 'claws dipped in blood', 'their clothes adorning nakedness not hiding it, with their false painted mouths', and 'short hair that looked like [a] mad woman's whose hair was cropped to stop her pulling it out'. The room closes in on her, suffocating her, emphasizing the weight of her own 'bright rich clothes and heavy jewellery' (pp. 18–20); most significantly, she, 'the wife' now, as her husband calls her, is torn by the reality that by marriage she was in collusion with one of the 'destroyers'. No longer protected by the language of custom, she is forced to confront the imprisoning ties of a bond of loyalty to a husband still driven, even in a different context from her own, by patriarchal norms, where the choice is not one between East and West, tradition or modernity, but a realization of a situation within which she is already enveloped and from which there is no escape.

Hosain's female characters (of whatever class or age) are frequently suspended, caught within the conflicting demands of class, gender and tradition. The fractures these women experience are generated, however, as much from within the context of their traditional lives as by outside forces.

In stories such as 'The Street of the Moon', where Hosain describes the radical behaviour of one of her few named characters, Hasina, the servant girl who tantalizes and eventually marries the old opium-addicted cook Kalloo – only to betray him by seducing his son and leaving the house to become a prostitute – the angle of the third-person narration is used to expose and critique the norms of the hierarchical feudal context which form the backcloth to such actions. Like Munni in 'The Daughter-in-Law' which narrates a similar tale of rebellion – an act of resistance within the servant's quarters – Hasina is an outsider to the system, whose behaviour does not conform to the age-old patterns of the household. The rhythm and lyrical cadences of the prose emphasize both the continuities and the chaotic interruption of predictable rituals when Hasina's unconscious self-determination unsettles established roles and results in her demonization, though she still torments Kalloo's deluded fantasies, still beckoning him like a painted witch from carnival as she waits, cast out under a street lamp in the unsalubrious street of the moon.

As we saw earlier with Raja Rao, who raised important questions regarding the notion of translation well before the idea was itself *translated* into a concept metaphor for the postcolonial migrant writer in the late twentieth century, Hosain was acutely aware of the political and emotional implications of her choice to write in English and not in Urdu, her mother tongue. Yet it is her use of language which, as many critics have shown, reflects influences from her Persian and Arabic tutelage, as well as the cyclical oral tales of her native Oudh, that creates the possibility of a pluralist vision, an aesthetic which both bridges and extends its landscape to unravel, sometimes unevenly, the contradictory realities and subaltern voices of her fictional world. The collection *Phoenix Fled* can perhaps best be seen as a distillation of Hosain's pre-Partition experiences as the daughter of one of the fading aristocratic class growing up in a period during the 1920s and 1930s. It was a period when 'ill-digested modernities' lived alongside age-old feudal traditions in an increasingly anachronistic political world where 'time' as one of her characters, says 'is running out'.[67] In contrast, the more specifically rendered historical context of *Sunlight on a Broken Column*, set in the turbulent years prior to Independence and narrated through the orphaned consciousness of Laila, provides a more graphic explication. In the novel, Hosain blends the elliptical style of her short stories with the historical details of nineteenth-century realism, stretching the syntax of the English language with the poetic cadences of Urdu, to express a landscape previously unrepresented in English fiction. *Sunlight on a Broken Column* is often critiqued for lacking a firm structure and being indulgently 'exotic' or 'nostalgic' – an immature *bildungsroman* and barely disguised autobiographical mirror of its author's own divided childhood – failing therefore to meet the criteria of more self-consciously political and *postcolonial* renditions of Partition. It is more useful, however, to approach the novel as an early and courageous attempt to discover a narrative poetics by which to open up the unresolved discontinuities of a painful past through the filters of memory, which can both double and fracture, restrict as well as liberate, perception.[68]

As in V. S. Naipaul's *A House For Mr Biswas* which was published in the same year (1961), Hosain's novel charts the disintegration and eventual breakdown of a family caught amidst internal fractures and the turbulence of the ethnic anxieties generated by a society in transition. The house, which features prominently in the novel both as haven and prison, is the symbolic umbilicus of Laila's memories, which are narrated initially through the divided consciousness of a young girl (15 at the opening of the novel and 35 at its close) who grows up under the care of her elders, Aunt Abida and the ageing patriarch of the family soon to die, Hakiman Bua. Whilst Laila has no parents, she is also orphaned from other worlds: the conflicting expectations of her Western education (she was known, we are told by Mrs Martin, as *Lily* at school), and a growing inability to tolerate the corruptions of the mores of the traditional world that surrounds her. In a powerful scene where Laila questions the punishment her Uncle Mohsin inflicts on the servant girl, Nandi, for transgressing the rules of purdah when he himself is guilty of similar infidelities, Laila bravely breaks the codes of honour and decorum by openly questioning his actions:

> Uncle Mohsin's face was distorted as he raised his stick and hit her [Nandi] across the shoulders. She fell forward and as I ran towards her the next blow glanced across my arm and I screamed, 'I hate you, I hate you', and ran blinded by tears to my room.
>
> (*Sunlight on a Broken Column*, p. 25)

Unlike Zahra, her cousin who fulfils the expectations of her role as the daughter of an aristocratic *taluqdar* family, Laila perpetually laments her isolation, the sense of always being 'torn apart', situated both within and outside the boundaries of decorum and tradition. Why, she pleads 'did you not bring me up like Zahra?' (p. 38). For whilst she does not physically leave Hasnapur like her male cousins who go to school in England, she nevertheless lived in two worlds, an 'observer . . . outside . . . solitary in my own' (p. 124).

The divisions of Laila's childhood are as evident in the world outside *purdah* and the gates of Hasnapur and Ashiana (a rural family seat) as they are within. Mrs Martin, once her English governess, always refers to England as 'Home' (though, as Laila observes, she had only ever been there for a few months with her husband), whilst Sylvia Tucker, one of her supposedly 'English' school friends, mocks Laila's idealistic and burgeoning political sympathies with Sita Agarwal and the Congress Party. Singing 'Rule Britannia' loudly whenever she sees them, she secretly withholds from public view the racial identity of her mother, who is 'dark' and 'not Italian'. Through a number of luminous and haunting episodes – not unlike the marooned atmosphere surrounding Antoinette Cosway at the opening of Jean Rhys's famous novel *Wide Sargasso Sea* – Hosain presents the disturbed consciousness of a society and family in transition, catching the strength of individual women's voices who did not fear to transgress, such as Aunt Abida. Until her enforced marriage immediately after Hakiman Bua's death, she could cut through the voices of patriarchy in the household 'like a blade'. Laila's 'difference' from the other women in the *zenana* is clearly 'a source of discomfort, even pain', but as Anuradha Needham has suggested, it is also 'productive of a vision of people and positions that simultaneously understands, even as it critically examines their investments'.[69] Although Laila ultimately betrays her Aunt's hidebound sense of duty to the family by following the freedom of her own romantic feelings and marrying Ameer Hussein – a man beneath her status – she does not ever reject or fail to empathize with the predicament of those who must make different choices on account of a wide spectrum of different influences – whether generated by religious belief, gender or politics.

On the surface, the structure of the novel suggests a predictable *bildungsroman* pattern which charts the coming-of-age of a young aristocratic Muslim girl. Divided into four sections, it counterpoints the public and private history of Laila's family, which is eventually broken apart by the competing influences of the National Congress, the Muslim League, Independence from British rule and the painful disintegration of the North Indian landowning classes (the *zamindars*) who following the first Independence struggle of 1857, 'the Mutiny', were coerced by the British to function as intermediaries, whilst still retaining their wealth, class and privilege. Yet as the nationalist struggle progresses, the *taluqdars* (such as Laila's Uncle Hamid) begin to witness the erosion of their elitist position and are torn between ancient loyalties to Muslim traditions, a disintegrating pact with the British and the realities of living in increasingly Hindu dominated states. Hosain dramatizes these shifting tableaux of conflicting positions and the gender conflicts they repress through a variety of voices: whether through the idealistic nationalistic fervour of Asad and Zahid (a passion leading to Zahid's death), Saleem's decision to support the Muslim cause against his father's wishes and migrate to Pakistan, or the tragic erosion of all Uncle Hamid's 'dreams and ambitions' (p. 111), 'crumbling' in an empty house where 'I longed to make . . . the stillness breathe' (p. 42).

Although Laila seldom identifies herself wholly with any one perspective, presenting herself as an observer who mediates and listens to a number of different voices, it is her ability to weave together the entire fabric of a multiple history of interlocking social, cultural and political relationships spanning the varied locations of her character's lives, which gives the novel a force beyond that of a *bildungsroman*. Hosain is less concerned with the chronology of either her main protagonist's life – the surface plot – or a linear narration of the fissures of a tortured political history, than with discovering an aesthetic to express the power of memory as a device to both contain and expose the heterogeneity of a broken past. As with the short stories, it is the voices and symbols of the past which stir and provide a unifying thread in Laila's consciousness, an associative narrative method which relies on flashback and the suggestive splinters of nodal moments – overheard conversations, partially recounted arguments, mood and atmosphere – to reconstruct a world, which like the old house if only in its stillness, continues to breathe.

In the final and fourth section of the novel – the section where Laila returns after 14 years to Ashiana, now a house for the refugees of Partition and disfigured like 'the skin of a once beautiful woman struck by leprosy' – time collapses into an epiphany which condenses her life 'as in a summary', where 'Fourteen years were as fourteen moments, but the years that had gone before were as many centuries' (pp. 271–2). Although this last section has most frequently been dismissed by critics as an indulgent 'orgy of sentimentality'[70] and an unnecessary adjunct to the novel's already weak chronological structure – it is in fact the coda that explicates Hosain's purpose and provides a 'double screen'[71] for the substance of Laila's earlier recollections. For it is through the spaces of memory embodied by the broken columns of the house that Hosain is able to piece together the multiple determinants of Laila's life as they parallel her potentially 'alternative account' of the 'nation in the act of making itself'.[72] There are many examples throughout the novel which demonstrate the extent to which Laila's consciousness is framed by the translated realities of memory, creating pools of insight in her developing consciousness. But such insights are not intended to be cumulative or developmental, as we see by Laila's own self-confessed failure throughout to overcome an inability to act either for one side or the other, a passivity engendered in part by the eclecticism of her broad education as much as by the circumscriptions of her location. Nor does the novel expose issues which it can pretend to resolve. Instead, it demonstrates the difficulties involved in attempting to sustain an imaginative fidelity to an unflinching portrait of historical truths, the grotesque effects that abuses of power and repressions of human freedom have on individual lives – whoever are the rulers, or the ruled. As Asad puts it: 'The people rotted under the rulers of our own race, as they do under the English, and as they will do if we rule ourselves again' (p. 218). And it is Asad, too, who supports Laila's courageous determination at the end of the novel to embrace the forces of change alone, to stay on in India despite her husband's death, and to live with the inexorable difficulties of redefinition demanded by a new social order.

Although Hosain's work was well received both in India and in Britain when it first appeared and although she was encouraged by many leading critics of the day including Cecil Day Lewis who edited her novel, Mulk Raj Anand who prefaced the Indian edition, and Leonard Woolf who was keen to publish it, she disappeared from public view as a writer until the republication of her work by Virago in the 1980s, following a resurgence of interest in fictions by Indian writers in English in the wake of the popular success of Rushdie's novel of Indian Independence, *Midnight's Children* (1981). This is a fate which seems to have also befallen Aubrey Menen and G. V. Desani, perhaps for different reasons, since, following the Second World War, there was a distinct reluctance amongst English critics to confront the extent to which the scale of recent atrocities in Europe bore any relationship to the 'holocausts' engendered by Empire. Moreover, it was also clear as Aubrey Menen notes in his candid autobiography, *The Space Within The Heart*, that the apparently radical yet narrow prescriptions of a Euro-American modernity could not admit those 'foreigners' whose writing reflected a different colour:

> however high I rose in the creative arts, I would not be what *they* [my italics] were looking for. The whole trouble was that there were far too many talented foreigners and far too few British ones. And I knew this.[73]

Hosain's understated antipathy to the sweeping dogma of political causes is differently articulated in the work of Aubrey Menen. Unlike Hosain, who was bilingual and in no doubt about her Indian heritage, Menen strove from an early age to confront his mixed racial background and what he called the absurdity of misguided patriotism and national prides. Born only a year before Attia Hosain in 1912, Menen frequently drew attention to the triangular nature of his mixed racial and cultural heritage as an Irish-Indian by parentage and a brown Englishman by birth and education. Unlike Menen, Hosain never felt herself to be part of any diaspora even though she lived in Britain (apart from short visits back to India) for nearly 50 years, working in the early part of her career as a well-known and fêted journalist/broadcaster for the BBC Eastern Service. In an interview conducted at the very end of her life in 1997, and after the emergence of what she calls the 'younger British generation', she is adamant that she is neither 'in diaspora' nor, as V. S. Naipaul puts it in an early and complimentary review of *Sunlight on a Broken Column*, 'caught between'.[74] For unlike those writers (who include Salman Rushdie, Atima Srivastava and Hanif Kureishi)[75] whose work, she has said, celebrates the notion of being unhoused, 'I am rooted in India. My branches might be spread all around, but my roots are firmly planted in the earth. I belong to India, to England, to the Universe'.[76] Yet Hosain's work, when viewed with the benefit of hindsight, clearly looks forward to what Amit Chaudhuri has described as that confident body of contemporary modern Indian writing (whether written at home or abroad) which does not need to display its inherent duality or hybridity as part of an exotic national costume fulfilling the mimetic and essentially orientalist desires of Western critics, but which employs instead a number of less explicit but nevertheless imminently 'postcolonial' characteristics, in which representation is always a form of translation and language, even when apparently conforming to traditional usages or a realist mode creates a system of subtly altered meanings which hover on the edges of 'absence and recognition'.[77]

Whilst Aubrey Menen does not of course situate himself in the 1950s as a product of what later in the century came to be known as the South Asian *diaspora*, his work captures many of the features now associated with writers of mixed-race or dual cultural backgrounds whose conceptual vision straddles several worlds. In contrast to Hosain, who deliberately refused to write about Britain – for fear of being seen as an exile, an 'outsider . . . a person here looking for something',[78] Menen describes himself as 'native' of at least 'three' lands, all of which 'I can call my own'. In an illuminating collection of semi-fictional pieces, *Dead Man in a Silver Market: An Autobiographical Essay on National Prides* (1954), Menen satirically presents the details of how his ethnicity was constructed for him, whether as 'brown Englishman' at school, or equally by his Indian grandmother as the 'last descendant of an ancient family' of Malabar Nayars. Although ironic and humorous in tone, these essays present a sharp critique of the blinkered arrogance that feeds notions of cultural superiority, whether engendered by East or West. In the opening piece, 'How I was Initiated into the Best Tribe' (the first version being published in his school magazine 'The Highburian'), Menen's intimate and comic portrait of the details of his early childhood is accompanied by a painful unravelling of the blatant racism he suffered as well as by a deconstruction of the hypocritical ideologies of Empire. As a young child who grew up during the First World War, Menen explains how he was first 'made much of by the English . . . even given pennies by old gentlemen in the street'. Yet as the war progressed, and the populace at large forgot that 'Indians on the Western Front were cutting the throats of Germans with a specially shaped knife called a *kukri*', 'I was mistaken for a Turk', a change of attitude likely to afflict anyone with a 'dark complexion'. Moreover, the Turks, unlike the British, were alleged to be uncivilized, brutally 'cutting off the testicles of their English prisoners'. By 1918 and the age of six, it had all changed once more and, as Menen notes, 'I was popular again'. For 'Victory had been won and the Indians who had cut the throats of the Germans were to be seen in London', wearing their knives as patriotic banners.

As the essay develops, Menen ridicules the fickle shiftings of public opinion, but he also exposes the serious dangers of adhering to any essentialist notions of cultural 'truth', whether linked to a narrow identity politics or the partisan dogmas of cultural nationalism. Whilst he is fully taken in for a while by those who were 'only too anxious to make me like themselves', believing firmly in dictums like: 'An Englishman's word was his bond' or that as an 'Englishman', he would forever be 'at home in the process called human history', his brainwashing at school did not assuage his developing sense of difference, his awareness that, despite his successful performances of 'the adventures of [Rudyard Kipling's] *Kim* my colour adding drama to the recital', he might none the less represent the embodiment of one of the less-fortunate and untrustworthy figures in Kipling's fictional world, a 'half-caste' or Eurasian (pp. 9–14). From the outset, Menen's tone is caustically satirical. Referring to his parents' decision to educate him as English, he says:

> If it should be thought that the idea of bringing up an Indo-Irishman as a Briton had something of the whimsical in it, I should say . . . that in nineteen hundred and twelve it was nothing of the sort. The English were then masters of three-quarters of the earth, and in this three-quarters were both the Irish and the Indians. Had I been brought up as either

> of these I would have thought of the English as my equals but treated them as my masters. As an Englishman I was able to treat both the Irish and the Indians as my inferiors as long as I was careful to speak of them to their faces as my equals. This formula was the basis of an astonishing organisation called the British Empire and remained so until the formula was finally understood by the subject races, when the British Empire somewhat hurriedly became the Commonwealth. Since, however, it did not become a Commonwealth until the English had no wealth to share, the master race has been able to look back on the process without loss of self-esteem (p. 9).

The 'well-meaning' logic of such unshakeable national prides unfortunately added up to the fact that Menen's own father could only ever be a 'congenital liar'; a member of an alien and 'coloured' tribe, whom Menen had been taught to regard as a race of 'harmless, but dirty inferiors' (p. 14).

Menen provides a reverse mirror of the absurdities of this kind of blinkered vision in his next essay 'My Grandmother and the Dirty English', in which on a trip 'half way across the earth' to visit his ancestral home near Calicut, Southern India, at the age of 12, he encounters a similarly arrogant attitude. Travelling with his Irish mother, 'the Englishwoman' as his Indian grandmother calls her, and whom she finds difficult to accept because she is 'ritually unclean', he voyages to meet this formidable matriarch. Not aligning himself with either camp, Menen's sense of comedy (his description of his grandmother's Nayar formality which was to greet all visitors 'with her breasts completely bare', for she regarded all 'married women who wore blouses and pretty saris' as Jezebels, a costume which 'could only be aiming at adultery'), nevertheless masks a deeper sense of disquiet. Playing in this and subsequent essays on the use of the words 'civilised', 'history', and 'truth' as used both by the British, 'who constantly maintained they were the finest race on earth', and the Nayars, 'who thought the same thing but considered it so obvious that amongst themselves they never mentioned it', he says: 'how was I to choose? Each side maintained that it was the summit of creation. Each side maintained that the other was backward and dirty.' And although the young Menen is tempted to adopt his grandmother's advice to drink cow's urine, to embrace the rituals and rights of his Malabar heritage and to cleanse himself of his heathen defilement, he is plagued on return by the voice of his English headmaster, whose remedy for any such confusion was to 'play games', a skill which would 'make me a fine young man acceptable to *English* society' (pp. 27–9).

As Menen was later to reveal in the more serious reflections on his painful growth to adulthood in Britain (recollected in his autobiography *The Space Within the Heart*), gameplaying, however proficient, was not the key to transcending deeply embedded social injustices. Having been rejected by University College for the 'Rosa Morrison' bursary because he was not of 'pure English' descent, a rejection made more painful because it was executed by the then Jewish Master, 'who should', as he says, 'have known better and he probably did',[79] Menen's subsequent writing was frequently to expose, whether symbolically in his fiction and plays, or more explicitly in his journalism, the myopia of narrowly held positions whether on race, culture or sexual practices. Frequently radical and courageously outspoken in his approach, one of Menen's early works, *Rama Retold*,[80] was banned in India by Nehru himself in 1956 for his treatment of Vedic myths, his critique of traditional representations of the plight of Sita, and his clear sympathies for the predicament of Hindu wives. Whilst Menen characteristically took this censorship lightheartedly, seeing the publicity it caused as the making of himself as a writer, his antipathy to Aryan myths in India was equally directed against the Nazis in Germany, who also called themselves 'Aryan', and whose behaviour during the Second World War destroyed, once and for all, what Menen called the 'myth of a white supremacy'.[81] Like Mulk Raj Anand, Menen was keen to expose the blinkered tenets of a modernity – 'I think therefore I am' – which promised, but did not allow the freedoms his reading of Descartes had promised him as a student. Instead, its fundamental dualism set in motion a system which resulted in the reductive creation of an invisible and undelineated group of colonial 'others' and ended 'by showing that he [Descartes] was part of a mechanical universe even more rigid and predetermined than my grandmother's'.[82]

Menen eventually left Britain, on the proceeds of his writing, to live for part of his middle age in Italy, a space 'halfway between' India and England.[83] As the author of over ten novels, 12 non-fiction works and numerous journalistic pieces, he was quick to establish an international reputation as a reporter and critic.[84] Menen's fiction, however, was not the subject of a great deal of serious critical scrutiny. He has been frequently seen as little more than a transient 'Anglo-Indian curiosity',[85] more interesting for his mixed-ethnic background and a declared homosexuality which derives, he suggests in *A Space Within The Heart*, from his Irish mother's predisposition to flirt with men with brown skins, an exoticizing desire which heightened his own Oedipal relationship with her as a young boy and was to remain a destructive force in his later relationships with women. Menen's fiction, as Mary Jane Hurst has perceptively suggested, clearly reflects concerns that are now common features in the currency of postcolonial criticism – demonstrating a satirical and sometimes allegorical exposure of the injustices of colonialism, as well as pinpointing the inequalities of institutionalized social systems whether of East or West. Yet his work appears on the surface to adhere to traditional narrative forms rather than exhibiting any self-consciously experimental or explicitly modernist fictional techniques. In addition, whilst its humour often masks the complexities of Menen's own location as a mixed-race homosexual who did not fit in to any comfortable literary niche, it is clear on closer examination that the insights gained by the contradictory realities of his own cultural background form a 'radical subtext'[86] to the stories he chooses to tell.

It is not possible here to examine the full extent to which Menen's literary output was driven by the need to revision narrowly conceived notions of 'tradition' or 'modernity' – the idea, as he puts it sarcastically in an essay originally written for 'The Highburian', his school magazine, that: an 'elephant walking down the main street of Bombay' might not cause as much surprise and 'obstruction to the traffic – as would one of the mighty beasts if transplanted into the middle of Picadilly Circus'.[87] But it is worth commenting briefly on Menen's first novel, *The Prevalence of Witches*, which explores the process by which beliefs, however conflicting their biases and whatever their cultural derivations, become dangerous when translated into 'truths'.[88] Widely acclaimed on publication in 1947 for its use of an ironic satire and its rigorous examination of the subject of ethics and morality in a small Indian community – a biting critique of the potential fundamentalism of religious faiths – *The Prevalence of Witches* examines the nature of good and evil, the perpetuation of superstitions and false 'mysticisms' as they are lived out in Limbo, an obscure jungle area of India. As the setting suggests, Menen's characters – who include Catullus, a compulsive talker and British officer, Cuff Small, a misguided American missionary (who lacks vision and has only converted one person in 20 years), the local village chief as well as the newly arrived and unnamed education officer who narrates the tale – all cohabit a nowhere land where a number of different religious and political ideologies are played out. Dramatizing some of the issues already explored in Menen's non-fictional essays, the characters are literally and metaphorically involved in a dubious witch-hunt which results from a clash of different cultural systems, a confusion created as much by the supposed logic of the British legal system (when the local Chief is jailed by Catullus for murder in fighting the witches beleaguering his community) as by the pagan supernaturalism of the village itself. Menen satirizes the absurd inconsistencies in both systems, exposing the collusive relationship between Christianity and Empire as well as sending up the local Swami for being a conman and hypocrite. As Catullus says at one point:

> We got an uncomfortably large slice of our Empire not by being good soldiers but by being quick at languages. First we sent our missionaries to make grammars and translations of the Bible, then we sent the Civil Servants to use the grammars to write out treaties. The Americans got the Red Indians drunk on gin: we got our Indians fuddled with words (p. 30).

Yet it is the duplicity of language, too, that enables the Swami to reap his financial rewards as witch doctor of the village, when he unwittingly succeeds in performing a 'miracle' and exorcizing a young boy – a miracle we later discover has been set in motion by the political machinations of the villagers themselves who wished to free their Chief. Working through a series of swift comic reversals, the novel attempts to break down the false securities of any rigid system or faith as well as exposing comically the hypocrisies of individual lives. The Indian judge, for instance, Justice Bose, is more concerned with writing a treatise on the 'lunatics' of 'Limbo' (p. 222) than with the Swami's complicity in the inducement of such hysteria; similarly, the retrograde Swami himself becomes a natural philosopher, the voice amidst apparent madness of ethics and reason:

> Everywhere you turn you see it in people's eyes: 'What have we done? Where are we going? Why can't we stop it?' They are like a people bewitched.

The Swami's philosophy is summed up towards the end of the novel by a vehement justification of the truths of his forked tongue: 'people won't listen to the truth unless it has all the appearance of a thumping lie' (pp. 207–9). Perhaps partially, this reflects Menen's own position as a writer, as he sought to confront the troubled questions of his own racial and sexual identity whilst working for a short period (like his first-person narrator) as an education officer in a remote rural area of India in the years following the Second World War. As he has commented in *The Space Within The Heart*:

> The Western world is brought up to believe that black is black and white is white and anybody who attempts to muddle the two is an idiot . . . The

> Hindu has never thought in this manner. He has always felt that anybody who could prove that black is not black, white is not white, but both are *really the same thing* [my italics] is a very clever fellow and worth listening to (p. 8).

Menen's desire to widen the angle of the lens and to open up the essentially dualistic perspective of a Western modernity was to be a life-long project. It was a perspective he shared (unwittingly perhaps) with his contemporary, G. V. Desani, whose iconoclastic and self-referential 'novel' *All About H. Hatterr* appeared in 1948, a year later than Menen's first novel. In *All About H. Hatterr*, Desani confronts head on many of the issues which Menen had so painfully attempted to unlock both in his essays and in his fiction. However, whereas Menen's language still works within a framework that conforms to certain traditional Western narrative rules – employing a comic, satiric mode to expose the incongruities of his hybrid vision, as well as revealing the dangers in adhering to any rigidly determined version of 'truth' – Desani's method is determinedly subversive from the outset, deliberately exploding any settled notions the reader may have of genre, language or style. As Desani makes clear in both the self-conscious staging of the author/narrator in his irreverent preface 'All About . . .' and in the preliminary 'Warnings' he issues to the reader, this is no ordinary 'novel'. Nor does it conform, initially at least, to any easily recognizable structure, whether authorial, linguistic, or generic. For Hatterr, the anti-hero and first-person narrator of his 'Autobiographical' (as he describes the main section of the narrative which is *his* story) is like his creator, an unreliable author, a spinner of yarns, who, in attempting to discover a voice and the secrets of 'truth', voyages on a hazardous journey across the infinite sea of language itself. As we are informed in one of the many parodic frames that Desani constructs to mirror Hatterr's mock-Socratic quest, the method may confuse rather than elucidate. And as the book's original subtitle suggested, its apparently (non)sensical content may represent more of a 'gesture' than a 'novel'.[89] We are given a sequence of performances in which Hatterr, as a modern reincarnation of the trickster figure of ancient myths, is a comic survivor, a character 'who pays no deference to class [race], or sex because tricks defy categories'. In *All About H. Hatterr*, Desani provides a natural context for what Gillian Beer has called the radical exhilaration, not of narrative development, but of 'narrative swerve'. Rather than exhibiting any explicitly driven linearity, it is a performative text, a literary carnival, unmasking the fact that all words, (whatever their cultural derivations or semantic systems), are only ever 'pointers, indicators, symbols'.[90] For, as Hatterr says, 'there isn't a single word in any lingo, dialect or doggerel, which is absolutely cast-true, suggesting in the exact infallible, *Truth*' (p. 274).

At one level the book can certainly be read as a comic picaresque, detailing the transcultural and episodic adventures of a twentieth-century immigrant 'Everyman', in which Hatterr, the eponymous anti-hero, travels India seeking the wisdom (dubious and often fraudulent as it turns out) of seven ancient religious sages in seven different cities. As the 'fifty-fifty' son of a 'European, Christian by-faith merchant seaman' and a 'Malay Peninsula-resident lady', the semi-educated Hatterr is as much the creation, as he tells us, of the 'Greeks' as of the 'Barbarians'. Separated at the age of one from his Malay mother, he also suffers the loss of his 'merman' father soon after his voyage East to India. After a swift and merciful adoption by an 'India-resident Dundee-born Scot', he falls into the role of an inveterate Pilgrim, a natural philosopher who seeks his fortune by attempting to resolve life's age-old questions. Quickly learning as a budding journalist that language (and its deceptions) are his capital, he seeks to protect himself from 'further blows of Fate' by preserving his story for posterity, writing an autobiography of sorts, which is 'ALSO A MOSAIC-ORGANON OF LIFE' in a 'rigmarole English', an 'English' that, whilst 'staining your goodly godly tongue', might 'ensure against drifting from isolation to utter eclipse' – and, more importantly, 'deprivation of grub' (pp. 35–7).

There are several moments in the 'novel' when Hatterr draws our attention, despite the fast moving and exuberant surface of his narration, to the difficulties of his existence. He frequently suffers from hypochondriac nightmares, and in his episodic encounters with the venerable sages, he is regularly humiliated. As he tells us in the 'Mutual Introduction', although he is delighted to be in England, this 'demi-paradise, this precious stone set in the silver sea', he is, like many of the 'Bard O'Avon['s]' characters, 'a most poor man and a stranger'. In the description we are given of Hatterr's humble arrival at Liverpool dock – a journey he undertakes reluctantly on the advice of his brother-in-law, friend and adviser, Bannerji – we gain an insight into the deflationary as well as the comic effects of Desani's burlesque:

> All my life I wanted to come: come to the Western shores, to my old man's Continent, to the Poet-Bard's adored Eldorado, to England, the God's own country, the seat of Mars, that damme paradise . . . to the Englishman's Home, his Castle, his garden, fact's the feller's true alma mammy and apple-orchard.

> And now I had arrived!
>
> The realisation made me feel humble, and O.H.M.S. *post-haste*, thank Almighty for same! Forgetting all reserve, forsaking all Do-As-Romans-do etiquette, and in full view of Liverpool's sardonically inclined docker population . . . I greeted the soil, both in the true English and the Eastern fashion.
>
> I took off my tropical lid, the sola-topi, in sincere salutation and next, without a waterproof, in my white drill shorts, I knelt on the mud-beds of the old country, the soft depths of its textilopolis County Palatine, aye, Keeper, luv, the blessed wet earth of Liverpool, Lancs, in a thousand salaams. (p. 36)

The experiences of Desani's own life, of course, parallel in some ways the destiny of his fictional character, H. Hatterr. Born in Nairobi in 1908, he was the son of a Sindi merchant family who had migrated to East Africa in the nineteenth century. A class of seasoned 'travellers', they were, as Desani has explained, experienced middlemen and skilled mediators, 'brokers' of 'language', who used this facility in order to trade. Returning to India at the age of six, he ran away from his second childhood home in Shikarpur (once part of the ancient Indus valley civilization) at the age of 17, escaping for the third time his father's insistent demand to marry him off to a Hindu child bride. Arriving in London in 1917, alone with no money or 'language', as he has put it, Desani became a self-made man, remaking himself in the West as a raconteur, a journalist, and eventually a well-known and fêted rhetorician patronized by the English aristocracy, particularly Lord Zetland, a Governor of Bengal. What does it mean, Desani asks in 'Liars, Hypocrites, Imperialists and Sages', to find oneself with 'no language'?[91] Having arrived in London with only a smattering of Swahili (his first language taught to him by his *Kikuyu* ayah) and Sindi, the language of his parents, Desani learnt English whilst working as a repairer of watches, reading the Bible in his spare time, and stuffing newspapers under his shirt. Later, with an introduction to the Rationalist Association and the works of eminent philosophers such as Bertrand Russell, he began to piece together the diverse cultural influences of his mixed cultural background, recognizing that the superstitious 'Nadi' texts of South Indian sages – 'hand-written texts on palm leaf' – were as much a key to the 'truths' he sought as the supposedly rational speculations of Western philosophers. But one thing was clear: 'There wasn't a single problem in India . . . no matter how exotic it looked, which had not arisen in Europe, sometime or the other.' More significantly perhaps, given Desani's later career as a wordsmith, was his growing realization that all beliefs, whatever their cultural derivations, were 'verbal feats', built through language on a shifting sea of 'words'.[92]

Given Desani's own background, it is not surprising that he plunges his mixed-race narrator in *All About H. Hatterr* into a situation where language is primarily 'Invention' and where improvisation becomes the key both to survival and understanding. Not unlike the 'sense' learnt by Alice as she tumbles into Lewis Carroll's upside-down world in *Alice in Wonderland*, Desani's beleaguered H. Hatterr (whose name deliberately plays, of course, on the Mad Hatter of Lewis Carroll's fantasy) navigates a path through a bewildering maze of different voices and systems of belief. Hatterr's unselfconscious creation of his own vernacular – an iconoclastic creolized style which draws on a wide range of jumbled neologisms – is the tool by which he negotiates his existence. Yet unlike Hatterr, Desani himself was extremely clear both about the derivations of various voices and philosophies which he was deconstructing, and about the book's structure. As is evident from the complex Editorial Notes he submitted to his publishers, whilst the surface chaos of the book might suggest that it is simply a tale told by a confused immigrant signifying nothing, the underlying vision is built on the sustained investigation of a series of serious philosophical questions. Moreover he explicitly places Hatterr in a comi-tragic role as a man driven by fear ('a hypochondriac'), unable to find love ('motherless' by culture and birth), yet still refusing to be broken by 'Life', whatever his scepticisms about God[s] ('a kind of Mephistopholes') or faith.[93]

Most contemporary readings of Desani's novel place it as 'an early, and largely underrated (post)colonial text which makes full use of the literary strategies of postmodernism in order to come to terms with the colonial condition' in which 'no single truth' but only 'difference' will suffice.[94] Such analyses, however, inevitably followed in the wake of now-familiar theoretical paradigms and often underestimate the extent to which current academic orthodoxies still fail to contain the potentiality and prescience of the creative work in both anticipating and recognizing its own 'problems in advance'.[95] Yes, the novel's urbane cosmopolitanism and eclectic 'hybridity' pre-empt the work of writers like Salman Rushdie (most notably in his first novel *Grimus* and later in *The Satanic Verses*). And yes, like many postcolonial novels which were to follow, the book exhibits an impressive intertextuality, moving backwards and forwards in time and place, culture and history, simultaneously undercutting the canonical scriptures of India's ancient 'sages' as well as the 'grand narratives' of Western epistemologies. The cumulative and allusive nature of Desani's punning style is evident throughout, whether through his witty reinventions of Shakespeare, his parodic pastiche of snippets from Rudyard Kipling, his satirizing of the ancient classics of traditional Indian religious doctrine or through his misquotations of the empirical language of medical encyclopaedias. The linguistic shifts are swift and impressive, as Desani moves from the empty, bookish knowledge of a Bannerji, who breathlessly misquotes a jumbled conglomeration of 'classical and Indian references . . . western texts, whether . . . Freud, Whitman or Carlyle', placing them, like a recited prayer, as undisputed 'source of all authority' for the more reflective, but still disorientating experiences of Hatterr himself.[96] Yet Desani's purpose is less to analyse or argue than to dramatize, to illustrate the process by which Hatterr both remakes and is remade by language, creating a space which is not constrained by time or place so much as by the inherent mutability of language itself.[97]

Significantly, Desani does not restrict himself only to a juxtaposition between misused Standard English or a number of 'Indianisms', but draws instead on a medley of terms which come from outside the Anglo-Saxon world. The polyphonic range of the text points as much to incongruities between the differently articulated voices of the Indian Sages, whom Hatterr meets on his quest to seven different Indian cities, as it does to the many versions of British dialects he presents. Moreover, drawing on Cockney, Scottish and Welsh usages, Latin, operatic Italian, bad French, Yiddish, as well as an erudite range of references to world-famous philosophers, Desani both liberates Hatterr from his plight as a mixed-race outsider attempting to find his bearings both within and in spite of English, and highlights what is perhaps one of the book's more serious intentions and the ultimate metaphysical destination of Hatterr's voyage: the recognition that, as we are frequently told, 'Life is contrast', and that 'Truth', in whatever guise it might appear, is always shifting, always someone else's translation. As Hatterr explains, in his own creolized Hatterrese, there is no point in writing back in the 'antithesis school' of 'retributive! compensatory!' (p. 61), for:

> Why should one unique individual feller lose, and the other gain, whenever any two are brought together by deliberate design or by off-chance accident?
>
> Hell, what is *Truth*? as one P. Pilate once asked!
>
> Posterity expects: and no dam'use funking the issue.
>
> But can words ever communicate *Truth* – whatever it is . . .
>
> A *Truth*-thing, or a *Truth*-idea, might be an *a*. By the time the feller has

> the notion of this *a*, a sensation of it, its nature changes. What a feller has is not an *a*, but an awareness of an *a*.
> Below the belt! He hasn't the true *a* but a *translation*!

The point Desani is making here – that any cultural or linguistic adaptation always involves translation – is not, of course, particularly new, although it has now become a paradigm of postcolonial theoretical analyses. For as the novel repeatedly displays, 'all communicated and communicable knowledge' has historically been 'subject to this bashing up', particularly, in countries like India with an ancient history of diasporic movement and assimilation. Furthermore, as Hatterr self-consciously goes on to exclaim (pp. 274–5), drawing the reader's attention once more to the figure of the writer both as trickster and alchemist of language:

> What do you expect of a damme *writer* of words, anyway? *Truth*? Hell, you will get *contrast*, and no mistake!'

2

Crossing Over and Shifting the Shapes: Sam Selvon's Londoners

Migration was not a word I would have used to describe what I was doing when I sailed with other West Indians to England in the 1950s . . . We simply thought that we were going to an England which had been planted in our childhood consciousness as a heritage and place of welcome . . . It was the name of a responsibility whose origin may have coincided with the beginning of time.

George Lamming[1]

By openly fighting tradition we perpetuate it . . . revolutionary literature is a filial impulse, and . . . maturity is the assimilation of the features of every ancestor.

Derek Walcott[2]

you took the small
language used by the island
for picong and calypsoes
and stretched its vowels
across the mouth of the world.

Cecil Gray[3]

Now that, in the postmodern age, you all feel dispersed, I become centred. What I've thought of as dispersed and fragmented comes, paradoxically, to be the representative modern experience! This is 'coming home' with a vengeance

Stuart Hall[4]

Although a sense of the need to migrate clearly affected early writers born in the Caribbean such as the Jamaican Claude McKay, who left in 1912 for the United States, and the Trinidadian C. L. R. James, who arrived in Britain during the 1930s, the period immediately following the Second

World War was particularly important for the arrival in London of a number of talented young West Indian artists. As Henry Swanzy, the producer of the influential BBC Radio programme *Caribbean Voices* observed, London had become a 'literary headquarters', a place where writers from the various islands were meeting for the first time and attempted, paradoxically perhaps, to establish a firm West Indian cultural identity. Yet, as he also notes, the imaginations of these writers were not *formed* within the 'grey world city'; their 'mental furniture was strangely different'.[5] The status of London as such has always been a point of controversy in the criticism of postwar Caribbean literature.

Whilst the majority of the writers came to Britain with the intention of getting their work published and to escape from the parochial 'philistinism' of the West Indian middle classes common at that time, they did not come alone. Their departure from the islands coincided with a period when over 40 000 West Indians emigrated to Britain in search of employment. Originally invited to the 'mother-country' by the postwar government as an attempt to solve the temporary labour crisis following the Second World War, and commonly known as the *Windrush* generation, islanders from a wide range of backgrounds journeyed to Britain expecting to find the jobs they had been promised through a widespread advertising and recruitment campaign hosted by the British government in the islands. As 'ordinary immigrant[s]',[6] many of the writers were looking, as George Lamming puts it in *The Pleasures of Exile*, for a 'better break' to broaden their audience and to improve their standard of living. But the streets of London were not 'paved with gold', and the journey from island to city was in many cases initially one of disappointment and disillusion. Moses, the prophetic and sage-like figure of Sam Selvon's well-known epic cycle of novels on the immigrant experience in Britain – *The Lonely Londoners* (1956), *Moses Ascending* (1975) and *Moses Migrating* (1983)[7] – makes the following satiric observations (pp. 6–7) on the plight of his West Indian *emigrants* who were transformed after arrival in the metropolis into *immigrants* and later by the white British media into working-class 'black' Londoners:

> The alarms of all the black people in Brit'n are timed to ring before the rest of the population. It is their destiny to be up and about at the crack o'dawn. In these days of pollution and environment, he is very lucky, for he can breathe the freshest air of the new day before anybody else. He does not know how fortunate he is. He does not know how privileged he is to be in charge of the city whilst the rest of Brit'n is still abed. He strides the streets, he is Manager of all the offices in Threadaneedle

> Street, he is Chief Executive of London Transport and British Railways, he is superintendent of all the hospitals, he is landlord of all the mansions in Park Lane and Hampstead . . . He ain't reach the stage yet of scrubbing the floors of Buckingham Palace . . . There is a scramble amongst the rest of the loyal population for these royal jobs, but with time, he too might be exalted to these ranks – who knows? Instead of moaning and groaning about his sorrows, he should stop and think and count these blessings reserved solely for him. He should realise that if it wasn't for him the city would go on sleeping forever.

The black man is therefore the backbone of the city but we see him only at night and whilst, as Stuart Hall has suggested, his history shadows Britain's imperial past as an *intimate* presence that is inside the history of the English, being so to speak, 'the sugar at the bottom of the English cup of tea', his significance was seldom seen or recognized.[8] Even as early as 1780 Ignatius Sancho, one of London's earliest black writers, described his location in Britain on one occasion as 'a lodger . . . and hardly that' as he awkwardly straddled the fashionable world of eighteenth-century English letters.[9] Sancho's sentiments, evident in some of his letters and highlighted more generally in the pieces included in Caryl Phillips's anthology of migrant writings, *Extravagant Strangers: A Literature of Belonging* (which takes its title from the words of Shakespeare's Othello), have been echoed again and again in the history of black and Asian writing in Britain, both in terms of their critical reception and in the placing of those writers from elsewhere outside the gates of the nation's falsely constructed borders. As George Lamming intimates in the epigraph above, his arrival in Britain in the 1950s represented the simultaneous fulfilment of an ancient tyranny and a passionate desire – the colonial's relation to the *idea* of England which was both 'mother', a part of his familial heritage, and symbol of a perennial exile, imposed on him as the descendant of the rigid strictures of a manichean colonial historiography born out of his New World Caribbean experience. It was, however, a relation that opened up an 'ambivalent space' that 'separated but also conjoined metropole and colony'.[10]

In a memorial tribute to Sam Selvon delivered in London in 1994, Lamming attempted to reconstruct the atmosphere of the early days he shared with Selvon both on the boat journey to England and, later, as young writers struggling to earn a living through the guineas they earned from the BBC. 'Can you imagine', says Lamming, 'waking up one morning and discovering a stranger asleep on the sofa of your living room?'. This was exactly the situation many English people found themselves in when 'they awoke' to find 'these people [once comrades on the Second World War battlefields, now strangers and post-war immigrants] metaphorically on the sofas of their living rooms . . . On the one hand the sleeper on the sofa was absolutely sure through imperial tutelage that he was *at home*, on the other, the native Englishman was completely mystified by this unknown interloper.'[11] As one of the pioneers of a literary movement which was to transform the face of British fiction in the postwar period and has become identified as 'Black-British' writing,[12] Lamming is pointing here to a fundamental paradox which faced the writer after arrival in the 'mother-country', when Britain's so-called 'imperial chickens . . . came home to roost'.[13] It was a coming home, however, that was to replay the territorial contestations and inequalities of a 300 year imperial history, as the visitor on Lamming's sofa remained destined to be perennially caught as disappointed guest, both inside and outside the familiar doors he has just entered.[14]

The contradictory nature of the situation came to a head with the Nationality Act of 1948, which paradoxically opened Britain's doors to citizens from the colonies, a moment which has come to symbolize for many the starting point of a postwar black British history, as it coincided with the highly publicized arrival of the SS *Empire Windrush* which docked at Tilbury on 22 June 1948.[15] Yet this now mythical boat, whose symbolic voyage across the waters of the Atlantic has been recorded as marking the beginning of 'black' Caribbean settlement in Britain – the colonization as Louise Bennett has described it of 'Englan' in reverse' – was, in fact, like George Lamming's fictional boat in *The Emigrants*, carrying a number of passengers who came not only from Jamaica as was usually suggested, but from a range of different islands, each with a specific history. Moreover its passengers were not only 'black', but included a range of migrants of different cultural origins, whether white, black, Indo-Caribbean, Chinese, Portugese-Guyanese, men or women. And whilst its arrival in Britain signalled an important moment in the pattern of postwar immigration that was to follow, it has also 'come to conceal a number of other, contradictory pasts'.[16]

Importantly these new British citizens held equal rights of residence in the 1950s, but it was not long after, with the institution of the 1962 Immigration Acts, that non-white immigration began to be controlled by an explicit policy to keep 'coloured' citizens of the colonies and ex-colonies out. As Simon Gikandi has shown in *Maps of Englishness*, the exclusionary nationalist ideologies underlying Enoch Powell's infamous 'Rivers of

Blood' speeches in 1968, warning the public of hordes of Black and Asian immigrants flooding Britain's shores, were nothing new; his arguments were, in fact, simply the 'working hypothesis' of an embedded discourse of nationalism and a xenophobic policy of exclusion which had prevailed long before and been articulated by some of Britain's most eminent philosophers and writers.[17] The fact that Britain and her colonies were intimately connected had always been a reality of imperial history. However, whilst colonial occupation had created 'Little Englands' all over the empire, the discourse of nationalism 'at home' was sustained by the construction of rigid border lines which were not to be crossed. As Gikandi says:

> Empire gave England power and prestige but left its national character untouched. Even at the height of its empire, England remained an island [supposedly] untouched by the landscapes and subjects it dominated; now with postimperial migration, the blacks have come to contaminate the realm.[18]

Although, as some have argued, an English liberal tradition of fair play may be seen to stretch back to the Magna Carta, it is one, as David Dabydeen has ironically noted, that has always been Janus-faced, masking an equivocation which was particularly in evidence in the early nineteenth century at the height of the slave trade. For even within the well-intentioned rhetoric of the anti-slavery movement lay an attitude which still remained hostile to foreigners. The first tradition 'is polluted by the second, because the people who belong to the first . . . would seem to be troubled if you came too close'. Dabydeen cites examples from across the canon of English literature to highlight the hypocrisy of the English in maintaining double-standards over questions of race and nation and as far as the expression of their civility is concerned. Although Samuel Taylor Coleridge may have written a great poem against the slave trade ('Ode Against Slavery'), for which he was awarded the Cambridge Gold Medal, he could, Dabydeen reminds us, be 'appalled' at the same moment by the fact that Desdemona, in a production of Shakespeare's *Othello,* could hug a black man on stage. Not only was such behaviour apparently 'nauseating' to behold, but Coleridge actually doubts whether Othello can indeed have been a 'veritable Negro'.[19] In a similar manner, Winston Churchill is able, almost two centuries later, to appropriate the famous lines of the émigré Caribbean poet, Claude McKay (If we must die, let it not be like hogs), to rally the nation during the Second World War, without citing their source or perhaps even being conscious of the poem's original subject – the miseries of slavery – which was the original idea behind the lines.

Not surprisingly, the focus for both sides – whether you were outside or in, an alien colonial or a native – was on accommodation. The threshold of the nation was policed not only by a vigorous apartheid system, a 'colour bar', which was openly displayed in shop fronts and guesthouses with signs that read 'No Coloureds Here', but also by an ignorance and refusal to distinguish the diverse histories of particular immigrant groups who originated from a variety of different colonial, as well as Irish and Jewish backgrounds in the postwar period.[20] As Sam Selvon has said, England in the 1950s exhibited a polarized racial climate in which he, as an East Indian Caribbean man, found it hard to get a job even at India House because he was not, as he puts it, a 'real Indian' from India. And in many of his London works, Selvon humorously illustrates the absurd shifts and changes his immigrant characters have to go through to persuade hostile landlords to take them in. As Selvon was quick to recognize soon after his arrival, the 'mother-country' was not the 'fountainhead of knowledge' his largely colonial education had promised him. Nevertheless, the surprising ignorance of their own history overseas which he encountered amongst the English – a narrowness of vision which frequently reduced his native island of Trinidad to nothing more than an insignificant 'dot' on the imperial map – made him, in contrast, feel 'ten feet tall'.[21] One thing, however, was abundantly clear: 'as long as you were not white you were black, and it did not matter if you came from Calcutta or Port of Spain'.[22]

As we see in Selvon's 1965 novel *The Housing Lark*,[23] Syl (Sylvester), his East Indian/West Indian character, is constantly confused about his perceived racial identity in Britain. And whilst Selvon frequently points to the absurd contradictions at the heart of racial stereotyping, he also exploits the creative and ironic potential this opens up for many of his characters, who are natural trickster figures, well rehearsed before arrival in shifting the shapes of a rigid colonialist hierarchy, sidestepping and exploding conventions as in the transformations the legendary figure Anancy goes through after crossing the Middle Passage in Afro-Caribbean folk lore.[24] The reader is alerted early on to the fact that Syl is not an ordinary black man but an 'Indian', although you 'mightn't think' so for a 'lot of people don't know it have true-true Indians living in the West Indies'. To add to the confusion, Selvon's narrator explains (treading a barbed path between the gaze of his imagined and ignorant white reader and the 'black' community his narrator belongs to), Syl 'ain't . . . a Indian name'. For some of them 'get so westernise that they don't even know where the Ganges is', picking up 'all sort of fancy name instead of the usual Singh or Ram' (p. 29). Yet Syl's appearance, the marker of his 'Indianness', becomes useful capital, particularly when looking for rooms with English landlords who always exclude 'Kolors', but sometimes make an exception for those more educated visitors 'from the Orient' (p. 31). Despite Syl's desperate attempts, however, to adopt the pose of an 'exotic student', his experience of the East clearly only stretches as far as the 'East End', and his later attempts (following the black Battersby's advice) to dupe the landlord and sneak into a room as a 'true born Indian who grew up on the banks of the Ganges', backfires. In a powerful and carnivalesque scene (p. 126) which forms the climax of the novel, where received 'English' history is turned on its head by a day trip to 'Hamdon Court' developing into a Caribbean fete, Syl is teased by the others in the group:

> 'Syl, why you don't go back to India boy? That is your mother-country.'
> 'Brit'n is my country'.
> 'Yes, Syl, how comes you don't wear dhoti and turban?'
> 'I wonder if I ever get in trouble if the Indian High Commissioner would help me, or if he would send me to the Trinidad office?'
> 'Man, you don't know if you Indian, negro, white, yellow or blue.'
> 'All he know is he is . . .

Selvon translates the seriousness of Syl's predicament into only another part of the day's *bachanal* festivities as the immigrants attempt to conjure alternative realities out of their predicament through their fast-moving banter and verbal pyrotechnics. Comically rendering the party of immigrants as the perhaps incongruous inhabitants of a traditional English rural scene, basking contentedly on the banks of 'Old Father Thames' on a summer's day, Selvon exposes the extent to which their language – a creolized discourse of code-switching, double-entendre and linguistic improvisation spanning the entire social spectrum of the Caribbean continuum – will ensure their survival and mark their continuing presence despite the ironic contradictions of their existence. As he explains: 'It don't matter what the topic is, as long as words floating about, verbs, adjectives, nouns, interjections, paraphrase and paradise, the boys don't care. It like a game, all of them throwing words in the air like a ball, and now and then some scandalous laugh making sedate Englishers wonder what the arse them black people talking about' and if they are 'a party of *Jamaicans* [my italics] on the bank' (pp. 126–7).

Many fictional and non-fictional accounts have documented this period of West Indian cultural history which initiated, to draw on Seamus Heaney's suggestive words, the making of a series of different 'Englands of the mind'.[25] Whilst Sam Selvon's pioneering work, *The Lonely Londoners* (1956), was emblematic in its literary translation of a pluralist Trinidadian and 'calypso aesthetic'[26] into the ironically constituted monolith of a 'black' colony in the heart of the city, there are many others, such as George Lamming's seminal novel, *The Emigrants* (1954), as well as his groundbreaking collection of essays, *The Pleasures of Exile* (1960), Andrew Salkey's *Escape to An Autumn Pavement* (1960) and V. S. Naipaul's *The Mimic Men* (1967) which deal in different ways with the loneliness and disillusion of the early immigrant experience.[27] Few women writers, apart from Jean Rhys, whose work spanned the pre- and postwar period, were either published or visible at this time, and Jean Rhys herself was to disappear from public view for several years until her work was rediscovered in the late 1960s, leading to the publication of *Wide Sargasso Sea*. Other women writing during this period, such as the well-known poets Una Marson ([see Plate 3, p. 26) and Louise Bennett, or the novelist Beryl Gilroy, were seldom heard at all and gained little recognition in the publishing world although they were clearly prolific writers at the time.[28] This imbalance between the sexes is often reflected in the subject matter of many early works by male writers, where there is a notable absence of women, successful love relationships, children or any organic family life.

Jean Rhys's *Voyage in the Dark* (1934), too, interestingly portrayed a typical sense of dislocation and cultural confusion as Anna Morgan, her white West Indian creole heroine (who as she tells us, 'always wanted to be black') attempts to feel her way in an unwelcoming city. Her England is a world where no homes are experienced and Anna, like many of Rhys's later heroines, survives on the edges of the society in an almost surreal metropolis which is frequently reduced to nothing more than colourless rooms in sordid boarding-houses. Rhys's characters, like V. S. Naipaul's Ralph Singh in *The Mimic Men* (1967) or even the 'boys' in Selvon's *The Lonely Londoners*, remain adrift whatever their situation:

> It was as if a curtain had fallen, hiding everything I had ever known. It was almost like being born again. The colours were different, the smells different, the feeling things gave you right down inside yourself was different. Not just the difference between heat; light; darkness; grey. But a difference in the way I was frightened and the way I was happy . . . Sometimes it was as if I were back there and England were a dream. At other times England was the real thing and out there was the dream, but I could never fit them together (p. 7).[29]

This early representation in Rhys of the effects of a kind of cultural schizophrenia, a dream which will always be deferred, points to several fundamental issues which are still major preoccupations in the works of many contemporary black and Asian writers today, artists who are giving voice to the later diasporic experiences of their own generation, a generation often born in Britain and for whom the writing of 'home' can still create a sense of unease, of amnesia and double rupture. For the experience of Britain did not create a simple antithesis between tropical exoticism and darkness in a cold clime, nor is the meeting of the two worlds in the imagination easily reduced to a nostalgic vision of a lost paradaisical childhood with an alien world to replace it. More centrally, the problem is one of different ways of seeing, of different modes of apprehending and naming reality which have to be comprehended within a new context. Even for Jean Rhys in the 1930s (who as a *white* West Indian is commonly set apart from the later group of writers in the 1950s), the main difficulty was to come to terms with the idea of London as an illusion, as a dream built on the foundations of the colonial myth, a myth which has to be demythologized in the mind of the artist who comes from a previously colonized world and re-presented.

Ironically, it was London that created the possibility, in many cases, of a bridge between the past – a history of racial admixture, cultural disorientation and economic exploitation – and the present, which posited a strong need, amidst moves for Caribbean Federation to establish a 'West Indian cultural pedigree'.[30] As Donald Hinds noted in *Journey to an Illusion* (1966), escape from the islands was frequently a stage on the route to self-discovery, the source of the writer's 'exile' not beginning, but ending with departure:

> Deep down I knew I loved my persecutors. Our Caribbean background was shaped by English things . . . but at last I was coming to terms with myself . . . I am indeed grateful to the English. Grateful for forgetting me in order to discover myself.[31]

The desire to create an alternative world which deconstructed the masquerade of the colonial myth had far-reaching effects on the voices of this early generation of Caribbean writers who searched, often in vain, for the solid world of a metropolis, a world which had been built in their imaginations on the dubious and artificial literary foundations of a metropolitan colonial culture. In V. S. Naipaul's *The Mimic Men*, Ralph Singh's inability to possess the heart of the city reflects the pain of the necessary process of demythologization:

> Here was the city, the world. . . . I waited for the flowering to come to me. The trams on the Embankment sparked blue . . . Its heart must have lain somewhere . . . I would play with famous names as I walked the empty streets and stood on bridges. But the magic of names soon faded . . . my incantation of names remained unanswered. In the great city, so solid in its light – to me as colourless as rotten wooden fences and new corrugated iron roofs – in this solid city life was two-dimensional.[32]

Similarly, Sorbert, in Andrew Salkey's *Escape to An Autumn Pavement*, comes to the recognition that he has not inherited a language and culture from his British colonial education but a sense of the lack of it:

> I walk around London and I see statues of this one and the other . . . There's even Stonehenge. And do you know how I feel deep down? . . . I feel nothing . . . We've been fed on the Mother Country myths. Its language. Its literature. Its Civics . . . What happened to me between African bondage and British hypocrisy? What?[33]

This sense of something missing, the sense of a cultural and historical void beneath the excitement that a group identity in the metropolis can bring, is exacerbated by the whole question of a language acquired, but not possessed. As was evident from the empty signifiers in Ralph Singh's reverential incantation of names, the naming of a thing and the knowledge, understanding or possession of it can be very different things. Societies, like the individuals of which they are composed, need their own areas of privacy, areas into which they can retreat and refresh themselves. For the Caribbean writer abroad for whom the language, as V. S. Naipaul has said, was 'mine' though the 'tradition was not',[34] this cycle of disillusion and cynicism was a crucial stage in the process of decolonization. Because it was through this process, as well as the expansion and subversion of the discursive spaces of a predominantly Western modernity which had previously entrapped them, that the writer could begin to rescue his/her community from the illusory myths of the imperial centre. Frequently, as we shall see in Chapter 3 focusing on the work of V. S. Naipaul, an initial alliance with what have been called 'the [exilic] ideologies of high modernism',[35] a rhetoric derived from the European avant-garde which privileged the idea of cultural dislocation as a means of escape from the nightmare of history, only exacerbated the situation. Yet as George Lamming still remarks in 'Echoes of Columbus', an interview with Caryl Phillips which took place in 1997, 47 years after his initial departure:

> I don't care how remote you are, in Africa, or Asia . . . there is no part of the planet that can escape the triumph of modernity. What each culture has to try and do is to find how it incorporates modernity into whatever it imagines to be its specific destiny . . . there is no question of killing [Prospero] off. The great challenge is how that is to be incorporated in what you conceive to be your specific and special cultural space.[36]

Frequently when we talk of crossing thresholds, we imagine a shift in a lifestyle, a form of rebirth, the crossing of a frontier whether real or imagined: in short, a rite of passage. This sense of a crossing over applies whether we are concerned with an arrival or a leave-taking, a new relationship or a divorce. Thresholds signify, then, a space suggestive both of transition and transformation, a location that represents the borderland of both old and new possibilities, and sometimes even a limit beyond which our sensibilities can no longer discriminate. Whilst the birth of a Caribbean consciousness by confrontation with the 'mother-country', and the subsequent redefinition created by the juxtaposition of the two worlds, has been a central preoccupation in a great deal of West Indian fiction, the counter-discourses and aesthetic experimentations generated by that experience exist outside, as well as within the discursive fields of the colonial encounter. Often, as in George Lamming's work such as *The Pleasures of Exile* (1960), his remarkable series of non-fictional essays which anticipate later postcolonial readings of 'exile' not solely as a condition of loss or reclamation, but as inventive counterpoint,[37] redefinition can only be found by addressing this dilemma within the context of the Old World. A confrontation and a meeting between is(land) and metropolis, Caliban and Prospero, must occur, and is a necessary prerequisite to the evolution not only of a Caribbean consciousness, but of an aesthetic which extends the phenomenon of modernity itself, providing a new entry point into history, where 'the old blackmail of language will not work' and Caliban is 'at liberty to seize the meaning of the moment'.[38]

Like Mulk Raj Anand in his conversations with E. M. Forster discussed in Chapter 1, Lamming allegorizes Shakespeare's *The Tempest* as a means of representing the historically determined position of the 'exiled' colonial writer and his relationship to the canonical tradition of 'English' literature. It is only by meeting Prospero on home ground as it were (the so-called 'Old World' and 'metropolis') that the psychological legacy of their 'original contract can be annulled'.[39] In such circumstances, argues Lamming, Caliban will not only reverse the terms of the colonial equation, but will seize the power to transcend and transform the reductive oppositions that previously defined that relationship. For as he says:

> I am a direct descendant of Prospero worshipping in the same temple of endeavour, using his legacy of language – not to curse our meeting – but to *push it further*, reminding the descendants of *both* sides that what's done is done, and can only be seen as a soil from which other gifts, or the same gift endowed with different meanings, may grow toward a future which is colonised by our acts in this moment, but must always remain *open*.[40]

As a figure, therefore, who has carried the history of what the cultural critic, Paul Gilroy, has recently called the double-consciousness of a modernity which has been built on the experience of the black diaspora, he is not only able to shapeshift and transform from within, but is also able to push further the epistemological boundaries and legacies of a discursive world that had previously enclosed him.[41]

The idea of departure from the islands as a means of ending an ancestral condition of 'exile' has frequently been discussed by Caribbean writers and critics as a force for creative liberation rather than a negative repetition of an ancient history of dislocation. Lamming's voice was not alone in redefining the Caribbean New World experience as a crucible and paradigm for a modernity that was long familiar with strategies for deconstructing the march of a colonial history. In such readings, 'the journey by sea' – a journey which linked both the Middle Passage and the crossing of the *kala pani* (the black waters) by descendants of nineteenth-century indentured Indians – is not so much a rupture as an 'interlude between home and the Caribbean communities islanded abroad'.[42] In addition, the varied cultural and racial histories, which were the lived experience of these Caribbean writers who grew up under the shadow of a European cultural topography, had already created what Edouard Glissant has called the inevitable 'iruption into [a] modernity' which departed from the violence of the colonial tradition.[43] It was a modernity however which not only used the tools of the master to dismantle the master's house, but had also long rehearsed and evolved more flexible indigenous and androgynous frames by which to exist outside the effects of a dominant and often distorting colonialist historiography. For, as Jan Carew suggests in 'The Caribbean Writer and Exile', departure from the islands was not simply the other side of 'homelessness', a condition of cultural schizophrenia forever holding the artist in a passive twilight world between 'limbo and nothingness'.[44] It enabled instead a creative space, one necessarily 'compelled by the exegesis of [the contradictions of] history', but which nevertheless bred an inventive ethos of cultural survival, a facility for improvisation which is expressed in 'whatever regions', whether 'island . . . continent or the cosmos' that the 'imagination encompasse[d]'.[45] Moreover, as the experience of a colonial culture had repeatedly attempted to repress the expression of a pluralist aesthetic – the formal means by which the diversity of the Caribbean's own versions of 'history' could be inscribed – such journeys often led to what Wilson Harris famously described in 1967 as a series of revisionary dialogues. It was a process which both generated innovative textual strategies whilst at the same time consuming its own 'biases', thereby effectively subverting the linear trajectories of dominant narrative forms.[46]

This is not to suggest the inevitability of what Lamming calls a 'colonial relation' or a counter-culture in the Caribbean indissolubly tied to one of derivation. Clearly any counter-discourse is linked to a pretext, a context from which it emerges, and there are obvious dangers in attempting to set up the Caribbean as a paradigm for an alternative modernity that exists in isolation from its European intertexts.[47] However, as Stuart Hall points out in one of the epigraphs to this chapter, the experience of growing up within the often contradictory fragments of a history built on cultural mixing created a wide-angled vision of cultural diversity that long predated Europe's own questioning of the authority of its grand narratives. Bearing this in mind, it is worth viewing the group of Caribbean writers and intellectuals who migrated to London in the 1950s (amongst whom Hall was one) not only as a remarkably distinguished and varied body of writers who were central in making visible a tradition of 'black' and diasporic writing in Britain, but also as a group whose early articulation of what in postcolonial discourse is now termed the 'narrative of the damaged home', reflected a 'dialogue of conflicting methods about a *commonly* felt need'[48] – the need, in short, to discover the voice of an 'effective collectivity', whilst simultaneously discovering appropriate artistic forms to narrate a twentieth-century 'condition of immigration', a condition which, as Michael de Certeau has frequently argued, is 'endemic' to us all.[49]

George Lamming's description of the newly arrived colonial immigrant, poised halfway through the doors of Britain in the 1950s, is therefore a very telling one. And whilst literary and theoretical spaces have belatedly been opened up in the West, offering a useful grammar by which to interrogate and negotiate the complex nature of individual cultural locations as they affect contemporary Britain's mixed racial and diasporic populations, it is important to remember that these 'homes' were initially forged through the navigation of a differently defined territory. As Stuart Hall implies in the epigraph cited earlier, the quintessence of what was sometimes defined in the late decades of the twentieth century as the *postmodern* condition were already part of the lived and historic experience of Caribbean modernity. Thus it is important to relate the writing of what we might call an im/migrant genre or im/migrant imaginary to a context in which that literature 'stages the experience of exile, immigration and deterritorialization', a situation that may *now* be postcolonial.[50] For the early fictional explorations of many of these writers can be viewed as exemplary of literary strategies (which have perhaps become common now in contemporary diasporic fictions) to translate and transform the rigidity of oppositional racial and national categorization, intervening in and subverting traditional ways of narrating British identity.

The experience was one both of migration and immigration. The crossing of the waters and subsequent passage across the threshold of Britain enacted a symbiotic movement both linking island and metropolis as well as suggesting an intervention into what has recently been called 'the double time of national identity'.[51] This voyage across both enabled what Claire Alexander has called the 'transgression of absolute and historical boundaries, in which the migrants are placed outside and in opposition to the wider imagined nation', and also set in motion a discourse for diaspora in which the experience of im/migration could be seen as an active process, marking a stage on a continuum which was to develop into a poetics of migrancy within subsequent writings in the 1980s and 1990s.[52] I am deliberately signalling the term *immigrant* here, despite some of the more negative associations that have come to be linked to the term, in order to accurately present the atmosphere of the period in which these writers arrived in Britain, as well as to consider their relationship at this stage to the realities of decolonization. The literary solutions these writers invented became a means not only of shifting the boundaries of the nation space, but also of creating an aesthetic correlative for that search for accommodation denied Lamming's early interloper. As such, the immigrant experience can be seen as marking a crucial intervention into the narrative of twentieth-century modernity.

* * *

Sam Selvon's fiction set in London during the period 1950 to the mid-1980s, when he left Britain after 28 years to live in Canada, is a crucial milestone in the history and development of the literatures of the Caribbean diaspora. Selvon is frequently described by black and postcolonial critics as the 'father of black Literature',[53] an 'alchemist of language'[54] who has reinvented Britain. And his London works – which include the short stories collected in *Ways of Sunlight* (1957), *The Housing Lark* (1965) and the 'Moses' novels *The Lonely Londoners* (1956), *Moses Ascending* (1975) and *Moses Migrating* (1983) – do indeed span a crucial period in the growth of 'black' writing in Britain. With the use of modified forms of the oral vernacular, or what we should describe as a consciously crafted Caribbean literary English for both the language of the narrator and that of the characters, *The Lonely Londoners* was a pioneering work as it moved towards bridging the difficult gap of perspective between the teller of the tale and the tale itself. First published in 1956, this novel is perhaps best known for its 'songs', as Kenneth Ramchand has described them, of 'innocence and experience' and its almost surreal depictions of black life in London.[55] For Selvon created a world which not only gave voice to his largely unlettered immigrant characters, but created a new language for describing and mapping the city, a language which subtly revisioned the city's borders and its previous canonical inscriptions. As one of the first full-length novels to be written in this language form – now commonly termed 'nation-language' – it reflected an innovative departure from the more standard modes of portraying unlettered characters in traditional English fiction. In style and content, therefore, it represented a major step forward in the process of decolonization.

Selvon's experimentations with form and language in his London works were to have a significant influence on later generations of writers, as he liberated his immigrant characters from the stereotypical straitjackets that surrounded them in the city, creating a space for them to live in it. As Caryl Phillips has said:

> if I were to point to a writer who captures the tone, rhythm and texture of London as the austere fifties were about to give way to the swinging sixties, I would not cite the plays of John Osborne or Arnold Wesker, or the prose of David Storey or John Braine. For acuity of vision, intellectual rigour and sheer beauty of the inventiveness of language it would have to be the works of Sam Selvon which would figure pre-eminently. He did not only know the Caribbean but also the pages of London's A to Z, and was able to capture these with a haunting lyricism which remains . . . with the growing influence of his work, imprinted on the imagination.[56]

Like many others of his generation, Selvon's sojourn in London from 1950–78 acted as a creative catalyst in the development of his art, enabling links to be drawn between the two major preoccupations of his fiction – Trinidad and London. Through the encounter with London, it became possible to move, on the one hand, towards a more fully realized picture of the world back home, and on the other, to define and establish a Caribbean consciousness as it redefined itself within a British context. Only in 'London' says Selvon, 'did my life find its purpose'.[57] Selvon's crossing from Trinidad to London was not only a crossing from the Caribbean to the colonial 'motherland', but also represented a deliberate shift from a creolized East Indian/West Indian voice in Trinidad to that of a 'black' writer in London.

The settings of Trinidad and London formed the major focus of Selvon's work, although late in his life he also set some short stories in Canada. Yet, whilst the Indian cane community is carefully observed in the best-known Trinidad novels, *A Brighter Sun* (1952) and *Turn Again Tiger* (1958), Selvon did not come from a rural background himself, nor was he 'Indianized' in any sense, unlike his younger contemporary V. S. Naipaul. Although he was born in San Fernando in 1923 of East Indian parents, and his father was the descendant of a Madrassi, from an early age Selvon related primarily to the culturally mixed world of modern Trinidad. Speaking of the Hindi language, he has said:

> I just ignored it . . . I grew up so Creolized among the Trinidadians . . . Not as an Indian, but as a Creolized West Indian as we say.[58]

However, as Selvon indicates in a paper delivered at the University of the West Indies in 1979, 'Three Into One Can't Go – East Indian, Trinidadian, West Indian', this was not always a comfortable place to be. For although the 'creolizing process' he was subject to in his formative years affected a great number of other East Indians of his generation, a process which, as he says, was so effective that 'one even felt a certain embarrassment and uneasiness on visiting a friend in whose household Indian habits and customs were maintained, as if it were a social stigma not to be westernised', it did not seamlessly resolve many of the hierarchical racial rivalries which mysteriously perpetuated themselves at the same time. Divisions were often accepted without question and meant that 'White people came first, then Indians, and then . . . Blacks.' Yet it is precisely these forms of mindless indoctrination built on prejudices which keep the 'wheels of history' groaning and squeaking as it 'repeats itself' that motivated Selvon to pursue the perhaps idealistic route of creolization as a means of rescuing his characters from just such divisive repetitions. As he comments, describing his own ambivalent location: 'the Caribbean man of East Indian descent . . . was something else. He wasn't accepted by those from India, and he wasn't wanted by the others because he wasn't a Black man so he couldn't understand what was going on.'[59]

The tensions and conflicts implicit in the idea of creolization are a frequent theme in Selvon's art, whether his subject is the East Indian peasantry, the urban middle classes, the rootless trickster figures and largely black characters of his London fiction, or the mixed calypsonian characters in the short stories set in Port-of-Spain. Indeed, in the 'black' London that Selvon creates in *The Lonely Londoners* (1956), we are deliberately kept unaware of the 'boys' particular racial identities. So powerful is the shared dynamic of their blackness, a signifier imposed both from without and within, that even Cap, the Nigerian, begins to behave like a West Indian. Yet as Kamau Brathwaite has frequently stressed, creolization was not a neat method of assimilation, a means to create a melting-pot culture out of a number of diverse histories, but instead exposed the 'extraordinary complexity' of Caribbean societies, making 'the fragments/whole'.[60] Moreover, the use of a creolized voice in Selvon's works provided the narrative vehicle by which he was able to both envision the idea of an emergent national consciousness whilst simultaneously overcoming the fissures which had previously divided the East Indian and Black populations.

In his 'London' works, Selvon clearly translates his dream of what has been called a 'calypso aesthetic' into a more polarized racial context, a shift which demands some of the same cross-cultural skills of manoeuvre, but is contained within a context which both liberates and entraps him. In a sense his calypsonian characters, who move from Port of Spain to London town, are the figures of a double appropriation: first, as the immigrant representatives of a modernity which can only see them as the flat and two-dimensional black subjects of empire, but, secondly, as characters who are the natural agents of an alternative vision, which not only contests but transforms the white gaze, enabling the genesis of a diachronic narrative of the city to open out the postures attributed to them by the dominance of a Western historiography.[61] As we see in the early immigrant story, 'Working the Transport',[62] Selvon is centrally preoccupied, on the one hand, with the ways in which his characters are transformed after arrival into an anonymous sea of black faces, whose only role is to run the city's transport. At the same time, however, it is in 'working' the transport, that the boys change an ordinary red London bus into a vehicle of a different kind of movement, providing new steps by which to navigate the city. Whilst Small Change, the main character of the story, works as a bus driver for London Transport, we learn that he has already rehearsed for this important role by setting up a mock bus on board ship. Although we see him literally 'driving' the city after arrival (although the buses may well follow the wrong routes), he simultaneously attempts to get on top of the music scene in London. Riding high with his new girlfriend, and keen to impress her with his knowledge of the latest in the rock scene, Small Change emphasizes that, in the Caribbean, 'rock 'n' roll' is out but 'hip n' hit' (a new name he invents to impress on the spur of the moment), is in.

> You want to learn some new steps? Catch say, 'Give me a beat.'
> So Change sit down on the platform on a bus and start to beat the side and Allipang finish drinking tea and hitting the empty cup with the spoon, while Jackfish keeping time on the bar it have what you does hold to when you going on the bus.
> This bus have a good tone Change say looking up to see what number bus it is, as if the number makes a difference (p. 135).

As a humorous fable about how his black West Indian characters can bring new life and rhythm to the city, subtly changing its cultural codes as well as its fashions, Selvon's story of course powerfully illustrates the extent to which 'small acts', as Bruce Woodstock has observed, can bring about significant changes.[63] Yet perhaps most significantly, as Selvon himself has commented, the improvisations and inventiveness of the language form he used in his London narratives became a form of travel in itself. It was, he says, like experimenting with 'music . . . I sat like a passenger in a bus and let the language do the writing'.[64]

Like many other West Indian writers of his generation, Selvon came to London both to find work and to extend what Lamming has called the 'parochial habits' of both English and West Indian reading by broadening the international audience for his work.[65] Soon after his arrival in London, his first novel, *A Brighter Sun* (large sections of which were composed on the boat while reluctantly sharing his small Imperial typewriter with George Lamming), was published, which gained him international recognition and enabled him to give up other employment and become a full-time writer.

Before we move on to a detailed examination of Selvon's imaginative reinvention of Britain,[66] it is worth considering Selvon's literary apprenticeship before he left Trinidad, as it was in these early pieces (collected by Kenneth Ramchand and myself in *Foreday Morning* and often published under a variety of pseudonyms) that we can gain an insight into the heart of his artistic project: the means by which he experimented with a number of different voices prior to his self-conscious translation of London into a 'black' city of words in the 'Moses' novels – an achievement 'which was long in the making'.[67] In these early stories and non-fictional essays, we encounter a Selvon who was experimenting with the whole range of the West Indian linguistic, social and racial continua. Moreover, whether disguised as 'Ack-Ack', 'Michael Wentworth', 'Big Buffer' or 'Esses' (a name derived from the s's in his own name), Selvon, as Kenneth Ramchand has observed, reflects a sensibility of both the 'poet of nature and the human heart', as well as the 'natural philosopher' we find lurking underneath the superficial banter of his more well-known urban creole trickster stories.[68] Many of these early pieces which were published between 1946 and 1956 reappear in different forms in his collection of short stories, *Ways of Sunlight*, published in London, but the genesis for much of the material was formed during his days as a Wireless Operator for the Royal Reserve, and later as literary editor of *The Trinidad Guardian.* Moreover, the lyrical poignancy of many of these early pieces, evident in 'As Time Goes By' or 'Poem in London', point to a Selvon whom we meet again in famous love stories such as 'My Girl and the City', in which the narrator's love for his girl and the city of London is consistently counterpointed with a sensitive analysis of the role of the writer searching for a voice. Interestingly, this story, unlike many of the others in *Ways of Sunlight,* is written in a standard form characteristic of some of his non-fictional pieces which appeared in *The Trinidad Guardian.* 'At last I think I know', says his narrator, 'what it is all about. I move around in a world of words. Everything that happens is words. But pure expression is nothing. One must build on the things that happen . . . So now I weave' (p. 188). Similarly, once in London, Selvon recasts formative pieces such as 'Calypsonian', a ballad to the cultural genesis of calypso set in urban Trinidad, which reappears in *Ways of Sunlight* as 'Calypso in London'. This early story, first published in the Caribbean literary magazine *Bim* in 1952, is illuminating in its presentation of a fast-moving, oral and ironic voice which Selvon was later to modify to the tone of a more serious evocation of the immigrant's sense of 'ambivalence' both towards 'home and his place of exile' in 'Calypso in London' and 'Come Back From Grenada' – voices which were later worked into his full-length novel, *The Lonely Londoners.* Moreover, in 'Calypsonian', Selvon, through his character Razor Blade and his one-footed friend, indicates the possibilities of survival in a society which straddles the crossroads of several cultures, a world where the comic is not just a vehicle of a political satire, but masks instead the ironic presentation of what L. W. Brown has called 'the tragic or near-tragic'.[69] Yet it is Selvon's ability to build a song out of Razor Blade's malaise and deprivation, which holds the potential of his self-creation and liberation.

Selvon's talent as a writer, then, stemmed primarily from his ability to shapeshift through a number of roles, whether as East Indian/West Indian Trinidadian or 'black' writer in London. And as a natural trickster figure, like G. V. Desani before him, he explored a number of ways of translating the plural and creolized aesthetic of an alternative modernity, which he had inherited from his Trinidadian background, into a context in Britain, which was to change the way in which not only the city was seen but literature itself. *The Lonely Londoners* was the first of three works to deal with the archetypal immigrant figure Moses Aloetta, a 'veteran' black Londoner, and his experiences with a group of ordinary and unlettered characters, 'black immigrants . . . among whom I [Selvon] lived for a few years when I first arrived in London'.[70] As in his radio plays, *El Dorado West One* (adaptations of *The Lonely Londoners*), the novel represents a comi-tragic attempt to subvert and demythologize the colonial dream of a bountiful city. Characteristically, Selvon's reversal of the original myth in the plays – a myth linked of course to the European voyages of discovery in the sixteenth and seventeenth centuries – has several important reverberations as far as the economic base of nineteenth-century imperialism and Caribbean colonial history are concerned. But Selvon's political commentary is always implicit and the world of his Londoners not gold, but grey; his questers may be led and supported by the sage figure Moses, who descends like Orpheus into the underworld of the city, but they are limited nevertheless by the bleak realities of survival in an alien and alienating metropolis.

At the beginning of *The Lonely Londoners*, the atmosphere of Selvon's city is described: 'as if is not London at all but some strange place on another planet'. Typically, the narrator subverts the standard English in the novel's opening, 'One grim winter evening, when it had a kind of unrealness about London, with a fog sleeping restlessly over the city' (p. 7). Selvon, controlling the narration and using a modified form of Caribbean English, which also draws on previous canonical writings of the city, such as T. S. Eliot's 'Prufrock' or Dickens's *Bleak House*, creates a distance between the narrative voice and the object described whilst simultaneously establishing an intimacy between the reader and the storyteller. The unemployment office 'is a kind of place where hate and disgust and avarice and malice and sympathy and sorrow and pity all mix up. Is a place where everyone is your enemy and your friend' (p. 22). More generally, 'it have people living in London who don't know what happening in the room next to them, far more the street or how other people living . . . It divide up in little worlds . . . and you don't know anything about what happening in the other ones except what you read in the papers' (p. 74). We meet few white characters, enter few homes, and topographical description is scarce, yet the boundaries of Selvon's black enclave are carefully defined and always made accessible to new arrivals, who need detailed initiation into the games of survival. Black London is thus domesticated by the ritualistic repetition of the names not only of important and viable areas – it is bounded for instance in the west by 'the Gate' (Notting Hill), in the east by 'the Arch' (Marble) and in the north by 'the Water' (Bayswater) – but also by the stories of the 'boys' who return with exciting 'ballads' to relate after venturing out into uncharted territories, 'ballads' which strengthen and reinforce the fragile identity of the group's own mythology. Selvon has himself pointed out that the London these immigrants inhabited lacked any of the normal pillars of security or cohesion. His characters may see the sights or taste the bitter-sweet attractions of the metropolis, but they ultimately live in a restrictive, two-dimensional world.

With its apparently unstructured episodic style and the comic dexterity of Selvon's literary use of a modified 'dialect',[71] the novel when it first appeared was often mistakenly regarded by reviewers as being simply an amusing social documentary of West Indian manners; its primary intention being to reveal with pathos and compassionate irony the humorous *faux pas* of the black innocent abroad. Whilst the surface textures of the loosely knit sketches or 'ballads' recounted through the ambivalent voice of the third-person narrator may seem initially to support this view, the majority of early readings, as David Dabydeen has recently pointed out, repeatedly missed the supreme 'artfulness' of Selvon's so-called 'naturalistic' style, which deliberately concealed the seriousness of his aesthetic purpose, emphasizing instead that as an 'intellectual born in Trinidad' but of 'Indian parentage', he should know better than to present the 'black' immigrant experience in such a 'simple-minded' way.[72] As readers, however, we are swiftly drawn into the pace of the narrative and the initiation rites for the 'desperate hustlers', as they 'land up' on Moses's doorstep with 'one set of luggage, no place to sleep, no place to go' (p. 8). Similarly, the idiosyncrasies and eccentricities of Selvon's various characters, known collectively as 'the boys' are clearly delineated. We witness the first shocks of arrival at Waterloo in the almost surrealistic opening to the novel as Moses journeys to the station through the fog of a London winter, the endless and usually abortive search for employment and the constant hunt for the forbidden fruits of 'white pussy'. The boys (the term itself suggests the almost primeval innocence of the immigrants), picaresque and calypsonian rogues from a variety of islands, circle like vultures around their sage liaison officer Moses, who attempts at times to offer solace.

However, from a very early stage in the novel, the romance of the city is counterpointed by a frightening sense of dislocation. So whilst the city always remains bleak to figures such as Moses, who, like his biblical namesake, is lost in the wilderness, it is simultaneously remade in their own image: the walls of Paddington slums 'cracking like the last days of Pompeii'. Similarly, the uninitiated newcomer, Sir Henry Oliver (immediately deflated and renamed Sir Galahad, which of course plays on the ancient figure of British national legend as well as drawing on the burlesque tradition of calypsonian satire) has his initial buoyancy fractured when he ventures out alone for the first time:

> The sun shining but Galahad never see the sun look like how it looking now. No heat from it, it just there in the sky like a force-ripe orange. When he look up, the colour of the sky so desolate it make him frighten (p. 26).

Selvon's descriptions of Galahad's reactions to a different climate, particularly to the difference in the appearance of the sun, is fresh and enlightening as he uses terms of reference from a tropical world to describe the incongruities. The psychologically disorientating effects of the alien surroundings on the newcomer are created implicitly in the way the language is used. Most strikingly perhaps, the collision of the two worlds in Galahad's mind – of Trinidad and London – with the dreamlike image of the 'force-ripe orange', enables the reader to experience the extremity of Galahad's fear. Similarly, by imposing the language of his subjects on the city, Selvon remakes it in their own image, building a world which is simultaneously of epic and local proportions, stretching its boundaries across history. At times, as Gordon Rohlehr has pointed out, Selvon's characters shrink an overwhelming world by the use of reductive analogies. Alternatively, subtly interweaving the mood of other stories of the underworld such as Dante's *Inferno*, characters like Bart (whose name again echoes the more familiar 'ballads' of Arthurian legend), searches in vain for his lost girlfriend, Beatrice.

Moses's developing scepticism about the resources of this community, and his urgent need to discover a private identity, provide one of the major tensions in the novel, as the voice of the third-person narrator mediates between the consciousness of the group and the predicament of Moses himself. After a visit from Big City, who has ambitions to be a worldwide traveller but who cannot even 'full' up his forms for the football pools, we are shown Moses's growing awareness of the futility of his existence: 'after Big City leave him Moses used to think bout . . . money, how it would solve all the problems in the world. He used to see all his years in London pile up one on top of the other, and he getting no place in a hurry' (p. 82). Moses's sense of a pointless repetition here is significantly reflective of a voice that becomes more articulate as the novel proceeds. Set apart from the others as the sage figure, with the knowledge of years of ballads behind him, he also has to come to terms with a sense of loss. This is dramatized most clearly in his relationship with Galahad; from the opening pages at Waterloo Station, Moses tries to persuade the newcomers to return 'back home' immediately. His words reveal the pain of a superior irony.

Whilst Galahad's dreams of the city may be actualized, like those of V. S. Naipaul's Ralph Singh in *The Mimic Men*, by the phrase 'Charing Cross' or by the magnetism of Piccadilly Circus, Moses's consciousness becomes increasingly disturbed. Although he attempts to relive his own past through Galahad's love affair with the city, he has already reached a point of stasis. As he says to Galahad: 'All them places is like *nothing* [my italics] to me now' (p. 69). As Galahad's persona becomes increasingly inflated – he begins to feel more and more 'like a king living in London' – Moses is drawn further and further into his introspective reflections and desire to 'draw apart'. And the boys' protective self-caricatures and nicknames become identifiable as only a transparent form of camouflage within the black colony, working both for and against their fragile identities. Moreover, the nature of the language itself in the city of words they have created, with its reliance on repetition, drama and anecdote, can also become a regressive force – a form of restricted code with disturbing implications for the possibility of growth within or outside the community.

Selvon's 'ballad' style in *The Lonely Londoners* shifts easily between an oral and a literary tone and bears many correspondences, as has already been suggested, with the native tradition of Trinidadian calypso. The oral calypsonian ballad is well known for its use of a subversive irony, the melodramatic exaggeration of farcical anecdotes, subversive racial stereotyping, repetition for dramatic effect and the inclusion of topical political material. In addition, as John Thieme has shown, there are close parallels with Trinidad Carnival, a form that is essentially 'parodic, egalitarian and subversive' but constantly offers the possibility for renewal and regeneration. That being so, Thieme argues that *The Lonely Londoners* is a central Carnival text;[73] furthermore, as a dialogic and polyphonic cultural practice, Carnival enables a creolization of language and form that can bring together both the marketplace and 'yard' culture of Selvon's 'boys' within the world of the printed book.

Yet as Selvon himself pointed out when composing the novel, a work which he attempted to compose for the first six months in 'straight English', there were certain 'physical and emotional scenes' where 'the dialect' simply couldn't carry the essence of 'what I want[ed] to say'.[74] The language therefore had to move, to adjust itself to the situation and context demanded of it. The shifts Selvon manipulates in the novel to delineate different senses of place are particularly evident in the long, unpunctuated lyrical prose-poem to summer in the city which captures, like jazz or the blues, the communal consciousness of the boys as they learn to both love and hate the city (pp. 85–94). Yet interspersed within this is the developing theme of Moses's increasing sense of isolation as alter-ego to Galahad, a voice which becomes more individuated and resonant as the novel proceeds. Written in a highly self-reflective mode which evokes the characteristics of high modernism, Selvon exhibits the breadth of his narrative style as the grammar and syntax generates new and fresh perceptions of the city bringing to birth a distinctive literary voice. And this voice emerges again in the final choric sections of the novel as the 'boys' gather together in Moses's room:

> The changing of the seasons, the cold slicing winds, the falling leaves, sunlight on green grass, snow on the land, London particular . . . What it is that a city have, that any place in the world have that you get so much to like it you wouldn't leave it for anywhere else?
> . . . In the grimness of the winter, with your hand plying space like a blind man's stick in the yellow fog, with ice on the ground and a coldness defying all effort to keep warm, the boys coming and going, working, eating, sleeping, going about the vast metropolis like veteran Londoners (p. 122).

Selvon's boys originate from a world of language, 'a world of words through which they grope for clarity'.[75] Sexual themes are almost always present, but from a male viewpoint (which has created critics of Selvon in recent years), though they conform and parallel in many respects the classically chauvinistic attitudes of the urban trickster figures of calypso. Rather like the ultimately reductive and self-denigratory effects of their nicknames, their view of women as 'pretty pieces of skin' reflects ultimately upon the boys' own uncertainty and insecure sense of self. It is partly because the conflicting values of white society constantly reduce their own stature that they must adopt these postures. This technique of 'naming' or 'labelling' as a means of self-defence is evident when Sir Galahad sets off 'cool as a lord' to meet his white date and confronts the colour problem. Never easily deflated, Galahad is left talking to the colour black as if it is a person, telling it that 'is not he who causing botheration in the place, but Black, who is a worthless thing' (p. 72).

As Selvon once said, 'New plot or idea . . . There never was any beginning',[76] and there is also no beginning nor end to the experiences of 'the boys' in *The Lonely Londoners*. Although details about Moses accumulate – we know he is tiring of Britain and frequently dreams of a return to the village of 'Paradise' in Trinidad – they are unobtrusive and fitting to his development as the novel proceeds. The surface fragmentation or conscious disorganization of the novel's structure therefore expresses its main revelation, namely that, 'beneath the kiff-kiff laughter, behind the ballad and the episode, the what-happening, the summer-is-hearts . . . is a great aimlessness, a great restless swaying movement that leaving you standing in the same spot' (p. 125). By the end of the novel Moses is aware of a meaningless repetition and circularity in the group's existence.

The phrase 'what happening', which echoes throughout and is the fundamental rationale of its numerous episodes, comes to imply less a resilience in the face of complicated experience than a painful sense of futility and incoherence. Moses's basement room, which acts as a kind of surrogate religious centre, is where the boys congregate every Sunday morning to swap ballads, talk about this and that. But the stories are never finished, and the breathless narration of this section (pp. 122–5) emphasizes its lack of direction. The repartee of the community has become a self-undermining rhetoric; as the boys attempt to swap well-worn anecdotes, we witness Moses's detachment as he becomes almost a mythical repository, a Tiresias figure who can never escape the constant 'moaning and groaning and sighing and crying'. The oral and rhythmic nature of the prose adds weight to this as the synchronization of voices degenerates into a deflationary climax which then reverts to the original theme: 'So what happening these days?' Significantly, the questions are not addressed to any particular subject; they ring out like voices in the wilderness.

Only Moses, who has almost merged in consciousness by the end of the novel with the narrating voice, seems to be moving forward and can perceive the need to discover a new language for existence. The black London of Selvon's 'boys' has become by the close only a city of words;

there are no firm foundations (apart from Moses's basement room), and the surface security provided by this shared code, which has reduced the vast metropolis to a manageable West Indian colony within the city, will only perpetuate their isolation as there is no desire for integration. We leave Moses looking down into the River Thames and articulating this sense of a void: 'when you go down a little you bounce up a misery and pathos and a kind of frightening-what? He don't have the right word but he have the right feeling in his heart' (p. 126). This search for the 'right word', or an appropriate and individual voice to define a new reality for the Caribbean writer in London, is central to an understanding of Selvon's first experimentations with language and form in *The Lonely Londoners*, and becomes the main preoccupation of a new Moses who is still in Britain 20 years later in *Moses Ascending*. As Moses forewarns us:

> Daniel was telling him how over in France all kinds of fellars writing books what turning out to be best-sellers. Taxi-driver, porter, road-sweeper – it didn't matter. One day you sweating in the factory and the next day all the newspapers have your name and photo, saying you are a new literary giant. He watch a tugboat on the Thames, wondering if he could ever write a book like that, what everybody would buy (p. 126).

In *The Lonely Londoners*, Selvon faced the problem of both dealing with an early and exploratory response to the creation of a black London as well as discovering a suitable literary frame to express this experience. The slight area of narrative uncertainty in *The Lonely Londoners* is clarified in *Moses Ascending*, where Moses becomes very much the self-conscious narrator. In this novel we meet a Moses who is actively trying to draw apart from all the hustling of the early days. He is now endeavouring to construct a fully realized individual persona and at an important level; in the changed social and political climate of the 1970s, a world where the effects of oppressive Immigration Laws physically affect entry and departure, Moses's development is explored metaphorically. He buys his own, admittedly dilapidated, house (due for demolition in three years); he is no longer a tenant but a landlord and, furthermore, he wants to be a writer, and sets out to write his Memoirs in the uppermost room with a large view of the city, his fictional 'castle':

> After all these years paying rent, I had the ambition to own my own property in London, no matter how ruinous or dilapidated it was. If you

are a tenant, you catch your arse forever, but if you are a landlord, it is a horse of a different colour (p. 8).

Or, as Moses says to Sir Galahad (now a fervent representative of the Black Power movement): 'I just want to live in peace, and reap the harvest of the years of slavery I put in Brit'n. I don't want people like you around, to upset the applecart' (p. 9). Moses only ascends for a brief spell to live in the attic or 'penthouse' of his own house which, as the novel proceeds, becomes increasingly crowded with Bob (his illiterate white Man Friday from the 'Black Country'), Jeannie (Bob's girlfriend and Moses's sometime mistress), Brenda, and the Black Power Group – as well as some 'Pakis' (more recent immigrants) who enact a sheep slaughter in his back yard. His ambitions, to be 'Master' of his own house and an erudite Black man of letters, suggest the possibility, in fantasy at least, of gaining security and moving away from the stasis of the old days, the days of the 'what happening' and the 'kiff kiff laughter' we saw in *The Lonely Londoners.* Moreover, the image Moses evokes at the opening, of gaining a 'bird's eye view' of life, is indicative of his intention to achieve a measure of distance on his community. But the preservation of such a sanctuary, a literary haven in Shepherd's Bush, is not shown to be a viable proposition, and Moses's 'castle' (p. 46) is progressively undermined as the novel proceeds, perhaps illustrating that even after the attempted inscription of his life, 'ascendancy and success remain a matter of skin colour'.[77]

The atmosphere of *Moses Ascending*, like Selvon's earlier work, is initially congenial and suggests an innocently mocking comedy concerned with the idiosyncracies of the new generation of 'Third World' immigrants in the city. But Moses's attempts to separate himself from his own community in order to make an investment in 'truth', as he calls it, are barbed throughout by a subtle discursive method which attacks both the aspirations of the budding black writer, with his recently acquired Anglophile social graces, as well as those new political radicals who make up the Black Brit'n he now lives in. The tensions which were developing by the close of *The Lonely Londoners* have culminated in an almost total dissipation of the original group. The supposed security of the West Indian island in the metropolis, the strength created by the 'boys' shared sense of dislocation and cultural identity has collapsed. Tolroy and family are returning to Jamaica, Big City has gone mad, walking 'about the streets muttering to himself, ill-kempt and unshaven . . . as if the whole city of London collapse on him'; others, we hear, have gone up North and some, simply 'down in the underground' (p. 16), never to emerge.

Of the original group, only Galahad and Moses remain, and Moses has lost much of his faith in the idea of Black unity:

> I will tell you one thing that I have learnt in this life. It is that the black man cannot unite. I have seen various causes taken up and dropped like hot coals. I have seen them come together and then scatter . . . in all directions (p. 49).

Moses's attempts to shield himself from the suffering of his people however are not taken seriously and Galahad, as we shall see later, becomes a major contributive factor in his old friend's descent from his newly-won attic freedom.

Moses's developing scepticism concerning the question of commitment to an ever-continuing series of futile causes is comparable, as we shall see in Chapter 3, to Ralph Singh's in V. S. Naipaul's *The Mimic Men*, in which Singh strives through his writing of a personal history to move beyond those sequences of false behaviour in his past which led only to a barren cycle of events. Both Selvon and Naipaul have frequently commented on the dangers for the postcolonial artist in becoming over involved in what Naipaul has termed the 'corruption of causes'[78] and Selvon, too, despite his obvious political sympathies, voiced a need to develop his art further than what he regarded as the ultimately limiting strictures and preoccupations of a literature committed in the main to the assertion of a narrow literary nationalism. In addition, his desire is to break through certain reductive interpretative categories – whether of 'protest', 'hardship' or 'slavery' – often assigned by certain metropolitan critics to the supposedly 'naturalistic' work of writers such as himself.[79] Although Selvon does not indicate a withdrawal from the black writer's struggle for acceptance in an established literary world, or that he is retreating from his responsibilities to that world 'where I belong'[80] (which now includes the whole of the 'Third World' as well as Trinidad), he does suggest the need for an expansion of consciousness, a widening of horizons in the new literatures of the world, to include grounds of more universal applicability and significance.

Interestingly, Selvon made those observations in 1979, just after his departure from Britain where he had lived for 28 years, a period which also spans the creation of the Moses figure. Moses, however, does not simply present autobiography: as a representative voice of the old generation of immigrants, he typifies to Selvon 'all that happened (during that phase) . . . he also spoke in the idiom of the people which was the only way that he could . . . express himself'. Based originally on a 'true-life' character,

Moses, in spite of all his 'presumptions to be English . . . remains basically a man from the Caribbean'.[81] Yet by the close of *Moses Ascending*, with the growth of a new generation of Black Britons, the Black Power movement, and the festering hostility between Asian immigrants and Blacks, we become aware of the impossibility for Moses of forming an organic relationship either with his own community or the white world outside. He is outdated, a misfit, a black colonial adrift in the city, straddling or attempting to straddle both worlds.

From an early stage we are shown how Moses, with the status of a black landlord, attracts exactly those types he is attempting to avoid. Being 'unprejudiced', his only stipulation regarding tenants is that none of the old group live in his house, and he leaves all the house management in the incapable hands of his white Man Friday, Bob, an even-tempered, illiterate Midlands white. But the house becomes an illegal centre for the smuggling of Pakistanis as well as the headquarters for the local Black Power movement. Moses only becomes conscious of the real 'goings-on' in the house when he witnesses the assembly of a Black Power demonstration in the street below. Similarly, his attention is first drawn to the mysterious Faizull Farouk when he hears the bleating of a sheep – a victim for a Muslim sacrifice – in his backyard.

Whilst Moses's lack of awareness is treated humorously, his predicament has several disturbing implications. The episode of the sheep-slaughter for instance is representative of the seriousness of Moses's new situation. On one level, the description of this scene is a successfully comical account of an absurd event, which is symptomatic of the confused clash of cultural values affecting the new generation of immigrants in Britain. Moses is interested in the episode only because Galahad has pressurized him to research topical material for his writing, a project which in some ways seriously compromises his position. The 'Pakis', of course, according to Moses's own misplaced stereotypes, are religiose about the whole affair and attempt to adhere strictly to Muslim rituals. In contrast, Bob, watching from a window upstairs, reacts with horror:

> A solitary shriek of horror rent the atmosphere. It was so unexpected and piercing that Faizull lose his grip and slip off the sheep . . . I was the onlyest one to keep my cool: I look up to the penthouse and see Bob leaning out of the window as if he vomiting.
>
> 'I will get the RSPCA to arrest you!' He shout, 'You too, Moses!'
>
> Everything was going nice and smooth until this white man run amok (p. 63).

The position of Moses in relation to Bob compares interestingly here with that of Moses and Galahad in *The Lonely Londoners*, when Galahad tells Moses the 'ballad' of his attempt to catch a pigeon for his supper in Kensington Gardens. There is obviously one major cultural difference between the two episodes, and that is Bob's conventional English attitude concerning cruelty to animals as against Galahad's perspective as a human being who is starving in a strange world where animals (even pigeons) grow fat whilst human beings starve. Bob's lack of familiarity with the cultural context of what he sees curiously parallels that of Galahad when confronted with a universe of cosseted dogs and protected pigeons; a world with different priorities. But, most importantly, this parallel involves a further contrast: that between Moses as confidante or fellow West Indian in *The Lonely Londoners* and Moses as landlord, having to accommodate the sensibilities of a native Englishman in *Moses Ascending*. From being simply an outsider, listening to those similar to himself, Moses has moved into the more complicated position of attempting to be an insider, with responsibilities both to his tenants and his neighbours which require him to mediate between the black and white worlds. He therefore cannot remain the easy-going black radical of the early days; he is now a man with vested interests, who desires to fit in and to find a place in British society. This desire is emphasized by the exaggerated adoption of certain British customs which he considers to be proper to his class, such as a drinks cupboard and a white manservant. This difference is further emphasized by the language he speaks.

Moses's literary ambitiousness is gently parodied by Selvon, his faith in his ability to write 'Queen's English' is shown to be not so dissimilar from his recent rise in social status, and the language he uses further reflects the hybrid nature of his personality. The first-person narration modulates between the formality of nineteenth-century English, Trinidadian proverbs, Greek myth, American films, contemporary advertising jingles and the banter of the old days. Selvon's linguistic resourcefulness, his subversion of the 'Standard' and his iconoclastic methods, which unite calypso with Western literature, only serve to heighten our awareness that Moses cannot yet fully inhabit a 'home'; he is not yet Master of his own house, or of the language with which he wants to compose his Memoirs. Furthermore, his partial misunderstanding of many of the terms he is trying to appropriate, reflects once again the divisive effects of the acquisition of a second-hand language – a language used but not possessed. Moses, is not trying to own the 'magical' heart of the city but he is attempting to become a writer, and in doing so needs to discover an appropriate voice.

Selvon's portrayal of Moses's attempts to find a voice is one of total confusion: a confusion of notions of order and reality, and the creation of a conglomeration which one reviewer called a 'verbal salad of ungrammatical wit and literary and biblical references'.[82] However, whilst the iconoclastic effects of this hybrid language may be inspired, as in the following extract describing once more the sheep slaughter:

> Kay sir rah, sir rah, as the Japanese say. It was a motley trio Faizull shepherd into the house. I have seen bewildered adventurers land in Waterloo from the Caribbean with all their incongruous paraphernalia and myriad expressions of amazement and shock, but this Asian threesome beat them hands down (p. 74)

the result is ultimately one of pathos. Similarly, in Moses's innovative, highly ironic and lyrical 'essay', which he composes to the Black man early in the novel (pp. 11–15), the only coherent piece he manages to complete before Galahad's Black Power pressure disturbs him, we see the means by which Moses's potentially serious and political subject matter is parodied by Selvon and rendered absurd by the literary style he constructs.

The essay, as my earlier quotation shows, deals with the plight of black workers in a hostile white urban society, a position of deprivation and inequality, and an issue that might have most naturally found expression in a polemical attack. Yet Selvon's technique and the quality of the pathos that results moves beyond the basic facts of the issue itself, marking an intervention into the entire discursive field within which he, as an Anglophile black colonial, is entrapped. In its wide range of 'literary' effects and the eccentric usage of a mixture of 'literary' terms, the piece, which is too long to quote fully here, mirrors the growth of Moses's linguistic affectations since his retirement. Moses's range incorporates nation-language, standard English, the Shakespearean 'Fie' or 'Gods blood things have come to a pretty pass', as well as references by allusion to assumed historic moments such as the 'Black Watch'. At times, Moses even uses a modified form of Caribbean English to describe the white man's predicament, exposing and subverting the ways in which stereotypical usages of cliché have been naturalized into everyday speech, entrapping all who are their objects. This conglomeration of linguistic modes and Moses's very sincere attempt to write in the argumentative style of the traditional essay form, an attempt which achieves precisely the opposite effect, is typical of the novel as a whole. Whilst Moses sets out to present us with all the advantages of the black worker's position, he establishes with innocent elegance a very different picture. Moreover, it is a picture which undercuts Moses's prime desire, which is to demonstrate that, whilst he may have adopted 'the borrowed guise of a Western cliché',[83] as a writer inhabiting the attic, a room of his own, he himself has not yet arrived 'linguistically' although his creator clearly has.[84]

Moses Ascending is very much a novelist's novel, a self-conscious literary extravaganza. There are explicit references by Moses, the fictional author, to other real Caribbean writers living in London – George Lamming and Andrew Salkey, for instance – but more significantly, the predominant tension in the book stems from Moses's attempts to actually become a black writer and to establish an authentic voice that his own people will listen to and take seriously. The novel therefore dramatizes the difficulties Moses faces as a 'black' postcolonial writer in Britain. After careful study of the pros and cons of the writing process, Moses begins to feel that he ought to be able to write a book with a proper plot and theme. Furthermore, he must reveal the breadth of his education and knowledge by using a language that can display his erudition, incorporating for instance classical myth, legend, the bible and oral folklore. The result is, as Michel Fabre has pointed out, 'the sophisticated appropriation by "colonial writing" of a literary style formerly reserved for the British born'. Moses's voice inadvertently deconstructs and rebuilds his world as he blends outdated, jerky English phrases with Trinidadian syntactical shifts and turns. Through Moses as a 'writer-of-memoirs, Selvon as a novelist claims the right to depart from the naturalistic ways of using English usually prescribed to non-British writers . . . [he] does not assimilate into the . . . mainstream, he explodes it'.[85]

It may be worth briefly considering here the various counter-discursive strategies Selvon employs not only in comically subverting the systems of discourse that surround his character – whether derived from 'black' or 'white' cultures – but also in questioning the very foundations of 'the systems which would see such binary structures as inescapable'.[86] For whilst much of the novel is built on an extended parodic reversal of the Crusoe/Man Friday paradigm, Selvon not only constantly destroys Moses's misplaced desire to become a Crusoe in relation to Bob, his nouveau Man Friday, but also, more importantly, breaks down the illusory structures on which Crusoe rested his authority. And whilst, as Helen Tiffin has noted, the language of a Robinson Crusoe, or a Prospero might appear at one level to be transparent or 'unproblematical', the use of language in *Moses Ascending* is left 'deliberately opaque', therefore mocking the canon and 'language itself' as any norm or standard by which the outsider should be judged.[87] Caught between an out-of-date 'Englishness' and an ill-fitting

Caribbean colonial identity, Moses remains uncomfortable in his new clothes both as landlord and as writer. Moreover, this has implications for the English too; for, although Moses in some ways represents the archetypal caricature of a colonial mimic man, his thwarted attempts to rise up the social scale and gain linguistic power are set alongside a world of new black Britons who no longer need to mirror themselves via the signifiers of a world which no longer recognizes them.

Moses's relationship with Sir Galahad and the Black Power movement is instructive here. Throughout the novel, the development of Moses's private identity is threatened by the public and political world of Brenda and Galahad, and the avidly supported Black Power group. Moses does not withdraw completely from them (it is he, in fact, who *acts* when the 'Party' does not have enough money to rescue two of its innocent brethren who are jailed after an unfortunate encounter with the police). Yet, paradoxically, Moses's remaining sense of incompleteness and a doubting of his selfhood is created most strongly by the pressures his own people impose on him. It is because he is a *black* writer that the conflict between his personal wishes to write his Memoirs and the demands made upon him by a fast-developing political situation are exaggerated. As Moses becomes increasingly plagued by what his 'proper' subject should be, his private work is gradually stultified, and he, through conscience, becomes involved in events which do not really concern him. Furthermore, the possibility of further withdrawal is no longer a viable alternative.

Galahad and Brenda will not accept Moses's refusal to be involved in what he calls the 'bandwagon' of Black Power, whereas Moses regards the new movement only as an alternative to more 'ballads' and 'episodes', 'liming' or roaming the streets. Galahad, the political activist, is ridiculed by the narrator's wider vision, which penetrates beneath his Black Power 'glad rags' and the use of the latest and essentialist political jargon to expose a still profoundly vulnerable awareness of self. Selvon gently exposes the corruption at the centre of the party, but it is in Galahad's harsh criticisms of Moses's writing that Selvon pinpoints the serious damage which Galahad's unconscious self-contempt reveals. Furthermore, it undermines Moses himself, who begins to feel like a traitor:

> 'What shit is that you writing?'
> 'I am composing my Memoirs', I say stiffly . . . .
> 'You don't know one fucking thing about what's happening, Moses'
> 'Memoirs are personal and intimate' . . . .
> 'That's no fucking use' Galahad say. Nobody ain't going to be interested

> in anything you have to say. If you was writing about the scene today, and the struggle, I might of got the Party to back you. In any case, who tell you you could write?'
> 'I am not an ignoramus like you', I say, beginning to lose my cool.
> 'You think writing book is like kissing hand? You should leave that to people like Lamming and Salkey.'
> 'Who?'
> Galahad burst out laughing. Derisively too. 'You never heard of them?'
> '. . . You see what I mean? Man, Moses you are still living in the Dark Ages! You don't even know we have created a Black Literature . . .' (pp. 49–50).

This confrontation between Galahad and Moses is perhaps the most explicit demonstration in the novel of Selvon's concern to explore the difficulties facing the writer who remains caught both within and outside the borders of the nation. *Moses Ascending* does not present the reader with any comfortable resolutions, but a sense of continuity is created by Selvon's demonstration of the impossibility for the postcolonial writer in Moses's circumstances to achieve such an end. Selvon repeatedly emphasizes the absurdity of the whole situation, and Moses's movements in the novel (whether upwards or sideways) create a cyclical satiric pattern framed by the 'goings-on' in the house, and culminating in Moses's final return to life in his own basement room. At one level Moses seems only to have moved from basement to attic and back again during his twenty-odd years in Britain; he is still living an underground existence and his fall from power at the close of the novel almost verges on the tragic. But Selvon's ambiguous ironic tone holds good even in this final moment of humiliation, when Bob, Brenda and the 'Pakis' have all turned against him to further their own interests:

> Thus are the mighty fallen, empires totter, monarchs dethrone and the walls of Pompeii bite the dust. Humiliated and degraded I took up abode in Bob's erstwhile room while he and Jeannie moved into the Penthouse (p. 143).

Having failed to set up home in a city of words, Moses resolves to sell up and return to Trinidad. The gauntlet that he flings at his former tenants in the form of an 'epilogue up his sleeve' becomes the central theme of *Moses Migrating*, in which Moses finally decides to leave London and return home to play 'Britannia' at Carnival. The novel opens with the reality of departure, and is illustrative of Selvon's continuing preoccupation with the theme of migration and diasporic displacement, as Moses writes a concerned letter to Enoch Powell, thanking him for his generosity in helping Black Londoners to return to their native lands:

> Dear Mr Powell, though Black I am writing you to express my support for your campaigns to keep Brit'n White . . . I have always tried to integrate successfully in spite of discriminations and prejudices according to race (p. 1).

The comic-grotesque reversals of the colonial encounter are developed as Moses, travelling third class in a liner – Selvon mock-seriously invokes the trials of the Middle Passage – ends up in the literally 'upside-down' world of the Trinidad Hilton – a tourist, in other words, in his old country. The metaphorical possibilities of rooms and houses as a correlative or frame for the lack of a firm cultural identity are thus extended; but it is neither basement nor attic, but hotel room which bears the weight of significance. The quintessential transitoriness, artificiality and unreality of the hotel room (under ground too) image the special hollowness and disorientations of Moses's now postcolonial identity. Moses seems fated to find no true home in either Britain or Trinidad. No more than in *The Lonely Londoners* or *Moses Ascending* does Selvon's character arrive at a promised land. Significantly, too, in Selvon's portrait of the masquerading Moses, playing a Black Britannia, we are shown his white Man Friday, Bob, beneath him, pulling the chariot. But even here, Moses, so to speak, represents both sides of the coin. For in reinvoking the icon of an imperialist stereotype, Selvon simultaneously suggests an alternative interpretation from the one Moses originally intended, as Bob literally performs an act both of physical labour and of a metaphorical mobilization, setting the original image, as it were, 'spinning'.[88] The lack of a resolution, and perhaps the lack of a possible resolution, is demonstrated in the open-ended quality of the novel's final episode – with Moses caught still clutching the 'cup' of the Holy Grail in a kind of suspended state, just outside the doors of Heathrow airport, 'like I was still playing charades' (p. 179).

PART 2
Imaginary Homelands

3

If the 'House' Falls Down: The Enigma of Writing Survival in V. S. Naipaul

A yearning for escape is, in fact, a search to find oneself; which is when all is said and done, a return to oneself

Alejo Carpentier[1]

One of the main problems facing the West Indian writer is how to write a novel about houses. A house suggests clearly defined boundaries: physical, emotional, traditional. The traditional English/European novel is a 'house' and is usually, in one way or another, about houses.

Kamau Brathwaite[2]

I've spent a lot of time . . . trying to define why one felt out of it, why one felt one didn't belong to this tradition of English letters. It was because its assumptions about the world were assumptions I could never make myself

V. S. Naipaul[3]

The structural potential and peril of the world, the structural understanding . . . is related intimately to the human being. That to my mind is the situation of the West Indian artist . . . the architectural problem that confronts him . . . Man is frequently overwhelmed by the immense and alien power of the universe . . . man's survival is a continual tension and release of energy that approaches self-destruction but is aware of self-discovery.

Wilson Harris[4]

V. S. Naipaul's writing career can be seen in terms of a journey, an 'infinite rehearsal'[5] and meditation on his diasporic experience as an East Indian West Indian and a continual revaluation of the situation of his double exile. A journey as an im/migrant writer in Britain and the location of that self in a world that is now not only post-imperial but also postcolonial – a country 'whose recent history of immigration ensures that the conflicts of postcolonial identity are now enacted on the site of the imperial power itself'.[6] This journey and the enigma of its many arrivals have been expressed over a period of nearly 40 years and through a variety of narrative forms ranging from fiction to travelogue, to autobiography and history.[7] Naipaul's fiction and non-fictional writings trace a symptomatic response to the need to discover an appropriate literary form for the representation of a psychic and symbolic sense of 'homelessness'. A need, as Bharati Mukherjee has suggested, to write constantly about 'unhousing' whilst still remaining 'unhoused',[8] to discover a new architecture for the imagination which would move beyond a sense of recurrent 'shipwreck', and give expression to the 'restlessness' and 'disorder' brought about by the psychic and physical upheavals resulting from a history of Empire. Importantly, we are told through the words of Ralph Singh, narrator of *The Mimic Men* (1967),[9] that 'the empires of our time' have been 'short-lived' but 'they have altered the world for ever: their passing away is their least significant feature' (p. 32).

Naipaul's project can be seen to be one which is firmly located in the need to come to terms with the effects of the 'passing away' of Empire, but, more significantly, in the writing and rewriting of the self within the trauma of that history, which he has viewed as the psychic losses created by being both a participant and victim of the imperial process. In attempting over a long career, to write and revision his own location as twice-born 'immigrant', both within Trinidad as the descendant of an indentured Indian and again within Britain, he has constantly shown that the stories of colonialism and its post-imperial aftermath engendered what could be called 'narratives of anxiety'.[10] For in such narratives, the process of writing itself becomes a performative act of intervention and survival. It is a process that is delicately balanced, representing a search for a cultural and psychic equilibrium which constantly approaches 'self-destruction' but contains within it the seeds of 'self-discovery'.[11]

It has been observed that Naipaul frequently draws attention in his work to the 'obsolescence of his own discourse'; displaying an 'anguish of affiliation' to the canonical house of 'Englishness', which is both the source of his betrayal and the means of his potential liberation. Naipaul has often described his work as being caught in a transitional space, which he calls a 'kind of limbo [where] I am a refugee in the sense that I am always peripheral'.[12] It is an 'in between' space which has consistently bred ambivalences but also created correspondences in his perspective as a writer caught outside the boundaries of empire and nation. Writing 'in limbo' may well have enabled what Naipaul terms an individual 'way of seeing', but it has also resulted in an inevitable entanglement with 'the excessive novelty of postcolonial history' as well as 'the excessive anachronism of the canon'.[13] If we read Naipaul in this way – as a writer caught between the lure of the canonical 'house' of Englishness and the need to reconcile and comprehend the broader dimensions of his diasporic inheritance – his tenacious experimentations with language and form, over the entire trajectory of his writing career, can be seen as an illuminating paradigm for contemporary critics attempting to define the complex parameters of a postcolonial discourse and its relationship to the narrative of migration and exile.[14]

Unlike many writers who have followed – such as Salman Rushdie and a whole generation of postcolonial writers born *after* independence – Naipaul was born a colonial in Trinidad in 1932, 30 years *before* independence. As a 'thorough colonial',[15] he needed to come to terms both with the fantasy of the 'idea' of England, as umbilicus implanted from his educational background, as well as the mythic notion of an equally potent 'idea' of India, created by his childhood experience as an East Indian growing up as the son of a Brahmin in Trinidad. As is seen in the last chapter in George Lamming's *The Pleasures of Exile*, the writers who migrated to Britain from the Caribbean in the period immediately following the Second World War exhibited a 'commonly felt need' to evolve an alternative vision, an aesthetic which could move beyond the reductive oppositions of a colonial consciousness. It was a period best characterized by the crisis of a dying colonialism in the wake of which, as we have seen in the previous chapter, alternative narratives of nationalism and different versions of 'Englishness' were born.[16] This was a period when the 'authority' of the hegemonic myths of empire began to be displaced by the evolution of a cultural grammar which questioned the epistemological bases of a received history, and thus enabled the creation of new narrative forms. It was a moment, therefore, which held enormous potential for the creative writer keen to forge a language by which to redefine the colonial past, to develop a way of seeing and reading the world free from the dialectics of a metaphor of place that stressed above all the need either for a culture of 'belonging', or its shadow, a space of 'unbelonging', hovering outside in a process of constant suspension. It was primarily the discursive world within the creative texts themselves which enabled the process of discovering new 'truths', as well as the charting of new literary spaces and locations. And it was these early explorations, which charted and reconfigured the literary territory which was later to be defined by theories of migrancy and the advent of the grammar of postcolonial theory and cultural studies in the 1980s. Naipaul's writing, then, can be placed firmly alongside that of Selvon, Lamming and others[17] in its struggle to articulate an appropriate language and form by which to frame and unravel a complicated and multilayered colonial and diasporic history. Whilst approaches by individual artists of course differ, Naipaul's writing can be seen to inhabit a growing body of work encompassing the ambidextrous vision of both a colonial and postcolonial consciousness. As such, it forms a crucial bridge between those who preceded him and those who have followed after.

Whereas Salman Rushdie has been applauded for making the very pain of cultural translation – its fracture and hybridity – the 'startingpoint'[18] for the source of his creativity, Naipaul's work has often been condemned by critics for its 'mimicry', for being forever locked in a colonialist manichean divide, striving obsessively for an essentialist dream of a pure time, a period before the betrayal of colonial history or that moment which Homi Bhabha has called the 'separation of origins and essences'.[19] This is a tempting division perhaps, and one common in contemporary literary criticism, where 'exile' or 'hybridity' are set up as two different stages on the path of the 'becoming' which defines a postcolonial identity. However, as we will see, it is one which does not survive close scrutiny, for whilst Naipaul was clearly troubled in his early work by the manacles of colonial mimicry and the shackles of inherited literary forms, he was simultaneously aware of the creative possibilities of translation present in the plural realities of his Indo-Caribbean background, a diasporic background which posited difference as the cultural norm.

The difficulty was not so much with the question of the range of his perception – seeing beyond a blinkered 'colonial' vision – but more with the difficulty of moving beyond what he has called his literary 'apprenticeship', to discover the formal means by which to distance himself from the linguistic and conceptual system that had framed his imagination from childhood. 'It might', he comments ironically in *The Overcrowded Barracoon* (1972), 'have been more profitable for me to have appeared in translation.'[20] Naipaul and Rushdie are not so much opposed to each other, as Michael Gorra suggests in his illuminating study *After Empire*, but 'illustrative of different stages in the chronicle of Empire, two aspects of a single historical process, [which they share] in which colonial mimicry eventually gives way to the postcolonial collage of the self'.[21] We should not therefore view the work of the two writers as being *separated* by a falsely erected colonial/postcolonial divide, but recognize that a multiplicity of different personal and cultural histories, as well as different periods of reaction to those histories, are necessarily involved in any reading of im/migrant literatures, whose fictional representations are reflected in the emergence of a whole range of different literary strategies and forms.

Although there are clearly grounds for the contempt which Naipaul's perceived stance – in his representations of what he has called 'half-made societies', as well as some of his public pronouncements – have evoked,[22] it would be misleading to suggest that Naipaul remains trapped in a dream of wholeness and fulfilment, whether from the point of view of the colonial 'mimic man', attempting to assimilate into the 'English' canon, or as the diasporic 'Asiatic',[23] attempting to return constantly to the ever-receding millenarian dream of a lost homeland. His work, in fact, frequently dwells on the pain of the realization that the dream will always be deferred and that attainment of such essentialist ideals is impossible. A more fruitful approach to reading Naipaul may be made by an examination of his constant attempts to move beyond the limitations of such binaries – whether of the perpetually tainted detached Brahmin and the exiled colonial Anglophile – through the associative process of writing itself. This process, as 'une course de vitesse', becomes coupled with a persistent and self-conscious desire to interrogate and dismantle the tyranny of the texts and language of the traditional house of English fiction that had always both seduced and betrayed him.

Naipaul's non-fictional essays are as revealing of his development as a writer as are critical studies of his work, if only because of their painful awareness of the writer's need to extricate himself from the predetermined plot of an inherited imperial history, and to 'let his memory, rather than his pretension, [as a colonial], speak'.[24] In his two essays, 'East Indian' (1965) and 'Jasmine' (1964), republished in *The Overcrowded Barracoon*, Naipaul expresses from an early stage the complex nature of the incongruities framing his ethnic and cultural identity. As in his colonial 'fantasy' described in 'Jasmine', of Britain as 'motherland' where the 'language was mine' but the 'tradition was not' (p. 27), India for the New World East Indian immigrant was not a place but 'a word', what he calls, in *An Area of Darkness* (1964), a space 'inhabited by the imagination'.[25] In 'Jasmine', Naipaul highlights, as George Lamming does in *The Pleasures of Exile*, the difficulty for the colonial writer who is misled and betrayed by the imposed authority and mythology of Prospero's language, leaving him caught in the gap between the naming of a thing and a knowledge of it. Whilst the author recognizes the scent of the flower from his youth, he does not know its name: 'to me it had been a word in a book, a word to play with, something removed from the dull vegetation I knew'. And although the plant was a part of his everyday landscape – growing in an old lady's garden in Guyana – he is unable to bring his knowledge of the word (instilled in him by his English colonial education) together with the flower itself. As we saw earlier with Anna Morgan in Jean Rhys's *Voyage in the Dark*, Naipaul cannot fit the landscape of his Caribbean childhood together with that textual world distilled from books, for the 'word and the flower had been separate in my mind for too long. They did not come together' (p. 31). The language inherited from his colonial background, the discursive world of the English text, only distances him from the reality of his background. 'Everything in books was foreign; everything had to be subject to adaptation; and everything in . . . an English novel which worked and was of value . . . at once ceased to be specifically English' (p. 29). Much later, in *The Enigma of Arrival* (1987), Naipaul is still, as we shall see, revisiting the difficulties of that early insight found in 'Jasmine', in which he now attempts to make sense of the anguish of his continuing relationship to the 'romantic' vision of a literary England in a decaying post-imperial world where 'the signs were without meaning or without the meaning intended by their makers' (p. 120).

A similar sense of cultural ambivalence created by the language of naming is expressed in 'East Indian', which was first published in 1965 and represents a different aspect of his cultural vision. Here we witness an early attempt to unravel the several layers of diasporic history, which constitute what he has recently called the 'fragments of his inheritance, a fragment of the truth' in *A Way in the World* (1994). In this essay, Naipaul comically highlights and ironically contrasts the differences between himself and a 'real' Indian from India in his rendition of a brief encounter with a journalist in Kensington airport terminal. Unlike Naipaul, the diasporic figure twice removed from the 'homeland', who adheres, perhaps over strictly, to the rituals of his vegetarianism, the Indian journalist is free to be sacrilegious when he is out of the country; he only maintains religious customs, he emphasizes, when he is 'at home'. As Naipaul says:

> To be an Indian from Trinidad is to be unlikely. It is, in addition to everything else, to be the embodiment of an old verbal ambiguity. For this word 'Indian' has been abused as no other word in the language; almost every time it is used it has to be qualified. There was a time in Europe when everything Oriental and everything a little unusual was judged to come from Turkey or India. So Indian ink is really Chinese ink and India paper first came from China. When in 1492 Columbus landed on the island of Guanahani he thought he had got to Cathay. He ought therefore to have called the people Chinese. But East was East. He

called them Indian, and Indians they remained walking Indian file through the Indian corn.[26]

Interestingly, Naipaul is not only anticipating here the discursive power of stereotyping and the exoticization of the East in the imagination of the West, which Edward Said was later to develop in his important and influential study *Orientalism* (1978), but also illustrating the degree to which his bifurcated and hybrid identity – as a 'colonial' and an East Indian West Indian – has been constructed by those very same discourses. And it is important to notice that from a very early stage in his thinking, Naipaul was already highlighting the extent to which his imagination was fired and educated by the indeterminate cultural landscape of diaspora. What, he asks, do we mean when we talk about an 'Indian' from Trinidad? And he continues, describing the historical context for indenture: 'So long as the *real* [my italics] Indians remained on the other side of the world, there was little confusion. But when in 1845 these Indians began coming over to some of the islands Columbus had called the Indies, confusion became total' (p. 36). It was a confusion, however, that was to be both disturbing and creative for whilst, as Naipaul argues, the East Indian must remain in perpetual exile, a restless 'immigrant' of the New World for whom there can be 'no true return', no El Dorado, his situation nevertheless holds the potential for revolution: a 'revolution' which, for the writer, 'takes place in the mind' and is essentially one of the imagination (p. 40).

It is significant that the nature of Naipaul's exilic consciousness – in which the 'memory of home becomes paramount in narratives where home itself is but a memory'[27] – differs considerably from those well-known modernist figures, Joyce, Conrad, Nabokov or T. S. Eliot. These writers were individuals who left their countries by choice to live as metropolitan exiles, whereas Naipaul's East Indian ancestors were part of a larger historical process, twice dispossessed, both as nineteenth-century indentured labourers in Trinidad and, later, as subjects of the British Empire. As such, they were representatives of the global history of indentureship, a crucial element of Naipaul's diasporic imagination in which, as Satendra Nandan has observed, the 'East Indian of the West Indies' has been given epic status, written back into history, and has become an alternative metaphor for 'our modernist fate'.[28] It is crucially an exilic consciousness that originates from a notion of displacement differing considerably from the tradition of imperial expatriate writing, where the metropolitan outsider is thrown into relief against an alien background, although in its romantic posturing it may be seen to bear some resemblance to the figure of the 'exile' commonly associated with 'modernist art'.[29] For Naipaul's characters, to use an oft-quoted phrase of Salman Rushdie's, have come 'unstuck from history'.[30] To be twice removed, as Shirley Chew has convincingly shown, is not only, as with Conrad, to confront isolation and the indifference of the world in a faraway place, but 'to occupy as well the "ambiguous", "shifting" and "not . . . infertile territory" of "a translated man" '.[31]

It may be worth considering briefly the historical background to the East Indian presence in the Caribbean islands, a historical process that has been described as the 'second system of slavery', in order to understand the extent to which the 'coolie odyssey'[32] acts as a symbolic repository in Naipaul's work. When slavery was abolished in 1833, there was a labour shortage in the plantations as many of the ex-slaves refused to work. Accordingly, indentured labourers were brought in from India, China and Portugal as sources of cheap labour. The indenture system lasted from 1845–1917 and whilst the labourers were offered a passage back home after their indentureship had expired, some were never able to make it 'home' on account of debt, and others were encouraged to stay and take land in lieu of the chance to return. Their descendants make up a large part of the Indian and Chinese population in the Caribbean today and are the subjects of several of Naipaul's, as well as Sam Selvon's, Trinidad novels. Vijay Mishra has described this phase of the Indian diaspora as the 'premodern phase', the crossing of the *kala pani* which 'signified the loss of caste [purities] as well as a new form of socialization' created by *jahaji-bhai* or ship-brotherhood.[33] Interestingly, whilst the image of the 'Black Atlantic' and its slave ships – crisscrossing the Middle Passage – has often been cited as a powerful trope and image for the 'double-consciousness' of contemporary modernity,[34] a means by which we can perceive the extent to which the borders of the modern world have always been mediated and transformed by the black presence in European history, little attention has been given to the parallel effects of the experience of the Asian diaspora, a series of historic and cultural passages which have involved similar crossings of national and political boundaries. It is an identity (like the process of creolization discussed in the previous chapter) that is built from the outset on the historic admixtures of different cultural groups and the need to recognize and live alongside difference. And whether we are focusing on the descendants of that early 'premodern' phase, in which there is a constant attempt to hold on to the essentialized rituals of the past, or the more recent, later twentieth-century phase, in which the migration of peoples has largely been voluntary, there is not usually any possibility of permanent return. Returns, such as they are, are usually figurative or metaphoric, symbolic and imaginative reconstructions of the 'homeland' – *fictions* – the creation not of 'actual cities or villages, but invisible ones . . . Indias of the mind'.[35]

Indeed, the majority of figures we encounter in the Naipaulian world are framed by just such a background, whether we are talking about the apparent 'security' of the subjects of his early social comedies, set amongst the East Indian community in Trinidad – *The Mystic Masseur* (1957), *Miguel Street* (1959), *The Suffrage of Elvira* (1958) and *A House for Mr Biswas* (1961) – or in his later explorations of the diasporic imagination in *In a Free State* (1971), *Guerrillas* (1975) and *A Bend in the River* (1979). Biswas represents in many ways the culmination of the early phase of Naipaul's writing, where the Tulsis build their world on the need to both somehow preserve the past – that lost world of India that will never fully return – while at the same time replacing that nostalgic desire with what inevitably becomes a creolized local version. Hanuman House, like Biswas's life, is a house built on shaky foundations, constantly shifting and shored up by the perpetual enactment and performance of ancient rituals, many of which have become bastardized – emptied out of meaning – but which simultaneously build on the power of the remaining original fragments to replace the original desire. The Tulsi household thus 'aspires to the "lost condition" of India whilst at the same time replicating a space' where 'centres and peripheries, motherlands and diasporas – . . . enter into relationships of mutual reinforcement as well as uncanny displacement'.[36]

Throughout the novel, the literal search for a house becomes a metaphor for the ever-increasing difficulty of establishing a centre, however makeshift, within the society and creating a structure from which to write. In fact, when Biswas finally achieves a roof over his head, a space where finally 'their lives would be ordered, their memories coherent' (p. 523), we can hear an overt echo of Naipaul's own displacement as he struggled to write his novel about Biswas, living in a solitary attic room in Streatham Hill. It was a period, as Naipaul describes it, of anxiety and destitution, a period when, having no money, 'I went to London from Oxford . . . in 1954 . . . to make my way as a writer'.[37] The book would not immediately come; its writing took several years for its subject (the life of his father and the loss of a rejected colonial childhood) was too close. And it was the anxiety of that time – in a room in suburban London surrounded by 'old furniture', the objects of 'homelessness' – which lay 'below the comedy of the book'.[38] Naipaul was unable to read the novel again for 20 years. With the completion of the novel came calm, but also the realization that the house of fiction which it represented, where 'I might adapt Dickens to Trinidad',[39] could never be revisited again, for he had exhausted the possibilities of the form and the material of its local setting.

In the period that followed the writing of *A House for Mr Biswas*, Naipaul has been portrayed as a 'man threatened by desolation, driven deep within himself, reduced to homelessness'.[40] Contemptuous of the Trinidad he revisited in 1960–1 and which he describes in *The Middle Passage* (1962) as 'unimportant, uncreative, cynical . . . a society which denied itself heroes', and disillusioned with the realities of the life he witnessed in India and described in *An Area of Darkness* (1964), like England an untainted world of his imagination in childhood, Naipaul's confrontation was with the wider dimensions of his diasporic inheritance, the fear of perhaps being forever lost in translation. This was a fear epitomized by his memory of his father's breakdown, when 'He looked in the mirror one day, and couldn't see himself',[41] and in his own experience of invisibility, recounted in *An Area of Darkness,* when 'faceless' at Churchgate Station in Bombay, he imagines he might 'sink without a trace'[42] into the Indian crowd. The escape to London 14 years earlier had also proved to be illusory, for 'London was not the centre of my world. I had been misled; but there was nowhere else to go. It was a good place for getting lost in', where 'I was confined to a smaller world than I had ever known. I became, my flat, my desk, my name.'[43] Interestingly the intense sense of cultural displacement expressed in *An Area of Darkness* – which refers both to his time in London as well as his search for an ancestral home in India, a 'resting-place for the imagination' – points in tone and perspective to his next major work and novel of exile, *The Mimic Men* (1967). Despite Naipaul's long residence in Britain, it is the only fictional work, apart from *The Enigma of Arrival* (1987), to explicitly focus on the experience of being an im/migrant in Britain. Naipaul's unnamed narrator – a fictive autobiographical figure – intimates in *The Enigma of Arrival* that he failed, unlike many of his other contemporaries, to see the true potential of the cross-cultural material that could have been his subject, 'because in 1950 in London I was at the beginning of that great movement of peoples that was to take place in the second half of the twentieth century – a movement and cultural mixing greater than the peopling of the United States', where 'Cities like London were to change . . . to cease being more or less national cities' and 'become modern day Romes' (p. 130). His failure to 'see' the relevance and drama of the 'stories' that surrounded him was not only built on his preconceived and essentially linguistic notions of 'Englishness' learnt from afar, but was also premised on a false idea of what the proper subject for a 'writer' should be, whether a J. R. Ackerley, a Somerset Maugham, an Aldous Huxley: 'wishing to *be that kind of writer* [my italics], I didn't see material in the campers [immigrant tenants] of the big Earl's Court House' (p. 125), the boarding-house where Naipaul first lived on arrival in London.

II

The remainder of this chapter will examine two works which focus particularly on questions of im/migration and exile in Britain. *The Mimic Men* was published in 1967 and is related closely in its search for form to those 'immigrant' novels by Sam Selvon and others discussed in Chapter 2. *The Enigma of Arrival* appearing 20 years later excavates more fully some of the very same questions, but which are now addressed from within the 'heart' of Englishness itself. It will be argued that the 'diasporic' character of Naipaul's vision, though painful, has enabled him to interrogate, subvert and translate those areas of the im/migrant imaginary previously bounded by the discursive world of English letters, and to break out of what have been called the 'hinges'[44] of an imperial history, in which postcolonial action is read primarily as a 'reaction' to a specific cultural void, an endeavour to replace the sense of 'something missing'.[45] However, it is not so frequently read as a creative intervention into the ways in which the symbolic universe of the creative texts themselves can actually transform our way of reading. As Helen Tiffin has frequently illustrated, the 'writing back' involved in any counter-discursive strategy involves the creation of what she calls a 'semiotics of resistance', where the colonial or postcolonial writer inevitably questions the European textual 'capture' of specific places and peoples, but, more importantly, makes an intervention into the 'whole of the discursive field within which those texts operate'.[46] In this sense, the writing becomes not only a means of moving beyond specific inherited models – or versions of literary and mythical 'truths' – but also what is fundamentally a journey into the nature of the defining qualities of language and form itself.

Naipaul's personal expression of his fear of extinction in *An Area of Darkness* (the fact that 'I had been made in Trinidad and England; recognition of my difference was necessary to me') is rearticulated in an important and suggestive essay, 'Conrad's Darkness', in which he expresses the literary effects of this personal fear and his anxious need to create a form which might provide a fitting correlative for his themes. To be a 'colonial', he says, 'was to know a certain kind of security' but one had to abandon that 'fixed world'; it 'was necessary to lose one's preconceptions of what the novel should do', for the 'romantic' fantasy of England as a 'purely literary region . . . untrammelled by the accidents of history or background' could not be sustained. Nor, indeed, could the other side of the fantasy, the vision of his colonial background and the history of empire as a history of disorder, being repeated in all the previously colonized regions of the world. The essay is significant both in its illustration of the extent to which Naipaul was in awe of Conrad as a model – a writer who 'had been everywhere before me' and whose achievement derives 'from the *honesty* [my italics] which is part of his difficulty' – and in its rehearsal of Naipaul's difference from Conrad. Furthermore, the essay is also revealing in its preoccupation with the possibilities of 'narrative' not merely as a linear form, but as an 'orchestration of perceptions', the potential key to unlock and effect a necessary process of decolonization and transformation.[47] As he has said in an recent interview:

> [narrative] occurs all the time . . . Your coming here is narrative . . . It's all narrative. [But] it's a matter of choosing. It's when you're doing the other kind of writing – you start looking for a thing called plot and you get into trouble . . . Narrative is something large going on around you all the time . . . Plot assumes that the world has been explored . . . Whereas I am still exploring the world. I don't know the world yet. And there is narrative there, in every exploration. The writers of plots know the world . . . I began to understand that quite late.[48]

Unlike Sam Selvon and George Lamming, who travelled to Britain on the same boat as 'ordinary immigrant[s]', Naipaul arrived in Britain in 1950 as an 18-year-old student, on a government scholarship to study English at University College, Oxford, harbouring an adolescent and 'romantic' desire to become a writer. This was an ambition which was not to be fulfilled until several years later, with the acceptance of *The Mystic Masseur* for publication by André Deutsch in 1957. Like many of the other writers who were later to form the influential Caribbean Artists' Movement,[49] Naipaul struggled after his university days in Oxford to earn a living, to cope with the disillusionment of his arrival and the difficulties of finding a voice in a literary world which was essentially indifferent to his art.[50] His actual experience of Oxford turned out to be a mockery of his expectations; the teaching of literature there did not encourage him to write:

> I had looked forward to wandering among large tracts of writing. I was presented with 'texts' . . . The fact was, I had no taste for scholarship, for tracing the growth of schools and trends. I sought continuously to relate literature to life.[51]

The gap between 'literature and life', between a world and a society founded precariously in the imagination, but rooted in a different and alien cultural context from his own, echoes in interesting ways many of the observations made in George Lamming's *The Pleasures of Exile,* in which the construction of the colonial's 'idea' of England was based primarily on the 'tyranny' of having been indoctrinated by the entirety of the discursive world represented by Prospero's 'texts'. The pleasures and pains, however, of Naipaul's exile, and the recognition that came 'with knowledge' that the 'vision' of English literature was 'alien' and 'diminished my own',[52] has often been misread as simply one of a supercilious 'mimicry', in which Naipaul, like those mimic men described in Frantz Fanon's famous work *Black Skin, White Masks*, was not able to perceive his 'difference' through the performative and potentially liberating elements of his colonial background. A mimicry, which to paraphrase Homi Bhabha's positive reading of the colonial condition, enables the articulation of an alternative space where one is 'the same, but not quite; the same, but not white'. Instead, Naipaul adopted the dangerous refuge of being an Anglophile, a 'double agent'[53] keen only to impress his views on the receptive ears of the white literary establishment.

Naipaul was set apart in the early phase of his writing career, both by critics and the writers themselves, due to the perceived distance he created between himself and his subject matter. It was George Lamming, in fact, who was the most outspoken in condemning Naipaul's apparently Oxonian perspective. Although, as we have seen, Lamming was concerned to analyse the extent to which literary colonization had influenced the development of the Caribbean novel in its creation of a linguistic and textual culture that came from 'outside', he was unable, in the 1960s at least, to accept the tone of Naipaul's writings of the East Indian into the diasporic history of the Caribbean in his early social comedies.[54] Dismissing Naipaul's work in favour of Selvon's, he writes in *The Pleasures of Exile*, that

> His books can't move beyond a castrated satire . . . When such a writer is a colonial ashamed of his cultural background and striving like mad to prove himself through promotion to the peaks of a 'superior' culture

> whose values are gravely in doubt, then satire, like the charge of philistinism, is for me nothing more than a refuge. And it is too small a refuge for a writer who wishes to be taken seriously.[55]

Clearly Naipaul's 'satire' in his first three books set in Trinidad – *The Mystic Masseur*, *The Suffrage of Elvira* and *Miguel Street* – was frequently directed at the illiteracy and disordered, anarchic lives of his East Indian subjects, and it was a sense of the 'oddity of people' in my 'early books', combined with a narrative voice which appeared to ridicule the subjects described, that tended to irritate local critics. Whilst Lamming's observations were partially accurate in the context of the 1960s and the heated debates that were going on concerning literary nationalism, he set up a political opposition, particularly between the work of Selvon and Naipaul, which was an oversimplification of the fundamental issues that both writers have addressed.

Naipaul's adaptation of a borrowed form, the 'satire' of his early comedies of manners, may well have been a 'refuge', but it was neither an uncomplicated nor a comfortable one. Frequently, the tone of these early works is held in balance by the combination of an apparently contemptuous satire and a sympathetic irony. Whilst Ganesh, for example, in *The Mystic Masseur*, is ridiculed for his ambitions to be a fraudulent masseur, a pundit and later politician, the writing of his story – despite its deflationary mock-epic qualities – still remains an important reinscription, as a 'history of our times'. When commenting on the question of satire in his early fiction Naipaul has stressed that:

> It is . . . fear that underlies a good deal of what is called satire, or the attempt to be contemptuous of what you fear. This can't be done; rather you will be contemptuous of what you love, and exalt what you fear.[56]

In *Finding the Centre* (1984), Naipaul provides a moving account of the desperation of his search for a literary 'voice' as a young writer in the freelancer's rooms at the BBC, and the breakthrough he achieved when he composed the opening lines of *Miguel Street*, his first written but third published work – a series of sketches set in Trinidad amongst a group of working-class characters not at all dissimilar to Selvon's 'boys', who are translated from the mock-heroic calypsonian street world of Port of Spain to the urban world in *The Lonely Londoners*. And, interestingly, it was a model from home – his father's persistence in the writing of *Gurudeva and Other Tales* – stories written from '*within* [my italics] a community' which became his inspiration. 'There is nothing of . . . protest . . . the barbs are all turned inwards . . . I stress it because this way of looking, from being my father's became mine.'[57]

In fact, Naipaul, as Sam Selvon before him, was to break his creative 'block' as a writer living in London by turning away from attempts to manipulate standard English forms to the immediacy of the popular Trinidadian vernacular idiom.[58] *Miguel Street*, like *The Lonely Londoners*, is a series of loosely related 'ballads' or 'episodes' set around a backstreet in Port of Spain. Naipaul, like Selvon, makes use of the oral calypsonian tradition, using nicknames for his characters and dramatizing their eccentricities. Names are drawn from the inanimate, the trivial and the arts – Hat, Bogart, Big Foot, Eddoes, Razor and Wordsworth the poet; these figures even recite similar 'gaffs', such as the ballad of Brackley and the Cross recited in both *The Lonely Londoners* and in *Miguel Street* as the story of Man-Man who sets himself up for crucifixion. In both novels the phrase 'what happening' reverberates throughout and beneath the humour and fast-moving oral banter, whilst a sense of futility and emptiness predominates. Bogart plays cards all day even though he doesn't like them; Eddoes, like Big City in *The Lonely Londoners*, projects a loud and noisy image of himself to cover his embarrassment; and Moses's revaluation of what kiff-kiff laughter really hides is, as Hat says of Dolly's giggling when George arranges her marriage, 'She ain't giggling, you know. She crying really.' Yet the final effect of Naipaul's stories differs considerably from Selvon's ballads due to the narrative perspective of the boy-narrator, who recounts these experiences in retrospect and whose linguistic code (Standard English) sets him apart from the characters on the street. Selvon, in his works, is more obviously on the same side of the 'yard' – the Caribbean literary fence – as Hat and the narrator in *The Lonely Londoners* moves imperceptibly amongst the characters modulating between various levels of his invented idiomatic scale. However, in *Miguel Street* the final irony is reserved for Naipaul's young narrator. His apparent linguistic authority is dramatically diminished in the final story, as he departs Trinidad with a deep sense of foreboding: 'not looking back, looking only at my shadow before me, a dancing *dwarf* [my italics] on the tarmac' (p. 222).

If *The Lonely Londoners* can be seen to be an emblematic novel of 'immigration' in which Sam Selvon's 'boys' translate themselves into black Londoners, making us read the city differently, V. S. Naipaul's *The Mimic Men* represents an emblematic novel of colonial 'exile' in which the split consciousness of the alienated intellectual Ralph Singh comes to be representative of that divided self, the brown man with a 'white mask' perhaps, familiar to some from the theoretical writings of Frantz Fanon. It is not usually common practice to draw correspondences between the London works of Sam Selvon and V. S. Naipaul, because Selvon, as one of the pioneers of black writing in Britain, has normally been associated with creolization and syncretism, creating humane and humorous parodies which sensitively subvert the notion of any dominant textual authority from within, and which reveal that culture to be incapable of 'supporting either its own fantasy of identity or the fantasies of its colonial subjects'.[59] Conversely, Naipaul, as winner of the first David Cohen Prize, and knighted in 1996 for a lifetime's work in 'English literature', is seen to have taken up the elitist and comfortable position of a 'universal' exile, concerned only to put his own past (and the rest of the 'Third World') into 'order' by adopting the dubious narrative authority of Western literary forms. However, the illusory sense of a colonial belonging to inherited literary forms – 'the tradition of civility'[60] – was not to provide a solution to Naipaul's ambivalent location as either a West Indian in Britain, the divided subject of Western discourse in Trinidad, or the carrier of his diasporic Indian inheritance. Indeed, Naipaul is as centrally concerned (although he explores this differently) with the process of interrogation, subversion and revision as is Sam Selvon in his London novels.

As Sara Suleri has powerfully argued, Naipaul's fascination with the clichés of colonial mimicry and the literary quality of his alienation 'may be his only means to arrive at an idiom' by which to confront himself as participant and stereotype of the clichés themselves.[61] It has been suggested that the narrative authority of the colonial text is lost 'precisely because the very objective of narrative – its plenitude, its signification of a unitary real' is always inevitably 'interrupted or left incomplete'.[62] Naipaul's *The Mimic Men* can be seen to explore the complexities of this 'incompleteness', in which the mode of writing acts as a correlative for the experience, and where the text itself becomes the vehicle for an analysis of the deceptions inherent in the colonial fantasy of order and cohesion, a 'circuit of betrayal',[63] as well as an interrogation of the impossibility of ever achieving such a position. Naipaul employs the form of *bildungsroman* as a self-consciously constructed metafiction, not only to confront the extent to which the notion of an unified self must always be an agent of deception for the hybridized colonial subject, but also to question the dubious assumptions of a dominant culture which has created the possibility of such fantasies. If Naipaul can in some measure be identified with the narrator of *The Mimic Men*, Ralph Singh makes several illuminating observations concerning the tone of this work, in which escape into the ordered idealized past – whether of sheep in Soho Square, or, in the vision Ralph frequently recites, of Aryan horseman riding over snowclad hills – or even into the order implied by the clarity of register in Naipaul's earlier novels is no longer possible. In *The Mimic Men,* style and subject matter come together in an attempt to face 'truth' rather than withdraw from it into colonial fantasy. As Ralph says:

> I wish to avoid satire; I will leave out the stories of illiteracy and social innocence . . . It is that [the] situation satirizes itself, turns satires inside out, takes satire to a point where it touches pathos, if not tragedy (p. 209).

And in this first novel by Naipaul to explicitly address the experience of exposing the myth of origins in the 'mother-country' – source of the colonial 'fantasy' – the narrator is as *involved* with the subject as is the incisive imagination of Naipaul, the artist. The narrator, if anything, points only to himself as the main object of satire in the novel; he is trapped in a cycle of events from which there is no easy escape or simple resolution. Ralph's dreams turn to nightmares as he gradually comes to see that the malaise of his past that he describes as 'shipwreck', an image clearly echoing Defoe's founding text of colonialist fantasy, *Robinson Crusoe*, cannot be rejected or ignored, for it is a part of him and the only past he has.

Moses's vision at the end of Selvon's *The Lonely Londoners* – a moment that expressed his developing awareness of an essential stasis in his existence, coupled with the threatening sense of a repetitive entrapment within a recurring pattern of events – provides an interesting parallel and an instructive starting-point for the discussion of Naipaul's exiled politician and narrator of *The Mimic Men.* At the close of *The Lonely Londoners*, Moses, the archetypal prophet figure, wished he could 'draw apart' from the hustling and bantering of the 'boys', for he could see a 'great aimlessness which leaving you standing in the same spot' (p. 125). At the opening of *The Mimic Men*, Ralph Singh also appears to have been involved – in the active part of his life when he adopted the Western postures of student, businessman and politician (a phase the narrator later describes in retrospect as a 'period in parenthesis') – in what he regards, when he begins to write, as a predictable and barren cycle of actions. Like old Moses, who eventually retreats in *Moses Ascending* into the 'attic' of his own house in order to compose his 'Memoirs', Ralph Singh stresses above all his need for withdrawal from the syndrome of his colonial fantasies. He retreats to the anonymous room of a hotel in an outer suburb where:

> I do not wish to become involved in battles which are irrelevant to myself. I no longer wish to share distress; I do not have the equipment. No more words for me, except these I write, and in them, the politician, chapman in causes will be suppressed as far as possible . . . My present urge, is, in the inaction imposed on me, to secure the final emptiness (p. 10).

Ralph's self-scrutiny here and his perception of the 'final emptiness' as the inevitable culmination of his career as 'mimic man' where he sees, from 'play-acting to disorder: it is the pattern' – are in many ways evocations of a comparable crisis of displacement and futility that Selvon points to as Moses stares down into the swirling waters of the River Thames.

Clearly then, the particular nature of Ralph Singh's various attempts to escape from the disorder of his colonial past on the fictional island of Isabella (closely modelled on Trinidad) – as student dandy, businessman, politician – may not immediately appear to constitute a mode that is comparable to the various 'ballads' of the boys in *The Lonely Londoners*. However, the fundamental impulses and insecurities underlying Ralph Singh's role-playing persona lead finally to the creative expression of an existential and psychological condition, which is directly comparable with Moses's growth in understanding at the close of *The Lonely Londoners* regarding his need to protect and preserve the 'wholeness' of the individual psyche against a stream of undermining forces. In many ways, Naipaul's novel can be usefully read as a fictional inquiry into some of the very sources of the difficulties that Selvon humorously dramatizes in his Caribbean island in the metropolis, as well as an example of the difficulties involved in creating a new language and form for the expression of that survival. Through the writing of his 'memoirs', Ralph Singh attempts to reconsider the chaos and disillusion of his past life by probing beneath the 'surface' actions or reactions, in order perhaps to discover an imaginative truth beyond the pattern of colonial mimicry. The writing of the memoirs thus becomes the means to explore the significances of Ralph Singh's hyphenated subjectivity – the gaps in his history, the 'period in parenthesis' – which 'can never be fully written out'.[64] 'Colonial' may not be an appropriate term to describe the fictional island setting which Naipaul creates in this novel – Isabella – as it is independent for at least half of the novel, but it is apparent that the problems and structures within Isabellan society are condemned for their neo-colonialism even if, like the politicians themselves, they assume the masks of Independence.

The Mimic Men presents us with an alternative vision of 'exile', and an alternative mode of response in fiction to a dilemma which creates a number of structural and phenomenologically kindred elements in the 'London' novels of Selvon and Naipaul. Certainly, Naipaul's canvas and concerns – the corruption of postcolonial societies, the exploration of the flight into exile of a fraudulent politician and the setting both in Isabella and London – differ considerably in scope from those discussed in *The Lonely Londoners*; but if we regard the comparable features as the bases and the conditions for the evolution of a im/migrant sensibility or a developing poetics of migration, an important generic affinity becomes evident in the artistic frames moulded by the two writers for their themes. Whereas in Selvon's work the use of a creolized idiom openly subverts the centre, Naipaul undermines the centre's assumptions of literary and cultural authority; whilst *The Mimic Men* is narrated in Standard English, it embodies the panic of a growing recognition that a gap of silence exists between that language and the narrator's need to articulate his experience.

One of the predominant concerns of *The Mimic Men* is to examine and redefine, not by the means of a logical analysis but through the fractured memories of a reflecting consciousness, the underlying patterns of colonial fantasy and education that can lead to the creation of such hollow myths. Responses to island and city are explored as symptoms of the same malaise and as the basis of the narrator's racial and cultural schizophrenia, his psychological restlessness and dispossession. *The Mimic Men* enacts what we might call a fictional reappraisal and rehearsal of Naipaul's earlier position as a writer, originally from the Caribbean living in London, and of the nature of his detachment from the society he left at the age of 18. In Naipaul's earlier work, as indicated previously, escape to an ordered world outside the island had always provided an alternative to the entrapments of mimicry, or the limiting and claustrophobic nature of the East Indian community. Even in *A House for Mr Biswas*, where some attempt is made to accommodate the 'hero' to the landscape of his birth, Biswas's son Anand eventually leaves to study in England. In *The Mimic Men*, the city no longer provides an ideal or a means of solace, a mode of security or of release. In fact, it serves only to increase to almost nightmarish proportions the very absence of the possibility for such a refuge. Visions of 'order' are now relegated to a pre-Renaissance world, a world before the 'voyages of discovery' that is unspecific in time or place, and which evokes, in the brief glimpses Ralph gives us of it, a lost Eden.

The encounter with London does, however, remain important. It provides both a point from which the exiled politician and narrator Ralph Singh can begin to measure the chaos of his past existence, and a means by which he can attempt to come to terms with his intimation – one which develops as the writing of the memoirs proceeds – of a modern predicament of displacement which is the summation of his diasporic inheritance. The room in which he is finally 'washed up' (one of many in the novel), and from which he begins to recount his past, is situated symbolically in the outer reaches of the metropolis. After an active career as a leader on the newly independent island of Isabella, the exiled politician flees to compose his memoirs. He survives, like Selvon's Lonely Londoners, on the edges of the metropolis, and through the composition of his memoirs unintentionally exposes, as does Moses in *Moses Ascending*, the fact that the unity initially suggested by the inherited *bildungsroman* form cannot be the 'inevitable condition of the colonial text'.[65] Whilst Moses's 'memoirs' in *Moses Ascending* can be seen to be ultimately parodic – in their renegotiation of 'the status of the "memoir" as a sign of literary authority'[66] – reducing the borrowed form to Moses's 'own level', Ralph Singh is engaged, in his need to move beyond his misguided attempts to inhabit the clichés of 'Englishness', in an equally difficult task – a process which finally exposes the cliché itself to have been a falsely constructed facade. Moses's clichéd pose in *Moses Ascending* – as the English writer (Black Englishman) and landlord – provides an ironic contrast to the predicament of Naipaul's narrator who is also attempting to compose his 'memoirs'. And as in Selvon's Moses novels, the room from which Ralph writes – whilst providing an image of the hollowness of his final displacement – also acts as a transient fulcrum-point both in terms of the narrator's present predicament and the novel's overall structure.

It is from this room – 'rooted in nothing, it linked to nothing' (p. 36) – that Ralph Singh, after 14 months of anxious labour, begins to perceive some patterns of meaning in a seemingly random and inchoate world.[67] It also allows the narrator the possibility of gaining a developing perspective in the narration of a past that is entrapped within the repetition of both a linguistic and a historical cycle of actions. It provides, in other words, a union of character and setting to which all the book's meanings can be related, and it is in this suburban hotel on the outskirts, a half-way house between past and present, island and city, order and chaos, hovering on the threshold of the 'nation', that Ralph Singh confronts the 'shipwreck' and 'violation' that he had always sought to escape, the 'shipwreck' becoming a literal metaphor for the debris of empire:

> It never occurred to me that the writing of this book might have become an end in itself, that the recording of a life might become the extension of that life . . . Order, sequence, regularity: it is there every time the

> electricity meter clicks accepting one more of my shillings . . . This is the gift of minute observation which has come to me with the writing of this book, one order, of which I form part, answering the other, which I create (pp. 244–5).

It is worthwhile noting that Naipaul himself, in the actual composition of the novel, faced the difficulty of creating a base, of placing the narrator in a fiction where the teller of the tale is as displaced as the subject itself and in which alternatives of escape to an external idea of 'order' are no longer possible.[68] On receiving the W. H. Smith award for the book, he commented to Francis Wyndham that he had attempted to write *The Mimic Men* three times. After the third attempt he realized that the work needed a physical centre – and this would be the place where the man was writing his memoirs. Ralph Singh makes a similar observation towards the end of the novel:

> I was overwhelmed as much by the formlessness of my experiences, and their irrelevance to the setting in which I proposed to recount them, as by the setting itself, my physical situation in this city, this room . . . And this became my aim, from the central fact of this setting, my presence in this city which I have known as student, politician and now as refugee-immigrant, to impose order on my own history, to abolish that disturbance which is what a narrative in sequence might have led me to (p. 243).

The 'disturbance' referred to here clearly involves a primarily private and psychological malaise. And as we shall see later, the ultimate end of what Ralph calls a 'narrative in sequence' or what we might call the conventional development of a linear plot, would have been a pointless exercise. To have elicited only an external, sequential narrative from the material of his life would have been to refuse the essentially cyclical character of his actions and to have led back again to the 'greater disorder' the 'shipwreck which all my life I had sought to avoid' (p. 7).

Accordingly, then, *The Mimic Men* is cyclical in structure. Its three sections are linked, not so much by chronology or the piecing together of Ralph's life, as through a poetics of 'association', a process of accretion that develops as the novel proceeds. The 'events' in a sense are clear. We move in the linear sense from Isabella to London where Ralph is a student, to his marriage to Sandra, to his return almost like a tourist in his own country, to a career in politics, the breakdown of his marriage, his exile and the writing of his memoirs, not the memoirs he originally intended, which were mainly historical in intent, but to an autobiography, confessional in tone, with a first-person narrator who is both participant and spectator – the young protagonist and the older man written into being from his hotel room. Ralph also goes through several reinventions of himself during the course of the narration, from student dandy who anglicizes his name from Ranjit Kirpal Singh, to the hard businessman who creates a mock Romanesque fortress in his Isabellan suburb (later called Crippleville), to the fraudulent neo-colonial politician, to exile and eventually to the reclusive Brahmin writer who has fulfilled the fourfold Hindu division of life.

The form as it is constructed by the older narrator enables an exploration into the whole process of writing, the deceptions of language and the impossibility of writing an objective history. As Ralph stresses at an early stage in the filtration of his past:

> It was my hope to give expression to the restlessness, the deep disorder, which the great explorations, the overthrow in three continents of established social organizations, the unnatural bringing together of peoples who could achieve fulfilment only within the security of their own societies . . . it was my hope to give partial expression to the restlessness which this great upheaval has brought about (p. 32)

But he is, as he openly admits, 'too much a victim of that restlessness which was to have been my subject' to ever write that history. The heterogeneity and disorder which form the fundamental characteristics of his past life make the standard writing of a history 'unspeakable', as the 'minimal conditions' for its narrative progression cannot be met. He can no more be the 'subject of his own history, in which he has no coherent identity, than he is of History itself'.[69] In the first section of the novel the older Ralph, reflecting on his past, can see that 'the warning signs were so clear', his mimicry could only lead to perpetual dislocation, the inability to find a thread on which to hang his various roles. Later, having recounted his life, the narrator begins to see that 'certain emotions bridge the years' and the 'recording of a life might become an extension of that life' (p. 244). The difficulty, however (whether we believe Ralph Singh or not), is to decide whether at the close he is simply enacting yet another pose, whether the 'final withdrawal' is genuinely that of the Hindu recluse in the final stage of his karma, or the symbolic posturing of the postwar writer in exile.

The ending, and indeed the whole tone of the narration, raise a number of important questions in terms of how we read the book. Is it a thinly disguised allegory – as some have suggested – of the inevitable corruption of newly formed postcolonial nations? What is the relationship between the exiled politician's perspective as narrator and that of the author? Ralph Singh has been seen as an 'alter-ego' of Naipaul himself, 'a man more limited than his creator . . . but almost as close to Naipaul, one suspects, as Marlow is to Conrad'.[70] To what extent is the self-conscious form of the fictional autobiography misleading? There are often at least three levels of consciousness interacting in any particular scene: the ironic distance between Naipaul and his narrator, Ralph Singh's own distance from the narration within his hotel room, and the immediacy of the descriptions of the protagonist involved in the events themselves. It becomes increasingly clear that what is described in the analysis of past events – his early days as a student in London, the chaos and segregation of his Asiatic childhood on Isabella, or even his fatal entrance into the drama of colonial politics – matters less to the purpose of the novel than does the growth in awareness which is achieved by the process of recollection itself. As Angus Calder has observed: 'The book is not a narrative, it is an ordered system . . . of attempts at explanation, evolving ideas, moods and memories, states of mind, changes of mind.'[71]

In the first section (which is composed of disjointed memories covering the entire spectrum of Ralph's past), we follow in a seemingly random and circular fashion, the starts and turns of the narrator's wandering consciousness, as he oscillates between the recollection of a past event and the insights of a later scrutiny. The second and third sections provide a more detailed exploration and an amplification in personal and political terms, of patterns and intimations merely glimpsed amidst the initial 'formlessness'. The novel therefore functions on two levels. Ralph reveals to himself and to the reader that growth in awareness which develops as his past is painfully unravelled. At the same time, the reader is able to perceive how the memories themselves relate a growth in experience, deriving from those actions which result in Ralph's final withdrawal. New definitions and images begin to replace and translate the rejection of those insubstantial colonial ideals that the novel progressively records. By intentionally allowing Ralph Singh to be involved in the anguish of placelessness as well as an interpreter of it, Naipaul comes to terms with his own problem of how to achieve the right perspective and tone in a novel so closely linked to his own experience.[72] This interchange between the two levels of apprehension in the novel leads beyond negation, cynicism, anti-climax, and the narrowing of possibilities to a more mature evocation and acceptance of the complex and often contradictory forces controlling the individual born into such a world. Importantly, too, the struggle of the narrator in *The Mimic Men*, in his search for 'ideal' landscapes and the preservation of the psyche against a backcloth of disintegrative forces (race, sexuality, history etc.), also offers an interesting perspective on Naipaul's own position at this time and an appropriate artistic correlative for his themes.

It is useful to pause here for a moment to examine the 'snow episode' as a typical passage, in which the doubling of narrative perspective allows for a translation of an earlier memory beyond the binaries which first constrained it. The description concerns Ralph's first significant memory – the incredible experience of his first snow which opens the novel, when the student Ralph rushes to the top of Shylock's boarding-house in Kensington (pp. 7–8). There are three planes of awareness registered in this passage. On the one hand, we have the initial excitement and apprehension of the student viewing snow for the first time; this is followed swiftly by a sense of deflation and disappointment. Lastly, we see the later perspective of the writer reflecting back, and attempting to place both the sense of 'beauty' the snow evoked and the 'forlornness' which so swiftly superceded it. It is the juxtaposition of the opposing forces at work in this episode and the tension in tone and emphasis between the contrasting reactions to the experience, which heighten its significance. The use of a double perspective illustrates both the immediacy of Ralph's enchantment as he climbs the stairs to the attic to view the 'airiest crushed ice', but is also suggestive of a more realistic and less mythical world, which contrasts with the student's 'ideal' element. The fulfilment of his dream is undercut by the surroundings from which he views the snow – the dinginess of the room, bare boards, a mattress on dusty sheets of newspaper, a dead fluorescent light.

In the second paragraph – 'Standing before the window – crooked sashes, peeling paintwork: so fragile the structure up here which lower down appeared so solid – I felt the dead light on my face. The flakes didn't only float; they also spun' – we only see at first Ralph's vision of so 'complete' a beauty, but within this enchanted view we gradually become conscious of the potential disintegration of the ideal scene, as he also perceives the smoke from ugly chimneypots and the decaying plastered wall of the house next to the bombsite. As he turns back to the empty room with the mattress on the floor, the 'magic' of the city soon vanishes, and he has an 'intimation of the forlorness and the people who lived in it'. This intimation of a reality, out of tune with his ideal, defines the mode in which the student Ralph gains a momentary glimpse of a postwar society which he had previously been unable to see due to his single-minded desire to fulfil his expectation. The perspective of the older narrator Ralph is distinguishable from the early enthusiasm and sense of beauty and the early disillusionment and sense of forlornness – although it subsumes both. This implicit third plane of awareness signifies a more fully realized expression of the original forlornness and is illustrative of a technique which unfolds as the novel proceeds, where the narrator is able to hold the perception of two memories together at the same time and discover new relationships between them.

At first Ralph's intimation of 'forlornness' defines only a sense of decay and increases his awareness of isolation and the corruption of his ideals. But as he attempts to describe the relationship between the forlornness he has perceived in the city and his own sense of displacement, he is unable to find the right words, and can only describe his own tragic sense of inevitable 'shipwreck': 'Even as I tried to put words to what I felt, I knew that my own journey, scarcely begun had ended in the shipwreck which all my life I had sought to avoid' (p. 7). Nevertheless, the association implied here between Ralph's despair after the vision of snow and the 'shipwreck' he fears is instructive, for in the intimation of 'forlornness' lie the seeds of the discovery of a more ironic pattern, a pattern of correspondences between his own life and the one he observes in the city. By attempting to physically inhabit an 'ideal' landscape, a dream nurtured in his imagination as a boy, Ralph recognizes that his geographically-based hope to escape the disorder of his makeshift society prefigures the 'forlornness' overwhelming him in the city, the location of the dream. Shipwreck therefore becomes Ralph's 'geographical metaphor'[73] of 'forlornness', and the growth in understanding, which develops from the oppositions inherent in this image, reverberates and amplifies as the writing continues. As Ralph remembers the frequent withdrawals and escapes of his past life, he begins to see that his private visions of Aryan horsemen, or the lone Asian boy standing outside the hut at dusk, are no different from his impulse to identify with his first snow in London, or even with the sacramental order of political power in the Roman House in Isabella. The recounting of that seemingly inconsequential memory early in the novel, enlarged upon by the developing awareness of the older Ralph, thus provides a central clue to the novel's structure and ultimate poetic unity. And it is by confronting these divisions in his own nature that Ralph is able to begin the process of demythologizing.

Space will not allow a full analysis of the ways by which 'meaning' is unravelled in the text through the shifting and meditating consciousness of the narrator, but insights can be gained by the mode in which Ralph Singh, in the second and third sections, revisits images and metaphors, using an associative technique which takes the reader and the narrator beyond the particular circumstances of their usage to the significance of their emotional currency and power to transform. These images will be all too apparent to any reader – shipwreck, snow, sea, celebration, violation, fear of flesh, private worlds. Moreover, their significance rests upon a careful repetition which in different circumstances provokes different emotional insights enabling a widening of perception. As Naipaul has recently indicated:

> The English language came with a literature, came with certain forms. The forms helped when I was writing about the smaller, complete world. But they didn't help at all when I was trying to get at the true nature of my wider experience.
>
> I always felt the need to establish the identity of the writer, the narrator, the gatherer of impressions: to make the point that, whatever associations came with the language, this English-language traveller in the world was not English but colonial, and carried different pictures in his head.[74]

In the conceptualized preservation of ideal romantic landscapes, Ralph's intellectual fantasies and literary expectations certainly contrast with the nature of the myth-making in Selvon's *The Lonely Londoners*. The 'ballads' of the boys, as we have seen, were more in keeping with the double-edged humour and play-acting of the calypsonian trickster figure than with the overarticulate, but alienated intellectual Ralph Singh. Yet the fundamental dilemma affecting both types of immigrant is similar – though Selvon clearly dwells more on topical details of the day such as unemployment, racism, cultural clashes – as in the need to be a 'performer', an actor in disguise wearing the uncomfortable clothes of his constructed identity. In London, Ralph says; 'I had no guide. There was no one to link my present with my past, no one to note my consistencies or inconsistencies. It was up to me to choose my character' (p. 20).

By escaping to London and later back to Isabella, Ralph attempts to live out an illusion which stems from the dubious and artificial assumptions of a literary world, a world of words, concepts and systems, of an 'order' or a 'truth' which was inappropriate to his own cultural background. The acquisition of such myths, rather than being a means of crystallizing a sense of belonging, only enforces a more profound awareness of displacement, which is coupled with the lack of a known code of new signs by which to view the world. Ralph cannot possess either landscape – whether of his childhood or in London – because the language he has inherited cannot adequately frame the multiple dimensions of his world. It is only in retrospect that he begins to recognize the extent of his misconceptions and the significance of memory. Referring to a scene where he remembers taking apples to the teacher at Isabella Imperial he adds: 'We had no apples on Isabella. It must have been an orange; yet my memory insists on the apple. The editing is clearly at fault, but the edited version is all I have' (p. 90).

The language of narration in *The Mimic Men* is 'Standard English', and Naipaul's method is basically analytical and reflective rather than dramatic. However, this language, acquired by Singh in his youth with all its associated implications for the colonial of division and artificiality, what Ralph later calls a facility for a 'superficial realism', is finally shown to be a limiting rather than an exploratory means of apprehending the world. It builds up a series of seemingly unresolvable tensions and oppositions (as we saw in the discussion of 'Jasmine' earlier), and is a form the older Ralph becomes deeply sceptical of as he recognizes the degree to which words can deceive as well as clarify. Describing his earlier experience of writing in a journalistic essay whilst he was a politician, Ralph admits that the 'article was deeply dishonest . . . it was the first of many such pieces: balanced, fair, with the final truth evaded, until at last this truth was lost' (p. 189). Written at a time 'when words came easily' due to his continued reliance on the 'game of naming', and the use of phrases which were not his own, 'we [believed] we spoke as honest men. But we used borrowed phrases which were part of the escape from thought, from that reality we wanted people to see but could ourselves now hardly face' (p. 198).

Through the composition of his memoirs, Ralph, it would appear, attempts to release himself from the glib and 'balanced style' of his previous works to 'rediscover that truth' which the borrowed words had always evaded. In order to break open the limiting, desensitizing frames imposed upon him by his inherited but not entirely assimilated linguistic modes, Ralph does not seek to evolve a new language as such: he does not attempt like Selvon in the Moses novels to reinvent the metropolis through an idiomatic Caribbean form. What he does is to use this conventional language in unconventional narrative or structural patterns, making it work in new ways, allowing it to generate new, highly *individual* meanings. Narrative coherence in *The Mimic Men*, emerges not as the result of a chronological and linear narrative structure, but through a cumulative method achieved by the repetition of a cycle of negative actions which only begin to gain signification as the writing advances. A reading demands the apprehension of a growing vision, the deciphering of a metaphysical and poetic order which stems from the original binaries – island/metropolis, centre/periphery, sea/snow – on which the imaginative order of the novel is based. A new conceptual order beyond dream or nightmare, ideal landscapes or shipwreck, only begins to surface as the divisive and discordant forces inherent in Singh's 'hollow man' fantasies recur, to the point at which the causal sequences in his past can be transcended by a simultaneous growth in understanding.

The character of these oppositions are in essence remarkably similar to those explored in Selvon's 'immigrant' works. Escape and arrival in the metropolis are accompanied by disillusion: the drama of Singh's active life is played out alongside a recurrent sense of emptiness and futility. Play-acting is a further evasion of the self and, most importantly, perhaps the 'final emptiness' and the lack of a spiritual anchorage either in London or Isabella are linked to the barrenness of the anonymous room from which he writes. In both Selvon's and Naipaul's novels, the limitations facing the protagonists derive from an attempt to protect the vulnerability of the private or, in the case of *The Lonely Londoners*, the communal self by an adherence to the codes of a private world of words, each with its own restrictive and isolated system of order and reality. The limitations of such a language of displacement – whether a language for or against identity – is exposed, either by the double-edged nature of the ironic humour in *The Lonely Londoners*, or by the use of a fragmentary and dissolving narrative method in *The Mimic Men*, to be the basis of a greater disturbance which stems from the confusion left by the impact of colonialism in all its phases. In both novels, the supporting 'myths' and 'labels', whether acquired or created, are demythologized through an understanding gained by the *process of survival* and the necessary invention of new literary forms, and by the recognition that whilst resolution may not be possible in what Wilson Harris has called 'the gloomy paradox'[75] of a world, understanding and creativity is.

In *The Enigma of Arrival*,[76] Naipaul transfers his setting from the suburban location of Ralph Singh's hotel room, perched on the edge of the metropolis, to the rural 'heart of Englishness', the illusory source of Ralph Singh's pastoral colonial fantasy. In this first work for 20 years to revisit the vexed question of Naipaul's 'arrival' in Britain, the unnamed narrator (a middle-aged writer from Trinidad like Naipaul himself) is situated as the cottage 'tenant' of an English country manor house in Wiltshire, a house built on the spoils of Empire, a world now decaying but linked indissolubly to the narrator's 'presence' as 'stranger' in the valley, and descendant of those indentured Indian labourers whose labour on the sugar estates in the Caribbean had made its 'apotheosis' possible (p. 174).

Throughout the book, a first-person narrative described as a 'novel in five sections', but which deliberately eludes either the description of 'autobiography' or 'fiction',[77] the landlord, who suffers from 'accidia', a degenerative disease of the soul, is set up as a strangely refracted version of the narrator himself, related but at 'opposite ends of wealth, privilege, and in the hearts of different cultures' (p. 191). We never meet this figure, who always remains remote, only catching glimpses of him passing by in a car, or through the partial vision of a naked leg as he sunbathes in the secluded manor grounds. Like the narrator, he is unnamed, a writer who chose to 'withdraw' from the world, an escape that occurred at precisely the same moment – '1949 or 1950' – that the narrator departed from Trinidad, a parallel coinciding also with the beginning of the narrator's 'exile' in England, the 'split' between writer and man which the writing of the novel seeks to redress (p. 197). Initially, however, it is as if both landlord and narrator are 'secret sharers of a historical pattern and a vision of decay'[78] that is caught up in the representation of a colonial world, a world built on the authority of economic and cultural privilege and the myths of a decaying memory of Empire. Although this world, like everything else that surrounds the narrator in this valley, is subject to constant flux and change, its patterns and rituals are also strangely preserved by the staff who work there (the Phillips's, Pitton, Mr Bray, the car-hire man), even though they themselves are shown as the novel progresses to be as displaced – 'rootless' people (p. 200), migrants from the town of Salisbury rather than indigenous residents of the countryside – as the narrator himself. The manor landlord, whose world is metaphorially strangled by the rapacious 'ivy' which he refuses to cut down, writes deluded and anachronistic poetry, riven with clichés – orientalist Indian 'romances' – or alternatively, creates almost cartoon versions of imperial sexual fantasies revealing a 'joke knowledge of the world' (pp. 281–2) which is trapped in the repetition of old rhetoric. Interestingly, 'each time the narrative focuses on the physical helplessness of the landlord as a synecdoche for imperial devolution',[79] the narrator is able to gain a greater sense of his own visibility as a post-imperial presence in the valley. He also begins to recognize the symptoms of his earlier *dechirement,*[80] the sense of exile which had resulted in a splitting between the self and the world, a literal and figurative 'shipwreck' where, as we saw in *The Mimic Men*, the narrator was constantly entrapped by the fantasy of a false vision of order, and a desire for 'belonging' which would always evade him. In *The Enigma of Arrival*, Naipaul begins to revision that early moment of arrival in Britain, and comes to see the experience as one not only enacting the 'panic of ceasing to feel myself as a whole person', but as a moment signalling the possibility of change and transformation, creating the chance not only to see but to *read* the world anew:

> Twenty years before, when I was trying to write at the Earl's Court boarding house, residence in the grounds of the manor would have seemed suitable 'material'. But the imperial link would . . . have been burdensome. It would have tormented me as a man (or boy) to be a racial oddity in the valley. And I would have been able as a writer (at that time) to deal with the material only by suppressing certain aspects of myself – the very kind of suppression and concealment that narrative of a certain sort encouraged and which had led me, even as an observer, eager for knowledge and experience, to miss much (p. 174).

And whilst Naipaul's 'tenant' of the decaying English manor house feels a curious kinship with his landlord, he also 'sees' that the owner's time is past, that his 'house' would press in on him and lead to 'non-doing and nullity' (p. 175), whereas for the tenant, his temporary residency provides the chance for a new 'way of looking' (p. 58), the writing and rewriting of another 'version' (p. 91). It would be a 'second childhood' in which he might unlearn his colonial 'exile', an unlearning and rebirth which might lead, after much excavation, to the discovery of a new synthesis. 'It wasn't that' he was 'unformed at the age of eighteen or had no idea what . . . to write about', but that the idea of writing had been a false one, not bred by the emotional knowledge of his own 'colonial-Hindu self', but bred out of the assimilated ideas of 'empire, wealth and imperial security', transmitted to him as willing subject in Trinidad. This concealment of the self beneath the 'writing personality', as he admits, did my 'material . . . much damage' (p. 134).

In *The Enigma of Arrival*, Naipaul confronts the intimations of his early essay 'Jasmine', where 'word' and 'object' could not come together – a gap in perception between the knowledge of a thing and the naming of it – and discovers the means by which he might attempt, through writing and remembering, to heal and bridge the 'gap' in his consciousness between 'man and . . . writer' (p. 102). As in *The Mimic Men*, we witness a complex exploration and unravelling of the deceptions of memory and language where now, 'The past for me – as colonial and writer – was full of shame and mortifications . . . as a writer I could train myself to face them. Indeed, they became my subjects' (p. 245). Perhaps, as has been suggested, the 'equanimity' of Naipaul's tone in the later novel is 'anchored in the difficulty of what has already been written',[81] and the difficulty of what was already written out. As Mrs Deschampneufs warned Ralph Singh in *The Mimic Men*:

> where you are born is a funny thing . . . You know you are born in a place and you grow up there. You get to know the trees and the plants. You will never know any other trees and plants like that. You grow up watching a guava tree, say. You know that browny-green bark peeling like old paint . . . Nobody has to teach you what the guava is. You go away. You ask 'What is that tree?' Somebody will tell you, 'An elm'. You see another tree. Somebody will tell you 'That is an oak'. Good; you know them. But it isn't the same (p. 171).

Set on Salisbury Plain, close to Stonehenge and in a rural and 'literary' landscape which has been inscribed into the canonical culture of 'Englishness' over several centuries,[82] the narrator embarks on a series of literal and imaginary journeys during which, as he retraces his steps (literally dramatized by the narrator's daily walks), he begins to recognize that he is necessarily engaged both in the process of unpacking his previously constructed notion of what this landscape and its past implies, as well as learning to understand the emotional significance of his particular relationship to it as an Indo-Caribbean writer now living in Britain. Covering ten years of life in a rural literary retreat, the narration deliberately highlights its own fictiveness – whether we read it as autobiography or 'novel' – in order to create adequate *depth* and the possibility of an alternative perspective, from which the narrator may see the extent to which his apparent arrival in England and his subsequent creation of an 'England of the mind' is as much an imaginary construction as was his previous construction of his departure from Trinidad. Importantly, neither turn out to be what they seem and both are subject to radical deconstruction and revisioning as the narrative proceeds; the subjectivity of the narrator is as multilayered, in the end, as the form itself, which, in its constant oscillation between its various points of departure and arrival, creates the potential for the possession of a new dwelling space. It is a space framed by the narrator's reconceptualization of landscape not as 'land alone' – marked out by specific historic and cultural borders, whether those of England or Trinidad – but as what we 'breathe into it, touched by our moods and memories'.

The narrator of *The Enigma of Arrival* dates the period of the writing between 1984 and 1986, a time, of course, which (surprisingly perhaps) did not differ markedly in political temper and racist rhetoric from late 1960s Britain when *The Mimic Men* was published, the period of Enoch Powell's infamous Rivers of Blood speeches.[83] As Salman Rushdie puts it in 'Outside the Whale', 1980s Britain was in a state of decline, and experiencing a 'condition of cultural psychosis', a condition that was heightened by the anxiety engendered by the inevitable loss of the myth of a supposedly 'great' imperial past, and the 'growing poverty and the meanness of spirit of much of Thatcherite Britain'. In addition, the essentially fevered patriotism of the Falklands War, combined with Mrs Thatcher's plea for a Victorian revival, increased the nostalgic desire for a return to the 'lost hour of their precedence',[84] to recreate a lost past imaged by the cultural investment in one of the icons of 'Englishness' – the country house – or in films of latter-day imperial glory such as the last days of the Raj. It is in such times, as M. Griffiths has noted, that the 'collective imagination *may* turn to those phenomena which already carry ideological freight to try and reinvest them with solidity and moral value . . . It is also a time when an intervention can be made by writers intent on an appropriation of such sites for different purposes.'[85] Interestingly, Naipaul's focus in *The Enigma of Arrival* is not so much on the 'empire within' Britain, a subject that Moses parodies, for instance, in *Moses Ascending*, and which forms the material for the work of later second-generation writers who followed on and who were born or raised in Britain – a post-immigrant generation – such as Hanif Kureishi, Meera Syal or Ravinder Randhawa.[86] Naipaul examines instead the ways in which the ending of Empire has enabled an interrogation of how its enabling myths were constructed, and how the 'lies of its [previous] representations'[87] retained their homogenizing power.

The subversive potential of the novel lies in its ambivalent and equivocal positioning in relation both to a decaying imperial past and the acceptance of the complex, and ambivalent, realities of a diasporic and postcolonial present. The fascination with 'Englishness', the world represented by the manor house in which the narrator, as tenant in the grounds, is both 'insider' and 'outsider', acts ironically throughout as point of departure and repetitive symbol of deception, thus enabling an interpellation and transformation of the polarized notions of 'home' and 'abroad' recurrent in some of Naipaul's previous representations of the divisive experiences of colonial 'exile'. As with *The Mimic Men*, the process of narration becomes the means of unravelling the illusion of 'purity' as being a myth of origins, as well as the tool by which the narrator is able to deconstruct the 'linguistic' and abstract sources of the fantasy itself. As such, the process of narration also provides an illuminating and intertextual dialogue with many of Naipaul's previous writings on return, displacement and identity, ideas which anyone familiar with Naipaul's earlier works will swiftly recognize as being embedded in a whole host of other texts, particularly *In a Free State*, *A Bend in the River*, and the non-fictional works *A Middle Passage*, *An Area of Darkness*, and *A Search for El Dorado*.

Divided into five sections, 'Jack's Garden', 'The Journey', 'Ivy', 'Rooks', and 'The Ceremony of Farewell', *The Enigma of Arrival* enacts a series of recurring journeys which become increasingly intertwined 'in time and space'[88] as the narrative proceeds. The journeys are both literal – whether dramatizing the initial shock of arrival after departure from 'home', and the sequences of foreign travel which follow, or the narrator's daily walks on the Wiltshire downs around Waldenshaw – and figurative, in his painful digging into the soil of his past misconceptions to discover that it is 'change' and 'difference' (p. 51) that is the constant, rather than 'decay', which 'implied an ideal, a perfection in the past' (p. 190). At the heart of the journeying is also the literary voyage of the narrator himself, the self- invented 'writer figure' who attempts from the opening, when 'I could hardly see where I was' (p. 11), to learn to read and see differently, to find the key to unlock the riddle of Giorgio de Chirico's painting from which the novel takes its title.

The question of seeing differently and the consequent process of reorientation lies at the heart of the narrator's struggle to achieve a different reading of his past and his present life as a 'stranger' in the Wiltshire valley. Unlike Sam Selvon, who reinvents the city of London through walking the streets, Naipaul's narrator walks the countryside around Waldenshaw, digging beneath the surface appearance of the landscape and reformulating the words he has imbibed from his literary education to describe it. We are frequently reminded that, although the narrator recognizes and indeed initially wants to share and be part of the literary landscape of the many writers who have walked on similar soil – the 'emanations' (p. 25) of Jack in his garden as a version of the Book of Hours (pp. 20, 31), a peasant figure of Wordsworthian proportions, or a sudden understanding of Kent's speech in *King Lear* concerning the geese on Sarum plain – such readings can be deceptive as imagined and romantic representations of a coherence that has perhaps never existed.

Naipaul's description of the setting is precise: 'the river was called the Avon; not the one connected with Shakespeare' (p. 1). It is clearly the 'Avon' (which as he tells us only means river anyway, and there are several in England), which flows through 'Salisbury, and near Stonehenge, through Wessex [Hardy country], where real and fictitious places coexist'.[89] Yet this literary 'knowledge' often leaves him 'still in a kind of limbo' (p. 12); his feelings of 'out-of placeness' (p. 19) are not assuaged by his intimacy with the works of writers before him, for 'I didn't know what I was looking at. I had nothing to fit it into' (p. 12). Furthermore, abstract knowledge does not provide understanding: Jack is not as he first imagines, a 'man fitting the landscape' (p. 19), a labourer rooted in the antiquity of the valley, but a recent arrival like himself; Waldenshaw, despite the suggestiveness of the etymology of its name, was not surrounded by 'woods'; its apparent fairytale setting was as much an 'illusion' as the narrator's initial perception of the sheep-shearing ceremony as 'something out of an old novel' (p. 18), untouched by the passage of time, when, in fact, what the narrator witnesses is a shearing by an Australian, an outsider like himself, passing through (p. 18). Words, like the places they seem to represent, also mislead although, in their repetition and the narrator's analysis of the history of their construction, they also ironically bring the narrator closer to a language of representation that can connect him with his past. The resonance of the manor gardener Pitton's description of refuse, his compost heap, as 'refuge', is a particularly glaring example of this as the notion of the history of the valley for the narrator as a 'refuge' made up of the subsoil of a complex cultural past, is also the striking image that links the narrator's past to his present. The vision of Jack digging his garden, then, is not just embedded in a wilful vision of an antique pastoral order but brings back 'very old memories to me, of Trinidad, of a small house my father had once built on a hill and a garden he had tried to get started in a patch of cleared bush: old memories of dark, wet, warm earth and green things growing, old instincts, old delights' (p. 31). It intimates the possibility of making a connection between Jack and his father, Trinidad and Waldenshaw. The narrator's learning about English 'gardens' from within, being able to recognize by sight the individual plants, when previously he was barely able to 'disentangle one plant from another' (p. 32), provides in the end a wider metaphor for his (re)learning not 'English' but England as a second language, seeing that the 'gladiolus . . . to my delight . . . flourished in both the climate of England and the tropical climate of Trinidad' (p. 33). And it is in Jack's persistent tending of a garden that will always be open to the 'constancy of change' (p. 34), a change that comes into immediate effect following his death, that ultimately allows the narrator to see that he is, in fact, relearning the emotional bases of a language that he has always known but never used, a language linked directly to the multilayered history of his Trinidadian and East Indian diasporic past.

The developing recognition that the soil of Salisbury Plain (p. 15) may be as littered with the 'ruins of a century' as the Gulf of Paria, viewed from the top of Laventille Hill (pp. 146–7), is a significant one, for in both descriptions the narrator – whilst being caught up in the fantasies of a literary and imaginary quest – is able also to forge new correspondences, a 'continuity' (p. 24) between the 'old' and the 'new', the 'world imagined and the world lived':[90]

> to look for the aboriginal pre-Columbus island, I had to ignore almost everything that leapt out at the eye . . . The landscape of the past existed only in fragments. To see one such fragment I looked at the drying-up mangrove swamp – green thick leaves, black roots, black mud – outside Port of Spain, ignoring the rubbish-strewn highway and the bent and battered median rail and the burning rubbish dump and the dust-blown shack settlement beyond the highway and the shacks on the hills of the Northern Range. From the top of Laventille Hill, among the shacks, I could imagine myself at the beginning of things if I looked selectively down at the Gulf of Paria – grey, leaden, never blue – and the islets in the Gulf (pp. 146–7).

As Shirley Chew has argued, these moments of selective perception in the novel are 'in many instances acts of intervention, involving [the narrator] persistently in the rereading and retranslation of the landscape and the literature which produces it'.[91] And whilst his familiar walk to the viewing point for the 'Henge' (as he now calls it) evokes a sense of temporary elation, provoked by his attempt to inscribe himself into a landscape of Wordsworthian antiquity, it, too, is contaminated by intrusive figures from the present and curious absences – the tourists in their red dresses or coats, the scars the big landowners have left with their recent planting of windbreaks – constantly changing the view. The narrator is self-consciously parodic at his own expense about his attempts to ground himself in the soil and landscape of 'Englishness', but at the same time he enacts, through his continued looking, a process of subversion as he highlights the ambiguity of his relation to it.

Texts weave within texts as the narrator attempts a number of different literary impersonations. We are frequently told, for instance, that he has been engaged in the writing of a book, amongst many others, which has caused him trouble, a book about 'Africa', which (if we are reading the novel as a thinly disguised autobiography) clearly bears close relation to Naipaul's *A Bend in the River* (1979). But he is also haunted by the image and title of a painting, 'The Enigma of Arrival', found in an art book left in his cottage by former tenants. Painted by de Chirico and taking its title from the poet Apollinaire, it bore correspondences in a 'poetical way' to 'something in my own experience' (p. 91). Depicting a desolate, misty and ghostly scene of arrival in the port of an ancient Mediterranean city, the painting, with its evocation of a 'mast', 'muffled figures' and a sense of desertion, suggests a story to the narrator of a traveller who has arrived at the gateway to this place, and who moves through its gates to the frenetic activity of an 'Indian bazaar scene' which envelops him; later, experiencing the disorientating feeling that, despite all this activity, 'he is getting nowhere', he attempts to return to the scene of his arrival, the deserted quayside beyond the gates, but as he passes through the door of this unnamed city, he realizes that there is no longer any mast or sail for 'the . . . ship has gone. The traveller has lived out his life' (p. 92).

The significance of this traveller's tale lies, of course, in its allegorical relationship to the narrator's own predicament, first as colonial arrivant, later as 'exile' and, finally, as migrant writer living in the period after Empire in Britain, a 'version of the story I was already writing' (p. 93), which is modified as the narrative unfolds. As we see in the last section, 'The Ceremony of Farewell', the parameters of the story shift their subliminal symbolization in the narrator's imagination: 'fantasy and the ancient world setting' are dropped. The story becomes more personal: 'my journey, the writer's journey, the writer defined by his writing discoveries, his ways of seeing, rather than his personal adventures, writer and man separating at the beginning of the journey and coming together in a second life just before the end' (p. 309). And it is in this final section, too, that crucial connections are made, linking, for instance, the ritualized occasion of the narrators' sister Sati's death and cremation in Trinidad to the story of Jack and his garden in Wiltshire (whose story opens the novel and symbolizes the narrator's changing perception of death, decay and change). This later section also creates a moment of illumination, like 'the shock of memory' that erupts, as Walter Benjamin has written elsewhere, in a moment of danger, like his debilitating dream 'of the exploding head' (p. 309). Being forced to confront the boundaries of his own mortality, the narrator begins to accept as well as to translate the 'multiple anchorages',[92] the emotional and historic realities, which make up his postcolonial and diasporic present.

On departure in 1950, the narrator had edited out of his memory and his diary notes, the significance of his family's farewell, his 'Asiatic' background, a 'remnant of peasant India in my life' (p. 100) for it did not fit the 'epic' vision of the world, constructed by the imagined sense of what his 'real' material should be, he then wished to describe. The moment seemed irrelevant and did not relate to the 'setting of magic and wonder' he had constructed, looking down from the plane at the island landscape he was leaving behind, where the island was 'like the landscape in a book, like the landscape of a *real* [my italics) country' (p. 97). Several years later, after Sati's cremation (and after several other reinventions of the island), he sees the rituals and celebrations of his family's history, not as inconsequential acts of a confusing 'Asiatic' hybridity producing clannish acts of ritualized irrelevance, but as a key to understanding the potential synthesis of his diverse past and a contemporary creolized present. It is the acceptance of the possibility of living with the inevitable discordances and mutations of a diasporic past – the way in which layer upon layer of history and culture, whether rural or urban, has transformed and changed, even within his own small family community – that enables the narrator to see the extent to which his 'sacred worlds' (p. 318), whether of childhood memories of 'home' or fantasies of order 'abroad', had vanished.

Recognition comes as he participates in the almost comic incongruities of the religious ceremony conducted by his pundit cousin on the terrazzo floor of a suburban verandah in Port of Spain. Initially, the narrator is disturbed by the seemingly cavalier mode in which his first cousin misrepresents the Hindu sacred texts – translating key concepts such as 'karma' and 'reincarnation' into creolized Western readings, or selling versions of the 'Gitas' – as well as by another guest's almost ludicrous misreading of the island's 'History' (p. 318). But later, as with the sudden valuation of the significance of Jack's garden, he comes to identify with these 'composite' versions, for they stem from the evolution of a language in which 'we' could make ourselves 'anew' (p. 317), a language built on an emotional life he had previously repressed, enacting a chronicle of survival and syncretism in a world which had always been without clear lines, without maps: 'one we had partly made ourselves, and had longed for, when we had longed for money and the end of distress; we couldn't go back. There was no ship of antique shape now to take us back. We had come out of the nightmare and there was nowhere else to go' (p. 317).

The novel is an elegy upon the middle-age of the writer, to a series of individual deaths which occur in almost every section of the narrative and underlie its composition in Naipaul's dedication of the novel to his brother Shiva, who died in 1985. Grieving, whether for Jack and his life of action in his garden in Wiltshire, or for the narrator's sister, unites everyone. And it is death, too, that provides the rationale for the narrator's passionate desire to begin the novel, to tell Jack's story and attempt to negotiate the paradoxes of a new life rooted in the soil of a landscape that had always previously alienated him. The narrator's creativity returns as he unlocks the riddle of Apollinaire's title, recognizing that 'there is nowhere to go perhaps because there is no need to go elsewhere'.[93] Life in the manor and its cottages has moved on – the Phillips's have gone, migrant labourers seem to staff the old house and garden. The narrator moves away from his 'tenanted' cottage in the manor grounds, which is about to be taken over, and creates a new space as resident of two tithe cottages nearby, literally knocking through the walls to make one dwelling where there were previously two.

Unlike Sam Selvon and many other writers of the early generation, who left Britain for the USA or Canada in the late 1970s, V. S. Naipaul has 'stayed on'[94] and still lives in Wiltshire. In many ways the shift in perspective from *The Mimic Men* to *The Enigma of Arrival*, a shift from a vision of divisive 'exile' to one accepting the condition of a transient belonging, becomes a 'metaphor of survival'[95] and a 'mode of living' in a location which will always, perhaps, remain ambivalent. Naipaul's new fictive space is situated within such a landscape, a landscape of 'Englishness' unmasked and then remade in order to come closer to a body of thought, the connections between 'man' and 'writer' that have made him. By the end of the novel the renovated cottages, situated in what was the 'heart of Englishness', signal a different position from Ralph Singh's 'far-out suburban hotel' in *The Mimic Men*. As a space of engagement rather than estrangement and dislocation, the renovated cottages, rebuilt according to the narrator's desire, are suggestive also of the aesthetic means by which the writer/man has come to see the creative potential of the contingency of his ' material' – simultaneously a part of his past: 'my island and my community . . . the ways of our colony' (p. 110) and manifesting his relationship to an everchanging present.

In his 1992 Nobel lecture, 'The Antilles: Fragments of Epic Memory', Derek Walcott examines the power of the creative imagination to revision and transfigure. Watching a dramatization of the *Ramayana*, the Hindu epic, performed by descendants of East Indian indentured labourers on the edge of the Caroni plain in Trinidad, he searches initially for the words to articulate a sense of elegiac loss fitting to this contemporary enactment of an ancient ritual in an East Indian village, a village far removed from the original sources of its diasporic history. Yet he comes to realize that the condition of loss – 'evocations of a lost India' – with which he wants to frame the scene are misplaced: 'Why "evocations"? Why not "celebrations of a real presence"? Why should India be "lost" when none of these villagers ever really knew it, and why not "continuing"?' For 'the love that reassembles the fragments is stronger than the love which took its symmetry for granted when it was whole'.[96] And it is loss, he suggests, that frequently rekindles the desire in the artist to recreate, to give shape to the past and to see the world anew.

Walcott's revelation here is an instructive one, for Naipaul's understanding of his diasporic inheritance can also be seen to facilitate a process of 'making' and 'remaking' the fragmented memory of an Antillean and diasporic past, illustrating in his most recent works that while 'something always gets lost in translation . . . something can also be gained'.[97] In terms both of cultural and historical displacement as well as imaginative reconstruction, Naipaul can be seen to be writing identity through a process of symbolic and aesthetic renewal. Like the many interwoven journeys in *The Enigma of Arrival*, his work can be seen to represent the enactment of a 'single journey', where the textual spaces created by the writing process itself become a fictional frame, an 'imaginary homeland'[98] built on the fragments of memory and desire that enable the heterogeneous elements of his complex past to be constantly negotiated and refigured. As one of his characters in *A Bend in the River* points out: 'home was hardly a place I could return to. Home was something in my head. It was something I had lost.'[99] For whilst diaspora is about 'exile' – about separation from one's *desh* or homeland, it is also about migration, transformation and constant renewal. No longer is 'Home' the object of a geographical quest, the fulfilment of a need to *belong* so much as the representation of an attempt to resolve a 'deeper, undefinable need',[100] a need expressed through the symbolic textures of writing itself. As Said has said, describing the modern condition of migrancy and exile: 'Our truest reality is expressed in the way we cross over from one place to another . . . in but not of any situation in which we find ourselves.' It is in facing the reality of this condition that we can discover connections, connections that frame the 'deepest continuity in our lives'.[101]

4

Writing Home: 'Unfinished Business' in Salman Rushdie and *The Satanic Verses* (1989)

But I, too, have ropes around my neck, I have them to this day, pulling me this way and that, East and West, the nooses tightening, commanding, choose, choose. I buck, I snort, I whinny, I kick . . . I choose neither of you, and both. Do you hear? I refuse to choose.

Salman Rushdie[1]

History is an interplay of various peoples, and it's gone on forever. I can think of no one culture that's been left to itself. It's a very simple view that borrowing just began the other day with the European expansion. Think of all that was brought back by the crusaders of the Middle East. The tiles in churches, the pulpit . . . There's always been this interplay.

V. S. Naipaul[2]

Wherever one looks, whether in the West or in the societies of the Third World, it would seem that moral being cannot be divorced from a deepened cycle of creativity through which we may visualize a breakthrough from absolute violence. Such a breakthrough requires us to accept the adversarial contexts in which cultures wrestle with each other but descend as well into camouflages and masks as flexible frames within the mystery of genuine change.

Wilson Harris[3]

The experience of diaspora can be a blessing or a curse or, more commonly, an uneasy amalgam of the two states. It is not a coincidence that the Hebrew root for exile or diaspora has two distinct connotations. 'Golah' implies residence in a foreign country (where the migrant is in charge of his or her destiny), whereas 'Galut' denotes a tragic sense of displacement (where the migrant is . . . the passive object of an impersonal history). Both words, in current usage, have a pejorative feel about them because they suggest an undesirable exile from an autochthonous 'homeland' . . . the distinction . . . is worth keeping as it encapsulates a sense of differing historical possibilities in our current idealization of an abstract 'diaspora'.

Bryan Cheyette[4]

'Do you hear?' exclaims the narrator of Rushdie's short story 'The Courter', 'I refuse to choose'. Unlike the 70-year-old Ayah, nicknamed Certainly-Mary, whose desire to return 'home' in the end outweighs her newly found passion for the Eastern European porter (turned 'courter') of the London block of flats where she now lives, Rushdie's young narrator remains adamant about keeping the lines of communication open between East and West despite the potential silencing implied by the choice. The title of Rushdie's collection of short stories, *East, West* (1994), echoes, ironically of course, the proverbial rhetoric of Empire 'East, West, Home's Best',[5] a discourse built on the myths of Empire and the notion of England forever as 'home' wherever in the world you may be. It also evokes the possibility of a late twentieth-century postcolonial and diasporic reading where not only is the notion of 'home' increasingly mobile, enacting a deterritorialization that, as Bryan Cheyette suggests in the epigraph above, can be both 'a blessing and a curse', but is also perhaps an illusory and fictional place constructed through the myths and fragments of the migrant imagination. The shifting and ambivalent boundaries of 'home' and 'abroad' have been the preoccupation of Rushdie's work from the creation of his utopian fantasy in *Grimus* (1975) – set mainly on an island in the Mediterranean caught between East and West – to his 'imaginary homelands'[6] in *Midnight's Children* (1981) and *Shame* (1983), as well as the more focused and explicit exploration of the 'stresses' and transformations of the 'migrant' experience in London in *Satanic Verses* (1988).[7] Even in one of his most recent novels, *The Ground Beneath Her Feet* (1999), one of the central preoccupations is the theme of migration and the myth of transformation.

The narrator of 'The Courter' – an immigrant Indian boy living in London in the 1960s, where he is joined for a while by his parents and his old 'ayah' – carries a number of significant autobiographical echoes. 'He has ropes pulling him in both directions' says Rushdie, but 'he's determined not to choose. In that sense, he is quite like me.'[8] Importantly, too, the *East* and *West* of the title of the collection are not divided, or hyphenated; they are placed side by side as *simultaneous* realities existing in different and sometimes parallel temporal and spatial locations, not either/or, but both – separated only by a pause, a comma. And it is the 'comma', Rushdie has commented, that is the most important part of the title because, 'it seems to me that I am that comma – or at least I live in the comma'.[9]

East, West was published five years after the *fatwa* which forced Rushdie into a political rather than a voluntary 'self-exile',[10] following the publication of *The Satanic Verses* in 1988. It is not my intention here to dwell on the contradictions and difficulties of the political events surrounding Rushdie's banishment from what he has controversially called 'my community' (Asian immigrants in Britain), 'from India, from everyday life',[11] for this debate has been recorded at length elsewhere.[12] However, it is significant to note that even after the pain of his forced withdrawal both from his ordinary life as a writer in London and his political exile from his two other subcontinental 'homelands', India and Pakistan (the fictionalized settings of *Midnight's Children* and *Shame*), he is able still to stress the significance of his self-declared location as one not simply of a continuing cultural suspension, caught in a limbo *split* between East and West, but one which instead celebrates the syncretism of 'cultural impurity',[13] a mongrelization fed by an emotional and intellectual identification with *all* the imaginative sources which have made up the multiple anchorages of his composite cultural past.[14] As he says:

> I am no longer Indian in the way that I would have been if I hadn't left, I'm *another* [my italics] thing. For a long time I would try and tell myself that this wasn't so, and that somehow *that* was still Home, and *this* [England] was still away. When I went back there I was going home. It's true that even now I feel 'at home' in Bombay, in particular, in a way I don't feel anywhere else in the world really. But I came to feel that I had to stop telling myself that: that there was a sense in which it had become a fiction that was no longer useful to me: it was a way of not looking at the real things about my life, which were that *that* isn't home, that *that* is away. *This* [England] is home. In a way, you can't go home again.[15]

The oscillation between 'here' and 'there' is instructive and characteristic, as is Rushdie's equivocation (almost despite himself) and reluctance to settle on a definition of 'home' either in England or India. It points to some of the major questions as well as the major sources for the figurative disguises explored in Rushdie's fiction and in his critical essays, where visions of 'home' and 'abroad' often shift uneasily amidst various 'camouflages and masks'. They shift between an emotional and cultural identification with the formative world of his childhood spent in Bombay and the need intellectually to redefine his physical departure – his leave-taking from a world to which he could not fully return and which, in some senses, no longer existed after Partition. It is suggestive, too, of the creative potential of the ambivalences inherent in his location as an Asian writer living abroad, still plagued by the contradictory impulses of the 'Galut' and the

'Golah', or what Vijay Mishra has recently defined as the narrative of the 'damaged home' (*East, West*, p. 93), which 'takes its exemplary form in what may now be called . . . diasporas of colour, those migrant communities that do not quite fit into the nation-state's barely concealed preference for the narrative of assimilation' and which are, he suggests, the most important markers of 'late modernity' in the contemporary world. Clearly, if we view the recent postwar migrations of Asians to Britain within the larger frame of recent postcolonial history, it becomes increasingly apparent that such narratives become the story of both 'its cause and effect'.[16] They thus, on the one hand, dramatize the cultural complexities of transplantation inherent in the losses and gains of im/migrant 'translations' and also move the 'question of culture's appropriation beyond the assimilationist's dream, or, the racist's nightmare' enabling a confrontation with the 'ambivalent process of splitting and hybridity that marks the identification with culture's difference'.[17]

We have already seen in the previous discussion of writers who emigrated to Britain before Rushdie how the double-edged experience of 'translation' involved a process of cultural metamorphosis, as these writers both invented alternative strategies for survival and at the same time reconfigured the monolithic notion of the imperial 'motherland'. In addition, as can be seen in the relationship between the Caribbean and Asian diasporas, such border crossings were not only 'mediated through the dominant culture', but also cut across the experiences of other subordinated groups resulting in new and not necessarily exclusive configurations.[18] Britain, by the time Salman Rushdie first began to publish, had not only been colonized in reverse, but had also become the potential, if still often invisible, archive of new mythologies, different histories and alternative ways of defining cultural identities beyond the limited spaces of a narrowly defined nationalism. This has always, of course, been a contradictory process and was never a painless one, since such transformations, like nationalism itself, were often Janus-faced, being both celebratory and reductive, expansionist and limiting, active and passive – simultaneously essentializing and universalizing ethnic difference.

As Stuart Hall, amongst others, has suggested, Rushdie's work has been exemplary in articulating the necessary doubleness of a migrant sensibility, a sensibility which can look two ways at once, existing both within and outside the nation's borders. Such writers of what he calls the 'new' and postwar diasporas often 'inhabit two identities . . . speak two cultural languages . . . translate and negotiate between them . . . without simply assimilating to them and losing their identities completely'. They also carry 'the traces of the particular cultures, traditions and languages and histories by which they were shaped'.[19] They must avoid getting lost in translation, and at the same time need to effect significant changes within the societies which they have entered. They do not only renarrate the metropolitan centre but also have to confront the often incommensurable nature of the 'unfinished business',[20] both within and without, at home and abroad, which their interventions inevitably raise. It is not just a question, to quote Toni Morrison's well-known dictum, of blacking up or universalizing out. The challenge is to both disrupt the essentializing discourse of the nation-state and retain at the same time the particularity of individual histories and cultures, thus enabling the 'Out there' to exist alongside the 'In here' against 'a binary logic of exclusivism'.[21] We must also remember, however, that the space inhabited by writers of the Asian diaspora, in Britain and elsewhere, is one which in itself represents a 'heterogeneous category'[22] differentiated along lines of class as well as gender. Like many other affiliated diasporic communities, it is 'contradictory at its heart, being both internationalist and particularist'[23] at the same time. The literary spaces of the diasporic imaginary will therefore always remain contested ones because, with its current and contemporary focus on dislocated histories and the crossing of borders, it can at the same time write over the equally strong desire for location which coexists within it; it both offers, in other words, a 'critique of discourses of fixed origins', whilst still needing to take account of 'a homing desire' which is, as we have seen, not necessarily the same as a 'desire for a homeland'.[24]

Rushdie's self-consciously chosen location as a diasporic Asian writer, joined both to East and West – as immigrant and migrant, exile and émigré – has acted as a central metaphor both in his fiction and in his critical essays, where the trope of migrancy has become renowned for representing a particular way of seeing, a way, as Bharati Mukherjee has observed, of 'partially comprehending the world'.[25] In *Shame*,[26] for example, Rushdie's narrator highlights the fact that he can only represent 'Pakistan by slices', in 'fragments of broken mirrors', for

> The country in this story is not Pakistan, or not quite. There are two countries, real and fictional, occupying the same space. My story, my fictional country exist, like myself at a slight angle to reality. I have found this off-centring to be necessary; but its value is, of course, open to debate. My view is that I am not writing only about Pakistan (p. 29).

However, whilst the narrator questions the legitimacy of the authority of his own view as 'Outsider! Trespasser!', a figure who has no 'right to this subject' and one speaking with a 'forked tongue', he stresses that he is still attached to its history – the referents of his past – despite the metaphoric leave-taking which the perspective of the narration partially dramatizes. Again, as before, we have the equivocation, this time voiced through his first-person narrator: 'I tell myself this will be a novel of leavetaking, my last word on the East from which, many years ago, I began to come loose. I do not believe myself when I say this. It is a part of the world to which, whether I like it or not, I am still joined' (p. 28).

It is not possible here to enter into the debates which Rushdie's barely disguised allegory of corruption amidst the ruling classes of Pakistan's elite evoked, either politically in Pakistan itself – where the novel was read as a traitorous act of betrayal – or, amongst those literary critics who have read his interventions into what, after all, is a serious critique of political corruption, as manifestations of an irresponsibility bred by his Western location, an irresponsibility fitting to the desires of his 'current metropolitan milieu', and an existential angst bred only by his relationship to a modernity built on 'linguistic quicksand'.[27] What I want to do is to examine the extent to which his self-conscious construction of the migrant as metaphor (inhabiting a literary poetics where cultural dislocation is no longer, as in Naipaul's work, linked to the pain and losses of exile but ostensibly to celebration) becomes a paradigm in the development of his art, and later a means to justify and explain, but not necessarily resolve, the literary and political questions which his diasporic location inevitably raises. The unresolved complexities of his diasporic location have, unfortunately, been taken up in recent years as a kind of manifesto by certain metropolitan critics. Keen to fetishize Rushdie as the contemporary postcolonial writer *par excellence*, they preach a barely disguised catechism of a universalized and aesthetisized 'state of homelessness that is at the heart of the new gospel of postmodernity',[28] a manifesto which has tended to prescribe and therefore eclipse the voices of many other writers of the diaspora who both precede and parallel his emergence. As Amit Chaudhuri, a contemporary, observes: 'the construction of the post-colonial Indian English novel, after Rushdie, has become inextricably entangled with the idea of "Indianness" and postcoloniality', a monumental edifice shadowing all that came before and much of what has followed after. Ideas of Indianness and Englishness which were historically opposed, like warring neighbours, 'are now wedded in a marriage that not only seems inevitable but health-giving; what might have been a tragedy has been turned, apparently, into a happy ending with numerous possibilities'.[29]

Rushdie has repeatedly stressed that 'stereoscopic vision' creates a peculiarly advantaged perspective for the writer living abroad. Though the 'past is a country from which we have all emigrated', the nature of the migrant writer's perspective – whose displacement is experienced on a physical as well as a metaphysical level – is intensified by being both 'out-of-country' and, in some cases, 'out-of-language'.[30] Moreover, the experience of border crossing can heighten perception and enhance vision. 'To see things plainly', he says, 'you have to cross a frontier.' For above all, 'the migrant suspects reality: having experienced several ways of being, he understands [its] illusory nature':

> The Indian writer, looking back at India, does so through guilt-tinted spectacles. (I am, of course once more, talking about myself). I am speaking now of those of us who emigrated . . . and I suspect that there are times when the move seems wrong to us all, when we seem to ourselves postlapsarian men and women. We are Hindus who have crossed the black water; we are muslims who eat pork . . . we are now partly of the West. Our identity is at once plural and partial. Sometimes we feel that we straddle two cultures; at other times, we fall between two stools . . . but however ambiguous and shifting this ground may be, it is not an infertile territory for a writer to occupy.[31]

Furthermore, the translations inherent in such passages do not only imply losses but also gains, for in confronting the ambiguities of the linguistic and cultural struggles that come with being 'borne across', sea-changes occur that may serve as cracked mirrors, but mirrors nevertheless, reflecting 'struggles taking place in the real world, struggles between the cultures within ourselves', and the adversarial conflicts of society at large. Thus he says, echoing many postcolonial literary voices before him: 'to conquer [and thereby to change and diversify the notion of Englishness] may be to complete the process of making ourselves free'. [32]

Such transformations inevitably involve rebirths, shifting identities which constantly reproduce themselves 'anew',[33] metamorphoses which involve not only renamings but a restaging of the journey into the symbolic, the '*unheimlich*' of the world of language and the imagination itself. As we witness in *Midnight's Children* (1981), the bottomless well of language is often the primal source for the shape-shifting processes of translation and change, for enabling the presentation of Saleem's many stories, his different 'versions'[34] of India. This bottomless well acts therefore as a metaphor for the writing process itself, at the very moment when the midnight child contained in the womb of the 'nation' is about to be born: 'What had been (at the beginning) no bigger than a full stop had expanded into a *comma* [my italics], a word, a sentence, a paragraph, a chapter; now it was bursting into more complex developments, becoming, one might say, a book – perhaps an encyclopaedia – even a whole language.'[35] Frequently in Rushdie's work therefore, the 'migrant' becomes the 'midwife' of language itself, 'as that language . . . is new-delivered'; for by entering into an 'alien language' as well as attempting to define a differently articulated imaginative territory, he is 'obliged to find new ways of describing himself, new ways of being human'.[36] Hence the boundaries of the text itself come to define the migrant's journeying in terms both of arrivals and departures, inventions and repetitions, as well as the necessary ventriloquisms generated by such divisions and transformations – 'the world of the book becomes the immigrant writer's home'.[37] And significantly, it is the journeying – a narrative process once theorized by Mikhail Bakhtin, in *The Dialogic Imagination*,[38] as a dialogic 'genre-in-the-process-of-becoming'[39] – that is the source of its desire rather than the initial port of embarkation or 'the enigma', to echo Naipaul of the 'arrival'.

Rushdie raised some of these issues in an early lecture, 'The Indian Writer in England', delivered at a conference to celebrate the Festival of India in 1982, one of the *first* conferences to be held on Asian writing in Britain. Now reprinted as the opening and seminal piece in his influential collection of critical essays, *Imaginary Homelands* (1991), and from which the title of the entire volume is taken, it continues to represent the basis of his thinking on the 'politico-aesthetics'[40] of the im/migrant writer, but was also prophetic, when first delivered, of a range of unresolved preoccupations he was later to explore in the fictions that followed *Midnight's Children* (1981), published the previous year. Interestingly, it was Rushdie, a new and young voice on the British literary scene at that moment (who had just won the prestigious Booker Prize), who was selected from amongst a whole range of more established elder statesmen of Indian letters – Nirad Chaudhuri, Raja Rao, Mulk Raj Anand, Sankharan Menon Marath,[41] also in attendance at that conference – to represent the voice of the Asian writer living in Britain. The majority of these writers had spent substantial parts of their lives in Britain and in more than one case were long-term residents.[42] There were no Asian women writers from Britain either invited to speak or, as far as I can remember, in attendance in the audience.

Rushdie, then, was clearly figured at this moment in the early 1980s as the representative of how 'newness' was entering what was coming to be seen as a burgeoning postcolonial literary canon in Britain, an idea developed several years later by Homi Bhabha's celebration of migrancy in his theoretical exploration of postmodern space, postcolonial times and the trials of cultural translation, *the location of culture*.[43] Whilst the paper Rushdie delivered in 1982 remains paradigmatic today for its early and sensitive articulation of a literary poetics by which his readers were later able to discuss and problematize the location of the im/migrant writer and his or her strategies for writing 'home' – the frequent need, for example, of literary invention or, the desire to create 'imaginary homelands' always only partial and fragmentary recreations of the past lost – it ironically also emphasized certain absences by its silences. For instance, there was a lack of attention given either to the previous history of a significant body of writing by other writers of Asian descent in Britain, or to the considerable influence that the *presence* of those writers, novelists such as Attia Hosain, G. V. Desani, Kamala Markandaya, V. S. Naipaul, Sam Selvon, may have had on preparing the ground – both imaginatively and theoretically – for the creation and evolution of that 'second tradition' which Rushdie describes as a particular asset of the Indian writer in England, a tradition 'quite apart from their own racial history . . . the cultural and political history of the phenomena of migration, displacement, life in a minority group'.[44] Rushdie acknowledges the fact that 'England's Indian writers [of the diaspora] are by no means the same type of animal. Some of us . . . are Pakistani. Others Bangladeshi. Others West, or East, or even South African' and 'Indian' is 'getting to be a pretty scattered concept'. But he admits that the main sources of influence on his own work are drawn – not from the diversity of these earlier migrant voices from the subcontinent who, apart from an acknowledged debt to G. V. Desani, had little conscious influence on him as a writer,[45] but primarily from an eclectic number of other international and mainly cosmopolitan sources – Latin American, Russian, Italian, American, Indian, English. In defining the polyglot nature of his literary family tree, Rushdie was of course attempting to place the recent history of postwar Asian ' immigration' within a broader context, a time frame and cultural range which might perhaps deconstruct the 'restrictive choices' and restrictive spaces allowed for the immigrant voice 'within English national culture'[46] at the time. For, as he emphasizes, 'the past to which we belong is an *English past*, the *history of immigrant Britain* [my italics]. Swift, Conrad, Marx are as much our literary forebears as Tagore or Ram Mohan Roy.'[47] However, there is a danger in these well-intentioned sentiments of either universalizing or flattening out the heterogeneity of the Asian diaspora of which he is a part, and creating instead yet another ' "great tradition" of international writers and thinkers who are beyond *any* historical or political contingency'.[48]

'Borrowings', as V. S. Naipaul suggests in one of the epigraphs to this chapter, have always created an 'interplay' between and across cultures. Moreover, 'cultural cross-fertilization[s]', to use Rushdie's more muscular phrase, have always been the norm even in the so-called 'English' canon – from Chaucer the supposed 'father' of English poetry to the multicultural world of Shakespeare's plays, or the linguistic 'abracadabra' of James Joyce's *Finnegan's Wake* (who is of course Irish and arguably one of the first postcolonial modernists anyway). This 'cultural impurity'[49] works across genres as well as narrowly defined national borders. Translation has always been part of cultural growth and particularly in the subcontinent, where the notion of 'syncretism'[50] is embedded historically, and does not need to be self-consciously displayed like 'hybridity' as a sign of difference. Describing the cultural admixture of his Indian childhood, Rushdie stresses again its eclecticism:

> As an Indian by birth and upbringing I had access to a second literary tradition which was also culturally multiple. Ethnically I belong to the group known as Kashmiri Muslims, not a very numerous group in India. But I am nevertheless used to thinking about such non-Muslim Kashmiri works as the Nritysahitya, in which in Sanskrit the principles of classical Indian dance were laid down, or the wonderful animal fables of the Shantra Trantra . . . The urban Indian environment in which I grew up offered the most culturally mixed environment it is possible to imagine, and part of that mixture, was . . . Western, so that now when I get asked – as I do get asked – why I mingle Eastern and Western elements . . . I find the answer perfectly obvious. In the first place both elements are mixed up inside me, because of where I have lived for a quarter of a century, and in the second place they were mixed up inside me in Bombay, long before I ever got to what we used to call 'proper London'.
>
> The world of rural India is no more homogenous than the cities. Here the old religions, Hindu and Islam, coexist with new ones . . . Pakistan, to which my family emigrated, is also a mass of cultures in conflict: immigrant bourgeoisie against the local bourgeoisie, north Indian culture versus the regional cultures, Urdu against the regional languages . . . I have been in [so-called] minority groups all my life, a Muslim in India, immigrant in Pakistan and then in England.[51]

This all seems eminently reasonable, and apparently circumnavigates what Rushdie has called the 'elephant trap of a ghetto mentality',[52] which 'immigrants' face in Britain, where minority groups only seem to speak and write to each other, their themes limited by a form of literary and cultural 'copyright'[53] created by the weight of an unbearable burden of representation, leaving the writing standing in the same spot. We can recognize here Rushdie's frustration with the sectionalism versus assimilation, 'ghetto' versus the mainstream argument, typical of many reductive contemporary critiques of black and Asian writing in the postwar period where, as Ben Okri once said, 'to be a writer and to be black in Britain is to be in a corner. If you are not published because of colour you are read because of it.'[54] Thus paraphrasing the prophetic voice of G. V. Desani's eponymous anti-hero, H. Hatterr (1948), Rushdie says:

> The migrations of the 50s and 60s happened. "*We* are. *We* are here". And *we* are not willing to be excluded from any part of our heritage: which . . . includes . . . a British-born Indian kid's right to be treated as a full member of this society, and also the right of any member of this post-diaspora community to draw on its roots for its art, just as all the world's community of displaced writers has always done (I'm thinking of Grass's Danzig-become-Gdansk, of Joyce's abandoned Dublin, of Isaac Bashevis Singer and Maxine Hong Kingston . . . Milan Kundera and many others').[55]

Yet, in order *to change the script*,[56] the writer who can look both ways at once also needs to make clear how he, as a 'first generation immigrant'[57] is reading the current 'ground beneath [his] feet',[58] and furthermore, who the collective 'we' of his statement really represents.

At an early stage in 'The Indian Writer in England', Rushdie warns the reader of the dangers in tackling a subject so broad as well as so specific; he makes plain that his use of the royal 'we' in the paper, an apparent pluralization of the experience of *all* Indian writers, needs to be treated with a good deal of scepticism. He, after all, is no representative but one of many different voices, both past and present. Yet the vacillation between first and third person in the paper, is indicative not only of Rushdie's self-ironizing as a spokesperson for such writers (and we are not sure in the paper who *they* are anyway), but is also the expression of a discomfort, an inability to be at 'home' with the local politics of race that such an identification perhaps demands. It is, in fact, the political insights of the African American writer Richard Wright, who wrote once that 'black and white

Americans were engaged in a war over the nature of reality', that Rushdie draws on for comparison when he asserts that 're-describing a world is the necessary first step towards changing it',[59] and not the black or Asian resistance movements in Britain, born through the political and literary efforts of a whole generation of im/migrant writers who preceded him. As Tim Brennan has noted in 'Writing from Black Britain', London for 'over a century' had 'been the home and training ground of anti-colonial intellectuals . . . It was the birthplace of the Indian National Movement, the pan African Congress, the launching pad for Jamaican Reggae, the site of Wole Soyinka's preparation, Chinua Achebe's coming out, and George Lamming's emergence.' And prior to the decolonization and independence movements of the early postwar period, there were the early narratives of 'the ex-slaves Olaudah Equiano and Ottabah Cugoano [who] worked for Abolition', as well as nineteenth-century Asian reformers such as the radical lawyer Cornelia Sobraji who attended university in Britain and wrote numerous essays and tracts.[60] In addition, as we saw in Chapter 1, 'Points of Departure', there was a broad spectrum of literary activity already taking place, which was partially stimulated by the ancient relationship between the subcontinent and Britain, as well as the numerous and differently motivated passages that Asian travellers and writers had already made to London prior to the large-scale migrations following the Second World War.[61] Moreover, as the examples of figures such as Sake Dean Mahomet, J. M. Malabari, Cedric Dover or Aubrey Menen have already shown, [62] the location and reception of Asian writers in Britain had always been an ambiguous one, particularly if the writers were not just representatives of the 'exotic' upper class or oriental travellers passing through, but were instead 'natives' of the country – black and Asian Englishmen and women – with leave to stay.

A large number of literary works published by black and Asian writers in the postwar period were fuelled, as we have already seen, by the need to discover an appropriate form, the necessity to develop alternative fictional strategies for defining a colonial and postcolonial relationship both to Britain and to the particular histories of their individual cultural pasts. It was a period of radical experimentation, involving formal and linguistic improvizations, as well as, in many cases, the creation of a literary poetics, flexible enough to translate the experience of exile and im/migration within the genre of the novel into a new architecture of the deterritorialized imagination, enabling aesthetic configurations secure enough to contain, as well as explode, the dialogic voices of a subversive discourse of postcolonial resistance. As we saw earlier, the motivation was not just one of constructing a 'counter-discourse', a discourse able to challenge the apparently irreconcilable oppositions of the hegemonic myths of nation, or simply to act as a writing back to empire, but one which could shift from within the epistemological and conceptual bases of the oppositions themselves, thereby perhaps changing fundamentally what George Lamming called in *The Pleasures of Exile* the parochial 'habits of English reading',[63] to enable a reception which did not simply continue to repeat the all-to-easy divisions of an ethnic allegory. As 'insiders' and 'outsiders', familial citizens of empire as well as ghettoized 'others', these writers carried with them their own differently constituted modernities, borne partially through the experience of the cultural transitions forced by the colonial encounter, but more significantly through the evolution of indigenous strategies for *survival* bred by the already familiar historical experience of living with, and alongside, racial and cultural difference.

We have already seen the extent to which the Indo-Caribbean diaspora was already a creolized culture – before, for example, Sam Selvon's creation of a black city of words in 'immigrant' Britain in the 1950s or V. S. Naipaul's belated translation of the significance of his exile from the rituals of his indentured Asian past in *The Enigma of Arrival*. The necessity for cultural improvizations, bred by living with cultural difference, was always, as Simon Gikandi and others have stressed, at the heart of Caribbean modernities whether at 'home' or 'abroad'.[64] As early as 1938, Raja Rao, in his famous Preface to what is arguably one of the first modernist Indian novels in English, *Kanthapura,* pointed out that English, like Persian or Sanskrit before it, 'may have been a colonizer's language', but had already been transformed into one of many Indian languages; for we are all, he said, 'instinctively bilingual'.[65] Similarly, as Rushdie himself has frequently illustrated, the process of cultural osmosis engendered by a long history of different colonizations and migrations, before the most recent English wave, was central to all aspects of 'Indianness'. The bases of this mixed cultural history had always been one of accretion and syncretism; plurality was a lived reality, a process which had always reflected the 'secular coexistence of various . . . cultures',[66] an indigenous adaptability and natural flexibility that came much later to be celebrated by the West as a form of modernity, which would perhaps bring release from the postwar and post-Holocaust 'savagery' of 'civilised man',[67] a modernity which was simultaneously able to produce, as Zygmunt Bauman has shown, both 'modernist art and culture as well as quintessentially modern forms of racism'.[68] 'Those of us', says Rushdie, 'who have been forced by cultural displacement to accept the provisional nature of all truths, all certainties, have perhaps had modernism forced on us,'[69] yet modernity in the Indian and diasporic context, as Attia Hosain's writing of the fragmented world after Partition in *Phoenix Fled* (1953) has already shown us, can be written in very different ways. To echo ironically Rushdie's earlier description of his polygot family tree, 'the list is endless'.

The ground for the entrance and impact of Rushdie's 'migrant' aesthetic in the 1980s had, then, been cleared in a sense, and staged not only by a wide range of literary figures, both black and Asian, who preceded him in their migrations to Britain, but also through the cultural history of his multi-layered subcontinental background, and the project of a Western modernity which sought to escape the double bind of a narrow and racist nationalism, and was keen to cast off the remaining traces of a colonial discourse, the repressed shadow of a Western civility.[70] It might seem unfair to castigate Rushdie for failing, in 1982, to draw specifically on the works of im/migrant writers who had preceded him in their writing narratives of 'exile' and 'migration' in Britain, thereby prescribing an imposed agenda for his talk, and setting up only another form of reductive politics, based on a 'rhetoric of . . . blame'.[71] But the omission of *any* explicit reference to the presence of a growing and heterogeneous body of black and Asian writing in Britain, or even the mention of fictions of individual writers who, like himself, were living in a state of 'double' dislocation – both from their autochthonous 'homelands' and from their now narrowly defined political status as 'immigrants' – is an important one. The absences are notable, not so much for the intimation of what may perhaps have been at this stage a predictable and understandable gap in Rushdie's classical and canonical 'English' education as an old boy from Rugby school – a gap signalling what Perry Anderson once described as the 'absent centre' at the heart of English intellectual life and the 'nullity of native . . . traditions' within Britain itself.[72] They also pointed to a general myopia in the cultural politics and reviewing practice of the mainstream publishing and literary world, a world still surprisingly entrapped in a patronizing and polarized 'canonical' colonial vision, despite the demise of Empire marked by the closure of the Suez canal in 1956. It was a world which failed to see, let alone recognize, the significance of the innovative and liberating modernities of these writers, even at this much later stage in the 1980s, well over 30 years after many of the first novels were published.[73]

Rushdie clearly became more conscious of the polarized politics of these issues later in his career and his acute awareness of the dangers of such 'pigeonholing' perhaps explains his reticence in becoming too closely identified with the word 'immigrant', as it had evolved in the nationalist geography of 'Englishness', particularly in the context of Thatcherite Britain in the 1980s when his work first began to be noticed. For example, in a passionate piece entitled 'The New Empire Within Britain', he described the inherently contradictory and racist character of Britain's revised immigration laws, whereby 'many Rhodesians, South Africans and other white non-Britons have automatic right of entry and residence . . . by virtue of having one British-born grandparent; whereas many British [born] citizens are denied these rights, because they happen to be black'. He also stressed how Britain's postwar postcolonial crisis – the society's loss of a sense of itself – has conveniently been transferred on to the citizens of this new Empire, an underclass still framed and politically disabled by the false equation of race, ethnicity and national belonging set up by Enoch Powell's inflammatory rhetoric in the 1960s – and perpetuated by Margaret Thatcher's and Norman Tebbit's infamous speeches of the 1980s. In the logic of that rhetoric, these 'immigrants' are not white but *always* 'black' or 'Asian'; they are repeatedly figured as people whose 'real "home" is elsewhere'. Living in 'what E. P. Thompson . . . described as the last colony of the . . . Empire', they represent, Rushdie suggests, the ghostly descendants of those 'new-caught, sullen peoples, half-devil and half-child', of Rudyard Kipling's 'The White Man's Burden'.[74] As we shall see later, many of the sentiments of this essay are fictionalized, as are the politics of many of his other essays, within his fiction, in the parodic Shaandaar Café sections of *The Satanic Verses,* and through the literal demonization of the 'fallen' immigrant, Saladin Chamcha, whose predicament evokes the fate of many previous arrivants on Britain's shores.

What is especially interesting in the essay, 'The New Empire Within Britain', however, is the clear indication that Rushdie was evidently aware from the start of the potentially dangerous refuge provided by his art – the luxury of 'the disguises that fiction permits',[75] as well as the political evasions that a retreat into what he calls a 'kind of aestheticism'[76] can be seen to imply – particularly in the light of the racial violence that was erupting in Britain in 1982, the time that the essay was published and to which Rushdie refers. His political agenda seems to be clear, particularly when he adds, condemning the us/them attitude of nationalist dogma, that a country which he says 'refuses to listen to its most threatened, most disadvantaged . . . citizens, until they start running through the streets burning things, is a creature which creates the crisis which it seeks to deplore'.[77] But his position as a privileged migrant intellectual, a 'cosmopolitan celebrity',[78] and literary spokesman for a metaphorical and universalizing rhetoric of migrancy, does not sit comfortably with these views. Despite the apparently unambivalent passion of his political affiliations in some of his more radical essays, as well as his clear identification with black and Asian minority communities in racial politics,[79] Rushdie clearly remained uncomfortable about the capacity of 'immigrant' to describe his diasporic presence as an Asian writer in Britain. This discomfort has been seen to be typical of what Tim Brennan has described as the privileged mainstream location of writers such as Rushdie where, 'in the interplay of class and race, metropolis and periphery', such cosmopolitans 'have found a special home'. For these writers both 'capture a new world reality which has a definite social basis in immigration', and at the same time fulfil 'the paradoxical expectations of a metropolitan public', thus bridging the 'literary world's Manichean spaces . . . by exhibiting a political-aesthetic that is itself double'.[80]

There are clearly some explicitly acknowledged personal difficulties here which relate to Rushdie's class background, questions of race and religion (both in Britain and the subcontinent), and a mosaic of diverse cultural identifications which stem both from the privilege of his cosmopolitan Bombay upbringing, and from the essentially colonial influences of his early schooling at the Cathedral and John Connon mission school, and later at Rugby (the English public school) from the age of 13:

> In common with many Bombay-raised middle-class children of my generation, I grew up with an intimate knowledge of, and even sense of friendship with, a certain kind of England: a dream England composed of test matches at Lord's presided over by the voice of John Arlott, at which Freddie Truman bowled unceasingly . . .; of Enid Blyton and Billy Bunter, in which we were even prepared to smile indulgently at portraits such as 'Huree Jamset Ram Singh', the 'dusky nabob of Bhanipur'. I wanted to come to England. I couldn't wait. And England has done all right by me; but I find it a little difficult to be properly grateful. I can't escape the view that my relatively easy ride is not the result of the dream England's famous sense of tolerance and fair play, but of my social class, my freak fair skin and my 'English' English accent. Take away any of these, and the story would have been very different. Because of course the dream England is no more than a dream.
>
> Sadly, it's a dream from which too many white Britons refuse to awake.[81]

Rushdie's description here of England as the dubious fulfilment of an illusory 'colonial' dream is not markedly dissimilar from those of the early

Caribbean writers who migrated to London in the 1950s, described by George Lamming in *The Pleasures of Exile*. But, unlike the Caribbean writers of this earlier generation, who grew up as colonials and arrived in Britain often both literally and metaphorically seeking 'rooms' within the 'motherland', Rushdie was born in 1947, two months before Indian Independence, and came to England as a young schoolboy, following the Anglophile educational aspirations of his father. Whilst Rushdie arrived in Britain during 1962, a period of widespread Asian emigration from the subcontinent, he was not underprivileged in any way nor did he later become part of any specific literary group as such. His educational, cultural and class background may have been similar in some ways to that, say, of an Attia Hosain or Kamala Markandaya, who were of a much earlier generation of Indian writers resident in Britain, but was very different from that of either V. S. Naipaul or Sam Selvon, who were not only twice-removed from their Indian origins, but also schooled primarily in one literary tradition – English.[82] Unlike Rushdie, they did not read or consciously use the languages of the subcontinent, which were the historic heritage of their indentured forbears, although the 'myth' of India as an 'imaginary homeland' was very much present, particularly in the case of V. S. Naipaul,[83] but also in Selvon's more explicitly East Indian and Trinidadian works.[84] Furthermore, the sophistication of Rushdie's urban and well-heeled liberal Muslim childhood in Bombay would have equipped him very differently from V. S. Naipaul's colonial education, for example,[85] for the encounter with the middle-class elite at Rugby School and the hypocrisy of the Arnoldian traditions of 'tolerance and fair play'.[86]

Although, in interviews, Rushdie's accounts of his early years in England signal the pain of the explicit racism he encountered as one of the only 'wogs' at the school, he has always expressed an anxiety – perhaps a guilt – about the ease with which he could don disguises, 'pass' for white, and thereby seem to retain a relatively easy rite of passage through the class and racial divisions which were glaringly evident on the other side.[87] As he puts it in *The Satanic Verses*, in an episode where he is clearly dramatizing a painful autobiographical moment regarding the rituals of how to eat kippers at Rugby School: 'these exclusions [differences from the other boys] only increased his determination . . . to act, to find masks that these fellows would recognise, pale-face masks, clown-masks, until he fooled them into thinking he was okay, he was people-like-us' (p. 43). His literary voice, however, could never be closely identified – whatever his personal sense of political affiliation – with the black and Asian communities in Southall or Brixton – nor, indeed did he want it to.[88] Yet his work, however, was often applauded for providing a bridge, a form of mediation between these worlds. Describing his preference for the implied mobility of 'migrant', as opposed to 'immigrant', to describe the imaginative world of his fictional characters, he has said:

> I don't like the word 'immigrant'. I didn't like it for this book [*Satanic Verses*] although I use it in other contexts, because it seems to me by now to have acquired a whole body of cultural and political baggage, which I wanted to strip away, to write . . . about the actual condition of change through movement. Immigrant has become a sociological word, whereas migrant seemed to me a truer word for what I was writing about; an immigrant is also an emigrant and the people I am writing about are as much emigrants as immigrants, as much defined by what they leave behind as what they meet on arrival.[89]

Being an immigrant suggests arrival and entrance; migrancy, on the other hand, highlights the possibility of constant movement, the refusal to be contained by any one position. Yet the two concepts, as their history and etymology suggests, are inextricably intertwined. It is tempting, as many recent critics have done, to see Rushdie's valorization of 'migrancy' as one which gives the dislocated/entrapped 'immigrant' wings, mapping a new imaginative territory, and enabling a movement beyond the familiar racist stereotypes of white British nationalist politics, thereby creating an aesthetic enabling freedom of movement, both literal and figurative, beyond the walls of the ethnic ghetto and borders of the nation state. But it is also important to remember that Rushdie's fashionable profile as a spokesman for the deconstruction of the fixity implied by the term 'immigrant' – the period essentially of the early 1980s – coincided with, and was to some degree enabled by, the simultaneous articulation of the cultural grammars of postmodernism, postcolonialism and the evolution of a liberal black diaspora politics in Britain. These grammars stressed diversity and heterogeneity as a new anti-essentialist politics of representation, a politics which had already gone a long way towards breaking down the reductive oppositions implied by the earlier ghettoization of the 'ethnic minorities' in the 1960s and 1970s.[90] Moreover, unlike some other earlier representations of the immigrant Asian experience, such as Farrukh Dhondy's more realist depiction of the problems of the second-generation Asian communities in *East End At Your Feet* (1976), Rushdie's literary strategies – narratives which overtly demonstrated a critique of a monolithic nationalism, and a preference for nonlinear, plural and often surrealist perspectives – were ripe for an easy assimilation into the increasingly popular theories of the postcolonial and postmodernist mainstream.[91]

If V. S. Naipaul was condemned at times for upholding the detached position of a universal exile, Rushdie's attempt to articulate and define a new imaginative territory (which celebrated the dislocations of migrant unbelonging) was attacked for its failure to engage properly either with indigenous politics in the subcontinent or radical black politics in Britain. Moreover, in its explicit aestheticization of the economic realities of im/migrant experience, an aestheticization which seemed to dehistoricize crucial questions of class and gender, as well as the specific historic and religious affiliations of those groups whose diasporic experience did not necessarily conform to his vision, Rushdie was condemned, as the furore over *The Satanic Verses* affair clearly demonstrates, for a secular and liberal positioning which was tied indissolubly to the philosophical and literary traditions of Western modernism.[92]

Clearly, the usage of 'migrancy', like 'exile' before it, was not intended to be more than a literary construct, and could not relate directly to the economic realities or the cultural transplantations of the majority of the twentieth-century Asian diasporic labour force, who had largely emigrated to Britain, the USA and the Middle East in the period following the Second World War. It did, however, carry with it a well-intentioned desire to effect political changes from within the realm of the aesthetic, an aim which infuriated many of Rushdie's harsher critics, who interpreted his articulation of a migrant location as a liberal politics with an excessively 'figurative flexibility', a flexibility which threatened to severely undermine the 'oppositional force of postcolonial politics' itself.[93] As a metaphorical grammar then, for what Bharati Mukherjee has called 'levitation'[94] rather than gravity, it provided a seductive lure to a metropolitan readership, as it allowed both an existential acceptance of the im/migrant and diasporic condition of homelessness – 'a belonging everywhere by belonging nowhere'.[95] Such a discourse also marked out an apparently subversive literary terrain for the surfacing of 'new' discourses of empowerment, a space where those historically located at the margins have come, as many have recently noted, to change the history of the nation. As Rushdie characteristically puts it in *Shame*:

> I, too, know something of this immigrant business, I am an emigrant from one country (India) and a newcomer in two (England, where I live, and Pakistan, to which my family moved against my will). And I have a theory that the resentments we *mohajirs* engender have something to do

> with our conquest of the force of gravity. We have performed the act of which all men anciently dream, the thing for which they envy the birds; that is to say, we have flown.
>
> We have come unstuck from more than land. We have floated upwards from history, from memory, from Time (p. 87).

The shift in terminologies from 'immigrant' to 'migrant' (a shift from the period of Sam Selvon's black Londoners to Rushdie's creation of Asian 'Brickhall' in *The Satanic Verses*) may have been no more significant than a reflection of the development of racial and cultural politics in Britain in the postwar period, a reflection of the limited spaces allowed within national culture and the classifying effects of critical terminologies concerning the formation of postmodern and postcolonial identities. However, the interrelationship between these various 'namings' is not so simple. As Aijaz Ahmad, amongst others, has suggested, Rushdie's migrant aesthetic is not so easily detached from history or time, for it bears a close kinship both to the philosophical basis from which poststructuralism derives, and to the familiar and well-established grammar of Western modernism. Thus modernity favoured the tortured metropolitan experience of European or American 'exile', but failed to see the crucial 'effects of colonialism on the concept of exile itself',[96] let alone the writing of a different kind of modernity already evident in George Lamming's *The Pleasures of Exile* and represented in the innovative experimentations of a large number of im/migrant novels already published by that time.

It is hardly surprising, as Lamming had already noted in the 1960s and Mulk Raj Anand in the 1930s, that the discourses of European humanism and a modernist poetics of exile were partially constitutive of the often excluded, but parallel modernities of the colonial psyche. However, what we have to ask ourselves here is how far the later evolution of the idea of a migrant aesthetic really takes us. Do Rushdie's perpetual migrants really fly free of older concepts such as 'exile' or 'immigration', thus detaching themselves not only from land (the nation), but also arguably from some of the more radical politics of decolonization, or are we, as Simon Gikandi has so powerfully argued, merely looking at old wine in new bottles, where migrant novels such as Rushdie's may be read as innovative 'exemplars of [a] postmodern historiography',[97] but are still linked in essence to the modernist trajectory of exile? Do such narratives provide a 'new' means for breaking down the polarized binaries generated by an essentializing colonial culture, 'destroying the epistemologies of the sources themselves',[98] or are they in the end just metanarratives, sophisticated commentaries on previous narratives of return and identity, still tied to the paradoxes which were part and parcel of the earlier experience of colonialism, immigration and exile? If this is the case, the 'new' diasporic space of migrancy may still be inextricably intertwined with its historic past, in a symbiotic relationship to the very narratives from which it is trying to escape. Is one of the central tensions and difficulties of Rushdie's work, then, created precisely because of the incommensurable relationship between these seemingly incompatible and intractable positionings? Are we contending with the difficulty of defining his own relationship both to a multilayered and eclectic cultural history in the subcontinent and to the heterogeneous character of the Asian diaspora in Britain?

It would not be difficult, for example, to construct a simple division between the narrative strategies of V. S. Naipaul and Rushdie, slotting one into the modernist trajectory of 'exile' and the other into a postmodern valorizing of multiplicity and plurality, but as we saw in the previous chapter, Naipaul is at pains – particularly in his later works – to deconstruct the protective irony of the exile and to embrace the constancy of change, translating and reading the world anew. Similarly, Rushdie cannot entirely separate his notions of migrancy expressed in several of his essays from immigration or indeed, exile. For if the migrant is a composite figure – both 'emigrant and immigrant, exile and émigré' – the various positionings, whether articulated through the canonical literary grammar of modernism or the parallel, but differently articulated modernist geography of the novel of colonial exile and immigration, are intimately related. Similarly, whilst it might be tempting to compartmentalize the works of Asian writers who preceded him, whether of supposed 'ghetto' or 'mainstream', within the neat trajectories that have largely been imposed by the Western literary critical industry, thus creating another canonical hierarchy and polarizing the diasporic range of their works still further, it is clear, as we shall see in the discussion to follow of *The Satanic Verses*, that Rushdie's concerns and aesthetic strategies are not only related to the 'high culture' and fashionable agendas of the cosmopolitan mainstream – as are Naipaul's, of course, in a different way – but also to the preoccupations of a number of earlier and less immediately visible writers of the Asian and black diasporas in Britain. The voices of these writers were not necessarily bound only by an equivalence generated by the ethnic allegory of alterity but more substantially by their different aesthetic experimentations with language and form, the common need to evolve a literary poetics of *survival*, to create what Wilson Harris has called the birth of 'flexible frames' from within the 'adversarial contexts in which cultures wrestle with each other', and from which writers have arguably been able perhaps to effect the 'mystery of genuine change'.[99] Diaspora, as we have already seen, is a contradictory and ambivalent space, holding together both the old and the new, the local and the international, exilic narratives of return as well as migrant narratives of dispersal and dislocation, along a continuum that can both reaffirm as well as deconstruct misconceived certainties and the essentialist notions of a monolithic ethnicity. Moreover, depending on how the various groups within the diasporic space are specifically differentiated, individual subjects may occupy 'minority' and 'majority' positions simultaneously.[100] Rushdie's refusal to 'choose' between 'East' and 'West', whether before or *after* 'exile', therefore becomes ironically restaged in the domestic arena of racial and literary politics in Britain.

No writer wants to be constrained by particular agendas, whatever their political sympathies, and Rushdie is acutely aware that not only are all metaphors 'capable of misinterpretation',[101] but that the trouble with 'theory is that it supposes all creative talent to be of the same kind'.[102] If Lamming had marked out the territory of the Caribbean novel of exile as a means to radically shift the limitations of the class and racial prejudices he encountered in Britain – citing Selvon's work as exemplary in giving voice and consciousness to the plight of ordinary, black and unlettered immigrants – Rushdie has also attempted, albeit in a very different way, to map out the imaginative territory of the novel, as an arena where some of the unresolved and perhaps unresolvable political ambiguities of his diasporic location might be addressed. Theory, at its best, enables the reader to ask more questions about the texts they read, but the creative text may be a more equivocal vehicle for such explorations. 'Writers and politicians', Rushdie has said, 'are natural rivals. Both groups try to make the world in their own images; they fight for the same territory. And the novel is one way of denying the official, politician's version of truth.'[103] Moreover, the novel has always 'been *about* the way in which different languages, values and narratives quarrel'. It does not 'seek to establish a privileged language, but insists on the freedom to portray and analyse the struggle between the different contestants for such privileges'. As an imaginative space, not necessarily limited by the constraints of any one particular agenda, it provides the possibility of a fictive arena where such often contradictory issues can be addressed, questions which may not always be answerable, but which may perhaps open 'new doors in our minds'.[104]

Such descriptions of the role of the literary imagination were evident in many of Rushdie's non-fictional essays and reviews published before the

Satanic Verses affair. They became more urgent in his subsequent attempts, following the *fatwa* issued by the Ayatollah Khomeni in 1989, to justify his position following that crisis, and the limitations on freedom of speech that it implied. However, the political furore following the publication of *The Satanic Verses* was not fuelled only by the supposed blasphemy of Rushdie's questioning and satirization of the certainty of religious 'truths' in his parodic treatment of the figure of the Islamic prophet, Mohamed, but more fundamentally by an intractable conflict which lies at the heart of the diasporic imaginary itself. In the irreconcilable controversies which followed the banning of the book – controversies between the philosophical traditions of Islam and the West, the outraged Muslim Asian communities in Bradford and the Western intelligentsia, a quarrel between 'the ancient (ascriptive migrants) and modern (ironic) metropolitans'[105] – was an ancient contestation not only over the legitimacy of particular 'ideological and epistemological' formations where, from either perspective, each point of view is 'equally true and valid', but a further manifestation of the inherent duality of the diasporic condition itself. Once the secular, defined through the modern and 'global politics of migrancy' (a movement stressing fracture and heterogeneity), intervenes too far into the 'sacred' (the old and unifying idea of a mythological and religious past), diasporas can retreat swiftly into 'versions of millenarian rememoration', the securities of an 'essentialist discourse, even though they know full well that the past can no longer redeem'.[106] As Rushdie attempted to explain, following the political impact of his novel:

> The *Satanic Verses* is not, in my view, an antireligious novel. It is . . . an attempt to write about migration, its stresses and transformations from the point of view of migrants from the subcontinent to Britain. This, for me, is the saddest irony of all; that after working for five years to give voice and fictional flesh to the immigrant culture of which I myself am a member, I should see my book burned, largely unread, by the people it's about . . . I tried to write against stereotypes; the zealot protests serve to confirm, in the Western mind, all the worst stereotypes of the Muslim world.[107]

II

Published only one year after V. S. Naipaul's *The Enigma of Arrival*, *The Satanic Verses*[108] is haunted, like that earlier novel, by a series of ghosts and chimeras, memories and transfigurations, that take on the powerful force of both sifting and excavating the unfinished business of the past. It is also centrally concerned with a wilful exposure and explosion of the now familiar oppositions of a diasporic present, negotiating the troubled relationships between visions of 'home' and 'abroad', exile and migrancy, tradition and modernity, faith and doubt, love and loss – in an attempt to change the script, to allow 'newness', to reiterate Rushdie's phrase, to enter the world. As such, the central characters of *The Satanic Verses* are migrant travellers who, transformed by the dislocating experience of 'arrival' in Britain, are reborn and attempt to reinvision the world. The novel both interrogates past histories in terms of constructing new 'ways of seeing' yet reverts, perhaps surprisingly, to a painful narrative of rememoration and return. In keeping with the nature of the narrative strategies explored in *Midnight's Children* and *Shame*, Rushdie creates a form which is dual in focus, polyphonic in voice and hybrid in intent. It is postmodern and realist at the same time, a multilayered story which constantly metamorphoses, shifting its focus not only between Bombay and London, the temporal urban spaces of his two major characters' lives, but also – through the mediations of 'Archangel Gibreel's' schizophrenic fantasies and the frame of a dream narrative which structures at least a third of the text – to a series of other parallel and interlinked stories. These sequences range from travelling across the boundaries of time to the Arabian desert in the seventh century; to the now infamous 'Mahound' section, which presents the revelation of the 'Satanic Verses' to the prophet; to the story of Ayesha, the butterfly girl who leads a pilgrimage from Pakistan to Mecca; to 'Return to Jahila', which depicts the historical and political background of the birth of Islam itself. And in keeping with the doubling of the narration, many of the characters are either metaphorically twinned, as is the case with the two im/migrants, 'Gibreelsaladin Farishtachamcha' (p. 5), who literally fall to Britain from the sky at the opening or, alternatively, are linked by name to what appear almost to be previous reincarnations or mirrors of themselves. Places, too, are yoked together across time and space, and cartographic boundaries dissolved: whether Bombay and London, the shifting sands of London and Jahila, the epic mythological landscapes mapped by the Bombay movies – the 'theologicals' – or the allegorical terrain of Ayesha's 'Parting of the Arabian Sea'.

Despite the enormously ambitious scope of the text, Rushdie's primary aim was to write a comic novel about migration, and to set it in im/migrant London, a city which had always existed, was 'visible' but had remained largely 'unseen', and which in his earlier work had largely remained absent.

'I wanted' the novel, says Rushdie, 'to be rooted in the kind of London that I actually do know about that has been very little described in literature. It has been largely invisible – when you think that the big migration into Britain happened in the late 50s and early 60s.'[109] *The Satanic Verses* clearly extends preoccupations that Rushdie had already rehearsed in his earlier works, the search for an appropriate frame to shape his large metafictional schemes, exile and migrancy, the relationship between nation and narration, the questionable 'certainties' of historical 'truths' whether of 'East' or 'West'. However, its focus is less on 'imaginary' countries of the mind, countries which in many ways were part of a past he had left behind and which, particularly in *Midnight's Children*, he had been attempting to reclaim, but on a *lived present* as an Asian writer residing in Britain. If *Midnight's Children* was an attempt to write about India as an 'insider' counteracting the orientalism of Western versions of the 'East' (which Rushdie has described fully in his essay 'Outside the Whale'),[110] the narrative perspective of *Shame* was complicated by the distant and partial filter of Rushdie's own relationship to Pakistan, a country he had only lived in for short periods and from which he had always felt estranged. Whilst the three novels are often seen as a trilogy representing the triangular history of the author's own diasporic background, it was in the writing of *The Satanic Verses* that Rushdie finally agreed 'to tell myself that I had left', and to write from the perspective of being part of the 'amazing phenomenon of the Indian diaspora'. Moreover, it was the first time that 'I have managed to write a book from the whole of myself. It is written from my entire sense of being in the world.'[111]

If '*The Satanic Verses* is anything', says Rushdie, 'it is a migrant's eye view of the world. It is written from the very experience of uprooting, disjuncture, metamorphosis . . . that is the migrant condition, and from which I believe, can be derived a metaphor for all humanity.'[112] However, whilst that experience of disjuncture and uprooting can be a liberation, a sublime liberation of the imagination, it is not without its pain, as Rushdie's epigraph, taken from Daniel Defoe's 'The History of the Devil', and which prefaces the novel, implies:

> Satan, being thus confined to a vagabond, wandering, unsettled condition is without any certain abode; for though he has, in consequence of his angelic nature, a kind of empire in the liquid waste or air, yet this is certainly part of his punishment, that he is . . . without any fixed place, or space, allowed him to rest the sole of his foot upon.

Migrancy is therefore a punishment as well as a freedom, and the airy 'empires' and liminal spaces of the im/migrant imaginary are open as much to demonization as to celebration. With hindsight, Rushdie's epigraph can now be seen as an ironic comment on the political fate that was to befall him following publication of the book. However, if we consider it in its literary context, he was clearly pointing to one of the book's major aims, which was to create a suitably eclectic and versatile literary frame from which both to interrogate the silences in English history and to ridicule and parody the continuing and noisy articulation of a demotic racist discourse in Thatcherite Britain, where 'they have the power of description and we succumb to the pictures they construct' (p. 168). The epigraph is also, of course, suggestive of the ambiguities of Rushdie's own location as a migrant writer who, without any secure ground beneath his feet, was attempting nevertheless to extend the literary landscape of the contemporary novel in English by bringing the South Asian diaspora centre stage, a subject previously ignored by the modernist avant-garde.[113] As Rushdie has said:

> Writers like Thomas Hardy, or William Faulkner . . . who are very rooted in community and a place, and have that territory which they know is their territory . . . are the writers that I really envy. Because of the accidents of my life, I don't have that sense of community, I don't have a natural group of people to write about, I don't have an automatic place, what I have is a plurality of places and peoples, none of them being, so to speak, home turf. [114]

Interestingly, as we saw in V. S. Naipaul's early work, Rushdie's initial focus was not on the complex class, gender and racial affiliations of the diaspora in Britain, where he had lived for most of his adult life, but instead, on the exploration of what Sara Suleri has called, in a different context, a series of literary 'ploys'[115] – an experimentation with an impressive repertoire of fictional strategies for rehearsing the condition of migrancy – which both helped to define the fractured memories of his own past, and provided, at the same time, the literary tools to build an alternative imaginative territory, creating a 'new angle at which to enter reality'.[116] As we have already seen, Rushdie had explicitly addressed in *Shame* the question of how migrants are to survive amidst the constant mutations of change:

> When individuals come unstuck from their native land, they are called migrants. When nations do the same thing (Bangladesh) the act is called

> secession. What is the best thing about migrant peoples and seceded nations? I think it is their hopefulness . . . And what's the worst thing? It is the emptiness of one's luggage . . . I, too, like all migrants, am a fantasist. I build imaginary countries and try to impose them on the ones that exist. I, too, face the problems of history: what to retain, what to dump, how to hold on to what memory insists on relinquishing, how to deal with change (p. 85).

The difficulty, however, which confronted Rushdie in the writing of *The Satanic Verses*, was how to write a novel about migrancy in a mode which did not simply repeat or reinvent the very categorizations which he was trying to shift. To find a means to move beyond what seemed the irreconcilable Manichean opposites of location and dislocation defined by colonial discourse and the modernist rhetoric of 'exile' in a historical and political context which may not have been so to speak 'home turf', but in which he was forced to face political questions which touched the realities of his everyday life. The question of 'exile', we are told in *The Satanic Verses*, is an 'endless paradox', a 'looking forward by always looking back' (p. 205). Similarly, whilst migration may be the supreme act of 'translation', the ways in which migrants reinvent themselves may not always be new. Saladin Chamcha, who, like Ralph Singh in V. S. Naipaul's *The Mimic Men*, anglicizes his name and attempts to reconstruct himself in London as an Anglophile actor 'with a thousand voices', is mortified by how his 'haughtiest English pitch' is suddenly transformed against his will into the 'Bombay lilt' of an earlier self on a plane journey back to India (p. 34). Moreover, despite the years he has spent fabricating his various selves, he cannot escape from the entrapping closure determined by his immigrant status – the 'prison of his skin' (p. 34) – in the white Britain he tries to enter via the route of assimilation, symbolized by his marriage to Pamela Lovelace, a representative of 'Yorkshire pudding and hearts of oak, that hearty rubicund voice of ye-olde dream England which he so desperately wanted to inhabit' (p. 180); or, in the literal demonization that his brown face provokes in those racists (the witch-like police force who guard the borders of 'white' culture) who are responsible for his surreal transmogrification into a goat, the devil incarnate with an enormous penis and cloven hooves.

In addition, as his Indian lover, Zeeny Vakil, warns him on his first return to Bombay, he will also remain forever 'giddy' in the city that used to be his 'home', for he has become a 'ghost', a shadow lost in the mutations demanded by his departure. The voices of India's Babel threaten:

'Don't come back again. When you have stepped through the looking-glass you step back at your peril. The mirror may tear you to shreds' (p. 58). These words are later echoed by Sufyan, the proprietor of the Shaandaar Café, in the Indian/Pakistani ghetto of 'Brickhall' in London (an obvious amalgamation of Southall, Brixton and Brick Lane). Attempting to provide a haven of solidarity in adverse conditions, he, too, urges Chamcha to *choose* affiliation, to stay where he is safe, 'among your own people, your own kind'. But here too Saladin refuses: 'I'm not your kind . . . You're not my people. I've spent half my life trying to get away from you.' And later he adds: 'Yes, this was Hell, all right. The city of London, transformed into Jahannum, Gehenna, Muspellheim' (pp. 253–4). In the real im/migrant world of *The Satanic Verses*, the airborne, celebratory dimensions of Rushdie's migrant aesthetic, complicated by issues of class and race, take on more disturbing implications, whether of dream or nightmare, as we also gain some profound insights into the author's own strategies for masking pain. As his narrator explains at one point:

> A man who sets out to make himself up is taking on the Creator's role, according to one way of seeing things; he's unnatural, a blasphemer, an abomination of abominations. From another angle, you could see pathos in him, heroism in his struggle, in his willingness to risk: not all mutants survive. Or, consider him sociopolitically: most migrants learn, and can become disguises. Our own false descriptions to counter the falsehoods invented about us, concealing for reasons of security our secret selves (p. 49).

It has often been said that the immigrant is 'either a performer, or has no personality'.[117] Rushdie's born-again migrants in *The Satanic Verses*, Saladin Chamcha and Gibreel Farishta, are clearly descendants from this tradition. They are both actors, 'cultural chameleons',[118] made-up brown men – Gibreel, a larger than life Bombay movie star, and Saladin, the familiar but invisible voice-over of the advertising industry – and use, in different ways, the performative as a means of survival, a strategy we already witnessed in the comi-tragic antics of the calypsonian trickster figures of Selvon's 'boys' in the Moses novels, as well as in the role-playing of V. S. Naipaul's shipwrecked narrator of *The Mimic Men*. However, by the late 1980s and *The Satanic Verses*, the problems of a divided colonial consciousness or a hyphenated subjectivity no longer lead to Ralph Singh's repetitive panic at a gap in his history or to the sad pathos of Sir Galahad's prophetic encounter with the 'colour problem' in *The Lonely*

Londoners. Instead, they lead to a deliberate and self-conscious attempt to explode and renegotiate such polarities, creating a 'third space', an empowered site of enunciation from within the conflicting and diverse cultural spaces of the diaspora itself.[119]

Selvon had, of course, already navigated this territory before such a theoretical grammar existed, in his early inscriptions of black London with what are arguably comparable generic methods for writing a creolized and parodic language of migration in the Moses novels, by using the anti-epic, the comic and the iconoclastic as a means of deflation and inversion, a mode of both interrogating the age-old myths of the colonial centre, and transforming at the same time their apparent immutability and dominance. And his humour, like Rushdie's later, does not stem from the security of a focal vantage-point, but is targeted at a number of different groups and objects; the reductive rhetoric of Sir Galahad's Black Power politics in *Moses Ascending* is as much the source of his humour as the ways in which the main character, with his writerly ambitions, is constantly deflated as a budding black scribe in Britain. And Moses, again like Rushdie's later migrants, Saladin and Gibreel, is also a figure of pilgrimage, an iconic prophet in the wilderness which is the im/migrant city, the object both of romance and nightmare, the source of a different kind of Holy Grail. As in Rushdie's work, Selvon is acutely conscious of the need to parodically reverse traditional views of 'English' history. Selvon's vision is ultimately a more sympathetic and less violent one; he may ridicule the lives of his im/migrant characters, but Moses in the end is happy to share his newly built house of fiction with them.

Saladin and Gibreel, in *The Satanic Verses*, not only belong to a different era, but they are also not part of any community. They do not belong either in Brickhall or the pastiched representations of the media and film world; they have both lost faith, and exist ultimately in a much more threatening and postmodern migrant world. It is a world where the potential splittings of self may take on a subversive quality that can also lead to certified schizophrenia as well as demonic transmogrifications. However, the difference is of emphasis rather than kind, although an obvious danger for Rushdie, in his playful usage of postmodernist techniques to break down genres as well as different discursive and linguistic fields in *The Satanic Verses*, is that 'the world may seem to offer nothing truly new, only a history to be reconstructed, an endless exploration of a worn-out past'.[120] However, *The Satanic Verses* ingeniously inscribes the presence of a subterranean im/migrant city, where a number of different cultural registers constantly intermingle and undermine the dominant landscape of a narrowly conceived 'Englishness'. As Rushdie has said:

> *The Satanic Verses* celebrates hybridity, impurity, intermingling, the transformation that comes of new and unexpected combinations of human beings, cultures, ideas, politics, movies, songs. It rejoices in mongrelization and fears the absolutism of the Pure. *Melange*, hotch-potch, a bit of this and a bit of that is *how newness enters the world* . . . It is a love-song to our mongrel selves.[121]

Situated precariously at the apex where all binaries meet, *The Satanic Verses* was an extremely ambitious undertaking, for it not only had to negotiate the difficult political terrain of a range of different versions of the narrative of im/migration and exile that preceded it, but also attempted to raise questions about the limits and deceptions of language itself in the construction of any religious or historical 'truths'. The varieties of 'English', and the linguistic and kaleidoscopic cultural range of the heterogeneous discourses which consistently collide in the text – discourses which range from the sacred to the secular, the Bombay film industry to suburban Indian English, the talk of Hobson-Jobson, the eclectic narratives of Hindu and Islamic epics, colonial English, London West Indian, second-generation Asian English, the language of pastiche and the advertising world – frequently draw our attention to its major purpose which is to demonstrate that no one position will or must suffice. It represents an attempt to embrace a whole variety of different 'Englishes', stemming from a literary and linguistic heritage which includes a vast range of conflicting and competing discourses: whether the modernist techniques of a James Joyce, the syncretism of Indian narrative forms, the religious texts of Islam, the fundamentalist voices of a revivalist and muscular Hinduism, the post-modernist pastiches of Mimi Mamoulian's advertising jingles, or the abracadabra of *The Arabian Nights*, voices which all help to account for the novel's insistent and slippery refrain, 'it was so it was not in a time long forgot' (p. 544). Yet the very attempt to forge new relationships between previously incompatible positionings and epistemologies leads, in *The Satanic Verses*, not only to a 'hybrid' celebration of the migrant condition – a desire to rename and rewrite the narrative of the *metis* – but also to a simultaneous eruption of the repressed dynamic of national 'purities' and 'tradition', voiced through both the 'Black Maria' witch-hunters of 'Maggie Torture's' Britain and the potentially essentialist religious narratives of the diaspora itself. As a deliberate 'intervention into the project of modernity', then, Rushdie's *The Satanic Verses* is also ironically forced to address the ambivalent paradoxes which are situated at the heart of modernity itself.[122]

The difficulties generated by Rushdie's project are reflected not only in the novel's structure, which threatens, as Rushdie himself has commented, to 'fall apart', but also in the deliberately oppositional positionings and stereotypings of some of his major characters and subjects who act at times – despite the moving *bildungsroman* narrative which underlies the stories of the two main protagonists – as vehicles of ideas rather than fully realized human beings. In a book which constantly metamorphoses, the cross-referencing, paralleling of themes and doubling of names is impressive, providing a kaleidoscopic quality to its multilayered mirroring. Hind, the sad wife of the Bangladeshi, Sufyan, and who holds the Shaandaar Café in Brickhall together by her cooking, shares her name with the wayward wife of the ruler of Mecca; Mishal, the name of the second-generation Asian British, eldest daughter of Sufyan, is also the name of Mirza Saeed Akhtar's wife; 'Cone' is not only the mountain where the Rushdie's renamed prophet 'Mahound' hears the revelations, but is also the family name of Otto and Allie Cone, Polish Jewish emigres and holocaust survivors of yet another story of twentieth-century diaspora. Whilst the narration makes clear that the paralleling of these various namings is partially a result of Gibreel's deluded psychological state, and the characters appear largely as figures in his fantastical dream narratives, the various refractions provided by such mirrors are clearly also part of Rushdie's purpose, and highlight the difficulty of the authorial task in attempting to design such a constantly shifting canvas. Rushdie's depiction of the scene in which Saladin makes love to Zeeny Vakil, only 48 hours after his return to Bombay, is perhaps indicative of the potential hazards of such narrative conjuring: 'the first thing he did . . . was to faint, to pass out cold, because the messages reaching his brain were in such disagreement with each other, as if his right eye saw the world moving to the left while the left eye saw it moving to the right' (p. 51).

Yet the novel's bifocal structure, if closely examined, is very tightly organized and also illuminates the book's major themes. As Milan Kundera has observed, the book is divided not only in its thematic exploration of questions of dislocation and reintegration, continuity and tradition, but also by its own structure, the odd and even numbered sections. Almost all of the 'odd' sections (*I to VII*) are set in London, apart from the last (*IX*), which is set in Bombay. These sections comprise by far the largest part of the novel's attention. The remaining 'even' sections (which are also, curiously, the same in length) are made up primarily of Gibreel's fantastic serial dreams, which provide the structural key to this part of the narration. However, it is in the 'handling of the interface between the "two" texts' that

Rushdie's narrative skill is tested.[123] Whilst it is beyond the scope of this chapter to deal in depth with Gibreel's dream sequences, for they have been covered extensively in criticism elsewhere, it is worth noting that the complex exploration of questions of faith and doubt, whether religious or secular, which they enact are a central part of Rushdie's overall design. That is an enquiry into the limits of the imagination and the contradictions which exist at the heart of all 'truths'.

Characteristically, in a narrative which is both self-consciously borrowing from and critiquing Western postmodernist techniques, the author appears in several guises, often commenting on and critiquing the action, whether as the poet satirist, Baal, who, representing the figure of the artist as 'whore', expresses the book's provocative desire to simultaneously embrace the true and the false, 'to point at frauds, to take sides, start arguments, shape the world and stop it from going to sleep' (p. 97), or as Jumpy Joshi, the amateur poet, who voices the transformatory power of the imagination in opening up the locked languages of politics and sociology as voiced through the radical lawyer, Hanif Johnson. We are frequently reminded that it is only through the revisioning power of language itself that 'the poisoned wells' (p. 281) of intractable positionings – such as Enoch Powell with his 'rivers of blood' rhetoric – might be mastered and renamed, turning 'insults into strengths', and enabling 'whigs, Tories or Blacks' to 'all choose to wear with pride the names they were given in scorn' (p. 93).

As Catherine Cundy has suggested: 'To be that which is designated as "other" is to be reinvented. To stem the tide of abuse and remake the abuser's language anew is to be privy to a rebirth', a movement which is reflected in the novel as a whole.[124] Rushdie's construction of the author as trickster figure is therefore part of the novel's purpose, and continually transforms and unsettles our reading, whether in his appearances as the explicitly fused autobiographical sign of Salman/Saladin, or as Salman from Persia who, in the now controversial dreamscapes of the deluded Gibreel – the 'Mahound' and 'Jahila' sections of the book – tricks the Prophet in his writing of a 'satanic' version of the sacred verses. Rushdie also critiques the limitations of some of his own literary techniques through this process, stressing through the deliberately constructed postmodernist voice of Mimi Mamoulian (Chamcha's onetime advertising partner) that whilst the creation of 'pastiche' may only lead to a 'flattened world', it is a world she nevertheless embraces with full knowledge, 'understanding what I am doing and why' (p. 261). And as Rushdie implies elsewhere, forms which are apparently 'new' in the Western canon often have other, more ancient antecedents. For the inbred eclecticism of Indian culture – whether of the modern Bombay movies or the more traditional epic narratives which are equally part of his literary intertext – may enable you to 'become a post-modernist writer' by also being a 'very traditional one'.[125]

Where V. S. Naipaul's unnamed narrator in *The Enigma of Arrival* suffers from a repetitive nightmare, fearing the explosion of his head into a series of ever spinning fragments, Rushdie's starting point is the explosion itself. Where Naipaul, as we saw in Chapter 3, 'If the House Falls Down', recoils from the mirror of his own invisibility, standing outside Churchgate Station in Bombay in *An Area of Darkness*, Rushdie jumps through the mirror into a 'crowd of stories', and insists instead on listening to the polyphonic babel of India, as well as the babble of 'Babylondon', enjoying the noisy dialogue of a narrative which constantly seeks, through the articulation of a number of different perspectives, to undermine its own biases. In many ways, Rushdie's novel takes off from the ground that Naipaul and others had so painstakingly created and opens with the literal explosion of the hijacked jumbo jet *Bostan* on New Year's day (or thereabouts) over the English Channel.[126] With this dramatic and carefully staged opening, Rushdie not only makes a powerful and courageous intervention into previous inscriptions of im/migrant 'arrival', but also confronts the potential chaos of the resultant splittings of the self, the carnage of fractured stories and histories that such migrations imply. Importantly, as the aircraft cracks in half, high above the shores of Albion, literally blown up by the violent act of Sikh terrorists – it conjures both the imagined, fantasy world of 'Vilayet', 'Ellowen Deeowen', 'Proper London', as well as the landlocked realities of an immigrant city, the *gravitas* of a 'city visible, but unseen'. The miraculous descent of Rushdie's two migrant protagonists is similarly orchestrated, suggesting both the surrealist and mythical possibilities of rebirth, reincarnation, transmutation and translation, whilst simultaneously presenting us with an intimation of the grimness of the immigrant's fate: 'just two brown men, falling hard, nothing so new about that, you may think: climbed too high, got above themselves, flew too close to the sun' (p. 5).

Rushdie sets up from the outset the questions he is later to develop, as he negotiates not only who has the 'best tunes' (p. 10), but who has the best songs for survival once his migrants are washed up on Britain's shores. Is it Gibreel's obsessive desire to hold on to a 'continuous past', to atone in 'Vilayet' for his previous blasphemies as a pork-eating Muslim, and remain 'at bottom an untranslated man', or Saladin's equally passionate desire to become a 'creature of *selected* discontinuities, a *willing* re-invention; his *preferred* revolt against history being what makes him, in our chosen idiom, "false" ' (p. 427). With this pyrotechnic scene, which dramatizes both the terror and the exhilaration of this 'drastic act of immigration', and the consequent Satanic 'fall', Rushdie not only situates his narrative in a long lineage of previous im/migrant arrivals, but also marks out its difference, as he reroutes the 'millenarian through the space of travel (replacing the ship with the aeroplane)', and situates his migrants in a faithless world, which is no longer neatly defined by the boundaries of land-space or the securities of any one tradition.[127] England, in *The Satanic Verses*, is no longer a 'space in which a divided consciousness is reconciled to its defining other; on the contrary, the appointed zone of the immigrant's reincarnation is the waters of the English channel'; it is a 'liminal zone between countries and continents'.[128] As his migrants literally fall into each other's arms, and miraculously descend the 29 002 feet to the icy shores of Britain, Rushdie introduces his major themes and suggests the multilayered mirroring that his narrative will enact. Characteristically, the surrealist elements of this scene are held in tension with the 'unfinished business' of his migrant's previous lives, buoyed up not only by Gibreel's optimistic faith – his belief in the possibilities of reincarnation – but also through their joint will to survive.

As they touch down on the snowbound English beach, Gibreel's refrain: 'Born again Spoono, you and me. Happy birthday mister; happy birthday to you' (p. 10) echoes as Saladin Chamcha, differently constituted, strains to gain vision in a 'void' where he would have to 'construct everything from scratch, would have to invent the ground beneath his feet, before he could even take a step' (p. 132). As with Selvon earlier, Rushdie presents these two migrant arrivants as anti-heroes, mythologizing and deflating them at the same time, and parodically reversing other interwoven stories of heroic invasion, such as Rosa Diamond's eternal waiting for 'William the Conqueror' (p. 129).

The idea of rebirth is not, of course, a new one in the writing of im/migrant fictions. Not surprisingly, then, Rushdie's twinned Bombay urbanites also undergo a series of reinventions both before and after departure. Gibreel Farishta (formerly Ismail) is the darling of the 'Bombay talkies', a film star who has risen to almost God-like proportions from his origins as the son of a lowly Bombay lunch-runner, before he falls into the delusions of insanity in Britain. Having taken on the name of *farishta* (angel) to fulfil his mother's dreams, and to emphasize his iconic status in the fantasies of his audiences, he is recast as the 'Archangel Gibreel', where the fantasies of his cinematic career are deliberately fused with his schizoid psychological state. However, even as we meet him, tumbling through the sky singing a mixture of *gazals* and Indian popular movie songs, his constructed image is already beginning to disintegrate, as suggested in the cracking image of his paper face on the Bombay street hoardings. He is reconstructed again, of course, as the obsessive lover chasing the dream, not of 'Proper London' like Saladin, his alter-ego, but of Allie Cone one of the objects of his jealous sexual fantasies. Saladin, originally Salahuddin before his first departure from Bombay and his rift with his father Changez Chamchawalla, also goes by the nickname of 'Spoono', his very name suggesting his sycophancy and the 'mimicry' he attempts to embrace, as he sells his soul not only to 'Englishness', but to the oblivion of the 'flattened' media world of advertising and *The Aliens Show*. These two characters – Gibreel the 'good' immigrant, who falls from the sky to become a modern 'Shaitan', and Chamcha the 'mimic man', haunted by the ghost of his Indian shadow and similarly 'fallen' in his surrealist reincarnation in Britain as a kind of 'elephant man', the bestial embodiment of the monstrous stereotypes of a white racist society – becomes the frame from which the narrative attempts to move beyond its own predetermined starting point. It is an opening which reverberates with the 'equally fragmented, equally absurd' questions of other im/migrant's lives, a cacophony of questions made up of 'broken memories, sloughed-off selves, severed mother-tongues, violated privacies, untranslatable jokes, extinguished futures, lost loves, the forgotten meaning of hollow, booming words, *land, belonging, home*' (p. 4).

Clearly, whilst part of Rushdie's purpose was to explode the potentially restrictive closures of the im/migrant novel by writing a novel in a form which was itself 'hybrid . . . part social commentary, part fantasy, part psychological investigation, part farce', and which represented a 'yoking together' of how these 'different worlds' might make one 'grafted world', he was also plagued by the difficulties of sustaining a story which might in the end read just as 'an endless series of performances'.[129] As he pointed out in an interview with Blake Morrison:

> the point about *Satanic Verses* is that it's a novel that begins in a pyrotechnic high-surrealist vein and moves towards a much more inner emotional writing. That process of putting away the magic noses and cloven hoofs is one the novel itself goes through; it tells itself by the end it doesn't need that apparatus anymore.[130]

And as we witnessed in the laborious process of unravelling that is, in the end, the key to the dream of the Chiroco painting which forms the subtext of Naipaul's *The Enigma of Arrival*, partially embedded in Rushdie's text is an autobiographical narrative, fictionalized through the story of Saladin Chamcha. Although Rushdie situates Chamcha as one unlike himself who returns, and maybe finds his way back, he has also admitted that in writing the novel, he was unconsciously confronting 'a thing I find difficult even to admit to myself, which is that I left home'.[131] A careful comparison between the author's biography and Chamcha's background soon reveals a number of obvious parallels: Chamcha's first and difficult trip to England with an alcoholic father, his baptism by fire into 'Englishness' in a public school, his career in advertising, his relationship with Pamela Lovelace, an absent mother, an affluent and sophisticated secular Muslim upbringing, and a difficult relationship with a father who, by the end of the novel, represents the sustaining love that redeems him; these have all been documented in biographical sources. There is also a parallel in Chamcha's ambivalent relationship to, and distance from, the im/migrants of Rushdie's Asian ghetto in Brickhall, the real inhabitants of the 'city visible, but unseen', and in his love affair with the memory of a childhood world lost in Bombay.

Chamcha negotiates – along with Gibreel, who perhaps represents a distorted version of the lost religious dimensions of his reinvented secular self – every aspect of 'Proper London', whether in the labyrinthine mazes of the city's irreconcilable opposites, 'the locus classicus of incompatible realities' (p. 313), which Gibreel attempts to map and 'tropicalize' with an 'A to Z', or in the subterranean underworld of the Shaandaar Café, which is ultimately burnt down by the fires of racial violence in a hallucinatory scene, where Saladin rescues Gibreel (whom he has been tormenting by impersonating a series of different voices on the telephone inciting him, like Othello, to insane jealousy). Whilst the inhabitants of Brickhall are carefully depicted – we have the older immigrant voices of the educated schoolmaster Sufyan and Hind, his wife, who, refusing translation, still longs for 'home'; the caricaturing of their two adolescent Asian-British daughters who speak a different language of Englishness and, in the case of Mishal, cross over to the parallel experience of the Afro-Caribbean diaspora; the parodying of radical black decolonization politics through the figure of Dr Uhuru Simba; and an impressive range of the figures of black history, commemorated through their waxen images by the gyrating East Indian albino, dub poet, Pinkawalla – Saladin is unable to enter fully into any of the spaces he is offered here. Moreover, the nature of Rushdie's parodying and stereotyping of this group does not invite us, as in Selvon's Moses novels, to laugh with the characters, but rather to remain with Saladin, hovering on the outside.

This section of the novel comes to a climax with two parallel scenes: the synthetic media party, in which Gibreel and Saladin come together again at Shepperton Studios, against a mock backdrop of a Dickensian London cast in fog, and the violent burning down of the Shaandaar Café which, like the dilapidated house in Selvon's *Moses Ascending*, had become the symbolic space for survival and resistance in the city. The paralleling of these scenes is instructive, as both in the end represent impossible resolutions for Saladin's predicament and in both he is reunited with and confronted by Gibreel, his 'mirror-self' and 'conjoined opposite'. Yet it is also this love–hate relationship which in the end redeems and enables his restoration from his devilish shape to his humanized self. If, as Gibreel suggests, 'the splitting was not in him, but in the universe' (p. 352), Saladin still remains locked, by the end of these scenes, in the repetitive dilemma of being unable to choose, and unable to accept, the mutated realities of his reincarnation as the monster of a postcolonial Frankenstein. It was still the same 'old dispute': 'Native and settler . . . continuing on these soggy streets with revised categories. It occurred to him now that he was forever joined to the adversary, their arms locked round one another's bodies, north to south, head to tail, as when they fell to earth, as when they settled' (p. 353). Importantly, too, while the fires of racial violence kill and maim the Sufyan family at the end of the novel, and violence rages through the streets, it is the burlesque orchestration of the carnivalesque images at the Club Hot Wax (p. 292) which remain most potently inscribed.

By the time the novel closes, we have been witness to a number of deaths and suicides. Otto Cone kills himself, as does Allie, in a similar manner to Rekha Merchant (both lovers of Gibreel) at the beginning, jumping to her death off 'Everest Villas' in Bombay. The Sufyan parents die in the Brickhall fire. Pamela Lovelace is implicated along with Jumpy Joshi (her new lover) in a police cover-up of a racially motivated murder enquiry, and they both die with their unborn child. And it is the terminal illness of Saladin's father, Changez Chamchwalla, which prompts his final return to Scandal Point, his childhood home in Bombay. It is here that he strips away his past selves, encouraged by the redemptive voice of Zeeny Vakil, who brings his shadowed Indian self back into the light. In one of the most moving scenes in the novel, Saladin reverts to his old name, Salahuddin Chamchawalla, and nurses his father towards death, recovering the magical Urdu stories of his youth, and the mysteries of the 'copper-and-brass lamp reputed to have the powers of wish fulfilment' (p. 525), which his father had saved for this moment of reconciliation. As in the 'Ceremony of Farewell' section in Naipaul's *The Enigma of Arrival*, it is through a confrontation with love and death, the familial and instinctive languages of the past, that Saladin's life is redeemed: 'The world, somebody wrote, is the place we prove real by dying in it' (p. 533).

Gibreel had also returned to Bombay after the Brickhall fires. Unable to restore his relationship with Allie Cone, he was in the process of 'ship-wrecking' his life once more, now playing drunken, lecherous roles in bad movies, still haunted by the ghosts of his past. And Gibreel, too, has to die, killing himself with a gun hidden in Saladin's magic lamp. But Gibreel's death is easier to comprehend than Saladin's return, since Gibreel's actions remain continuous, as Simon Gikandi has suggested, with the persona of the 'demented performer' we have encountered throughout the text, 'writing his identity – and *ressentiment* – in acts of blood and fire'.[132] Saladin has not previously exhibited a desire either for reunification with his father, who is the source of this emotional reidentification with the 'homeland', or to throw off his earlier embrace of the masks of 'Englishness'. Moreover, Saladin is not only seemingly restored to the shadows of his past, but also to a future with Zeeny Vakil where, as she warns him: 'If you're serious about shaking off your foreigness, Salad baba, then don't fall into some kind of rootless limbo instead . . . Try and embrace this city, as it is not some childhood memory that makes you both nostalgic and sick. Draw it close . . . Become its creature; belong' (p. 541). The 'unfinished business' of the past, it seems, must be left behind, the ghosts laid to rest, but the solutions posed by the novel's conclusion for each of its protagonists are very differently framed.

In the final pages of the novel, as Saladin looks out from his window across the Arabian Sea, the vision is one of rebirth, rejuvenation, a living in what he calls 'the present moment of the past' (p. 535). Yet, we are not sure as readers, whether the questions which have been the novel's main subject have been resolved. Clearly, whilst his reconciliation with his dying father is crucial to his final rebirth, the return is potentially a dangerous one. Does Rushdie shift in the course of the writing, as he himself has suggested, from a fractured, fantastical and episodic narrative style to a more traditional and linear *bildungsroman* narrative of return and reunification with the paternal order, or has the noisy wrestling match between the different discourses of diaspora, migrancy and exile been silenced through the atoning powers of love, the food that fed the creative process in the first place? Is he, as one commentator has persuasively argued, not naming the unnameable but renaming the already named?[133]

Whilst *The Satanic Verses* is without doubt a text which seeks to oppose and explode the limited stereotypes of a racist Britain, and make present the diverse realities of an im/migrant London, we may wonder at the end whether Rushdie has succeeded in his aim. Is the world of Brickhall any more visible, closer to the reader, than that of Selvon's earlier rendition of a black London in the Moses novels? Are the differently articulated metaphysical dilemmas of Saladin's and Gibreel's migrant lives resolved? Clearly, the ambitiousness and courage of the novel's project has made it one of the most discussed books in the English language. And, clearly, it has also acted as an important bridge not only in linking the contradictory voices and often incompatible political positionings of different im/migrant groups in Britain, but also in opening up spaces for other parallel histories to be written and to be heard. Yet, as I have argued, both its innovations and its interventions owe much to the vast range of im/migrant diasporic writing that came before it. As Rushdie intimates in *Haroun and the Sea of Stories* (1990), a children's fairytale which has the stifling of human freedom imposed by the *fatwa* as its subtext, and the freedom of the creative imagination, the never ending 'sea of stories', as its central metaphor:

> the water . . . was made up of a thousand and one different currents, each one with a different colour, weaving in and out of one another like a liquid tapestry of breathtaking complexity; and Iff explained that these were the Streams of Story, that each coloured strand represented and contained a single tale. Different parts of the ocean contained different sorts of stories, and as all the stories that had ever been told and many that were still in the process of being invented could be found here, the Ocean of the Streams of Story was in fact the biggest library in the Universe.[134]

It is not possible within the scope of this chapter to examine in detail the novels which followed *The Satanic Verses*, but it is worth noting that even in *The Ground Beneath Her Feet* (1999), a mythical 'rock n' roll love epic' which spans three geographical areas – New York, London and India between the period of the 1950s and the 1980s – there lingers a reluctance to bid farewell finally to an India which will always remain a major part of Rushdie's literary and imaginative inheritance.

PART 3
Homes Without Walls

5

'Homing In': Opening Up 'Asian' Britain in Hanif Kureishi and Ravinder Randhawa

It is the British, the white British, who have to learn that being British isn't what it was. Now it is a more complex thing involving new elements. So there must be a fresh way of seeing Britain and the choices it faces: and a new way of being British after all this time.

Hanif Kureishi[1]

All 'Asians' are ipso facto *British Asians, indeed they are only 'Asians' because they are British 'Asians'. Being 'Asian' is always already a hybrid form, a condition of cultural bilingualism, or . . . perhaps polylingualism.*

Robert Young[2]

The pleasure of writing as an Asian woman is the pleasure of exploding stereotypes.

Meera Syal[3]

England's Indian writers are by no means . . . the same . . . [They] include political exiles, first generation migrants, affluent expatriates whose residence here is frequently temporary, naturalized Britons, and people born here who may never have laid eyes on the subcontinent . . . fiction is in future going to come as much from addresses in London, Birmingham and Yorkshire as from Delhi and Bombay.

Salman Rushdie[4]

In a suggestive essay named after the northern town of Bradford, Hanif Kureishi has explored the uncomfortable terrain of a *hybridity* which is 'Englishness' for a new generation of Asians born and raised in Britain. Kureishi's portrait of Bradford as a 'microcosm' for what he calls the potential of a 'larger' Britain, a Britain that might acknowledge its cultural and racial diversity as being *inside* rather than *outside* its borders, points to some of the major preoccupations of his art, as well as those of a number of other contemporary Asian British writers. The discordant polarities of the world Kureishi exposes in Bradford are both exhilarating and threatening; it is the home of competing racist groups – whether white, black or Asian – the birthplace of the Yorkshire Ripper, the site of British workingmen's clubs, deprived white housing estates, boarded up 'Asian' houses, Pakistani taxi drivers with Yorkshire accents, single sex Muslim schools. It can invoke nostalgia, memories for Kureishi of his English grandfather, and a 1960s childhood in a London suburb – 'pigeon-keeping, greyhound racing, roast beef eating and pianos in pubs'[5] – whilst simultaneously highlighting the 'discrepant', yet increasingly syncretic, 'attachments'[6] of a tense and newly emerging Asian British culture. It is a culture tied as much to Western rock'n'roll as to the mosque, and dynamic in its resourceful appropriation and reconfiguration of a number of differently inflected languages, whether Yorkshire English, Asian British English, Urdu, Punjabi, or the popular iconographies of the movie world, whether of East or West. In stressing the need to unlock the static notion of a monolithic vision of citizenship and ethnicity – the 'mimetic self' of an imaginary nation shaped both by 'stories of imperial greatness'[7] and the lingering political rhetoric of such figures as Disraeli, Churchill, Enoch Powell and Margaret Thatcher – the negotiations of the diverse population of Kureishi's Bradford stage what Stuart Hall has described as 'a contestation over what it means to be British', as well as the necessary coming to birth of 'new ethnicities' in 1980s Britain.[8]

Bradford is 'another country' and was not one easily recognizable either in T. S. Eliot's famous catalogue of the characteristic activities of the British people or in the false talk of national 'unity' by politicians of the New Right in 1980s Britain under Margaret Thatcher. Whilst 'culture' is everywhere in Bradford – in the streets, the schools, the discos – it is not 'Culture' as T. S. Eliot or George Orwell would have defined it in the early postwar years. In Bradford, and by implication in Britain at large, the ossifying characteristics of T. S. Eliot's famous list defining the habitual pastimes of the English people, or George Orwell's equally myopic vision of a longlived tradition of tolerance and gentleness need to be redrawn.[9] For Eliot, says Kureishi, culture was 'a *whole* way of life' epitomized by 'Derby Day, Henley Regatta, Cowes . . . a cup final, . . . Wensleydale cheese, boiled cabbage . . . nineteenth-century gothic churches and the music of Elgar'.[10] Today, such a vision of what Eliot called a 'unity in diversity'[11] is not possible; the list would have to be extended to include:

'yoga exercises . . . Indian restaurants, the music of Bob Marley, the novels of Salman Rushdie, Zen Buddhism, the Hare Krishna Temple as well as the films of Sylvester Stallone . . . hamburgers, visits to gay bars, the dole office and the taking of drugs'.[12] Kureishi's playful juxtapositioning here of competing versions of 'Englishness' does not simply attempt to quantify the momentous effects that postwar migrations have had on the revisioning of vernacular cultural identities in post-imperial Britain. It also highlights a significant gap in ways of seeing and reading the world crystallized in what he calls the false and distant order of an 'Ox-bridge common-room' (largely inhabited by those governing the country), and the apparent chaos of those 'barbarians and philistines' outside. Like many other writers of the so-called 'second generation', Kureishi has described such differences – differences between what is supposedly distinguished as 'high' and 'low' culture as well as gaps in ways of inscribing 'Englishness' – as being indicative of a yawning 'hole' at the 'centre of English writing',[13] an absence which, as Caryl Phillips put it in *The European Tribe* (1987), left Britain's black and Asian children 'starving'.[14] And whilst issues of race, later redefined unproblematically in government parlance as the minority politics of 'ethnic' groups, clearly exacerbated the need to shout across what Rushdie has called the ever-increasing 'gulf[s] in reality'[15] witnessed in Thatcherite Britain, the schisms were not only engendered by convenient constructions of racial difference. For if Bradford, as Kureishi makes abundantly clear, contains all the potentially dynamic elements of a previously invisible plural society 'struggling to find a sense of itself', it was also still a world trapped in an outdated, but nevertheless still virile nationalistic rhetoric, a rhetoric which sought to repress any real assertion of diversion from the status quo – whether of region (North/South), class, economics, or sexual preference. And as Kureishi has consistently illustrated in those fictions, plays and screenplays which focus particularly on Asian Britain,[16] issues of class and gender are as central to redefining Englishness as are questions of race.

Kureishi has frequently highlighted the difference between his experience as a *British* writer of mixed Pakistani and English parentage, and that of what he calls an earlier 'immigrant' generation who, like his fictional characters, Haroon in *The Buddha of Suburbia* (1990)[17] or Omar's alcoholic father in *My Beautiful Launderette* (1986), have 'stayed on'.[18] For such figures can revert, he argues, whenever necessary to the memories of a lost past, the invented refuge, however fragmentary, of an 'imaginary homeland'. Thus Karim, the protagonist of Kureishi's first novel, can *home in* on English culture in a way that Haroon, his father, who is still in many ways caught up in a Naipaulian discourse of arrival and loss, cannot. As Karim graphically illustrates: 'Dad had been in Britain since 1950 – over twenty years – and for fifteen of those years he'd lived in the South London suburbs. Yet still he stumbled around the place like an Indian just off the boat' asking questions like 'Is Dover in Kent?' (p. 7). And as Kureishi himself once put it in an interview: 'people think that I'm caught between two cultures, but I'm not. I'm British; I can make it in England. It's my father who's caught. He can't make it.'[19]

Kureishi's representations of 'Englishness', whether in his early stage plays such as *Borderline* and *Outskirts* (1981), or in his now well-known screen plays and novels, have consistently pointed to the fluid and constructed nature of all identities – identities, which, as Stuart Hall would argue, are constructed within, and not outside, representation[20] – as well as the need to forge new affiliations across a range of previously exclusive and excluding cultural discourses. The effects, therefore, of the world of Western popular culture (the Rock movement of the 1960s and 1970s, the Beatles, the Rolling Stones, David Bowie, the punks and new romantic) on his mixed race and adolescent narrator Karim in *The Buddha of Suburbia* (whose history mirrors Kureishi's own)[21] are as pivotal to his representations of a new way of writing 'Englishness' as is the need to re-angle and revision the myths of 'high' culture, whether Orientalist, colonial, or caught by the narrowly parochial vision of the suburbs and the Home Counties. The patriotic remnants of Norman Tebbit's 'cricket test' Little Englandism,[22] or William Blake's powerfully sustained image of a green and pleasant land, can no longer be shored up to provide a comfortable illusion of the continuing 'greatness' of an ever-receding imperial past.

If Kureishi's depiction in 'Bradford' was one version of a postcolonial Britain, it remained in 1986, at least, a world that was largely invisible to those who governed it. Furthermore, as the explosive effects of the *fatwa* demonstrated only three years later when *The Satanic Verses* was banned and burnt by Asian British Muslims in the very same city – a crisis which split open any easy notion of ethnic homogeneity or consensus amongst the Asian diasporic communities within Britain – it was a world which, having long endured the fate of an imposed interregnum, had suffered many deaths and was waiting to be born. As Kobena Mercer puts it in *Welcome to the Jungle* 'from . . . the Brixton and Toxteth uprisings in 1981, to the rage and despair brought about by . . . the burning of books in Bradford in 1989', the 1980s in 'Black Britain' were 'lived as a relentless vertigo of displacement'.[23] Moreover, in a postmodern age where the certainties of the past were fast diminishing – despite the British film industry's attempts to reinvoke patriotic nostalgia for the lost days of the Raj, in films like Richard Attenborough's *Gandhi*, or the BBC's televised series of Paul Scott's *Jewel in the Crown*[24] – it was the previously unseen, but already experienced, cultural navigators of the black and Asian diasporas who were best able to shift the angle of vision, to 'open up new ways of seeing' the heterodox nature of the incongruities which had always resided at the centre of Britain's imperial past, and might contain the key to radically shifting the boundaries of its postcolonial future.[25]

Unlike the figures of Saladin and Gibreel, who remain migrant figures, as we saw at the close of *The Satanic Verses*, who eventually return to the geographical realities of their '*imaginary homelands*' in Bombay, Kureishi's central characters, like many others of the so-called 'second generation' of Asian British writers – who by the late 1980s included a large number of women's voices – are 'here to stay'.[26] Furthermore, they are engaged in the complex process of redefining their relationship both to Britain and to the limiting prescriptions of an Asian British past, the 'folkloric straightjacket of [an] authenticity' (*The Satanic Verses*, p. 52), imposed by the signs of their racial difference both within and outside the Asian communities. In *The Satanic Verses*, Rushdie clearly focused on tropicalizing London, and creating a phantasmagoric im/migrant city, always visible but rarely seen. But his willed celebration of the utopian potentialities of mongrelization and hybridity as narrative device and conceptual tool does not in the end penetrate deeply enough into the economic, social and historical realities of his characters' lives. Nor does it offer any indication of how those who cannot return are to achieve the possibility of agency or self-determination which the advantages of their *cultural translations* supposedly imply. In fact, Saladin's self-confessed inability to fully read the signs of a character like Mishal Sufyan, the Asian Brit, or her political attempts to highlight what Paul Gilroy once termed the 'black in the Union Jack',[27] are indicative of a surprising shortsightedness, not only in Rushdie's protagonist, but also in the extent to which the novel is really able to engage with the future potential of the second generation of Britain's black and Asian diasporic communities, the subjects on which it partially draws.

For Mishal's 'Englishness', as Saladin openly admits, is differently constructed from his own. It derives from another story, the story of having lived within the context of the often conflicting signs and shifting cultural codes of an Asian British childhood. And Mishal Sufyan, like many other female characters in a whole body of Asian British novels, such as Kulwant in Ravinder Randhawa's *A Wicked Old Woman* (1987), or Jamila in Hanif Kureishi's *The Buddha of Suburbia* (1990) clearly speaks a different language from either Saladin (the Anglophile migrant) or her schoolteacher father, Sufyan (a first-generation immigrant), who holds on tenuously to the position of inhabiting the essential unchanging purity of a true self. Moreover, Mishal's strategies for survival – her need, as she says, to redefine the terms on 'home turf' – aim to effect change from *within* the geographies of a reinvented Englishness which is coming to define the local borders of her diasporic 'home'. As she says: 'Bangladesh in't nothing to me. Just some place Dad and Mum keep banging on about' (*The Satanic Verses*, p. 259). Or, as Ravinder Randhawa puts it in *A Wicked Old Woman,* when she describes Kulwant's initially optimistic attempts to open up the full dimensions of her Asian British identity: 'she had wanted everything, wanted to be Indian and English, wanted to choose for herself what she wanted out of both [but] . . . Thinking of all that, she rubbed the colour on her skin, which wasn't ever going to rub off.'[28]

Before going on to a discussion of Ravinder Randhawa and Hanif Kureishi, I wish briefly to explore the term 'hybridity' and its usefulness as a conceptual and critical tool. In the 1980s, contemporary literary theorists and cultural critics were keen to stress the transformative potential for Britain's black and Asian 'minorities' of living in what came to be called the 'hybrid', thus not only creating a new space for agency at the interstices of the nation's borders, but a space where formerly antagonistic and polarized versions of cultural identity could be realigned and renegotiated.[29] 'Hybridity' (as a strategic renaming of the previously negative signifiers of miscegenation or contamination) quickly developed amongst postcolonial critics into a theoretical grammar for moving beyond the old, imperializing and hegemonizing forms of a static ethnicity[30] long experienced by 'minorities' within Western metropoles. Yet insufficient attention was paid to the historical realities by which this was to be achieved. As was frequently argued, 'ethnicity' as a concept had to be redefined, opened out, to break down the differences which had always anyhow existed within any constructions of 'ethnic' groups – whether white or black. In addition, it was no longer possible, as had been the tendency in the politicization of the label 'Black' in the 1970s and early 1980s, to counteract racist stereotyping by a simple reversal of the binary logic of black or white. For as Stuart Hall puts it in several of his essays:

> Ethnicity can be a constitutive element in the most viciously regressive kind of nationalism or national identity. But in our times, as an *imaginary community*, it is also beginning to carry some other meanings, and to define a new space for identity. It insists on difference – on the fact

> that every identity is placed, positioned in a culture, a language, a history. Every statement comes from somewhere, from somebody in particular.[31]

Hall was clearly attempting to recast the essentialist signifiers of 'ethnicity', the notion, for instance, of any authentic or 'true self', alongside the apparently contradictory insights of a pluralist poststructuralist position, in order to make the boundaries of the term and its possible significations more permeable. In short, he was attempting to make 'ethnicity', and the wide range of communities and people it referred to, mean differently. One of the central elements of this was to recognize that the person 'who speaks and [he/she] who is spoken of, are never identical'.[32] As such representations were clearly formulated within language itself (whose shifting signifiers have always been open to flux and constant renegotiation), it followed that cultural identities, too, were fluid, defined as much by differences within sameness as by surface similarities, whether of colour or supposed cultural affiliations.[33] Hall's insights were further fuelled by the belated acceptance amongst postmodernist critics that the historic experiences of displacement and diaspora already lived by many of Britain's black and Asian population – the need to exist within what Paul Gilroy has termed the temporal dislocations and double consciousness of a black modernity – were, in fact, generally representative of the uncertainties of a postmodern and post-imperial age. Thus not only had the 'margins' moved to what has been called the 'frontline',[34] but as Kureishi puts it in *The Buddha of Suburbia*, the figure of the 'immigrant' becomes the physical sign and symbolic trope of late twentieth-century modernity, a professional mutator, the 'Everyman of the . . . century' (p. 141).[35]

We have already witnessed in previous chapters the fact that 'hybridity', whether we accept contemporary definitions of it or not, can take many forms and be expressed through a variety of different narrative solutions. Moreover, it is worth remembering, as Robert Young has shown in his book *Colonial Desire: Hybridity in Theory, Culture and Race* (1995), that the notion of the 'hybrid', so popular now in contemporary critical discourse, was not a new one. It had clearly been pivotal to a number of debates in the nineteenth century which focused on race and miscegenation, and was even a part of the vocabulary of how the Anglo-English at times described themselves. What is significantly different in its contemporary usage, argues Young, is the fact that questions of cultural hybridity in the postwar years became inextricably and almost obsessively focused on colour as a visible sign of racial difference. And this narrowing of the focus on to questions of colour was accompanied by the pressing need to disentangle the positive elements of cultural admixture and cultural fusion from an often exclusionary nationalist rhetoric of racism. Thus the more negative associations of the history of the term – associations which linked it to repressed ideas of colonial desire, miscegenation, and the dilution of cultural purities – were cast off by critics in an effort to rename that condition of 'blackness',[36] as Rushdie describes it in *The Satanic Verses*, which once was viewed with scorn. As Young says:

> Hybridity . . . works simultaneously in two ways: 'organically', hegemonizing, creating new spaces, structures, scenes, and 'intentionally' diasporizing, intervening as a form of subversion, translation, transformation . . . Hybridization as creolization involves fusion, the creation of a new form, which can then be set against the old form, of which it is partly made up. Hybridity as 'raceless' chaos by contrast, produces no stable form but [instead] a radical heterogeneity, discontinuity, the permanent revolution of forms.[37]

Despite the obvious attractiveness for contemporary critics of the more utopian versions of hybridity as 'organic' fusion,[38] or the politically reassuring notion of an intentional subversion of dominant forms, the idea of the 'hybrid' has also met with significant opposition. This is partially due to the fact that the widespread usage of the term began to lose any real specificity in terms of the actual histories of the migrant communities to which it referred.[39] In addition, in attempting to highlight what Kureishi signals at the opening of *The Buddha of Suburbia* as a 'new breed of Englishman', it has inadvertently shrouded some of the very differences within apparent sameness that it wanted to distinguish. This has been particularly apparent, as we shall see later, as far as questions of gender and class are concerned. Furthermore, in employing 'hybridity' indiscriminately as a universal concept, there is a danger of failing to recognize that the particular histories of specific writers and their individual locations determine the nature of the way they write, whether inside or outside the hybrid space.[40]

II

This section will focus on the background and context to a number of works by Asian British writers which were first published during the 1980s, and which attempted to chart a new territory. It seeks to discover new co-ordinates by which to write the uneven map of Englishness through Asian British eyes. Whilst migrant writing, as we saw in the previous chapter, had 'pushed the critical establishment' to identify voices of the international cosmopolitans as one of the 'most significant forces' of the eighties, 'smaller revolutions', less concerned with 'genre and classification', were taking place in England.[41] For it was at this time that a new generation of Asian Britons began to turn to the lived realities of their own lives as the subject matter for their fictions. The potential of 'diaspora' discussed in previous chapters, therefore, becomes differently inflected and modified in this still emerging genre of Asian British writings. These works are concerned, less with the search for geographic or cultural 'roots' than with a series of discrete navigations across the frontiers of race and class in Britain. Situated between what we might call a politics of belonging and a politics of location, these novels portray *local migrations* which seek to explore new 'routes'[42] for maintaining and domesticating 'the other within', the dynamic of the still 'unstable equilibrium'[43] which characterizes the dual heritage of many Black and Asian British lives. For these writers, as Caryl Phillips implies in the epigraph to his bleak novel of Caribbean migration, *The Final Passage* (1985), an epigraph which ironically (re)cites a passage from T. S. Eliot's poem 'Little Gidding', 'History is now and England'.

It is regrettably not within the scope of this chapter to elaborate on the many suggestive correspondences which, of course, exist across the fictional landscapes of the Black and Asian diasporas in Britain. Clearly, the central concerns of a number of black writers such as Caryl Phillips in *The Final Passage* (1985) or Joan Riley in *The Unbelonging* (1985), and later Diran Adebayo in *Some Kind of Black* (1996) or Andrea Levy in *Every Light in the House Burnin'* (1994), can be closely identified with those of a number of their Asian British contemporaries.[44] But it is important to note that in all cases, whilst many of these writers have followed on from and share literary and cultural links with the earlier generation of writers, they now write Britain from within the ' "racial" dialectic' of an Englishness which is their common home – 'the nation's inlaid "other" and yet endemically own history'.[45]

Stories, it has been said, never end but continue somewhere else, and following the furore caused by *The Satanic Verses* affair, John Berger's observation that 'Never again will a story be told as though it were the only one'[46] is an apposite one. The stories of the so-called 'second generation' of Asian Britons had of course already been written long before the appearance of Rushdie's novel and not only in contemporary works such as Farrukh Dhondy's pioneering collections of short stories set amongst the working-class black and Asian communities in *East End At Your Feet* (1976), and *Come to Mecca* (1978), or in the many anthologies published by women writers, *Charting the Journey* (1988), *Right of Way* (1989) and *Watchers and Seekers* (1987), many of whose authors are now well known.

Despite such antecedents as Aubrey Menen, Sam Selvon, Kamala Markandaya and their early explorations of living within what would now be called a 'hybrid' identity, Ravinder Randhawa's *A Wicked Old Woman* (1987) is arguably the first *explicitly* Asian British novel.[47] Unlike Kamala Markandaya's historic and haunting novel of Asian immigrant life, *The Nowhere Man* (1972), which dealt primarily with the harsh realities encountered by first-generation immigrants from the 1930s to the 1960s, Randhawa's novel focuses in the main on the lives of a younger generation of female characters, for whom return – whether literal or metaphorical – is no longer an imaginative possibility or aesthetic solution. It is worth noting here that the category 'British Asian' only came into general political currency with the Commission for Racial Equality's general recommendation in 1988, that peoples of Asian origin resident in Britain would no longer be classified as 'black', a recommendation which sought to replace the 'counter-politics of racial solidarity' common in the 1970s 'with one of ethnic pluralism'.[48] Hanif Kureishi's first novel, *The Buddha of Suburbia,* followed Randhawa's three years later in 1990, and gained wide critical acclaim in the aftermath of the commercial notoriety of his screenplays *My Beautiful Launderette* (1985) and *Sammy and Rosie Get Laid* (1988).

Many other works have subsequently appeared which write the Asian presence in Britain through what Prafulla Mohanti once called 'brown eyes'.[49] These include: David Dabydeen's *The Intended* (1991) and *Disappearance* (1993), Farhana Sheikh's *The Red Box* (1991), Atima Srivastava's *Transmission* (1992), Rukhsana Ahmad's *The Hope Chest* (1996), Meera Syal's *Anita and Me* (1996), Bidisha Bandyopadhyay's *Seahorses* (1997) and, of course, Kureishi's more bleakly rendered portrait of an Asian Britain in his second novel *The Black Album* (1995), written in the aftermath of the Rushdie affair, and in some of Kureishi's short stories collected in *Love in a Blue Time* (1997). Yet Randhawa and Kureishi's early novels were particularly significant in their pioneering and groundbreaking attempts to map out a new territory for the representation of the diversity of Asian British lives. Importantly, too, these two early texts by Kureishi and Randhawa can be seen to derive from what might appear at first glance to be opposite ends of the diasporic continuum.

When, for instance, Randhawa's novel initially appeared, it gained little critical notice, and was soon consigned to the literary 'ghetto' as a predictable apprenticeship novel of ethnic becoming from The Women's Press, penned by an unknown Asian woman writer.[50] Kureishi's text in contrast, was more readily taken up by mainstream critics as an innovative, if 'ethnic' *bildungsroman*, an alternative version of the social realist 'condition of England' novel, familiar from the works of David Storey or Alan Sillitoe. Alternatively, it was seen as exemplary of mainstream postcolonial concerns, a counter-discourse penned by one of the 'empire within' which, through its interrogation of both Western and Eastern intertexts, cast a different light on familiar Anglo-Indian versions of cultural admixture. Kureishi's central protagonist in *The Buddha of Suburbia* was most commonly received as emblem of a new kind of Englishman, the acceptable and upwardly mobile 'herald' of a 'hybridity'[51] that could easily be accommodated within the now increasingly post-imperial and fractured heart of 'Englishness' itself.[52]

The different critical reception of these texts, as we shall see in the discussion which follows, was not only indicative of blinkered readings by critics keen to stay within the predictable parameters of fashionable critical orthodoxies, but also reflected at times the difficulties experienced by many of these writers in breaking away from the labels of previously assigned racial and cultural stereotypes – whether of sectionalism, assimilation, the 'ghetto' or the 'exotic'. The double-edged qualities of diasporic consciousness discussed in previous chapters were therefore translated within the context of Thatcherite Britain, to re-emerge as a number of apparently antagonistic versions of community politics – the minoritarian and/or the ethnic, the majoritarian and/or the xenophobic – although, as has often been observed, such strategic positionings often displayed similar discursive fields, where ' "Englishness" as "ethnicity" is the forever receding vanishing point of "blackness" as "race" '.[53]

As any bibliographical survey will reveal, the majority of Asian British novels published during this period were by women.[54] Yet their works were frequently eclipsed by the cultural politics and reviewing practices of the publishing industry, which tended to sideline those 'ethnic' voices that did not fit the fashionable trends of a neo-orientalist exoticism. Thus while David Lean's *A Passage to India* was heralded as a film classic, or Rushdie's Booker prize-winning novel *Midnight's Children* could be acceptably seen as representing the 'voice of a continent', Hanif Kureishi's popular film *My Beautiful Launderette,* set amongst the Asian and white working-class communities in South London and transgressing a whole series of sexual, racial and class stereotypes, was condemned by the English press as representing 'sick scenes from English life'.[55] And this expression of critical double standards applied as much to the traditionalist voices of the Asian communities, outraged by Kureishi's iconoclastic portraits of Asian Britain, as it did to the establishment mainstream. Whilst Kureishi managed to leapfrog the 'ethnic' label, as well as the vehemence of the more traditionalist sectors of the Asian community, by deliberately setting himself up as an 'English' and not an 'Asian' writer,[56] the virtual invisibility in critical discourse of the writings of a large number of Asian British women was revealing. For like Kureishi, whom Rushdie explicitly applauds for breaking out of the 'brown man's burden',[57] treating his 'black and Asian characters in a way that white writers seem very rarely able to do, that is . . . as fully realized human beings, as complex creatures, good, bad, bad, good',[58] writers such as Suniti Namjoshi,[59] Leena Dhingra, Ravinder Randhawa and Meera Syal were all attempting in their early fictions to articulate a similar agenda, if from a different perspective.

Many of these writers were either linked to the Asian Women Writers' Workshop, a collective founded in 1984 by Ravinder Randhawa, or first published by small presses such as The Women's Press or Virago. These presses had come to birth in the early 1970s in the wake of the feminist movement. Furthermore, the enormous commercial popularity of Black Women's writing as a saleable commodity in the USA had encouraged publishers to give space to the retrieval of black and Asian women's histories in Britain, with a view to setting up a similar market in the UK. It was surprising in this context – given the general explosion of literary and theoretical interest in im/migrant and hybrid narrative forms, as well as the pressing need voiced by Black British cultural theorists in the 1980s, to deconstruct static models of ethnicity and gender – that little attention was paid to their works. In fact, Suniti Namjoshi's suggestive fable, 'The Blue Donkey',[60] like Leena Dhingra's essay, 'Breaking Out of the Labels', both highlight, at an early stage, the difficulties of attempting to write from within the limited creative spaces and prison house of an already prescribed language, whether determined by race or by conventional notions of gender and sexuality. As Dhingra puts it:

> I first came to this country nearly thirty years ago during which time I have fallen into, fitted and resisted a number of multifarious labels from: a girl from India, an Indian girl, a coloured, a Paki, a black, a wog, an Asian and recently graduated to becoming a member of an ethnic minority . . . Recently when I was asked to give a talk as an Asian woman, I

found myself reflecting more on what to say to fit the label than what to say to fit my own person.[61]

Dhingra was not only voicing the now familiar dichotomy of how to write from within the confines of such a restricted space, but also pointing to the negative effects which literary ghettoization can impose on imaginative freedom. For whilst the critical agendas of Western poststructuralism had opened up productive spaces for some voices of the Asian diaspora in Britain, they closed doors for many others which did not fit so neatly into its agenda. Moreover, in favouring the heroic and transgressive articulations of hybridity common in many migrant narratives, it left those with a differently articulated or more local and socially realist agenda standing in the same spot.[62]

I am not attempting here to set up a reductive antagonism between the migrant and cosmopolitan aesthetic of writers such as Rushdie versus the local articulations of those writing Asian Britain from the supposed 'ghetto' – a restaging of the familiar conflict between 'theory' and 'empiricism', or theory and the authentic voice of the 'native informant'.[63] As we shall see later, the texts themselves subvert any such neat categorizations, but it is worth noting that in order to gain full critical visibility, these writers not only had to negotiate the prescribed markers of their racial difference in Britain, but also had to deconstruct the flattening effects of a theoretical discourse which homogenized rather than distinguished the different constituencies from which their fictions derived. As bell hooks puts it:

> It is sadly ironic that the contemporary discourses which talk most about heterogeneity, the decentred subject, declaring breakthroughs that allow recognition of Otherness, still direct their critical voice primarily to a specialized audience that shares a common language in the very master narratives they claim to challenge. If radical [theories are] to have a transformative impact, then a critical break with the notion of 'authority' as 'mastery over' must not be a rhetorical device. It must be reflected in habits of being, including styles of writing as well as chosen subject matter.[64]

A number of critical 'labels' have currently been attached to this growing body of work by Asian British women writers which both constrict the potentiality of its visions and mark it off conveniently from the traditional postwar Anglo-English novel in which, as Suresh Renjen Bald has observed, citing George Orwell's essay 'Marrakech', 'people with brown skins are next door to invisible'.[65] Thus terms such as the now popular 'post-immigrant', 'second generation', or the 'ethno-English novel',[66] currently abound as descriptive categories for these works, and point in their proliferation to the difficulties of avoiding a seemingly inevitable restaging of the exclusionary rhetoric of nationalistic discourse in literary reviews. Such terminologies also highlight the urgent need to discover a critical grammar that can move beyond and open out a flexible space for the diverse subjectivities caught beneath such confining representations. For these writers, as Randhawa's character Kulwant so clearly enunciated earlier, are both *British* and *Asian* and deliberately inhabit a range of differently staged identities along a shifting spectrum which defines the particular histories of their individual lives. They are not caught between, in a state of never-ending becoming, but strategically invent a series of alternative locations, as a means to assert both their presence, and their difference from Anglo-British lives. As Meena puts it in Meera Syal's novel, *Anita and Me*, a largely autobiographical work set in the fictional landscape of Tollington, a northern, working-class mining community: 'I knew I was a freak of some kind, too mouthy, too clumsy and scabby to be a real Indian girl, too Indian to be a real Tollington wench, but living in the grey area between all categories felt increasingly like home' (pp. 149–50). Thus, rather than glorifying the 'immigrant movement' as a mode of perennial liminality, 'the diaspora self' seeks in these fictions to 'reterritorialize itself and thereby acquire a name'.[67]

Before we move on to a detailed examination of the novels themselves, it is worth considering briefly the ways in which literary discourse had itself served to reinforce stereotypical representations of 'Asians' in the years when many of these writers were growing up. For such already prescribed conceptions still linger on today in terms of how the fictions of these writers have been received. Despite a long and now well-documented history of the construction of the untrustworthy 'Asiatic' in colonial discourse, there is, perhaps unsurprisingly, a remarkable absence of the presence of Asian Britons in postwar Anglo fiction. 'When he (and it is always a male) does make an appearance he is presented either as a lovable overgrown child or as being respectfully silent. Ironically lurking behind these images is the fear of miscegenation.' Furthermore, as Bald's thorough survey of the invisibility of the Asian presence in British fiction has also demonstrated, the emphasis by Anglo writers in the years after the Second World War (and he includes such figures as Barbara Pym, Margaret Drabble, Jeffrey Archer, John Mortimer, Denis Potter, Kingsley Amis and

Anthony Burgess) was primarily on changes in the British class structure, but ignored completely the 'diversity introduced . . . by the racially and culturally different immigrants'.[68] In many of these novels, it is the black or Asian immigrants who become flattened by default into the new underclass. Such representations were not of course so far removed from the stereotypes, already common currency in the received political rhetoric surrounding the Immigration Acts;[69] and the accepted currency of such caricatures was of course heightened by the inflammatory language of Enoch Powell's and Duncan Sandys's infamous speeches in the late 1960s, recorded in Hanif Kureishi's early diaries, and fictionally dramatized in the violent burning of Srivinas's home by his long-term white neighbours in Kamala Markandaya's *The Nowhere Man* (1972).

Describing his childhood memories of growing up in the 1960s and early 1970s as one of the only 'Asian' boys in his school, Kureishi has commented on the difficulties of both coming to terms with an alien image of himself as a 'Paki', as well as having to negotiate an adolescence in a cloying South London suburb riven by class and social inequalities, where it was said 'that when people drowned they saw not their lives but their double-glazing flashing before them' (*Buddha of Suburbia*, p. 23). Yet it was a Britain of which he was a part:

> Parents of my friends, both lower-middle class and working class often told me they were Powell supporters – I was desperately embarrassed and afraid of being identified with these loathed aliens. I found it almost impossible to answer questions about where I came from. The word 'Pakistani' had been made into an insult. It was a word I didn't want used about myself. I couldn't tolerate being myself.[70]

Moreover, Kureishi's disassociation from his own image was so extreme that, when he first wrote his autobiographical account of this history in *The Rainbow Sign*, he was unable to place himself as subject of his own history, to write his own story in the first person.[71]

The memories Kureishi records are familiar ones to the majority of writers who grew up in Britain during this period. Ravinder Randhawa, who came to Britain at the age of seven with her Punjabi family, grew up under what she has called a sentence imposed by the naturalistic equation of gender, culture and race in British society, experienced first at school and later as the first generation of her family to go to university. Similarly, Meera Syal, who like Kureishi was born in Britain, has emphasized the need she felt as a child to constantly construct strategies for survival, to make up stories, even tell 'lies', as a means of creating a differently mirrored space, a space which could enable the ironic possibilities of 'double-entendre' and comedy to explode prevailing stereotypes. As her adolescent narrator, Meena, puts it in *Anita and Me*: 'The gap between what is said and what is thought, what is stated and what is implied, is a space in which I have always found myself.' There was a need therefore to create more room for manoeuvre, to discover a means to write the histories of Asian British lives and to exorcise the repetitive discourse of victimhood frequently attributed to the history of their presence. As Syal puts it later, when Meena attempts to place herself centre stage within her own narrative in order to contest and re-angle the previous dominance of her white friend Anita's story: 'I'm not really a liar, I just learned very early on that those of us deprived of history, sometimes need to turn to mythology, to feel complete, to belong.'[72]

As we have already seen, the literary voices of the Asian diaspora in Britain derive from a variety of different histories, and emerge from a number of diverse subject positions. They are both local and international at the same time. Moreover, the specific backgrounds of individual writers, and the nature of their various aesthetic practices, have been determined not only by a colonial or postcolonial relationship to Britain, but also as a consequence of issues of class and gender within, as well as a range of other cultural and linguistic factors. Whilst it might initially appear to be an easy and natural progression to move in this chapter from Rushdie's 'love-song to our mongrel selves' in *The Satanic Verses*, to a discussion of works by a younger generation of writers engaged in a parallel, if less visible, process of writing and redefining 'Englishness' in the late 1980s, the transition is not as simple or as seamless as it first appears.

As novels such as David Dabydeen's *The Intended* clearly illustrate, a work which charts the adolescence and early manhood of an 'Asian' boy from the Caribbean growing up in South London, the process of attempting to forge a system of alternative signs, by which to deconstruct the limiting strictures of a monolithic discourse can also lead to death. David Dabydeen, like Sam Selvon and V. S. Naipaul before him, writes Britain from an Indo-Caribbean perspective. Well known for his interventions into canonical versions of 'Englishness' in his critical and creative works, Dabydeen, in this first novel, attempts to examine the process of how to unwrite the mythologies of an already prescribed discourse.[73] In contrast, however, to the fictions by Kureishi and Randhawa, which will be discussed in the final section of this chapter, Dabydeen's novel retains a link with a past elsewhere, through the counterpointed childhood memories of the protagonist's

Grandmother in Guyana, a creolized voice, which sustains him in his attempts to move away from the prescriptions of both his race and class in Britain. More importantly however, the solutions Dabydeen posits for his narrator (whose story Dabydeen has compared to that of a fictional biography of the young V. S. Naipaul) are bleak ones, and result in his dubious assimilation at the end to a temporary refuge provided by the literary towers of Oxford.

Despite what appears to be a pessimistic conclusion, and one that seems only to repeat the familiar pattern of colonial mimicry, the novel also attempts on a number of levels to interrogate and dismantle such a reductive process. Yet the main figure in the book, who attempts to inscribe himself differently, literally burns off his skin and dies as an act of resistance to the negative effects of the images which frame him. Joseph, a black Rastafarian and friend of the Asian narrator, is portrayed, like the narrator, as a poor and underprivileged artist as a young man. As both *alter ego* and foil to the narrator's inflated colonial and canonical desires, Joseph's illiterate but visionary voice disrupts what would otherwise appear to be a seamless passage. However, whereas the narrator manages to escape from the confines of the 'Asian' urban jungle he shares during his schooldays, along with the unsalubrious and commercial exploits of his contemporaries (Shaz, the British born Pakistani, who has never seen the subcontinent, and the Gudjerati-speaking Patel), Joseph is unable to achieve the artistic freedom he desires. Yet it is Joseph's death, his confrontation with the nothingness which has defined his sense of being black in Britain, which enables the narrator finally to recognize that it is only through shifting the shapes of language and the deconstruction of its already established cultural and racial signifiers, that new meanings can perhaps be born. For, in contrast to the narrator, who significantly remains unnamed throughout, and whose literary consciousness has been largely determined through the conventional routes of what Dabydeen himself has called 'book-learning and technical competence', it is Joseph who is the 'genuine poet'.[74] And it is also Joseph who constantly returns to haunt the narrator as a recurring symbol of his repressed but frustrated creative desires, the shadow of his 'dark' self. As he says, soon after he has learned of Joseph's death:

> I take up a pen and begin to write in the broken way that he [Joseph] spoke . . . I write in a fit of savagery, marking the page like stripes. I think of the agitation of his mind as he emptied the can of oil over himself, shaking the last drop out, as I now rattle and shake my mind for expression.[75]

It is not possible here to do justice to the complexities of Dabydeen's novel, which hovers perilously on the edge of being and nothingness, survival and disappearance,[76] in a courageous attempt to unpack the discourses of modernity and its discontents signalled by its title, which derives directly from Joseph Conrad's novel *Heart of Darkness*. But I mention it here for two reasons. First, it is what we might call a transitional text, and relates both backwards to those narratives of migration and exile discussed in earlier chapters – to which it demonstrably, like many of Dabydeen's other works, bears an explicit intertextual relationship – as well as forwards to the Asian British novels set entirely in Britain, which are the subject of this chapter. But most significantly, it points to the fact that living amidst the contradictions of class and race, which define the realities of the hybrid spaces of the black and Asian diasporas in Britain is a journey which as yet remains fraught with difficulties, difficulties which are in many ways still unresolved. The voices of the new generation of Asian British writers of the 1980s should perhaps be seen to represent less a 'symphony' of polyphonic voices, celebrating the utopian possibilities of hybrid fusion or transcultural relocation for a new generation of Asian Britons, than what has been called an 'atonal ensemble'.[77]

III

The final section of this chapter will focus on Ravinder Randhawa's *A Wicked Old Woman* and Hanif Kureishi's *The Buddha of Suburbia*. At first glance these works can be perceived to derive from opposite ends of the diasporic continuum. Yet whilst Randhawa and Kureishi voice different versions of the Asian British story, in the context of the turbulent period of social change that characterized British society in the lead up to the Thatcherism of the 1980s, many of the questions their characters are forced to address are similar ones. The precise dating of Randhawa's novel is less clearly marked than that of Kureishi's (which closes, as Karim tells us, just before the General Election in 1979), although Kulwant's school years clearly take place just before Karim's in 'the pre-time to Beatle-time', the period when it was not yet 'chic to be ethnic' (p. 16). Both novels therefore locate themselves at a specific moment in 'British' history, the period of the 1960s and 1970s, and dramatize the difficult and inherently contradictory experience of living in what Randhawa has called the 'racist divide'.

The various journeys which these novels depict do not, however, seek to authorize or validate any one position. Instead, they illustrate that heterogeneity is the norm in any community, whether white or black, 'Asian' or 'English', and that differences between various groups are often as closely allied to issues of class as they are to race. As Shanti, one of Randhawa's older characters, puts it in *A Wicked Old Woman*, 'our children believe that by rushing into the English life they will leave behind all the Asian problems. When will they realise it's only an exchange? An English set of problems for an Asian set' (p. 38). Or as the white suburbanite figures of Charlie or Eva his mother illustrate in *The Buddha of Suburbia*, the need to relocate and redefine one's social and cultural location is not just a preoccupation of the 'immigrants' or their children. Like Karim, or indeed Haroon his father, who learns to survive in England by adopting the pose of a fraudulent spiritual guru, becoming the Buddha of the novel's title, Eva's obsession with the exotic potential of Haroon's culture-sell – the commodification of his 'otherness' for those lost in the spiritual desert of white, middle-class suburban society – represents a similar passage as she tries 'to scour [the] suburban stigma right off her body' (p. 134) by marrying Haroon and reinventing herself later in the city as a *nouveau arrivante* artiste. Similarly, Charlie, who becomes Karim's half-brother, dons the persona of a fashionable icon of pop culture, a working-class punk hero, who can flagrantly display his 'Englishness' in the USA via his false adoption of a cockney accent.

When Karim goes out to meet Charlie in the States, he comes to the realization that, however seductive Charlie's use of pop culture has been in his desire to break out of the conventional moulds of his suburban past, his particular form of iconoclasm is just another version of a saleable exoticization, an invented identity which does not differ significantly from Karim's father's fraudulent pose as 'a renegade Muslim masquerading as a Buddhist' (p. 16). For after 20 years of existence as an Anglophile Indian, surviving the prejudices of white society via the route of assimilation, Haroon, like Charlie, is keen to cash in on the marketability of a new, prepackaged identity. As Karim says, describing Haroon's rehearsals for his entrée as spiritual voyeur: 'He was hissing his s's and exaggerating his Indian accent. He'd spent years trying to be more of an Englishman, to be less risibly conspicuous, and now he was putting it back in spadeloads' (p. 21).

Towards the end of *The Buddha of Suburbia*, Karim comes to the recognition that 'home' is not necessarily linked indissolubly to questions of race or origin, but is determined more by an individual's particular location, the place, as he says, 'where you start from' (p. 249). And for both Hanif Kureishi and Ravinder Randhawa, as has already been argued, the *starting point* is in Britain itself, a Britain which comes to be reimagined and reinscribed in their fictions through both Asian and British eyes. Kureishi's narrative begins, so to speak, in the cloying and confining location of a white lower-middle class English suburb, where life was all 'familiarity and endurance', and 'security and safety were the reward of dullness' (p. 8). However, Randhawa's opens with the need for her central protagonist, Kulwant, to step out of the uncomfortable clothes imposed by her past life as an 'Asian woman', who has grown up within the restrictive spaces of an already allocated cultural identity as a member of an 'ethnic' community. Karim's departure from 'The Suburbs' (Part I of the novel) is clearly depicted by Kureishi as a necessary escape from the entrapping securities of a world where he had lived for 17 years holed up behind 'closed doors' (p. 4). In contrast, the second section presents the exuberant and romantic possibilities for Karim of 'the City' (Part II) as perennial 'playground', a 'site not only of appropriation and resistance but of performance, display and artifice'.[78] Interestingly, Kulwant's strategy from the outset of Randhawa's novel is also to step outside, to walk the streets as a means of revisioning and redefining the ethnic geographies of her past life. And whilst for Karim, the city was like a 'house with five thousand rooms, all different', where the 'kick' was to discover 'how they connected' (p. 126), Kulwant is more cautious in her explorations, fearing the fact that such passages into what she calls the 'in between spaces' (p. 104) of the city outside might also cause her to lose her way, to be sliced off by its 'jagged edge[s]' (p. 41). Yet as we see early in the novel, when Kulwant recounts a painful attempt to cast off her identity as the only 'Indian girl' at her school, by entering into a taboo love affair with Michael the Archangel, who 'creams' her as his 'Indian Princess', she was, like Karim, 'avid with hunger to learn, experience and experiment, to step out from her insulated, closed-off home life and dip her feet into the world's whirlpool' (p. 6). Later Kulwant's disguise as the wicked old woman of the novel's title – a homeless, Oxfam baglady – is employed by Randhawa both as literary device, a choric frame to present a retrospective narration of the kaleidoscopic sequences of Kulwant's many past lives and the literal sign of her need to deconstruct any predetermined notions of her authenticity as a representative 'Asian' voice.

In both texts, it is clear that the process of learning to live outside the already defined and known parameters of 'home' – whether as the imposed and familiar stereotype of the culturally divided Asian woman in Randhawa's novel, or alternatively as a semi-assimilated, mixed race suburban boy in Kureishi's work – is not an easy one. A tension between private desire and public responsibility, homelessness and what Randhawa has described as the 'dangerous territory' of the 'hybrid'[79] is the central dynamic fuelling both narratives. 'This country', warns Kulwant's mother, has 'put you in one of its mixers and whirled you round till you can't tell your inside from your outside, your duty from your rights, your needs from your responsibilities' (p. 54). Despite Karim's adolescent and avowed intention to avoid confronting such ethical and political questions in *The Buddha of Suburbia*, Kureishi persistently undermines Karim's hedonistic pursuit of pleasure by presenting a series of other narratives of Asian lives – such as the stories of the radical feminist, Jamila, her traditionalist father, Anwar, and Changez, the figure of her forced arranged marriage – which cast serious doubts on some of Karim's more irresponsible experimentations with a number of invented and constantly shifting personas. Whilst a celebration of cultural indeterminancy may be the means for the assertion of Karim's individuality in the early stages of his career as a professional actor, such strategies for empowerment are shortlived, and cannot fly free of wider issues of social, ethnic and gender classification which determine individual lives. And whilst Karim is keen to display constantly the hybridity which his body signifies, Kureishi often alerts us to the problematics surrounding its literary inscription. The artifice of carnival played out in the novel is therefore not without its serious masks. In fact, Karim lightheartedly voices this dilemma early in the novel, long before he begins to fully recognize the seriousness of its implications: 'Yeah . . . sometimes we were French, Jammie and I, and other times we went black American. The thing was, we were supposed to be English, but to the English we were always wogs and nigs and Pakis and the rest of it' (p. 53).

In a recent interview, Randhawa has said that her writing does not arise from any sense of 'certainty' – whether of race or of gender – but 'out of doubt'.[80] Her work has therefore been primarily motivated by a desire to discover and invent appropriate fictional and imaginative co-ordinates, by which to express the ambivalence of her cultural location as an Asian woman writer in Britain, and also to ask questions about the invisibility of the reality of women's lives in recent narratives of Britain's im/migrant past. In *The Rainbow Sign*, Kureishi has made a number of similar observations on the significance of imaginative vision, the invention of stories as a means of retrieving the painful absences of a past written over in dominant narratives of the nation:

> Stories . . . help me see my place in the world and give me a sense of the past which could go into making a life in the present and the future. This

> was surely part of the way I could understand myself . . . The pain of that period of my life, in the mid-1960s, is with me still. And when I originally wrote this piece, I put it in the third person . . . because of the difficulty of addressing myself to what I felt then, of not wanting to think about it again. And perhaps that is why I took to writing in the first place, to make strong feelings into weak feelings.[81]

Kureishi is referring here, of course, to the alienation he experienced as a young boy growing up in a Britain, where the visible sign of his 'race' bore little relation to the realities of his largely 'English' cultural background. And this was combined with his later need as a writer to inhabit a more broadly defined space than the one allocated to him at that time in English society. Unlike Rushdie, however, who set himself up as an authoritative voice, a spokesman for the writers of the 'Third World', Kureishi has always been reticent regarding questions of his viability as a 'middleman', a representative for Asian British lives. As he says in his authorial note to *Borderline* (1981), 'I wasn't keen on the idea of a project about Asian immigrants in Britain. I was afraid of being asked to write outside my own experience . . . I preferred familiar territory'.[82] And elsewhere, too, he has stressed the dangers of writing only from one location:

> If contemporary writing which emerges from oppressed groups ignores the central concerns and major conflicts of the larger society, it will automatically designate itself as minor, as a sub-genre. And it must not allow itself to be rendered invisible and marginalised in this way.[83]

Although Randhawa's work has often been closely affiliated with precisely the kinds of 'sub-genre' that Kureishi is talking about here, she has consistently expressed a number of similar reservations on the dangers of becoming the symbolic voice of the community. 'If we have a right to be here', says one of her characters in *A Wicked Old Woman,* 'don't we have a right to be human, warts and all?' (p. 105). Not surprisingly, therefore, both Kureishi's and Randhawa's novels focus their attention on the particular histories of individual lives in relation to general questions of representation rather than arguing a case for either a minoritarian or nationalist view of identity politics. They also attempt, albeit in different ways, to explore a series of performative narrative strategies as a means of voicing the diverse counter-histories of their characters – whether white or Asian, first generation or Asian British – who inhabit the hybrid spaces of their multiple homes.

As Mark Stein has observed, the use of the performative as literary device was often employed in Black and Asian fictions of the 1980s to provide a means by which reductive stereotypes of a static ethnicity could be ironically subverted and destabilized. Moreover, the strategic use of such techniques not only provided writers with a means of giving authority to previously marginalized voices, but simultaneously shifted the shapes of the narratives which had hitherto framed them. As we have already witnessed in earlier chapters, the poetics of the fictions themselves and the specificity of their discursive practices often become symbolic of wider processes in the society at large.[84] Thus, whilst both Kureishi and Randhawa may write their stories from within what could be called the general frame of the *bildungsroman* (a widely accepted and traditional genre for 'coming of age' narratives stemming originally from the familiar patterns of a European nineteenth-century and social realist tradition), the form is subverted, re-angled, manipulated and appropriated for their own purposes.

Traditional *bildungsroman* characters usually journey, as has often been illustrated, 'along the authorially controlled lines of a predestined plot, living through a succession of picaresque, but never desultory adventures which result in their accomplished transformation from dubious strays into worthy citizens'.[85] In contrast, narratives such as Kureishi's and Randhawa's, which are set in a postcolonial and diasporic context, can be seen to disrupt the seamless pattern of social integration typical of the genre, whilst simultaneously positing a need to invent an alternative means of inscription and identification. In fact, it is the tension of negotiating a space between the wider society's powers of cultural signification, and thereby recasting the traditional and restrictive 'frame of [the] *Bildung*',[86] that distinguishes, as we shall see, the mosaic-like actions of the characters in both texts, and liberates them from the spaces previously allocated to them by their pre-determined social and cultural positionings. In this context, it is perhaps also significant that both Kureishi and Randhawa have professed a commitment to popularizing the novel form, and making it speak to as wide an audience as possible. Whilst both texts clearly draw on a wide range of references – whether John Masters, Bhowani Junction, or Bonnie and Clyde in Randhawa's work, or Kipling, Flaubert and the history of 1970s rock music in Kureishi's – they refer largely to a familiar and contemporary discursive field, which locates their characters primarily *within* an English code of reference, and one which pertains to the realities of 1960s and 1970s popular culture amidst which both novels are set.[87]

A number of further correspondences can be drawn between the two works. Both Karim, whose nickname is 'Creamy', and Kulwant face the related dangers of exoticization and assimilation by well-meaning white liberals. Both writers propose a number of inventive, as well as defensive, strategies for code-switching between and across the mixed spaces of their individual character's lives. Like Karim's father Haroon, who is rechristened 'Harry' by his mother's working-class white relations, Ted and Jean, many of the figures in Randhawa's text often have to don Anglicized names in order to more easily negotiate the shifting dimensions of their dual identities in the narrow spaces allocated to them within English society, whether as Rani/Rosalind, Kuli/Kulwant, Arvind/Arnold and so on. Similarly, too, both texts seriously critique the perpetuation of a racist discourse in the generation of representative stereotypes, even if produced by well-meaning white liberals such as Shadwell, the theatre director who gets Karim to 'brown up' so as to present a more ' authentic', if totally absurd, image of Mowgli, when he acts the part in Shadwell's production of Kipling's *Jungle Book.* A more disturbing version of this commodification of 'otherness' or the 'exotic' is presented in *A Wicked Old Woman,* when Maya is commissioned to conduct a semi-ethnographic study of the causes of madness in the 'Asian' community by two white TV producers. Keen to receive a packaged piece of research from the 'inside' – the real thing – Randhawa's ironic presentation of the questionable objectives of this TV programme points both to the absurdities of the typecasting involved in such apparently well-meaning projects, and also raises important questions about the complicity of her own position as a writer, the unwilling producer of such images herself.[88] In fact, the guidelines for Maya's research mirror in many ways the difficulties Randhawa herself faced in trying to avoid packaging her novel for the gaze of a white audience keen to read about the Asian British experience. As she says, outlining the producer's objectives for the programme: 'Let's dissect the terrain. Where does culture turn the screws? How does imagination hallucinate the logic and the rational? "Is Asian Madness" ask the hungry producers "the same as English?"' (p. 58).

Both Randhawa and Kureishi are inevitably involved, as British writers of Asian origin, in the manufacture of images by which the lives of previously marginalized communities can be misrepresented or misinterpreted, whether by critics of the right or left, white, black or Asian. And one of the major difficulties that both Kureishi and Randhawa faced in these ambitious and groundbreaking first novels was to avoid becoming symbols of their own 'ethnicity', entrapped through their own representations in the very stereotypes they were attempting to explode. In apparently celebrating what has been called an 'aesthetics of impurity',[89] there was a danger in inadvertently resorting to the creation of allegorical types, and thereby flattening the very figures they were attempting to liberate. In short, both writers faced in different ways the problem of writing both within and outside the burden of representation. As such, there was a need to both distinguish and differentiate the realities of living in the hybrid, without falling into the trap of regularizing its fictional representations into the rigidities of a predictable form.[90] As Kureishi has said:

> You would flatter yourself if you thought you could change things by a film or a play or whatever, but perhaps you can contribute to a climate of ideas . . . It is important to ask questions about how we live sexually, how we live racially, what our relations are with each other emotionally. Asking these questions seems to me to be the things artists can do rather than change society in any specific way.[91]

Not surprisingly perhaps, Kureishi's and Randhawa's novels ask these questions in different ways. And whilst, as we have already seen, there are a number of obvious correspondences between the background contexts informing the two writers' choice of subject matter and theme, these two early *bildungs* ultimately differ substantially in their effects, as well as in the final political implications of their open-ended resolutions. The significance of the issues these differences raise will form the substance of the discussion which follows.

With Kureishi's novel, a literary genealogy can easily be traced back to earlier inscriptions by a number of male writers of a black and Asian Britain. Karim Amir is a professional actor, and like Rushdie's Saladin, and furthermore, in a similar way to Selvon's 'boys' in *The Lonely Londoners*, he represents a picaresque anti-hero who navigates the city, reterritorializing and renaming its spaces. Kureishi also draws, like Selvon, on the use of iconoclasm, polyphony and parodic inversion as means of both appropriating and subverting commonly accepted stereotypes to comic effect. And, like Selvon's 'boys', too, Karim is in many ways an amoral figure, an 'innocent abroad', who identifies himself first and foremost as a *Londoner*, and who inhabits, as John Ball has suggested, 'a cosmopolitan space not fully attached to or detached from either British nation-space or some nationless world-space'. In this sense, Karim's migration, from the outer London *suburb* of Beckenham to West Kensington, can be seen as a *local* version of the international migrations of a whole number of earlier fictions by black and Asian writers who have rewritten the city, 'a miniaturized version of postcolonial migrancy and culture-shock'.[92] And further parallels could be developed. Whilst Karim does not seek to establish a 'half-way house', such as we saw earlier in the case of Naipaul's Ralph Singh – a literary refuge on the outskirts of the city from which he can begin to come to terms with the ambivalences of his colonial past – he is, like Ralph Singh, both semi-attached to and semi-detached from the cultural signs of his hybridized racial body. But unlike the colonial Ralph Singh, Karim (the suburban London boy) is not, initially at least, particularly insecure about his identity. As he says in the oft-quoted opening of the novel:

> My name is Karim Amir and I am an Englishman born and bred almost. I am often considered to be a funny kind of Englishman, a new breed as it were having emerged from two old histories. But I don't care – Englishman I am (though not proud of it) from the South London suburbs and going somewhere. Perhaps it is the odd mixture of continents and blood, of here and there, that makes me restless and easily bored. Or perhaps it was being brought up in the suburbs that did it. Anyway why search the inner room when it's enough to say that I was looking for trouble, any kind of movement, action and sexual interest I could find (p. 3).

In this provocative opening (notably written in the present tense, whilst the majority of the rest of the novel is a retrospective first-person narration), Karim writes himself into English history through what have been called a series of 'British and Indian intertexts'.[93] And, as was apparent in Chapter 4 when we examined the dramatic opening of *The Satanic Verses*, Kureishi, like Rushdie, is clearly making a self-conscious and deliberate intervention into a number of differently angled stories, deriving from both migrant and Anglo versions of English life. Kureishi is, for instance, clearly echoing H. G. Wells here (who as Karim informs us was born in Bromley and believed that English suburbia consisted of 'roads that go nowhere'), as well as a number of postwar fictions which have charted similar journeys of a social or class mobility in what Steven Connor has called the 'condition of England novel'.[94] The opening of the novel also interrupts those bleak renditions of immigrant life dramatized in early Indo-English works such as Kamala Markandaya's *The Nowhere Man*, where Srvinas's leprosy both literally and metaphorically becomes a symptom of his position in society after 30 years in England. Furthermore, K(ar)im's mixed race background clearly signals a generic relationship to a number of earlier Anglo-Indian and Raj fictions, such as Rudyard Kipling's white but 'Indian' boy *Kim*, or the hybrid figure of Hari Kumar in Paul Scott's Raj trilogy; and we could also draw many direct correspondences between Kureishi's and Rushdie's work.[95] However, despite the novel's explicit and implicit affiliations with earlier writings of Britain and India, Kureishi's purpose, is not, as Karim says, to explore the 'inner room' or to constantly display the self-reflexivity of its eclectic heritage. Whilst the novel clearly interrogates and deconstructs a number of familiar colonialist paradigms, Kureishi's concern is less with the construction of what is now perhaps the predictable genre of a multi-layered counter-discourse than with finding an appropriate aesthetic frame to adequately portray the contradictory, and often antagonistic, social realities of Karim's indeterminate cultural location as a suburban 'Englishman born and bred almost'.

The opening of Kureishi's novel has often been cited as a kind of mission statement by those critics keen to stress the celebratory aspects of hybrid fusion. As the physical embodiment of what Homi Bhabha has called the condition of the 'vernacular cosmopolitan',[96] Karim's bold assertion that he is going 'somewhere' does seem at first sight to offer a possible means of circumnavigating and transforming the manichean spaces of a long history of racial exclusion. Yet Karim's apparently confident claiming of a space within the dynamic of a reconstituted English identity, however uncomfortable that space might prove to be, is undercut from the outset by a number of important equivocations, which are further elaborated as the novel proceeds. Kureishi's constant qualifications ('almost', 'some', 'funny', 'here', 'there') in the passage quoted above both point to the protagonist's prevailing anxieties and undermine the extent to which the reader wants to believe Karim's self-declaration. These equivocations systematically erode the reader's expectations as to the extent of the protagonist's supposed progression by the end of the novel: whether from the hidebound discourses of lower middle-class suburban culture, or the various manifestations of racism (both overt and covert) which he encounters as would be lover to Helen (whose father 'Hairy-back' sets his Great Dane on him for attempting to meddle with a nice, white girl) or, later, as the liberal symbol of a neo-orientalism.

Karim's local and intra-national journey can clearly be distinguished from that of Sam Selvon's black Londoner, Moses who, in attempting to relocate himself in Britain, only ever seems to be able to move in a metaphorically presented spiral of reversal from basement to attic and back down again. The youthful protagonist of Kureishi's *bildung* is in many ways similarly thwarted, although the nature of the difficulties Karim encounters stem more from his own refusal to commit himself to any one of the many homes to which he already belongs. In fact, Karim is shown from the start to code-switch across the standard discourses of a whole number of different communities: whether as son to his Pakistani father who maintains, like Uncle Anwar and Auntie Jeeta (Karim's 'second family'), that despite the length of his long sojourn in England, he will remain first and foremost an Indian man; or as bisexual lover to both Charlie and Jamila; working-class nephew to Uncle Ted and Auntie Jean, who can beat up a 'frog' in Calais; be a 'loyal' Indian friend to Changez; or, in various masquerades as a professional actor, play London itself, as much as the theatre world, for what he can get. The city is frequently presented as a metaphor for the theatre in the novel, the means by which Karim's personal quest, as Alamgir Hashmi has observed, becomes a performative correlative for the form of the narration itself. [97]

Kureishi offers Karim a series of multifaceted identities by which to act out his hedonistic desires to navigate the city, and in some senses the novel can be read as a portrait of a postmodern and consumer culture, in which the hybrid as im/migrant *Everyman* sells his wares without ethical or moral responsibilities. And whilst Karim clearly shares his father's philosophy to pursue personal desire as the only route to freedom and happiness, he slowly comes to acknowledge that despite his itinerant credentials as an actor on the stage of the postmodern city, where artifice and play has replaced any credo of responsibility and where if he 'wanted the additional personality bonus of an Indian past, I would have to create it' (p. 213), there is, after all, an important difference between his apparent freedoms. His ability, as he describes it, is to live in five places at once – 'carrying my life-equipment in a big canvas bag' (p. 94), without being attached to any one location, or the concomitant realities of political or moral affiliation. And it is only at a late stage in the novel, when he attends Anwar's funeral (after having appropriated his story as possible material for a play for the champagne socialist Pyke) that he begins to acknowledge any sense of ethical or cultural responsibility:

> I did feel, looking at these strange creatures now – the Indians – that in some way these were my people, and that I'd spent my life denying or avoiding the fact. I felt ashamed and incomplete at the same time, as if half of me were missing, as if I'd been colluding with my enemies, those whites who wanted Indians to be like them (p. 212).

Karim's belated recognition here of the need, perhaps, to take more heed of Changez's warning earlier in the novel not to 'leave his own people behind'

(p. 136), points to one of the central questions which the novel raises but does not adequately resolve, as Karim refuses to commit himself to the realities of any one of a number of possible political perspectives.

Whilst Karim is unconcerned by the exploitation of his 'Indianness' in Shadwell's production of Kipling's *Jungle Book*, a number of other characters warn him of its implications and the relationship between representation and power. Jamila, for instance, criticizes Karim harshly for his amoral involvement in a 'neo-fascist' production, his pandering to white audiences through 'showing off' his 'innocent and young' brown body, as well as reconfirming prejudices and 'clichés about Indians' (p. 157), whereas Haroon is distressed by Shadwell's invoking of colonialist stereotypes, as well as the translation of his son into the farcical figure of a 'Black and White Minstrel'. Similarly, as we see later in his involvement with Pyke, the left-wing radical director, Karim can both be feted for his 'immigrant' credentials whilst also becoming the subject of a political attack by a black actress for his exploitative use of his Uncle Anwar's story for his own ends. As she says:

> Your picture is what white people already think of us. That we're funny, with strange habits and weird customs. To the white man we're already people without humanity, and then you go and have Anwar madly waving his stick at the white boys (p. 180).

These two episodes of the novel, which notably take place within the milieu of the theatrical world, have received a great deal of attention by critics keen to discuss the implications of the relationship between representation and political responsibility, art and politics. However, it is arguable that Kureishi is less concerned with questions about the morality of Karim's supposed collusion with neo-orientalist versions of his 'otherness' than with the ways in which political positionings, whether of right or left, nationalist or pluralist, radical or traditional, can limit individual freedoms. Whilst Karim recognizes that Tracy is keen to present only positive images of the black community (despite the fact, as he declares ironically, that he is 'beige'), and that the conflict was now 'between "minorities" ' (p. 180), his apparently flippant answer to Tracy's plea that 'Truth has a higher value' is suggestive of Kureishi's overall and more serious purpose in the novel, to deconstruct the stability of any such positionings. Thus Anwar's reversion to the role of a traditionalist Muslim father, who forces his radical feminist daughter into an arranged marriage, is satirized by Kureishi both for the hypocrisy his position represents (as he beats his wife and carries on drinking alcohol) and the untenability of any essentialism. Similarly, whilst Kureishi is sympathetic to Jamila, who acts as *alter ego* and voice of Karim's repressed conscience throughout the novel, her politics are also caricatured, as she reads the works of Simone de Beauvoir, listens to the music of Bessie Smith and Ella Fitzgerald, and carries a photo of Angela Davis in her pocket. Yet the agency of Jamila's particular brand of radicalism is also portrayed as a strength by Kureishi when she moves into a commune, and succeeds in translating Changez from traditional and frustrated lover of a failed arranged marriage into a willing househusband.

Kureishi is not, of course, unaware of the serious elements underlying the various postures he satirizes. Clearly, Jamila's predicament is forced on her by the refusal of her father to accept an alternative to his patriarchal discourse. And Changez, like Jamila and like Karim earlier in his life, is beaten up in one of his daily confrontations with racism on the streets. Moreover, we are aware throughout the novel of the ways in which such overt racism affects individual lives. As we are told at the beginning of the novel, neo-fascist groups roamed the streets, 'beating Asians and shoving shit and burning rags through their letter boxes . . . There was no evidence that these people would go away – no evidence that their power would diminish rather than increase' (p. 56). And whilst Karim humorously sends up Jamila's preparations for the day when Asians might be forced into 'gas chambers' (p. 56) as victims of another twentieth-century Holocaust, the lives of Anwar and Jeeta are genuinely pervaded by a fear of violence. Although Karim feels he has escaped such physical threats by his migration away from the suburbs to the more protected location of the chic theatrical world, he becomes increasingly disturbed by the implications of its politics and the hypocrisy of its pretensions. As Karim indicates just after his failed affair with Eleanor in his satirical portrait of a liberal and upper-class English rose:

> we pursued English roses as we pursued England; by possessing these prizes, this kindness and beauty, we stared defiantly into the eye of Empire and all its self-regard – into the eye of Hairy Back, into the eye of the Great Fucking Dane. We became part of England and yet proudly stood outside it. But to be truly free we had to free ourselves of all bitterness and resentment too. How was this possible when bitterness and resentment were generated afresh every day? (p. 227).

It is at this point in the novel that Karim begins to unmask a number of distinctly unattractive elements in the blatant prostitution of his body for both materialist gain and sexual pleasure by Pyke and his radical theatre group. For, like Anwar's regressive shift into the position of a traditionalist Muslim, which Kureishi satirizes for its disingenuousness, Pyke can be seen to be repeating, despite the new camouflage of a left-wing philosophy of cultural diversity, yet a different version of an essentially colonialist discourse in using Karim to represent the acceptable face of an ethnic authenticity. Thus Pyke's 'manipulation' of Karim as ethnic construct, as Bart Moore-Gilbert has convincingly argued, 'develops [not only] into sexual exploitation', but 'effectively and economically symbolizes how a (neo-)colonial mentality underlies western radicalism's desire to help give voice to or liberate the oppressed'.[98] The hybridity of the figure Karim attempts to represent within the urban 'jungle' of London's agit prop world is therefore consigned once again to the figure of 'native'. His apparent liberation is contained within the very same binaries he was trying to escape in his passage away from the more overt displays of racism he had encountered in the suburbs. It would seem, then, that Karim has become caught up in what Sara Suleri has described as the repetition in contemporary discourse of the 'familiar' and imperialist 'category of the exotic'. For, as she says, recent 'rereadings of colonial alterity' in contemporary discourses 'too frequently wrest the rhetoric of otherness into a postmodern substitute for the very Orientalism that they seek to dismantle'.[99]

As the novel draws to a close, we become increasingly aware of both Kureishi's and Karim's inability to bring the narrative or the questions it raises to a resolution. Unlike Jamila and Changez (whom he regards as the only real family he has), Karim has not really progressed, either in his political thinking or in dealing with the anxieties expressed at the opening concerning the ambivalence of his cultural location. Whilst Karim is clearly not afraid to signal his racial difference, unlike Allie his younger brother, who chooses the arguably easier path of an unproblematic assimilation, it is difficult to see how Kureishi's courageous confrontation with the issues raised by Karim's deliberate donning of the costume of 'hybridity' can fully resolve the political issues of representation which the novel constantly dramatizes. And whilst, as we have seen, questions of mimicry and performance apply to white and Asian characters alike in a world where no values seem to be stable, Karim appears at the close not, in fact, to be 'going somewhere', but instead to be sitting on the fence, caught between a number of conflicting discourses. Whilst we might read his position as one which is *en route* to a recognizably postcolonial consciousness as he comes to recognize the full political implications of the power relations that have determined his cultural location, Kureishi does not posit such a neat conclusion.

In fact, the understated tone of Karim's final summation at the end of the novel only points, in many ways, to a repetition of the questions Kureishi has dramatized throughout. And it forces the reader inevitably to question whether the very contingency of the novel's transparent structure, its flagrant replacement of the notion of 'development' with a discontinuous and fragmented novel of 'episodic renewal',[100] is, in fact, part of Kureishi's message. If this is the case, Karim's conclusion can be read as a somewhat pessimistic one:

> I could think about the past and what I'd been through as I'd struggled to locate myself and learn what the heart is. Perhaps in the future I would live more deeply . . . I thought of what a mess everything had been, but that it wouldn't always be that way (p. 284).

And although Karim, like Sam Selvon's character in his well-known short story and love-song to London, 'My Girl and the City',[101] celebrates the romanticism of his location in 'the *centre* [my italics] of this old city that I loved' (p. 284), we wonder how far Karim has really moved from the predicament of Selvon's 'boys' in *The Lonely Londoners*, and whether the kind of narrative solutions that Kureishi proposes in this early novel can, in fact, provide an empowering frame for the political realities of his characters' lives.

Like Kureishi's *The Buddha of Suburbia*, Ravinder Randhawa's *A Wicked Old Woman* examines the contradictions of both living in Britain and making a 'home' in the hybrid. However, Randhawa begins her kaleidoscopic, flashback narration from a different perspective, the voice of a middle-aged Asian British woman, the daughter of immigrant parents, who has already lived out several lives in Britain. Whereas Kureishi's Karim, as we have seen, celebrates the fluidity of his multiple identities, and wears his difference like a costume which he can take on and off whenever it suits him, Randhawa's character Kulwant is more sceptical from the beginning about the ultimate effects of such performances. In fact, as a figure, Kulwant can more easily be aligned to Jamila in Kureishi's novel, both in terms of her political consciousness – her awareness of the causes and effects of stereotypical representations – and in her desire to explore a radical means to effect change both within and outside the community of Asian women around whose lives the novel is largely set.

Inderpal Grewal has suggested that whilst 'home' has often been constructed as 'the original site of nationalism', it can also be profitably read as the locus of feminist action, 'since it is here that women can resist nationalist formations by rearticulating them as a site of struggle rather than of resolution'. She also argues convincingly that such struggles are not only articulated in the 'so-called peripheries' (the colonies), but in those 'contact zones' which exist within the heart of the 'metropolis itself'.[102] Whilst Grewal is primarily concerned in her study *Home and Harem: Nation, Gender, Empire and the Culture of Travel* with exoticized constructions of the 'harem' in colonialist discourses, it is both possible and suggestive to read Randhawa's *A Wicked Old Woman* through a similar lens. For one of the main objectives of Randhawa's novel is to relocate the still lingering boundaries, in a 'post-imperial Britain', of similarly constructed nationalist myths of the im/migrant Asian woman as *victim* or exoticized 'other'. She thus translates the essentially xenophobic construction of the ethnic 'ghetto' or 'community' within Western metropolitan discourses into an active space for female agency, enabling a more three-dimensional representation of Asian women's lives. Ironically, then, the 'harem' as exoticized space, the prohibited home for gendered 'otherness' in colonialist discourse, is evoked once again by Randhawa's novel, but in a different context, within the terrain of the postcolonial metropolis itself.

The notion of the 'harem' as ghetto reappears in several ways in the novel, whether through the tunnel-vision view of a whole series of limiting stereotypes of the culturally entrapped and passive Asian woman, or through comparably restrictive geographical and discursive spaces available to them as they attempt to live their lives outside such narrowly defined binaries. And whilst Randhawa appears, as Sharon Montieth has perceptively noted, to be dealing like Kureishi with an urban setting, the landscape that she depicts functions more as an objective correlative for her character's 'mentalscapes' than as any easily recognizable physical space. As Montieth also notes, 'walls function' in the text as 'conceptual barriers' between the individual characters themselves – as we see in Kulwant's relationship with her daughter-in-law Shirley, who is kept out of her life with a 'wall-like dislike' (p. 91) – as well as acting as symbolic metaphors for the compartmentalizing effects of a number of patriarchal discourses, whether of East or West.[103]

The process, then, of attempting to mark out a new discursive territory in *A Wicked Old Woman,* as Randhawa frequently illustrates, is a complex one. For life, whether lived *within* the strictures and behaviourial codes of the supposed 'community', or *outside* in the as yet unmarked 'hybrid' spaces of the city, threatens to drive many of her characters such as Rani/Rosalind, or even Kulwant herself, to desolation or even 'madness'. And this continuing sense of an uncertainty in navigating the city is heightened by the fact that Randhawa deliberately avoids 'concretising her context'.[104] Unlike Kureishi, Rushdie or Selvon, Randhawa does not attempt to reterritorialize the physical geography of the city through a renaming or mapping of its places; instead, what becomes crucial in *A Wicked Old Woman* is a process of psychic reorientation, the creation of differently conceived imaginative spaces, through the slow accretion and inscription of a number of previously unheard stories of women's lives.

Unlike Karim, Kulwant is initially hesitant about stepping outside the boundaries of her traditional role as willing participant in an 'arranged marriage' and motherhood. These are personas Kulwant wilfully adopts, like Jamila in Kureishi's novel, as a means of avoiding falling between what Randhawa has called elsewhere the 'holes in the diasporic net',[105] where 'the framework of life' is so 'loose people [may] lose their way' and 'flounder between the spaces'(p. 102). Kulwant is shown initially to be casting off the uncomfortable clothes of her various 'ethnic' personas, strategically adopting the role of a homeless Oxfam baglady, who can traverse the streets of the city weaving a pattern of memory across her various past lives – whether as friend to Caroline, whose Englishness, as she says, should not be confused with England, or as reluctant member of a number of 'Asian' centres which, like postcolonial reincarnations of 'Frankenstein', are 'patched together with the flotsam of travel posters, batik work . . . traditional embroidery, cow bells' (p. 31). However, she comes to recognize that using disguise as a means of evading the pains of her experience of her identity as split rather than 'hybrid', cannot adequately address the political causes of her cultural (dis)location. As she says: 'No more trying to walk in the middle. There were too many pot-holes and she was like a blind woman without a stick. Safer to stay in the territory she knew' (p. 29).

Although Kulwant comes to recognize that the apparently safe spaces within the community are equally as constructed as any other identities she might choose to assume, her early attempts to negotiate between a misplaced sense of duty and the parallel need to develop a sense of independence and agency are dramatized within a context which 'floated in space without history to anchor the location of a future, to give it guiding reassurance' (p. 17). And when Kulwant's arranged marriage (which she goes into against the better judgement of her parents) predictably fails, Randhawa makes a telling comment on the difficulties of survival in Britain. The situation is summed up, as Lyn Innes has suggested, in Kulwant's parting exchange with her husband, who has left her for another woman:

'I never thought my life would be split like this. I didn't marry in order to separate.'
'Another one of England's gifts.'
'It's not England. It's what's wrong between us.'
'How can you tell the difference?' (p. 61).

Randhawa, like Kureishi in *A Buddha of Suburbia*, starts off from the premise that identities are not fixed, that they are open to reinvention and reinscription. And through the powerful opening image of attempting to paint a bindi on a Russian doll, Randhawa provides us both with an illustration of the ways in which multiple selves can be caught beneath a familiar exterior, as well as pointing to the possibilities of art as a form of political empowerment, a means perhaps of transforming the fixed face of the doll's exterior.

The kinds of faces that Randhawa sets out to redraw in her novel are shown in two early chapters which deal with episodes from Kulwant's past: 'Kuli's Cover-Up' and 'Kuli's Double-Up'. Here Randhawa deliberately contrasts what have been described as two familiar, but opposing stereotypes of the Indian which are common in Western discourse, 'the poverty stricken recipient of European hand-me-downs, the Oxfam Indian, an old and crippled victim', and an 'older British image . . . the Oriental princess'.[106] As we also saw in Kureishi's novel, Randhawa is keen to suggest the complicity of the paradoxical relationship between these two images, both through Kulwant's relationship with Michael, who attempts to win her as the exotic 'Mata-hari of his Heart' (p. 6), as well as in her retreat back into precisely the kind of cultural stereotype she was initially attempting to escape from, the arranged marriage, 'that special feature of [Indianness] emphasized by Europeans as the mark of difference and unacceptability'.[107] The predominant image of Kulwant in her transformed state as a homeless 'urban nomad' is therefore not one of empowerment, but one of instability, as we see from the refrain that frames the narrative of many of the stories that she recounts: 'Stick-leg-shuffle-leg-shuffle. Stick-leg-shuffle-leg-shuffle' (p. 2). And as Kulwant moves about the city in an attempt to reconstruct her past, we see that the ground, to echo the title of Salman Rushdie's novel, is not firmly beneath her feet. And whilst Randhawa clearly intends to satirize comically the image of the im/migrant woman as victim, the point is nevertheless a serious one, and contrasts dramatically with the image of Karim at the opening of *The Buddha of Suburbia,* who feels he can confidently claim a 'new' space within a variety of indeterminate contexts.

Randhawa's text then is situated *within* a closely-knit urban community of 'Asian' men and women, who carry the history of Kulwant's past life. However, as Kulwant frequently shows us, these characters derive from a widely diverse range of backgrounds and histories. Ammi, for example, comes to England after her husband but finds, when she arrives, that he is already involved with an English woman. Unlike Kulwant, Ammi does not have either the educational or psychological resources to cope on her own in England, and it is her two eldest daughters who partially assimilate and take on the role of supporting the family. Similarly, Kurshid and Big Sis differ from many of the younger characters in the novel, such as Kulwant's brother Parminder who also goes by the name of Pauli, or Arvind/Arnold, Kulwant's son, in that they are not unduly disturbed by issues of belonging.[108]

Whilst Randhawa, like Kureishi, marks the differences between the attitudes of the first and second generations, she also points to a number of class and educational variations. Whereas, for instance, Arvind marries Shirley, a white working-class English girl, Anup his brother is described as being a member of what Randhawa euphemistically calls the 'D.E.A.D', the buppie class of Asian social climbers (doctors, lawyers, accountants and dentists), who prefer to follow the path of invisibility, living out their lives with minimal resistance in order to get on. It is important to note that in Randhawa's novel, the 'community' as such is not linked through any cultural or historical nexus, whether of background or religious group, gender or generation, but through the personal relationship many of the characters bear to Kulwant's past and future life. And if there is any cohesive bond between the characters, it is created more by an awareness and acknowledgement, that develops as the novel proceeds, of their common predicament and *presence* as 'Asians' in Britain rather than by any political or cultural consensus.

Importantly, however, many of these characters are engaged in different ways in attempting to inscribe the realities of their presence in Britain. Kulwant's son Anup is writing *The Invisible Indian* (p. 99), Maya's ideas are appropriated by her lover in his Asian farce *Laying the Blame,* and Satwant Singh writes his version of the diasporic story in his 'notes on the life and "British" histories' of the people who come to his club (p. 155). And ultimately, of course, Maya the Myopic, as Patricia Duncker has pointed out, 'writes her own screenplay, where the community is gathered together, to tell their story to the small white screen and to the reader of Randhawa's text'.[109]

Interestingly, *A Wicked Old Woman* cannot be easily placed in terms of any literary antecedents or models. For, in contrast to *A Buddha of Suburbia* which, as we have seen, bears some relationship to an earlier and largely male tradition of im/migrant writings of Britain, Randhawa is unable to slide 'easily into a novelistic form conducive to her purposes', for there is 'no well-honed genre', as yet, 'that will sustain the characters and the ideologies she seeks to represent'.[110] And it is in this context, in the need to invent a fictional mode that can both represent and take possession of the previously unwritten stories of her female character's lives, that the experiences of Rani/Rosalind come to be pivotal for Kulwant, who learns that donning the disguise of a homeless outcast is no long-term solution, either for her or the group as a whole.

Like many of the characters in the novel, Rani/Rosalind has a dual identity, but unlike Arvind/Arnold or Parvinder/Pauli who manage to survive both within and outside the community, Rani runs away and assumes the life of a vagrant, living anonymously in desolate bed-sits and squats. Her escape into what she calls 'anonymity', a space where she can 'breathe and live' (p. 138), is a path which she feels will release her from a predetermined future as an ethnographic symbol of cultural division, the 'Asian' woman in Britain. It is also, however, an attempt to circumvent gender divisions in the society at large where, as she says, even amongst the English a woman 'is still nothing except her spot of blood, her vaginal passage. Judged by who she's with rather than what she is' (p. 123).

Rani's story, together with her subsequent voyage into a state of psychological instability and desolation, creates a number of significant political reverberations as the novel proceeds. In one sense, as Randhawa implies, her journey is just one of many others, a familiar version of the stereotypical narrative of cultural conflict created in media representations of the *problems* of the 'Asian' community, as yet another second-generation Asian girl leaves the strictures of 'home' to escape the confines of her past. Yet whilst Rani is able initially to disappear and to cast off her ethnic origins, her body remains open for exploitation. After a dramatic episode where she kills her flatmate Rosco who attempts to rape her, Rani retreats completely from society, and is rediscovered by her grieving mother and the rest of the community, lying in hospital staring blindly into space, literally refusing to shut her eyes.

The figure of Rani acts as an important framing device throughout, and brings many of the other women's narratives together at the close of the novel. More importantly, however, her healing, which results from the literal 'massaging' of stories 'into her body'[111] by the collective efforts of the whole community, who individually recite parallel narratives to her as she slowly regathers her consciousness, can be seen to be a significant political act. For it is through the collective vigil engendered by the telling of these stories that Kulwant abandons her persona as a crippled old woman and, with Caroline, Ammi, Angie and Maya, nurses Rani back from the edge of madness. Significantly, too, as the accretion of stories – the individual histories of the different character's lives – begin to infiltrate into Rani's consciousness, the community itself begins to visualize the possibility of growth and the creation of an alternative space to represent the contradictory realities of their existence.

If the ending of *A Wicked Old Woman* posits the ghetto as a hybrid space, a location situated outside the confining boundaries of either an essentializing nationalism or the patriarchal institutionalization of questions of gender, Randhawa also illustrates, unlike Karim in Kureishi's *The Buddha of Suburbia*, that it is only through the collective efforts of the community (however mixed that community may be) that significant changes will occur. Unlike Karim, who at the close of Kureishi's novel regrets that he, as an individual, has not lived more deeply, the politics of Randhawa's Kulwant are more mature. As Big Sis says at one stage in Randhawa's novel: 'Forget fiction. Real life is where the drama lies' (p. 79). And whilst it may well be the 'British . . . who have to learn that being British isn't what it was', as Kureishi suggests in one of the epigraphs to this chapter, such transformations in ways of seeing also have to be precipitated by changes in ways of thinking. And these changes, as Randhawa demonstrates, have to be generated as much from *within* Asian British lives as from a desire to construct counter-narratives of the 'nation'. The healing power of the community does not lie with its ability to generate fantastic and nostalgic illusions of a past lost, but with its capacity to participate instead in the transformation of the present, and the generation of more subtly nuanced modes of representation. Thus if the ending of *A Wicked Old Woman* celebrates the need, in its closing words, for 'ACTION' (p. 207), it is an action which can only be achieved through the women's communal engagement with and participation in the images of their own representation where, as we see in the making of Maya's documentary film, they can both confront media stereotypes of themselves as the passive, ethnographic inhabitants of Britain's ethnic communities, and simultaneously present themselves to British society on their own terms.

To conclude: it would seem that the solutions posited by both Randhawa and Kureishi in their respective first novels are difficult ones. And whether one takes the essentially postmodernist and pluralist route of embracing 'hybridity', as we saw in *A Buddha of Suburbia*, or alternatively attempts, as in *A Wicked Old Women*, to open up and deconstruct perceptions of the supposed 'ethnic ghetto', the journey is a precarious one. Furthermore, as I have already suggested, both writers have had to face the difficulty of not only confronting the question of the politics of their different representations, but of evolving appropriate fictional strategies to carve out new discursive spaces for the articulation of the diversity of Asian British lives. And whilst many narratives of an Asian Britain have subsequently appeared (including a number of filmscripts, such as Gurinder Chadha's *I'm British But* (1989), Meera Syal's *Bhaji on the Beach* (1993), or the recent comedy *East is East* (1999)), Kureishi's and Randhawa's first novels were particularly important in breaking the ground for others to follow. Kureishi's subsequent novel, *The Black Album* (1995), of course represented a further shift in his position as he attempts to deal with the consequences of the Rushdie affair head on. His vision in this novel, as has frequently been observed, is bleaker and less optimistic than in *A Buddha of Suburbia*.[112] Moreover, he was clearly aware, like Randhawa, of the dangerous effects of cultural misrepresentations and the appropriation of the power of representation by other voices, as we see in his short story 'With Your Tongue Down My Throat', where the power of the telling is wrestled away from the Asian voice of the story's subject. If, as Kureishi has frequently argued, it is 'the white British' who have to change, then the question of who is speaking and to whom is paramount. In attempting to write the local histories of individual Asian lives, Kureishi and Randhawa in their early fictions have not only opened up new spaces for the representation of the heterogeneity of the diaspora *within* Britain, but have also translated previously static notions of 'home' or 'abroad', 'native' or 'immigrant' into a series of differently conceived possibilities situated within the contested terrain of 'Englishness' itself. 'Home' in these Asian British fictions therefore can no longer be a *single* place, but represents instead a series of *locations*, an imaginative ground fertile for new improvisations. And if the characters that Randhawa and Kureishi explore in their respective fictions stem from a series of very different histories, they clearly share similar struggles. As bell hooks aptly puts it:

> At times, home is nowhere. At times, one only knows extreme estrangement and alienation. Then home is no longer just one place. It is locations. Home is that place which enables and promotes varied and everchanging perspectives, a place where one discovers new ways of seeing reality, frontiers of difference.[113]

6

Birds of Passage: The 'Rooms of Memory' in Romesh Gunesekera, Sunetra Gupta and Aamer Hussein

In my father's house are many mansions
Gospel according to St John[1]

Literature, like all living art, is always on the move. It is part of its life that its . . . form should constantly change
V. S. Naipaul[2]

Survival in fact is about the connections between things
Edward Said[3]

The island, to be fruitful, can never be intact. It is traceried by water, overflown by birds carrying seeds
Gillian Beer[4]

How does one write 'home' from a house full of mirrors? In this chapter the focus will be on the narrative poetics of making memory 'home' in the fictions of three distinctive and post-Rushdie voices of the 1990s. In our readings of these writers, it is important not only to examine the nature of what is remembered and what is forgotten, but also to consider the means by which the questions raised *en route* open up new cycles of resistance, alternative ways of writing, reading and *living* the world. For it is through a journey into the incommensurable spaces within memory itself that these writers enact individual passages, which can no longer be sustained by the recognition of any easily identifiable or firm boundary lines whether of tradition, language, place or time. In so doing, the sounds of their voices echo like those of migrant birds, whose perennial flights into other skies mark and name the permeable boundary lines of those im/migrant histories which have always existed, to evoke the title of Paul Gilroy's most recent study of 'homelessness' and diaspora, 'between camps'.[5]

All currently resident in Britain, these writers are of a similar generation to Hanif Kureishi and Ravinder Randhawa discussed in the previous chapter. However, their concerns are less with the need to open up the geography of Asian Britain than with a desire to explore the difficulties of writing the past, once the familiar contours of 'home' have gone. As such they share a preoccupation with the representation of an interior landscape of desire, a longing to enter the symbolic as a narrative journey not only defined by the border cartographies of a diasporic history, but, rather, as an active and ongoing process of negotiation with the present. Romesh Gunesekera was born in Sri Lanka and moved to Britain in 1972 after a brief period in the Philippines. Aamer Hussein, of a similar generation, was born in Karachi in 1955, and spent his early years and adolescence moving between Pakistan and India, migrating to London with his family in the 1970s. Like Gunesekera and Hussein, Sunetra Gupta travelled widely in her youth, being educated in several languages, and living in a variety of locations, whether in Calcutta, East Africa or the USA. Like Hussein, she has retained strong affiliations with the multicultural and cosmopolitan traditions of her subcontinental background, where, as a descendant of what she has called the 'ancient Bengali diaspora' – a diaspora internationally renowned for its literary eclecticism – she does not feel that either her bilingualism or her cultural mobility is anything new.[6] In seeking to write 'home' from a series of multiple locations, both within and outside Britain, the fictions of these writers represent a new and, as yet, largely unexplored aspect of contemporary migrant writing in Britain.

In contrast to Hanif Kureishi and Ravinder Randhawa, whose early writings (as we saw in the last chapter) exposed the racial and ethnic straightjackets borne by existing in the 'here and now' of Asian British identities, these writers focus less on an examination of the politics of place – an interrogation of the ambivalences inherent in their individual cultural locations – than on a gathering of the present through a rearticulation and reworking of the process of 'making memory' itself the subject of fiction.[7] These narratives construct a poetics of diaspora in which return is no longer possible, and the filters of fragmented memory no longer provide an untroubled or celebratory route to an 'imaginary homeland'. Instead, the multiple layers of a diasporic subjectivity are inscribed through a precarious journey into the gaps within the symbolic realm of discourse itself, where writing becomes the 'territory of loss and memory' and the act of narration enables the possibility of a '*re-turn* to selfhood through [a] dialogic and interrogative encounter', that is both a confrontation with an 'internal/external other' as well as the 'site' of an existential and 'unfulfilled journey home'.[8] Reflecting a shift in tone that has been called a 'changing of the seasons',[9] the subject matter of these fictions inadvertently directs the reader's gaze away from the 'giganticism'[10] and panoramic scope of the so-called 'India' novel of the 1980s, to a more inward contemplation of the problematics involved in writing the diasporic stories of individual human lives, lived through the eruptions of private memories in a variety of differently imagined geographies. Although echoes of home are still discernible in these texts, the lines of their cultural and linguistic parameters constantly shift as their chimeraic contours flow in and out of other landscapes, other histories, which reconfigure and disrupt the longing for such *stable* anchorage points.

On the closing page of Romesh Gunesekera's haunting and elegiac novel *Reef*, Mister Salgado warns Triton that 'we are only what we remember, nothing more . . . all we have is the memory of what we have done or not done'.[11] *Reef*, published in 1994 and short-listed for the Booker Prize, is a delicately shaped novella whose major preoccupation is as much with the fragments of memory, the recollection and naming of things past, as about Sri Lanka itself, the beleaguered 'island' where it is set during the 1960s to 1980s, a period of brewing political, ethnic and religious turmoil. Like Mister Salgado, Triton, Gunesekera's narrator, now lives in London and shares with his old master and mentor what he calls a 'refugee' existence, separated both from history and a 'far-away house of sorrow' (p. 190). But whereas Ranjan Salgado, a marine biologist, returns to the island after several years in Britain, summoned by a desire to hold on to a lost dream and the memory of a lost love, Triton, his one-time adopted houseboy and a culinary artist (whose assumed name of course echoes that of the sea-god of ancient mythology), remains behind. Alone in London, an orphaned figure, 'without a past, without a name', he remains committed to survival and transforms his makeshift existence by an alternative dream: to turn his small snack shop into a Sri Lankan restaurant and become a restauranteur in Earl's Court.

Despite the frames of its specific locations – whether in Salgado's house in Sri Lanka or in London – the predominant image in the novel is one of flux, as the vagaries of individual lives, the mixed histories of this 'teardrop' island (a 'salt' dot off the subcontinental mainland) are threatened and encroached upon by an all encompassing sea. It is a sea that may sweep up and scatter the debris of history, yet enables individuals to reconstruct themselves anew, by giving birth to a world revisioned and remembered by the force of the imagination. Whilst it is a force that destroys (as we watch the *paradisaical* barrier reef of the island being ransacked and depleted for economic gain), it is also a force, as Gunesekera demonstrates, that binds and frames experience, linking the two worlds of London and Sri Lanka in Triton's developing consciousness, a space where ideas can 'flow freely', as stories and memories germinate like seeds and migrate from one mind to another.

On a trip with Salgado to Wales before his departure from Britain, Triton wonders if the sea there, 'shimmering between . . . black humps of barnacled rocks . . . snuffling and gurgling', is the same as the 'coral-spangled south coast back home', if all the oceans of the world 'flow one into the other' making and unmaking the stories of diasporic histories – whether here or there, if we are not 'all refugees from something? Whether we stay or go or return' (pp. 182–4). Gunesekera's answer in this novel would appear to be not dissimilar to that intimated by Gillian Beer in the epigraph above. For although Beer, in her influential essay on modernity and Virginia Woolf, is referring to the necessary deconstruction of a different 'Island story' – one set amidst the cultural and nationalist myths of Fortress Britain as the inviolable and 'safe' home of Empire in the period immediately following the First World War – the narrative of Gunesekera's later and postcolonial 'island story' can be read not only in similar terms, but also sets up an implicitly radical dialogue with the landlocked binaries of a colonialist historiography.

The lines from Shakespeare's *The Tempest* ('Of his bones are coral made'), which preface the novel, signal Gunesekera's broad metaphysical concerns: a preoccupation with the effects of the passage of time, of loss, and the role of the imagination in the transformation of individual human lives. Yet the novel's location, at a particular moment of political turbulence in recent Sri Lankan history, unobtrusively extends the metaphor of the universal permeability of the human body to that of the colony and the newly independent island nation, which is riven within and without by internal contradictions and ethno-political conflict. The reef of the novel's title becomes, then, a suggestive metonym for forces not only of irreparable human loss, but also of connection and reconstitution, creating a palimpsest of a diasporic history built on the remembered stories of individual lives, which mutate and transform like the polyps on the Sri Lankan reef. 'You see', says Mister Salgado at one point:

> this polyp is really very delicate. It has survived aeons, but even a small change in the immediate environment – even *su* if you pee on the reef

> could kill it. Then the whole thing will go. And if the structure is destroyed, the sea will rush in. The sand will go. The beach will disappear. That is my hypothesis. You see, it is only the skin of the reef that is alive. It is real flesh: *immortal*. Self-renewing (p. 58).

As Gunesekera is keen to show us, the umbilicus of language, symbolic vessel of the human imagination, is like the skin of the reef itself, a delicate container not necessarily punctuated by arrivals or departures, or by willed acts of physical emigration or immigration, whether from the histories of diasporas lived within or imagined outside his native Sri Lanka. It is, rather, a fluid terrain defined by the 'sea in our loins' (p. 182), a space which calls, as Iain Chambers has put it, for a 'dwelling in language', rather than in 'place', where the shifting boundaries of time and geography enable the creation of migrant histories and identities that are 'constantly subject to mutation'.[12]

Gunesekera's creation of a home in language has been read cynically by some as the evocation of yet another 'imaginary homeland', a luxury enabled by migration, and sustained by a writer distant through residence in Britain from the political realities of his homeland. However, as will be evident later, it is less productive to read Gunesekera's work as a romantic or nostalgic attempt to come to terms with the *loss* of a *homeland,* or the parallel need to generate fictional forms of imaginative *return*, than as a sensitive unravelling of the ways in which the discontinuities of time past and time present constantly collapse spatial and temporal boundaries, creating, as T. S. Eliot once put it, a 'still point' in a 'turning world'.[13] It is a point, however, which for Gunesekera has multiple anchorages, whether historical, cultural, religious or linguistic. In addition, it exists on a perpetually shifting axis, caused by a narratological desire to constantly reshape, whilst at the same time exposing, the inevitable and perhaps intrinsic fictionality of all 'homes'. 'Home', then, is expressed as much by a mental geography as through the representations of a physical landscape; the writing process itself becoming an 'intrinsic attribute of home'.[14]

Although this process may be intensified by the mixed cultural heritage and 'double time' (to use Homi Bhabha's phrase) of Gunesekera's diasporic location – as a Sri Lankan who has lived in Britain since 1972, and who now sees himself as a British writer – the question of location, as he has frequently pointed out, is not the major issue. What is more significant is the mode of the telling and the discovery through fiction of voices and tones, moods and landscapes, of a language which can shift and re-angle the material realities of the present, whether 'here' or 'there', still leaving the many unresolvable questions of life open. As Gunesekera has explained, 'for me' writing is 'a bit like making a sculpture. It's only through writing that you discover a way of seeing the world, a *way of living* if you like.'[15] The Sri Lankan setting of many of the stories in *Monkfish Moon* (1992), or his rewriting of the island from a different perspective in *Reef* (a preoccupation which reappears, despite the London base of the narrator again, in *The Sandglass* (1998)) is not 'necessarily a physically real place, but [rather] the imaginative equivalent of all those other places that you can go to without moving your feet'.[16] And whilst it may still be convenient for contemporary critics or literary historians to 'talk of how stories are located in places' – searching for signs of cultural authenticity or racial identification – the 'best stories', says Gunesekera, are not necessarily located anywhere; rather, there are 'invented' and sometimes recognizable 'places' that 'exist in them'.[17]

Gunesekera's artistic vision may be read by some as a Sri Lankan version of a now-familiar late twentieth-century and postcolonial tale of disappointed love, where the process of writing provides a 'shelter' allowing 'space to that which otherwise would be hidden, covered over, crossed out, mutilated'.[18] Yet, his 'island' stories do not only figure a migrant sensibility built solely on a desire for an imagined return, a homesickness bred by separation from a natal homeland. Instead, they vividly dramatize the difficulties of imposing a false historiography on the discursive discontinuities of diasporic lives, an experience which also needs to account for the complex task of representing the past 'in and through its very displacement'.[19] Moreover, as Gillian Beer has argued, 'islands' – whatever their particular geographical locations or cultural and historical contexts – have always been innately permeable, open to change. As she explains: the word 'island' – as seductive symbol for an imagined nation[20] – is itself an intrinsically unstable one. For 'isle', as the *Oxford English Dictionary* tells us, in early Middle English usage meant 'watery' or 'watered'; 'land' was added later 'to make a compound: "is-land": water-surrounded land'. Water and land, continents and islands, colonies and histories of Empire are thus, Beer suggests, implicitly interconnected, not so much mapped by linear or imperialist cartographies, but 'overflown by birds, carrying seeds'.[21]

Narrative (whether ancient or modern, oral or literary) has always, of course, been a form of travel, a passage through time and space signalling movement like the poetic metaphors which are its frame, whether literally dramatizing a journey from one place to another or exploring a voyage inwards, into the country of the past, the landscape of another's mind.[22] Similarly, the idea of translation (whether literal or metaphorical) and its accompanying signifiers in the recent grammar of contemporary postcolonial discourse – which emphasize, as we have seen in earlier chapters, transition, crossings and the transformation of identities – was a notion already embedded in the heroic tales of migrancy and exile characteristic of ancient classical epics (whether of East or West) as well as in the mixed cultural and linguistic sources of canonical 'English' works such as Chaucer's *Canterbury Tales* or many of Shakespeare's most famous plays.[23] As we see, too, in Derek Walcott's late twentieth-century epic *Omeros* (1990), a long poem which revisions the migrant geography of Homer's *Odyssey* from the perspective of the Caribbean diaspora – the 'new Aegean' as Walcott calls it – such literary voyages, whether of the past or the present, have always involved an architectural process of rebuilding, rewriting and rememoration, the construction of a *poetics of home*. Of course, the difficulty in this is that the ancient power of narrative to transform – to change our 'ways of seeing' can be exploited in very different ways depending on who is doing the telling: whether through an agenda (as has often been the case in the past, or even currently in an age of decolonization) for national reclamations, or alternatively as a potentially fertile image (frequently used in a postcolonial context) of the cross-cultural fluidity of contemporary diasporic histories.[24] As Edward Said persuasively argued in *Culture and Imperialism* (1993):

> no one can deny the persisting continuities of long traditions, sustained habitations, national languages, and cultural geographies, but there seems no reason except fear and prejudice to keep insisting on their separation and distinctiveness, as if that was all human life was about. Survival in fact is about the connections between things . . . reality cannot be deprived of the 'other echoes [that] inhabit the garden'.[25]

By the mid-1990s, a general scepticism was evident in Western critical debates concerning questions of nation, memory and history. This scepticism was partially fuelled by the growing popularity of poststructuralist and postmodern theoretical strategies to open up the buried heterogeneity of *les petit récits* concealed within the supposedly homogenous 'grand narratives' of the past.[26] For writers of the South Asian and black diasporas, however, the dismemberments created by a colonial and postcolonial history took on a greater significance. David Dabydeen, for example, amongst many others of his generation, graphically illustrated the need to redress and reconfigure the imposed silences of the past in his much-applauded long poem *Turner* (1994),[27] a work which focuses on the sea as trope for both the potential of diasporic transfiguration and the birth pains of a historic amnesia. Taking Turner's famous painting 'Slavers Throwing Overboard the Dead and the Dying'[28] as its point of departure, Dabydeen's poem highlighted the submerged head of a black slave who had been 'drowned in Turner's (and other artists) sea for centuries'. Dabydeen's ancestral slave, a figure who is metaphorically reborn in this poem, attempts initially to give voice to a newly imagined and idyllic homeland, but his romanticized vision is constantly frustrated by already being placed and 'named' within the remembered remnants of a too 'grievous' history. Yet Dabydeen's later exploration in the poem of a vision of hope for the slave's diasporic descendants is a powerful hymn, not only to the potentiality of contemporary im/migrant *survivals*, but also to the future patterning of '[c]hronicles which will write the world through different eyes'.[29] As the magician figure Manu, holder of the secrets of the tribe, prophesies:

> . . . in the future time each must learn to live
> Beadless in a foreign land; or perish. . . . Each
> will be barren of ancestral memory
> But each endowed richly with such emptiness
> From which to dream, surmise, invent, immortalise.[30]

As was the case with Gunesekera's novel *Reef*, Dabydeen is drawing here on the sea as a creative repository for the diasporic imaginary, a space which exists both *within* and *outside* the geographical, temporal and spatial frames of a linear historiography, a sea which opens a passage to the vision of other skies.

Interestingly, the imaginative exploration of such connections as a means to open up the 'faultlines' of the West's selective remembrance of things past began, by the end of the century, to represent a new departure in the works of a number of other writers of the black and Asian diasporas, whether in Britain or elsewhere.[31] As Bharati Mukherjee, for example, was to suggest in a short story, the movement of the planet's tectonic plates as a form of 'continental drift' could be read as a suggestive metaphor for the cultural collisions and dislocations of the contemporary experience of the Asian diaspora.[32] Moreover, this idea has recently been taken up by several critics keen to find new ways of defining the transnational links which exist between, and across, an increasingly large body of international diasporic writers. Such links, however, also stem from the very nature of narrative itself which, as an ancient form of migration, has always generated an 'interdiscursivity';[33] a means of cross-cultural travelling, creating translations, rewordings, reworldings, rememberings which revise and frame the world anew. As the author-narrator of Aamer Hussein's short story, 'Skies', explains:

> we all, probably . . . live in three rooms at once: the room of memories, the room of dreams and the room of the chore-laden, work-burdened present . . . Being a migrant is something like that . . . only more complex, because we inhabit not only these three rooms but about as many houses too: but our continuities are broken and even words play games with one another as memories suffer the distortions of other languages.[34]

It has often been argued that all narrative is a form of memory, a means of giving shape and substance to a past lost, combined with the possibility of envisioning new 'homes' within an imagined future. Moreover, within what today has been called a 'postcolonial genealogy of modernity',[35] memory has been seen not only as a route to historicizing the past, but also as an active agent, a participant in making audible the voices of previously buried and displaced histories. As Tim Middleton and Peter Woods suggest when referring to Toni Morrison's influential novel, *Beloved*, 'contemporary writers rely increasingly on scenes of recollection, witness and amanuensis to represent historicism in action' and memory is 'assumed' to be a presence in the 'making of history'.[36] Moreover, in texts where time and space is not so much 'recovered . . . but brought into being, invented, made and unmade', the reader's role is an integral part of the cultural poetics.[37] For the relationship between reader and writer is often an interactive one, a memorial process which expands perception, crossing temporal and spatial boundaries to enable an engagement with a broader and less narrowly defined 'public . . . space'. The reader is actively engaged then, like the writer, with the processes of narrative formation and rememoration, looking forward and backward, not necessarily travelling to a potential destination, but instead to an awareness of the irreducibility of a discontinuous and heterogeneous past.[38] Within the realm of contemporary diasporic fictions, such a journey acquires

> the form of a restless interrogation, undoing its very terms of reference as the point of departure is lost along the way. If exile presumes an initial home and the eventual promise of a return, the questions met with *en route* consistently breach the boundaries of such an itinerary. The possibilities of continuing to identify with such premises weaken and fall away.[39]

This is not to suggest that questions of cultural identity and/or regional affiliation are no longer important concerns in these fictions. As will be demonstrated, in the analysis which follows of *The Sandglass* (1998)[40] by Romesh Gunesekera, *The Glassblower's Breath* (1993)[41] by Sunetra Gupta and selected short stories by Aamer Hussein in *Mirror to the Sun* (1993) and *This Other Salt* (1999), the voices of all three writers clearly derive from their individual cultural backgrounds and histories. However, like those early writers such as Mulk Raj Anand and Attia Hosain whom we discussed in Chapter 1, they articulate both a 'local' and a quintessentially 'international' sensibility. It is a sensibility which may stem from a specific location, but which nevertheless creates an imaginative facility to live freely in the 'world at large'.[42]

The individual works of these writers vary markedly in terms of style and approach. They all, however, rehearse the difficulties in moving beyond the already prescribed contours of a narrative of reclamation, and draw attention to the complexities of rehabilitating the aporia of a post-colonial present, once the familiar call of 'home' is gone. As Aamer Hussein illustrates in the title story to *This Other Salt,* as he depicts Sameer's abortive attempts to first write a 'ghost story' and then a memoir after arrival back in Karachi, the lost city of his dreams:

> I wrote about the city by the sea . . . Of home as a forgotten song, a shared language, common consummation like bread. I wrote about my longing for another tongue, a mother tongue, the language of my longings: liquid, whispering, sibilant. I suppose by the time I reached its end I knew the call of home was gone. I had written about a Karachi that was lost, that I had left twenty-five years ago, and then I was looking for light again. But my book ended with images of all my cities on fire . . . I knew I couldn't keep grieving for that contagion (p. 17).

What Hussein is pointing to here is the need above all to move outside the seductive trajectory of forever dwelling on the fractal frames of a lost past. This is a process he sees as crucial to releasing the wings of the diasporic imagination from a mental geography set up by a repetitive recycling of the binaries inherent in the migrant condition. Interestingly, Hussein had already hinted at the dangers of journeying into such literary alleys in his first collection *Mirror to the Sun*,[43] which explores the difficulties not only of cultural displacement and rehabilitation, but of existing between the signs and cultural slippages of a number of different linguistic and epistemological systems. As he reminds us in several of the stories, the act of writing 'home', whether via narratives of 'emigration' or 'autobiography', constitutes a form of 'infidelity'; furthermore, each 'letter' home, whatever its ostensible shape, can now only be like 'a message in a bottle, a paper boat crossing uncharted spaces, eternal darkening oceans, never to reach the shore' (p. 228).[44]

This sense of embarking on an uncharted journey into the interior world of memory and language itself describes the creative impetus lying behind much of Hussein's fiction. For, as he tells us in the title story to *Mirror to the Sun*:

> You leave behind a land to make a home elsewhere, or cheat on a friend to tell the true story of a life. It's like holding up a mirror to the sun – catch as much light as you can, *celebrate the absence* [my italics] of the real thing. The lost and beloved object of the telling is gone, become a reflection of leaving, a fading trace of first words written in love and faced with absence (p. 210).

Whilst Hussein's quest could be seen in some respects to echo the example set up by V. S. Naipaul in *The Mimic Men* and *The Enigma of Arrival*, he is not caught within the essentially colonialist frame of Naipaul's 'anxiety of influence'. Instead, he begins, like many others of a later generation, from the confident possession of an inherently bicultural and multilingual background. It is a background which starts from the premise of a 'rooted cosmopolitanism',[45] a cosmopolitanism already inherent in the vernacular traditions on which he draws.[46]

The majority of the 13 stories collected in *Mirror to the Sun* are narrated in the first person, and for many of Hussein's characters, it is through the process of writing that a tension between a past lost and a current state of displacement is resolved. Frequently, as we see in 'The Colour of a Loved Person's Eyes', 'Karima' or 'Mirror to the Sun', Hussein's 'letters home' are inscribed less through an overt depiction of the diasporic dismemberments of Partition, which is their subtext, than through the transferred articulation of a language of desire, a longing which is often figured by a particular individual's sense of frustrated and unrequited love. Thus, for the narrator in 'Mirror to the Sun', two love objects, La and Layla – one from his adolescence and the other reincarnated in his twenties – become the illusory objects of a desire, transient surrogates for a 'homeland' lost, embodying the realities of a quest which can never be fulfilled. Interestingly, such figures disguise several other enforced translations taking place, as the narrator's insatiable yearnings are interwoven with memories of the lost syllables of Urdu, his mother-tongue. As he tells us, 'La' is a sign for nothingness, 'an absence'; 'Sometimes I feel I've identified myself with that name: I'm a sign of negation' (p. 231). Interestingly, Hussein is playing here on the double signification of 'La', a word which means 'No' in Arabic but also has a religious resonance in being the first syllable of the Muslim credo, 'there is no god but God (*la illa ha ill allah*)'.

Like those in Hussein's later collection *This Other Salt,* the stories in *Mirror to the Sun* traverse a number of different cultural and geographical landscapes, where people, places and memories – whether we meet them in Jakarta, Java, India, Karachi, Rome or London – hide like masks behind each other, reappearing at different times in new configurations. The cumulative effect of the mirrors in Hussein's stories is not only to focus our attention on the dissonances of migrant displacement, but also to illustrate an existential scepticism with 'the claims that passports make on our souls'. Moreover, if the act of writing provides a free passport into the simultaneity of lives lived elsewhere, it is never rendered as a state of irresponsible privilege bred by an easy fusion. Rather, the creative juggling of the signs of differing epistemological systems heightens our awareness of the need for constant acts of 'cultural ambidexterity',[47] the need to be engaged in a process of negotiation, where absence is transformed into desire and the migrant self is renamed within the fissured realities of a diasporic present.

This process is not buoyed up by a self-referential or unproblematic shape-shifting of the binaries separating the twin poles of home and/or abroad, but manifests itself through the intertextual excavation of a fundamentally 'bi-literary' and cross-cultural linguistic terrain.[48] This fictional project is exemplified by a rhythmical movement across the English language and Urdu (the author's and many of the other characters' mother-tongues), which knits together the quintessentially polyglot nature of his literary world. Writing therefore becomes a process of moving both from left to right and, as in Urdu, from right to left. It is a means of bonding, as one of his characters says: the closest one 'can get to loving, to sailing out in silence, waiting for an answer, filling the gap between the silence and the scream'.[49] Hussein's stories thus 'cull' their 'images from Urdu poetry and ghazals, the cadences of Rajastani and Sindhi folk songs . . . the Indonesian gamelan, not to mention 1960s pop music'.[50] And these sounds reappear, as Firdous Azim has observed, in the cosmopolitan world of many of his London characters, as well as in those of 'other' cultures, such as Jai, in 'The Blue Direction', or Benedatta in 'Benedatta, Amata'. What becomes clear is that the axis determining the narration gains its nourishment from being part of a shifting linguistic terrain; for 'loss of home' is not only denoted by 'migration to the west' but invokes instead the impossibility of ever finding a refuge in an imagined 'home' whether in Pakistan, India or 'elsewhere'.

As is evident in 'Painting on Glass', one of Hussein's only stories to focus explicitly on the problematic of writing Britain, it is not only questions of race or place which entrap the voice of his budding Pakistani journalist narrator, but the clashing signs of language itself. First published in a general anthology of migrant writings in Britain, *Leave to Stay* (1996), this story linked Hussein's work with the writing of a wider community of migrant writers in Britain, many of whom, as its narrator tells us, were searching by the 1990s for 'higher ground'.[51] It reappears later as the penultimate story in *This Other Salt.* At first glance, 'Painting on Glass' seems to rehearse now familiar arguments concerning 'roots' and the burden of representation for the black or Asian artist in Britain; however, it also raises more complex questions about language, form, voice and translation. For whilst its Muslim narrator, Irfan Malik, is imprisoned within the straitjacket of his ethnicity in Britain, his sense of paralysis as a writer is further exacerbated by his location in the gaps between the sign systems of two different languages, each one constructing a different persona, a different version of his identity. As the story opens, we witness Malik attempting to find a register to describe his life in London. However, his words become increasingly stultified and surreal until, achieving a breakthrough, he turns away both from the English language and the recurrent symbols of his exile, a desolation epitomized by the graffiti of the London world outside his window. Once Malik begins to write in the 'syllables of my lost tongue', a tongue 'which licked my skin like fires', he discovers a voice more fitting to his predicament, and one which gains him the agency to turn the walls of his London world around. Interestingly, this moment in the story of an almost epiphanic vision, which lifts the invisible ink of Malik's immigrant experience back on to the centre of the page, is later rewritten and translated back to him through the lyrical rhythms and cadences of an elegant English prose.

This story not only exposes the complexities for the migrant writer of 'living in translation', but also illustrates that such acts of 'cultural stammer[ing]'[52] are an inevitable part of the pain that gives birth to fictions unfettered by the contingencies of already predetermined forms. As Malik says at one point, reflecting on the question of distance and his role as a writer in London:

> I had my material – you only had to read an article about Pakistan or watch a documentary to get it – and I had apartheid, intifada, Ethiopia,

> Timor . . . We carry our histories on our backs, I wrote, in our blood and our bones. But . . . I knew somewhere in these bones of mine that what we were doing was only ranting and raving and preaching to each other and the ranks of the already rallied, our words couldn't get us to where we really wanted to go, our well of words was running out of fresh water as if a cow or worse still a pig had died in it. That we didn't have the courage to face an era which had placed us in a safe asylum, where we could scream the screams of dumb bright birds just as long as we didn't make a noise in the neighbourhood, disturb the local residents by shattering the glass walls of our aviary (p. 237).

The need to create a new 'well of words', which can both make and unmake the boundaries of a past no longer containable, either by the walls of what has becomes a form of aesthetic 'asylum' or by the comfortable securities of a 'monogamy with language', form the major preoccupation of many of the stories in *This Other Salt.* Whilst Hussein returns in this collection to questions already raised in *Mirror to the Sun*, the growth in awareness displayed by the cyclical structure of the ten stories reveals that it is only in confronting the unformed signs, which exist *behind* the 'cracked mirrors of belonging', that his characters can move beyond the narrow confines of the repetitive symbols which have previously defined their discontinuous pasts.

The narratives of Sameer, whether as academic, poet or prodigal son, emerge in a number of the stories. Whether we encounter him through the dream voice of the child in 'Birdcries', or as the lost lover in the title story, or later as 'cross-eyed critic' and frustrated writer in 'Skies', he is driven by a need to unravel the indirections of the mirrors of memory, a quest which becomes his subject. And whilst, as was indicated earlier, he first returns to Karachi in 'Skies' to dig up his past and write a social history of Urdu, his lines constantly slip out of his grasp, as he recognizes that even the apparently indigenous group of 'nationalist' Pakistani writers (who are his daily companions) are as unsettled by their own versions of diaspora as he is. The divisions in the story, subtitled 'Four Texts for an Autobiography,' dissolve ultimately into a mosaic of shifting traces: the search for a lost but legendary literary manuscript of his great-uncle Rafi, an elegiac requiem to a Muslim father recently interred on sacred ground in London, and an unfolding of the history of his extended Indian and Pakistani family, a history which finally exposes itself by the presentation to him of a series of fragmentary letters and newspaper cuttings following his father's death. Interestingly, towards the end of the narrative, fiction and reality merge, linking Sameer with his creator 'A's' own past. Sameer thus writes himself and is rewritten from a number of different locations, and comes to see, as we do, that not only are the most significant 'melodies' hidden 'between the lines', but that even the matrilineal songs of childhood have become 'birds with broken wings', never to 'find written shapes or forms' (p. 119).

The 'balancing act' involved in both recognizing and transforming the ghostly signs and eruptions of narrative shapes generated from, yet also dissolved by the uneven traces of a landscape of memory, also figures as a predominant concern in Romesh Gunesekera's *The Sandglass* and Sunetra Gupta's *The Glassblower's Breath*.[53] For both novels exhibit what we might call the creation of an illusory *simulacrum*, a skeletal frame which steadily recedes as the 'rooms of memory' unravelled in the respective texts open like Chinese boxes, and expose the presence of a number of hidden stories which are not immediately apparent from the initial design. As we have already witnessed in Hussein's work, this process of opening up and extending the literary parameters of a migrant sensibility is an ongoing one, a developmental process which is similarly evident in Gunesekera's and Gupta's published work to date.

In *Monkfish Moon* (1992), an early collection of short stories set both in Sri Lanka and Britain, Gunesekera draws our attention to the 'monkfish' of the title story as the potent, but illusory symbol of a world that cannot be regained unless through the shadow lands of memory and the imagination. For monkfish, the writer takes care to inform us, do not exist in the waters of the Indian Ocean around Sri Lanka. This particular story focuses its attention on a symbiotic relationship played out between the over-inflated yet narrow life of a business magnate and his artisan servant (a narrative perspective that he reverses in *Reef* his next work, with Triton the house-boy and Mister Salgado). Whilst we are made aware of the incongruities of power and history represented in these two character's lives, Gunesekera does not dwell on painting the exotica of a lost island paradise whose beauty (according to some critics) poignantly overshadows the bloody realities of a violent civil war, but examines instead the gaps, paradoxes and delusions which have led to the hollownesses at the centre of his ageing narrator's life. For, as in many of the other stories in this collection – whether set in London or Sri Lanka – the tragic epiphanies of individual lives occur in counterpoint with the haunting and beautiful landscape of an island which is not 'exoticized', but exists instead as a source of subliminal anxiety, always out of reach.

Similarly, Gupta, in her first novel *Memories of Rain* (1992),[54] explores and defines the limits of what pertains for the most part to be a modernist novel of exile. Her central female character, Moni, a woman brought up on both the songs of Tagore and the poems of Wordsworth, is first orientalized by her English lover and husband, and then betrayed after arrival in Britain. Whilst Moni's spirited return 'home' to Calcutta with her mixed race daughter suggests a form of resolution and agency, the novel is less concerned with gender politics, or the social issues suggested by Moni's physical displacement, than with the imaginative sustenance provided by the reworking of her memories, interwoven as they are with the legendary and mythical stories of her cosmopolitan Bengali past. In fact, as is characteristic of other texts of female 'exile', such as Jean Rhys's *Voyage in the Dark*, Moni's memories of home are most powerfully evoked at moments of extreme alienation. Yet Moni, unlike Gupta's later Indian protagonist in *The Glassblower's Breath*, is not able to break her umbilical relationship with her past; and whilst she creates an intensely inward recreation of 'home' narrated in a 'stream of consciousness' voice which pervades the emotional realities of *all* her worlds, her return is portrayed as the inevitable consequence of her emotional exile, a particular way of reading and seeing the world. As Debjani Ganguly has noted, whilst Moni is apprehensive about the possibility of a rejection by her maternal city, a 'city whose tired, blistered nipples she had pushed away with disdainful lips', her return to Calcutta is nevertheless rendered in mythical terms and enshrined by the ritualistic *Durga Puja* ceremony, a ceremony which enacts a welcome for the '*Goddess* [my italics] to her father's home'.[55]

Both Gupta and Gunesekera have frequently commented on the fact that writing is an 'act of personal and political independence', a way of living and being in the world, which depends on the powerful resilience of stories to map the interiority of an imaginative territory of desire. As Gupta has put it:

> creative writing allows me to develop a language with which to probe the deeper recesses of my being. Writing is, in this sense, as much about discovering a *new* language, as *using* the language to look further into yourself and those around you.[56]

A similar point is made by Gunesekera in *The Sandglass*, a novel concerned more with an anxiety about human impotence in the face of death, than with piecing together the life-history of the recently deceased Sri Lankan immigrant, Pearl, the story which purports to be its subject. As we are told at one point:

> Writing, I guess like reading, is about stopping time. Only then do we realize that we do live forever, in a way, as our consciousness rushes in to fill the black hole of a rounded full stop (p. 236).

As the investigative narrator attempts to slowly piece together a fictional jigsaw of Pearl's life (a life reconstructed in the novel from her son Prins's journal entries, assorted scraps of paper left to him in a biscuit tin, and the mysterious ellipses of an oral history cut short by illness and death), we see, as Chip himself comes to realize, that each fragment, whatever its particular history, told its own 'special story . . . hiding another between every line' (p. 268). Moreover, the various strategies Chip obsessively adopts to create surrogates for his representations of a past lost, reveal his own panic at the recognition that it is perhaps only memory that is left to define the migrant's true 'home'.

The main narrative of the novel opens with Prins, the eldest son of the deceased Pearl, returning to London for her funeral in 1993. It is a return that also begins the unfulfilled quest to untangle the 'truth', surrounding the mysterious death of his father Jason Ducal in 1956. However, Prins's 'hunger' for the reclamation of what becomes both a private and political history of Sri Lanka following independence in 1948 is thwarted at every turn. For, as he says at one point, in words that hint at the dynamic underlying Gunesekera's narrative itself:

> You know, nothing really fits. That's the trouble. It all pretends to fit, like someone has constructed it all for us to see exactly how the thing works, but really it is done to hide everything. To lead us completely in the wrong direction. I feel I have been given a puzzle with a ready-made solution to divert me from something else (p. 249).

On first reading, as many critics have pointed out, *The Sandglass* seems to 'fit' with a number of features characteristic of the late twentieth-century novel of diasporic reclamation. For it is a novel which painstakingly charts the history of a life knitted together by the fragments of memory and the previously 'untold' stories of a diasporic past. It is a past which is meticulously reconstructed, covering two countries, the dynastic histories of two families, and stretching by the end across three generations. In the opening sequence we meet Chip, an honorary member of the Ducal family and surrogate son of Pearl, in a 'low-lit hotel room' overlooking Colombo, a lost 'city which seemed to rise on a tide of rubble' (p. 1). Describing his present life as one fuelled by a desire to unravel the links between Pearl, the history of the Ducals, and the 'scheming' Vatunases 'who seemed forever coiled around them', Chip becomes the repository for a quest, which only seems to relate obliquely to his own location and the 'orphaned fragments' of his 'aborted past' as a one-time Sri Lankan student, now immigrant, living in London.

Moving swiftly away from this opening vista, which takes place two months after Pearl's death, the novel zooms in on an intensely worked scene of memory and recollection, lived out during 24 hours – from 'Dusk' till 'Dawn' – in Chip's London flat, amidst preparations for Pearl's funeral. Concentrating for the most part on a dialogic encounter between Prins (Pearl's long-lost 'emigrating immigrant' son) and Chip (her London confidante and ex-lodger), the novel weaves a web of interconnected stories, which tie Pearl and her children's personal stories to the larger history of colonial Ceylon and post-Independence Sri Lanka. Yet as Chip warns us at one point, pointing perhaps to a different agenda disguised in his material, and which mocks the reader's initial expectations: 'The imagination . . . likes an easy ride: familiar territory . . ., toeholds, and handgrips' (p. 239).

Like Chip, we become engrossed at first in tracing the gaps in the evidence presented to us. Was Jason Ducal murdered in 1956 or was he the unlucky victim of someone else's suicide? Why does Ravi, Pearl's younger son, seek a 'dreamland' in the United States, and then attempt to kill himself without trace and without a sound in Pearl's Almeida Avenue flat? Was he really Jason's son? Is Prins about to follow in the footsteps of his father who, as an astute opportunist, exploited a moment of 'heady' confusion during the Independence years to further his own interests with the manufacturing of Ambrosia, a local whisky? For Prins, despite his curiosity about his father's death, is also portrayed as a character who fears the secrets of the past, a counterpoint to Chip, who needs to carefully rework and re-examine the 'density' of the material which surrounds him but constantly eludes him. Instead, like his rival, Dino Vatunas, Prins is keen to sell the present: 'the paradise experience between death camps and suicide bombers who didn't care', mysteriously disappearing by the close, like his father before him.

Despite these many unanswered questions, the novel's structure and time-scheme are almost too tight and over neat in their design. We are given precise details of almost all the characters' lives. We hear of Jason Ducal's fascination with the 1936 process of 'Ceylonization', a dubious involvement with what, after independence, seems to be a neo-colonialist process of indigenous exploitation, later leading to his purchase of the house of his dreams, 'Arcadia', the house in which Pearl's children grow up. Similarly, Pearl recounts specific details of her honeymoon period with Jason in England in the 1930s, presenting a 'romanticized' and colonial vision of an England which she attempts to return to after his sudden death. Whilst Chip unravels the connections between the corrupt histories of both the Vatunas and Ducal families, at the same time exposing the post-1948 history of the corruption of the land-owning classes in Sri Lanka, the cumulative effect of all the fragments he pieces together does not seem in the end to either resolve or assuage his anxious desires. In fact, the novel's progressive opening up of the 'rooms of memory' disclosed by Pearl's revelations in her small flat in London only dramatizes further the extent of Chip's existential dilemma in ever coming to terms with a subject whose boundaries constantly slip out of his grasp. Moreover, as the narrative accelerates its pace, mimicking in its fraught time-scheme the never-ending ticking of a clock, we recognize that by its close its 'real' story has almost been hidden by the accessibility of its surface design.

At several points in the narrative, Gunesekera draws our attention to the misleading 'neatness' of his own form, as he leaves his narrator baffled 'by the too-sure closures of things, days, lives'.[57] However, this is a productive confusion, which for Chip is combined with a growing anxiety to attempt to move outside the limitations imposed on his story by the relentless passing of time. We are given an insight into this process by the novel's persistent exposure of the impossibility, either for Pearl's generation or that of her children, to ever realize the Utopian promises of their displaced 'dreamlines'. Jason's 'Arcadia' becomes a 'mausoleum', a 'teardrop' like Sri Lanka itself, situated on the edge of unresolved ethno-religious histories. Moreover, as we see through the narrative's progressive deconstruction of the various other fictional houses it builds – whether Prins's Shangri-La, Pearl's flat in 'England', or Ravi's failed attempt to find an 'imaginary homeland' in America (a homeland built on the poetry of Longfellow, Whitman and Ginsberg) – such individual co-ordinates of diaspora cannot be sustained. And whilst Gunesekera is clearly playing in the novel on subverting the received images of what some have perceived to be an irresponsible use of an 'orientalist exotica', he does so in a self-conscious manner which does not succumb to the notion of Sri Lanka as either a 'poisoned paradise' or a 'latter-day derivative of the colonial construction of Ceylon as Eden'.[58]

What becomes clear is that Gunesekera's major preoccupation, as in *Reef*, is less with questions of psychic or physical displacement engendered by his character's diasporic histories than with exposing the artist's dilemma of representing such histories, caught as they are through memory and the filters of the lens of time. And if, as is the case in *The Sandglass*, the borders between time and space appear to be indistinct, this is not only due to Gunesekera's deliberate refusal to set up such artificial divisions, but also due to the narrative's implicit interrogation of how the process of writing from memory itself blurs such categories. As Prins revealingly points out on more than one occasion, perhaps voicing Gunesekera's own preoccupations:

> Trouble is when I look back I see . . . everything . . . through so many filters. Nothing you can be sure of . . . It makes it all very difficult. I have to build it up, pixel by pixel in my mind (p. 239).

The hourglass of Chip's narration thus becomes the symbolic frame which signifies the novel's main subject. It is an image that acts both as a 'metaphor' for the passage of time and the need for the artist to capture that moment in the present, in what Gunesekera has called a continuous reworking of the 'process of transformation'. Moreover the two elements of sand and glass, which appear initially to be in opposition, are interconnected like the stories. As Gunesekera has suggested,

> sand is freemoving, opaque and porous . . . glass is hard transparent and non-porous. But there is a point, albeit at a different melting point when they are one and the same.[59]

By the close of the novel, Chip is less concerned with the material details of the stories which perpetually run through his hands than with the artistic questions raised by the act of mediation itself. Although Chip attempts to figure the birth of Pearl's grandchild 'Dawn' at the end of the novel as a symbol of the coming of a 'somehow better world', this sense of an attempted closure is too forced and unconvincing. Thus, in what appears at first to be a narrative built on reclamation, a series of stories which melt into a predictable diasporic quest for place, we see that place is no convincing determinant. Similarly, Chip comes to see that through the process of searching for the gaps in Pearl's life history, his quest for her reclamation has uncovered the repressed narrative of his own psychic survival. The stories of the 'whole of a life', counterbalancing perhaps, 'the nothing of one'.[60] For Chip's own relation to the narrative, a story which is reduced by his appropriation and reflection of the stories of other people's lives begins to emerge (as his name suggests) as yet another story untold. In addition, as Chip fervently continues to channel his material through the narrow neck of the sandglass, assuaging his longing to capture the realities of a world forever remade in 'the capricious acts' of disappearance which occur every day, we gain an insight into the complexity of Gunesekera's own task as a writer and his attempts in this novel to celebrate the 'resilience of all stories, even ones of disappearance to make new' (p. 87). As Pearl suggests to Chip:

> You see clearly only when it is empty, no? You can't go back until it is, but by then it's all over. Empty. Gone. You have to turn yourself upside down and start all over again (p. 159).

As Gunesekera indicates then, the sandglass is a potent symbol both for death and for life, for absence and presence, a conduit by which the artist can briefly hold the transformations wrought in human lives by the passing of time. For the act of writing 'flashes up' its own revelations (to use Walter Benjamin's image) when they are least expected, launching the writer and reader alike into a differently framed space. Interestingly, Gunesekera's concern with the poetics of transformation, the fictional strategies involved in making old stories new, is also a major preoccupation in Sunetra Gupta's work.

Although Gunesekera and Gupta are clearly two very different writers, Gupta has also made plain that it is the form of the telling and not the material of the story itself that provides the ingredients to avoid 'starving the guest'. For all stories, whatever the nature of their cultural derivations or individual subjects, have in one way or another been told before. And whether they stem (as is the case in her work) from a self-conscious rewriting and reconfiguration of myths and legends, already part of literature's wide cultural archive, or attempt instead to stretch the sinews of language to the limits of their symbolic and syntactical order, it is the process of invention that is her primary subject. For, as she has said:

> stories change . . . stories change in their telling, and that is why you must never yourself tell the story of your own life, for facts will stretch it taut and motionless, like an empty cloth upon a table, a feast that starves the guest.[61]

Gupta's purpose then, is to advance a narrative poetics in which memory provides the semantic reservoir for establishing a 'dialogue with the self'.[62] Its territory exists outside the temporal borders of space or the nostalgic memories of a past lost, reflecting many lives 'embedded within a life, and

. . . in another . . . and another'. Fiction enacts, therefore, a form of time travelling, a journey of discovery in which the migrant self is not only inscribed within the furniture of one room but, as Meena Alexander describes the process in her memoir *Faultlines*, can open up many more, 'each filled with [their] own scent'.[63] For as we shall see, in *The Glassblower's Breath* – a novel which attempts to break and change the rules of both language and form, by exposing the cultural and symbolic slippages which occur at the heart of discourse itself – Gupta is not only concerned with the complex task of translating the unformed territory of diasporic memory into a poetics for the present, but also explores the potential of textual miscegenations, the 'collisions' that result by constructing an intertextual dialogue between such differently constituted 'multiple selves'. As Sandra Ponzanesi has observed, the textual rehearsal of such migrant transformations is not only a question of 'overlapping, intertwining and fusing different aspects of identity', but also involves a 'jarring, jolting and tossing [away] of mutilated parts'.[64] In a sense, then, the fictional world of *The Glassblower's Breath* represents an aesthetic inversion of the process we have already observed at work in Gunesekera's novel, a novel in which a meticulously constructed and largely 'realist' frame is deliberately undercut and subverted by its own absences. For whilst Gupta's dissolves from the outset, the apparent transparency of the fictional 'glass' containing the passage of time in Gunesekera's tale, her construction of an associative and nonlinear narrative frame in *The Glassblower's Breath* threatens, as in *The Sandglass*, to undermine its own biases as it hovers between desire, memory and the inevitability of death.[65]

In many respects, the novel is exemplary, in Gupta's *oeuvre*, of an attempt to create a new home in language, one generated by a hazardous journey into the making of subjectivity itself. Set, like Virginia Woolf's *Mrs Dalloway*, on one ordinary day in London, this almost plotless narrative throws up all kinds of incompatible cohabitations. These range from the unnamed Indian protagonist's past, lived in the cities of Calcutta, London and New York, to a journey into a disjointed childhood and adolescence in Britain, which resists containment by either the frames of a past left behind or the refractions of a present, mediated to us through her relationship to the multiple voices of the male narrators who tell her tale. Gupta returns persistently to questions of self-referentiality and deconstruction, re-angling the popular and received myths of childhood and fairy stories, yet at the same time examining the jangling effects of a number of literary hypotexts, whose lines are cumulatively interwoven into the disjointed body of a narrative seeking to carry the often incongruous signifiers of a mixed cultural past. This interrogation of how texts frame each other is further developed in terms of gender and the predicament of the female 'you' protagonist, whose life is constructed through the voices of her male lovers.

In addition to the skeletal plot, which focuses on the female protagonist's active pursuit of an adulterous affair, arising from an arbitrary meeting on an ordinary day in London with a butcher, Daniel, the text constantly draws attention to its self-conscious artifice, creating a patchwork of literary references which derive, like the protagonist's consciousness, from a wide-ranging cultural history. Thus we hear, in different keys, the voices of modernists such as Nabokov, Virginia Woolf or James Joyce, who sit side by side with Rilke, Rabindranath Tagore, the nursery rhyme story of 'Mother Goose', Gepetto's *Pinocchio,* and the Bengali tales of the protagonist's Calcutta childhood. These literary intertexts are also framed by the voice of the thirteenth-century Persian poet, Jelaluddin Rumi. This is not, however, simply a postmodernist use of either an exoticized embroidery or a hybrid polyphony. For although the protagonist's links to her Indian past – what she calls a 'half-hearted courtship with nostalgia' (p. 35) – are progressively severed as the novel proceeds, the collective cultural codes of her childhood are transcribed into the adult agency and authority of her migrant voice. We know that this process of transcultural permeation has been going on for a long time, for she used, as a child, to write stories in two languages, English and Bengali, keeping both in the same exercise book. However, as her father once suggested, 'you [can] write the English stories in the first half', while, 'to write the Bengali stories . . . simply invert the exercise book and write from the back and somewhere they [will] meet' (p. 61).[66]

This desire to run several narratives in parallel, hoping that 'somewhere they would meet', is a strategy that recurs throughout *The Glassblower's Breath.* Two texts in particular stand out as a frame for Gupta's ten-part cyclical and poetic narrative which, 'embedded with layer upon layer of apparently irreconcilable and bizarre tales and metaphors',[67] constantly draws attention to the fragility of its own structure. Whilst some critics have stressed the significance of the novel's feminist.rewriting of the locus of James Joyce's *Ulysses* – a re-angling which brings the experiences of Gupta's female protagonist centre stage – her literary project is clearly not primarily concerned with the insertion of a counter-discourse into her text. One can, of course, read the refrain from the nursery rhyme 'Mother Goose' as the uncanny example of an 'Eastern appropriation' of the arbitrariness of 'Western patterns' in the novel, a strategy which transfers and subverts the received colonial wisdom of an Indian childhood on to the 'cultural landscape of the mother country'.[68] However, Gupta is clearly less preoccupied with the political effects of such metafictions than with the creation of what she has called elsewhere 'a labyrinth of tales for my readers to hide within, where one story dives into another and resurfaces without its fins'.[69]

Like the tale of 'Mother Goose', which recites the stories of the butcher, the baker and the candlestickmaker, the image of the glassblower's breath is a metaphor which recurs throughout. Its significance is signalled by Gupta's free translation of Rumi's original thirteenth-century version, which acts as a preface to the novel:

Last night the moon came dropping its clothes in the street
I took it as a sign to start singing,
falling up into the bowl of sky.
The bowl breaks. Everywhere is falling everywhere.
Nothing else to do.
Here's the new rule. Break the wineglass,
and fall into the glassblower's breath.

As these lines indicate, Gupta's primary concern is to explore the possibility of generating a new language in this novel, a language which can break down the existence of any stable mirrors of identity and exist in a new home without rules. It is a space which is both exhilarating and dangerous, brim full with the passions of desire – suggested by the 'obscene' implications embedded in the apparently harmless nursery rhyme of 'Mother Goose' with its sexual innuendoes to events taking place in bathtubs during country fairs – but constantly surrounded by the realities of death. The repetitive notion of 'breaking the wineglass' and falling into the breath of the glassblower recurs throughout and becomes the rationale, as Debjani Ganguly has pointed out, both for the narrative's 'metaphysic' and 'its creative principle – an abrogation of Order, Reason, Form and a celebration of the Amorphous, the Chaotic, the Semiotic, Vowelless, Primal Tongue'.[70] Such metaphysical and aesthetic concerns, enshrined behind the broken looking-glass of objective representation, are juxtaposed with the protagonist's walks across the landscape of contemporary London, her sexual liaisons, and imaginative flights back to the mental geography of an irretrievable house demolished in Calcutta. The ominous lure of the glassblower's breath grows ultimately into a limitless metaphorical space, filled with the metaphors of a new language that both author and protagonist keep returning to. Acting, on the one hand, as a literary surrogate for a permanent physical and emotional home, it more importantly also simulates the alchemical process of invention itself, as old patterns are forged into new forms.

Not surprisingly in a text that draws implicitly on the refractions of both a modernist and a postcolonial vision, Gupta's female protagonist is constructed as much in the mind of the reader as she is by the lovers (all second-person and unreliable narrators) who, through a prism of mirrors, tell her stories. There are no securities left in this world – what she calls 'beloved syllogisms' and 'comforting rituals' – although we are made conscious at several moments of their previous existence in the painful memory of her sister's death, her natal home in Calcutta and the stories of the child Rima, the daughter of her sister who lives with her in London. Yet these are temporary refuges which Gupta's homeless migrant characters cannot afford to participate in. Moreover, Gupta constantly makes us aware through her use of poetic imagery, as well as through the kaleidoscopic form of the novel itself, how unstable and thoroughly subjective our perceptions are:

> And here you are now, in the city of your dreams, in a houseful of mirrors that each scream your story . . . Some fissure your gaze into a thousand threads, others curve your smile to cruel rainbowed horizons, the odalisque-sized mirror that guards your bath still steamily flatters, but the glazed portals of the broom closet remain relentless in the examination of your features, surgical, under harsh kitchen light. Somewhere, among these, hide the lineaments of your destiny, that you will always search. Yet everyone of them, my love, down to the last looking glass, will tell your tale differently, as we will my love, all of us who have loved you (p. 10).

As this extract demonstrates, Gupta's language is fundamentally associative and fluid in its structure, an experimental mode which has led some critics to dismiss her work as the undisciplined and overblown wanderings of a writer whose narrative is not only apolitical, but going nowhere. Yet despite the novel's difficult style and its apparent meanderings, its purpose is not as arbitrary as it seems. For it attempts, through its cyclical and multi-focalized repetitions of numerous stories, to generate new meanings. Meanings built by a cumulative series of poetic and symbolic links to undo the subject–object oppositions of a past lost, so as to present a re-angled version of a now familiar twentieth-century tale of migrancy and belonging.

The exploration of migrant subjectivity is perhaps represented most powerfully through the novel's focus on language, and the possibility of creating a universe which can exist outside the binaries of the subject–object divisions generated by discourse itself. The character Jonathan Sparrow argues, for example, that vowels are always the 'essence of unambiguity' and that they actively restrict the freedom of the 'poetic', thus leaving us forever stranded on an arid plain of 'concrete communication'. In contrast, in a language without vowels:

> consonants [become] replete with dreams, as now only the hollows between words and images may be, the clashes of metaphor and reality have come to replace the conflict of sound and meaning contained within the single word (p. 133).

Yet as Gupta herself intimates at one point in the novel, invoking Flaubert: 'if all is metaphor, what becomes of fact?'[71] Rather like the Joseph figure in David Dabydeen's *The Intended* (whom we encountered in Chapter 5), Sparrow, a natural philosopher, envisages a world where subjectivity is not perpetually reduced by the flattening effects of a language which denies the complexities of cultural ambivalence. His points are significant, for they stress, as does Gupta herself, that an acceptance of an unregulated chaos rather than order is fundamental to creative freedom. Gupta's vision of disorder as a correlative not for 'dissipation', but 'a process inherent within the same rules that create and explain order' (p. 210) bears some relationship to the use of 'chaos theory' as a literary paradigm for discovering the potential of transformation inherent in 'apparently disordered and creolized or hybrid societies'.[72] Moreover, it provides a useful means of questioning the symbolic system expressed by the dominant society, thus enabling a reconstruction of postcolonial and migrant identities on the basis of an open, shared and equal set of discourses. The negative side, however, of the imaginative potential that Gupta invokes in breathing new words into the imaginative shapes released by the glassblower's breath, is that this world threatens to extinguish itself (like the form of the novel itself) by the demands of its own desire.

The novel recounts one day in the life of a woman when all three parts of her life collide: the physical, the emotional and the intellectual. The physical is represented by the butcher Daniel, as well as David, her first love; the emotional by Avishek the Baker, and the intellectual by Jonathan Sparrow the candlestickmaker. These characters, like the 'you' protagonist they construct, are all migrant figures, who confidently construct a multicultural geography of the once imperial city and the new populations who live within it. Most of the major characters we encounter in the novel have lived elsewhere: the protagonist's cousin Avishek, a one-time lover, now survives by creating gingerbread versions of popular Oxbridge 'English' icons; Sparrow, once a Platonic friend, is an American and worldwide traveller; whereas Ivanov is a Russian émigré. At the close, we encounter the protagonist returning to her house in London after her day of illicit sexual liaisons, where she rejoins her Iranian husband, the immunologist Alexander. But the home she enters, like the text itself, is nothing but 'a houseful of mirrors' in which she is surrounded by her three suitors – Sparrow, Avishek and Daniel. All three lovers eventually die, meeting the same fate in Alexander's bathroom as that suffered by the destiny of the 'three men in a tub' in 'Mother Goose'. And whilst we are not sure whether these deaths are 'real', or projections of a murderous deathwish inspired by Alexander's insane jealousy, the arbitrariness of the novel's ambivalent ending is part of its overall design. For in conjuring an effect which does not depend on any plot or realist base, the novel becomes a fictional prism of the multiple identities of her various characters. It therefore leads us, like its dissolving and elusive form, to a seemingly meaningless close which, like a house built with a pack of cards, just falls down.[73]

A number of critics have voiced difficulties in placing the imaginative world of Gupta's fiction. For her work is not only radical in its experimentations with narrative form and voice, but also resists easy categorization, whether in terms of gender, race or cultural location. In its refusal to either sit easily within the 'migrant camp' of contemporary postcolonial literature, or unproblematically within the dominant models of a Western modernity, it calls attention to the shifting cultural axes of its own genesis. And whilst, as we have seen, the realities of diasporic histories inform all of the texts that have been considered in this chapter, each writer has progressively turned their fictional lens inwards, shifting their material away from an overt consideration of either a politics of location or a politics of identity. This is not to say that these writers have freed themselves entirely from the sentence, as Aamer Hussein defined it in 'Painting on Glass'; of forever carrying their histories on their backs. Yet, in shifting the terms and expectations of their individual burdens of representation, they have not only cleared a space for the articulation of their individual subjectivities, but also opened up the critical geography of the 'namings' which have previously constrained them. As Salman Rushdie once put it, when pointing to the serious political impact that 'readings' of literary texts can have on individual lives:

Literature is the one place in any society where, within the secrecy of our own heads, we can hear *voices talking about everything in every possible way*. The reason for ensuring that that privileged arena is preserved is not that writers want the absolute freedom to say and do whatever they please. It is that we, all of us, readers and writers, citizens and generals and godmen, need that little, unimportant-looking room . . . Wherever in the world the little room of literature has been closed, sooner or later the walls have come tumbling down.[74]

Epilogue: Some Notes Towards a Conclusion

It has recently been suggested that the contemporary experience of the South Asian literary diaspora is an 'epic without a text', an 'ancient odyssey' replaying itself in 'modern historical guise', lived primarily within the imagination.[1] Unlike many other diasporas, it is not necessarily linked to the 'homeland' by the transportation of familiar cultural, economic, or religious institutions, but primarily by a sensibility rooted in 'systematic diversity', an imaginative facility imbibed, as Amitav Ghosh has argued, from an ancient 'subcontinental tradition' of living alongside 'complementary difference'. It is a tradition which has thrived, in spite of contemporary and ancient ethno-religious schisms, on a multicultural and multilingual heritage. Thus it is adept not only in daily transitions (between and across languages and cultures), but in the broader translations of a 'linguistic process' that has historically inscribed such heteroglossic transformations. Writers of the Asian diaspora thus carry an innate ability not only to adapt, to assimilate and appropriate, but also to hybridize, reshape and sometimes deliberately misappropriate. And if, as Ghosh suggests, the subcontinent has become an 'infinitely reproducible space', an 'empty space, mapped purely by words', its literary representations will inevitably take on a number of highly individualized and differently constructed aesthetic forms.[2]

If we accept the observation that the diaspora is, in one sense, 'an epic without a text', it also must be said that it is a modern 'epic' that has progressively redefined the grammar of its own history, naming its presence as an influential partner in the twentieth-century narrative of modernity. For the diaspora today has clearly spawned a vast range of different immigrant and migrant stories, stories which are both local and international in their scope, and which, when examined, reveal certain phenomenological preoccupations and generic affiliations. It has not been within the scope of this book to suggest *global* correspondences across the enormous and varied literary terrain of the international diaspora – comparing the work of writers such as Bharati Mukherjee (USA), Sara Suleri (USA), Rohinton Mistry (Canada), Moyez Vassanji (East Africa/Canada), Satendra Nandan (Fiji), Amitav Ghosh (India/USA/Britain), to name but a few – although suggestive comparisons and contrasts could certainly have been made across these individual diasporas and their different areas of settlement.[3] However, as has been evident in the discussion of the British experience, the diaspora has not only generated a substantial body of literary texts, whether of migration or settlement, arrival or departure, but has also manifested itself in a wide range of literary forms.[4] These texts have emerged, as we have seen, from a range of subject positions and varied historical and cultural contexts, located at different points of the diasporic continuum. Deriving from an eclectic range of literary and cultural intertexts, whether Western and/or Eastern, oral and/or literary, modernist and/or traditional, histories with which they are at different times both complicit and resistant, they do not necessarily conform to any easily identifiable formula. They do, however, share a preoccupation with the literary exploration of a *poetics of home*, exhibiting a 'homing desire',[5] which has belatedly shifted and reconstituted the borders of a modernist aesthetic of 'exilic' writing, derived largely from the epistemologies of a Western tradition. In so doing, these narratives have made visible the presence of alternatively constituted modernities, diasporic subjectivities which have always coexisted both within and outside the long 'immigrant' history of the 'British' nation.

Homi Bhabha's observation, in his influential study of the modern nation, that 'the "other" is never outside or beyond us', but emerges most forcefully 'when we *think* we speak most intimately and indigenously "between ourselves" ',[6] is frequently lived and inscribed, as we have seen, through the experiences of the black and Asian literary diasporas in Britain. And whilst the *home truths* that Bhabha's theoretical insights evoke are clearly drawn in part from the now institutionalized orthodoxy of French poststructuralism (combined with the insights of Freudian psychoanalysis), it is worth noting that the prime influences on his thinking did not derive either from 'the English authors' which he 'avidly read', or 'from the Indian authors with whom [he] deeply identified', but instead from the 'diversionary . . . exilic' insights of the fictions of V. S. Naipaul. For it was Naipaul's experience of living the diaspora as a twice-removed Indo-Caribbean (who, like Bhabha himself as a Bombay Parsi, had no 'originary' links to either a Muslim or Hindu tradition), which led 'to the historical themes and . . . questions' that were to form the 'core' of Bhabha's later critical interventions.[7] The *crucial* interrelationship, which Bhabha signals here, between creative texts and the theoretical discourses which surround them, is one which this book has sought to prioritize. Moreover, as Naipaul demonstrates in his description of Leonard Side in *A Way in the World* (1994), it is the reconstitution of the discourse of memory as active agent and subject of the present which holds the key to unlocking the doors of the manichean binaries of a migrant past:

> He knew he was a Mohammedan, in spite of the picture of Christ in his bedroom. But he would have had almost no idea of where he or his ancestors had come from. He wouldn't have guessed that the name Side might have been a version of Sayed, and that his grandfather or great-grandfather might have come from a Shia Muslim group in India. From Lucknow, perhaps; there was even a street in St James called Lucknow . . .
>
> With learning now I can tell you more or less how we all came to be where we were . . . I can give you that historical bird's eye view. But I cannot explain the mystery of Leonard Side's inheritance. Most of us know the parents or grandparents we come from. But we go back and back, forever; we go back all of us to the very beginning; in our blood and bone and brain we carry the *memories* [my italics] of thousands of beings. I might say that an ancestor of Leonard Side's came from the dancing groups of Lucknow, the lewd men who painted their faces and tried to live like women. But that would only be a fragment of his inheritance, a fragment of that truth. We cannot understand all the traits we have inherited. Sometimes we can be strangers to ourselves.[8]

As Naipaul implies here, history alone cannot provide the clues to the multiple inheritances and mysterious connections of a diasporic past. Nor indeed can *one* kind of theory or *one* kind of reading adequately frame the diverse particularities of present diasporic subjectivities.

As has been argued throughout, political, cultural or academic labels, invented to contain 'black' or 'Asian' identities whether at 'home' or 'abroad', only ever tell part of the story. And whilst the use of the label 'South Asian' has become a convenient taxonomy in contemporary Britain – like the political usage of 'black' in the 1960s and 1970s, used to create a sense of affiliation and solidarity amongst Britain's so-called non-white, black and brown 'minorities' – it can also be divisive and misleading in a literary context, when it erases the complexity of significant differences between the writers themselves. Attia Hosain and G. V. Desani, as we saw in Chapter 1, may have both been writing in 1940s London, but stem, like Aubrey Menen, Mulk Raj Anand or Raja Rao, from very different cultural and class histories, whether viewed from within or outside their subcontinental origins. Similarly V. S. Naipaul, the late Sam Selvon, and David Dabydeen may all represent aspects of the South Asian and 'black' diasporas as lived within Britain, but they are equally Indo-Caribbean and 'postcolonial' writers with links both to the nineteenth-century system of indentured labour in the Caribbean islands as well as to the narrative of contemporary modernity. And whilst Salman Rushdie and V. S. Naipaul, as we saw in Chapters 3 and 4, could be said to explore similar concerns in *The Enigma of Arrival* and *The Satanic Verses*, articulating a sensibility perhaps linked by exploration of the question of migrant arrivals and by the remapping of old imperial landscapes – whether urban or rural – their regional/national/caste/class backgrounds are very different, as are their aesthetic strategies. Furthermore, as we saw in the discussion of Ravinder Randhawa and Hanif Kureishi in Chapter 5, whilst both these writers are preoccupied to some extent in their first novels with writing 'Englishness' through Asian eyes, the mode and the form of exploration is suggestive more of complex differences rather than as neat correspondences.[9] Although the female protagonists in Randhawa's *A Wicked Old Woman* are forced, like Kureishi's Karim in *A Buddha of Suburbia*, to inhabit multi-layered diasporic identities and to negotiate a path between the often contradictory discourses which surround them, they are firmly located in the particular dynamics of gender and racial politics amongst the Asian female communities of which they are a part. In contrast, Kureishi's fiction – exemplified most recently in his confessional and autobiographical novel of a failed marital relationship, *Intimacy* – deliberately problematizes a seamless focus on questions of ethnicity, gender or race in Britain. Instead, Kureishi's concern, like that of a number of later British-born writers, is to explode the transparent geography of an Anglo-Englishness which fails to acknowledge the opaque and hybrid colours of its mixed racial, regional and imperial past.

The contrasts could go on. The literary strategies employed by South Asian writers of the diaspora in post-1945 Britain have been varied, ranging from the picaresque *bildungsroman* to the intimate autobiography, to comic and magic realism, the fabular, as well as to the referential and postmodern. Whilst many have been deliberately subversive in their individual experimentations, explicitly interrogating and reshaping the canonical terrain of received narrative genres, others have expressed their differences from within the structures available to them, stretching their boundaries, and writing stories whose colours of resistance are perhaps less immediately obvious to the critical eye. There are also clearly identifiable intertextual connections between many of the writers as is evident from the interrelationships which have emerged from the historical chronology this book has traced and the subsequent literary examples of fictions which have followed on. Whilst Salman Rushdie, to take one instance, cites G. V. Desani as the main 'Indian' influence on his fiction, it is also clear that

Mulk Raj Anand, Raja Rao, as well as V. S. Naipaul were important, if not consciously acknowledged as precursors. A similar pattern emerges in the work of David Dabydeen, a writer who has frequently drawn attention to both Sam Selvon and V. S. Naipaul as pivotal Oedipal figures in the development of his artistic vision.[10] Moreover, if we turn to the contemporary Asian British context, it is clear that both Ravinder Randhawa and Hanif Kureishi have been key players in pioneering a branch of diasporic writing, which is still proliferating today in the numerous fictions published by writers such as Bidisha Bandopadhaya, Meera Syal or Atima Srivastava, as well as a number of screenplays. Most recently, perhaps, the example of Zadie Smith's highly acclaimed novel, *White Teeth* (2000), reflects not only the continuing influence of diaspora as a mode of postnational survival in the present, but also reminds us of the extent to which its now attractive chic of 'vernacular cosmopolitanism',[11] a mode of existence where 'cultural translation' is the norm as an act of daily survival, had already been anticipated by the poetics of an earlier but less visible tradition of im/migrant writing in Britain. Although one could, with hindsight, make illuminating comparisons between, say, the creation of Sam Selvon's black city of words in the 1950s, and that of Zadie Smith's multicultural Willesden today, it is perhaps less useful to point to correspondences between these writers in terms of their individual histories or particular styles than to examine the genesis of a literary sensibility, the generation of a diverse tradition of migrant writing, derived from the cross-cultural influences of their individual diasporic conditions.

It is clear that 'home', like migrancy itself, is a perpetually shifting concept in these fictions. It is both here and there, past and present, local and global, traditional and modern. It may provoke a referential construction of a past lost, but may also be a deliberately invented construct, an imaginary homeland built on the shifting sands of memory, extending and reshaping the boundaries of both the familiar and the strange, whether encountered at 'home' or 'abroad'. In addition, if, as is the case for many second- or third-generation writers, the umbilicus to the past, to the *heimlich*, is fractured and destroyed by the lost traces of a diasporic history, the symbolic may no longer signify the possibility either of return or of settlement, but may invoke instead a desire to construct fictional *homes without walls*, homes which can exist in a present whose boundaries are always deferred, always in translation. As the final chapter of this book has argued, such narratives do not only seek to fulfil what has come to be seen as a postcolonial hunger for the rewriting of history. Instead, as Romesh Gunesekera demonstrates in *The Sandglass*, they thrive on the 'resilience' and capacity of *all* stories, even 'one[s] of disappearance', to make new.[12] And whilst the *ancient* diasporic reality of living 'between' has recently come to be assimilated into dominant modernist discourses as a useful and universal trope to define the character of 'global' modernities in the new millennium, we must remain cautious about the optimism of such sentiments.

Whilst many works by writers of the South Asian diaspora today feature prominently in critical discussions of the contemporary novel worldwide, the history of the process of its evolution, and the difficulties many writers experienced in making interventions into the narrow discourses of a closed, and largely Western, canonical tradition do not reflect either an easy or a painless journey. Moreover, 'new ethnicities', as critics such as Stuart Hall and Phil Cohen have frequently warned, still repeat 'old racisms'.[13] It is tempting, given the current climate in literary studies, to conclude with the observation that the story of the South Asian diaspora has belatedly come full circle and to reiterate the fact that the West has finally come to accept the wisdom of a viewpoint which has always been a lived reality in the historic experience of many marginalized diasporic communities: namely, that to be different in a 'world of differences' is 'irrevocably to belong'.[14] Yet for the descendants of the black and Asian diasporas now living in Britain, the ghostly echoes of the question, 'So what do we do with them now?' still unfortunately reverberate. 'History', as Romesh Gunesekera ironically informs us in *The Sandglass*, may be an argument rehearsed across time about whose 'arse' is on whose 'grass'.[15] Yet it is only when time, so to speak, has almost run out that one can see clearly and gather together the present in the as yet unborn songs of the future. In this lies a fable not only for the existential transformations enabled by the process of writing itself, a process which, as V. S. Naipaul once put it, has made him a 'free man', but also for the *vital* role that the diasporic imagination has played in extending our readings of the narrative of modernity and in making visible the *home truths* of history.

Notes

PROLOGUE

1. Julia Charlotte Maitland, *Letters From Madras During the Years 1836–1839: By a Lady* (London: 1843), p. 92.
2. Enoch Powell, Speech at Southall (4.11.71); quoted in Paul Gilroy, *There Ain't No Black in the Union Jack* (London: Unwin Hyman, 1987), p. 45.
3. Moniza Alvi, 'Arrival 1946', in *The Country At My Shoulder* (Oxford: Oxford University Press, 1993), p. 32.
4. See amongst others: Antoinette Burton, *At the Heart of Empire: Indians and the Colonial Encounter in Late-Victorian Britain* (Berkeley, CA: University of California Press, 1998); Rozina Visram, *Ayahs, Lascars and Princes: The History of Indians in Britain, 1700–1947* (London: Pluto, 1986) and *Four Hundred Years of History: Asians in Britain* (London: Pluto, 2001); Peter Fryer, *Staying Power: The History of Black People in Britain* (London: Pluto, 1984).
5. Caryl Phillips, *Extravagant Strangers: A Literature of Belonging* (London: Faber, 1997), p. x.
6. Linda Colley, *Britons: Forging the Nation 1700–1837* (New Haven, CT: Yale University Press, 1992); Alan Sinfield, *Literature, Politics and Culture in Postwar Britain* (Oxford: Blackwell, 1989); Raphael Samuels, *The Making and Unmaking of British National Identity*, Vol. 11, *Minorities and Outsiders* (London: Routledge, 1989); Judy Giles and Tim Middleton, eds, *Writing Englishness 1900–1950* (London: Routledge, 1995); Robin Cohen, *Frontiers of Identity: The British and the Others* (London: Longman, 1994).
7. See: Bart Moore-Gilbert, *Postcolonial Theory: Contexts, Practices, Politics* (London: Verso, 1997); Ania Loomba, *Colonialism/Postcolonialism* (London: Routledge, 1998).
8. Edward Said, *Culture and Imperialism* (London: Chatto & Windus, 1993), p. 403.
9. Two volumes of *Ariel* were published in 1995 on the theme of 'Postcolonialism and Its Discontents'.
10. Phil Cohen, *Home Rules: Some Reflections on Racism and Nationalism in Everyday Life* (London: University of East London New Ethnicities Unit, 1993), p. 3.
11. A distinction between immigrant/migrant has been signalled throughout this study to reflect different critical, cultural and historical perspectives in the way this writing has been defined in the post Second World War period.
12. See James Clifford, 'Diasporas', *Cultural Anthropology*, 9, 3, 1994, pp. 302–38 for a full discussion of this idea.
13. Robin Cohen, *Global Diasporas: An Introduction* (Seattle, WA: University of Washington Press, 1997), p. 128; I am grateful here to Anuradha Dingwaney Needham's discussion on diaspora in the 'Introduction' to *Using*

the Master's Tools: Resistance and the Literature of the African and South Asian Diasporas (New York: St Martin's Press – now Palgrave, 2000).

14. Needham, *Using the Master's Tools*, p. 13.
15. avtar brah, *Cartographies of Diaspora: Contesting Identities* (London: Routledge, 1996), p. 209; the phrase a 'homing desire' is also from brah, p. 16.
16. Rasheed Areen, 'A New Beginning: Beyond Postcolonial Cultural Theory and Identity Politics', *Third Text*, 50, Spring 2000, pp. 8–10.
17. I am aware, of course, that this discussion is a limited one in terms of the writers selected for discussion. Fruitful comparisons could be made elsewhere and across the writings of the black and Asian diasporas in Britain. In addition, my choice to focus on fiction does not, of course, take into account the significance of other literary forms such as poetry and drama during the period under discussion.
18. Simon Gikandi, *Maps of Englishness* (New York: Columbia University Press, 1996), p. 4. For an analysis of the ways in which literary discourses change predictable patterns of thought, see Ross Chambers, *Room for Maneuver: Reading (the) Oppositional (in) Literature* (London and Chicago, IL: University of Chicago Press, 1991). Ross argues that all literary texts are 'produced in historical circumstances whose features the text necessarily takes into account', p. 15.
19. Salman Rushdie, 'Is Nothing Sacred', in *Imaginary Homelands* (London: Granta, 1991), p. 422.

PART 1 PASSAGES TO ENGLAND

CHAPTER 1

1. E. M. Forster, *Howards End* (London: Arnold, 1910).
2. Raja Rao, *The Serpent and the Rope* (London: Murray, 1960).
3. Aubrey Menen, *Dead Man in the Silver Market* (London: Chatto & Windus, 1954), p. 118; all further references are to this edition.
4. Nayantara Sahgal, 'The Schizophrenic Imagination', in *From Commonwealth to Post-colonial*, ed. Anna Rutherford (Mundelstrup: Dangaroo Press, 1992), p. 30.
5. R. Radhakrishnan, *Diasporic Mediations: Between Home and Location* (Minneapolis, MN: University of Minnesota Press, 1996), p. xiv.
6. Sahgal, 'The Schizophrenic Imagination', p. 30.
7. Anne McClintock, 'Angel of Progress', in *Colonial Discourse and Post-Colonial Theory*, ed. Patrick Williams and Laura Chrisman (Hemel Hempstead: Harvester, 1993), p. 294.
8. See: R. Visram, *Ayahs, Lascars and Princes* (London: Pluto, 1986); *Asians in Britain: 400 Years of History* (London: Pluto, 2001); Peter Fryer, *Staying Power: The History of Black People in Britain* (London: Pluto, 1984); Ron Ramdin, *Reimaging Britain: 500 Years of Black and Asian History* (London: Pluto, 1999); my use here of the term 'voyaging in' derives originally from

Edward Said, in *Culture and Imperialism* (London: Chatto & Windus, 1993), p. 288.

9. As Visram, amongst others has shown, a number of words in common English usage such as 'pyjama', 'bungalow', 'loot' derive originally from Indian sources.
10. Michael H. Fisher, ed., with Intro., *The Travels of Dean Mahomet: An Eighteenth Century Journey Through India* ([1794]; Berkeley, CA: University of California Press, 1997). The spelling 'Mahomet' was used in the first publication of this book in Cork 1794. I am therefore using the 'Mahomet' spelling for the purposes of this chapter despite the fact that after Sake Dean's move to Brighton in 1812, he set himself up as a 'Shampooing Surgeon', a masseur trading under the name of 'Mahomed'. See Plates 1 and 2.
11. Antoinette Burton, *At the Heart of Empire: Indians and the Colonial Encounter in Late Victorian Britain* (Berkeley, CA: University of California Press, 1998), p. 8; see also Dorothy Sayers, *Unpopular Opinions* (London: Gollancz, 1946).
12. Visram, *Ayahs, Lascars and Princes*, p. 1.
13. See Fisher, *The Travels of Dean Mahomet*; S. D. Mahomed, *Shampooing, or Benefits resulting from the use of the Indian Medicated Bath: as introduced into this country by S. D. Mahomed . . . containing a brief but comprehensive view of the effects produced by the use of the warm bath, in comparison with steam or vapour bathing* (Brighton, 1822, 1826, 1838).
14. Fisher, *The Travels of Dean Mahomet*, p. xix. See also Lyn Innes, 'Eighteenth-Century Men of Letters: Ignatius Sancho and Seek Dean Mahomed', in *Reading the 'New'Literatures in a Postcolonial Era*, ed. Susheila Nasta (Cambridge: Boydell and Brewer, 2000), for a discussion of Mahomet's transcultural literary strategies.
15. Antoinette Burton, 'Making a Spectacle of Empire: Indian Travellers in Fin-de-Siècle London', *History Workshop Journal*, 42, 1996, p. 128.
16. Behramji Malabari, *The Indian Eye on English Life; or, Rambles of a Pilgrim Reformer* (London: Constable, 1893), p. 141; see also T. B. Pandian, *England to an Indian Eye* (London: Elliot Stock, 1897); Medhi Khan, 'London Sketched by an Indian Pen', *Indian Magazine and Review*, February 1890, pp. 142–7.
17. Burton, 'Making a Spectacle of Empire', pp. 141–3.
18. Lala Baijnath, *England and India: Being Impressions of Persons, Things, English and Indian and Brief Notes of Visits to France, Switzerland, Italy and Ceylon* (Bombay: 1893). In this series of essays he says: 'most [Indians] live in Bayswater, which has been nick-named *Asia Minor*, because almost all the Asiatics who visit London patronize the lodging houses to be met with in that locality', p. 29. Interestingly, it is Bayswater, too, that is the centre of Moses's world in Sam Selvon's novel about immigrant London, *The Lonely Londoners* (1956).
19. T. N. Mukharji, 'Introduction' to *A Visit to Europe* (Calcutta: Newman, 1899), p. 4.
20. This phrase is cited in Antoinette Burton's, 'Making a Spectacle of Empire', p. 133.
21. Burton, *At the Heart of Empire*, p. 7. I am following Burton's argument here.

22. Term originally coined by K. R. Srivinas Iyengar, *Indian Writing in English*, 2nd edn (Bombay: Asia Publishing, 1973), p.22.
23. Oudh was the Eastern part of a state known to the British as the United Provinces.
24. Salman Rushdie, 'Introduction' to *The Vintage Book of Indian Writing in English*, ed. Salman Rushdie and Elizabeth West (London: Vintage, 1997), pp. xviii.
25. Anthony Burgess, 'Introduction' to King Penguin edition of G. V. Desani, *All About H. Hatterr* (Harmondsworth: Penguin, 1972), p. 8. Originally published in 1948 by Aldor Press, London, the novel was reissued in 1950. A revised edition appeared in 1970 (London: Bodley Head) with a further revision and final chapter added in 1972. All further references are to the 1972 edition and are included in the text.
26. Desani, *All About H. Hatterr*, p. 15.
27. Desani, *All About H. Hatterr,* p. 31.
28. Ferdinand Dennis and Naseem Khan, eds, *Voices of the Crossing* (London: Serpent's Tail, 2000), p. 3.
29. Zulfikar Ghose, 'Going Home', *Toronto South Asian Review*, 9, 2, 1991, p. 15.
30. D. F. Karaka, 'The Barbarian is Born', in *Oh, You English* (London: Muller, 1935). *Oh, You English* critiqued the hypocrisy of the 'English' in writing over anyone else's stories and 'civilizations' but their own. In addition, as he points out in *All My Yesterdays* (Bombay: Thacker & Co., 1944), it is the 'attitude of white races throughout the world that must change', p. 11. A Parsi journalist, born in Bombay in 1911, Karaka was the author of several books and pamphlets on English life. See: *The Pulse of Oxford* (London: Dent, 1933); *I Go West* (London: Joseph, 1938).
31. H. J. Booth and N. Rigby, eds, *Modernism and Empire*. (Manchester: Manchester University Press, 2000), p. 2.
32. Stephen Collini, 'How the Critic came to be King', in *TLS*, 8 September 2000, p. 11. A letter was written in response to this by Susheila Nasta, 'Critics on the Air', *TLS*, 6 October 2000, p. 19.
33. For a full account of the connections that were evident between such writers in 1940s and 1950s Britain, see Lynda Prescott's forthcoming essay in *Wasafiri* – on *The London Magazine* and its relations with Indian and Caribbean writing. See also: Jessica Gardner, 'Where is the Post-Colonial London of *London Magazine*', in *Kunapipi*, XXI, 2, 1999, pp. 93–106.
34. Mulk Raj Anand, *Conversations in Bloomsbury*, (London: Wildwood House, 1981). These recollections record a critical period in literary history frequently absent in Euro-American versions and document Anand's discussions with a number of notable British writers including: D. H. Lawrence, Edith Sitwell, Virginia Woolf, Aldous Huxley, Leonard Woolf, Vita Sackville-West. See also: Cedric Dover, *Feathers in the Arrow: An Approach for Coloured Writers and Readers* (Bombay: Padma Publications, 1947), and his novel *Half-Caste* (London: Secker & Warburg, 1937).
35. Mulk Raj Anand makes this point in an essay dedicated to E. M. Forster. Entitled 'Prolegomena to a New Humanism', in *The Letters of Mulk Raj Anand*, ed. and intro. S. Cowasjee (Calcutta: Writers Workshop, 1974), p. 2.

In 'Towards a New Indian Literature', *Left Review*, II, 12, 1936, pp. 613–23, Anand also makes the significant observation that Iqbal, the Urdu poet and one of Anand's literary mentors, had already addressed many of the questions that T. S. Eliot was to raise in his famous essay 'Tradition and the Individual Talent'.

36. Anand, *Conversations in Bloomsbury*, p. 21.
37. Mulk Raj Anand was a regular reviewer and critic in academic journals and the national press. See his novels *Coolie* (London: Lawrence & Wishart, 1936), and *Across the Black Waters* (London: Cape, 1940).
38. Dover, *Half-Caste*, p. 18.
39. Anand, 'Prolegomena to a New Humanism', p. 48.
40. For further details of the *Progressive Writers Association*, a group of writers dedicated to the use of vernacular forms, see: Mulk Raj Anand, 'Towards a New Indian Literature', in *Left Review*, pp. 613–23 (includes early version of the Manifesto of the Association); Ahmad Ali, 'The Progressive Writer's Movement in its Historical Perspective', in *Journal of South Asian Literature*, 13, 1–4, 1977–8, pp. 91–7; Hafeez Malik, 'The Marxist Literary Movement in India and Pakistan', in *Journal of South Asian Literatures*, 26, 4, 1967, pp. 649–64. *The India League* was an organization founded in Britain and consisted of many left-wing writers and intellectuals, including Mulk Raj Anand, Aubrey Menen, J. M. Tambimuttu, Krishna Menon (Indian politician and founding editor of Pelican Books), Herbert Read, Bernard Shaw, Leonard Woolf and many others. Meetings often took place at India House, where a number of writers met on a regular basis. Much discussion focused on talks about how to open up notions of 'Englishness', as Indian British citizens worked against the oppressions of colonialism and racism in the metropole. For detailed discussion, see: Rozina Visram, *Asians in Britain: 400 Years of History* (London: Pluto, 2001).
41. Anand, *Conversations in Bloomsbury*, p. 74.
42. C. L. R. James, *The Black Jacobins* (London: Secker & Warburg, 1938).
43. Bryan Cheyette, 'Venetian Spaces: Old-New Literatures and the Ambivalent Uses of Jewish History', in *Reading the 'New' Literatures in a Postcolonial Era,* p. 69.
44. It is important to remember that Aziz's incipient nationalism in E. M. Forster's 1924 novel, *A Passage to India*, is always presented with an ambivalence that is often beyond Fielding's comprehension. For when Aziz chooses a form of self-exile within India by writing poetry and living as a Muslim doctor in a Hindu state, his desire to create a 'motherland' is complicated not only by his Islamic background, but by the fact that the figure of any 'motherland' only gained definition for him in relation to the incident at the Marabar caves in which he becomes estranged from the English. And whilst Aziz recognizes that there could not be a 'motherland' without 'the creation of new homes', it is the Hindu Professor Godbole's vision of 'internationality' which offers Aziz the most attractive resolution. It is here, as Godbole is quick to suggest, that the promise of Aziz's future work will be fulfilled – not through a rejection of his embryonic nationalist concerns or by losing the specificity of his love for Urdu and Islam – but by moving beyond the narrow parochialism of a monolithic or monolingual

vision and embracing instead the transcultural and inter-regional diversity which is the lived experience of Indian history, whether ancient or modern. For it is India, as Godbole points out, which may seem to the recent colonial power, the British, 'not to move', that 'will go straight there' and create new spaces for cultural expression 'while . . . other nations waste their time'. See: *A Passage to India* ([1924]; Harmondsworth: Penguin, 1978), pp. 273–4, 290. Interestingly, as Mulk Raj Anand makes plain in *Conversations in Bloomsbury*, he identified closely with the character of Aziz on his first reading of the novel after his arrival in London in 1925.

45. Raja Rao, *Kanthapura* ([1938]; New Delhi: Orient, 1971), p. 5.
46. Harish Trivedi, in *Literature and Nation*, ed. Richard Allen and Harish Trivedi (London: Routledge, 2001), p. 9. Interestingly many of these writers, particularly Mulk Raj Anand and Sankharan Menon Marath, married or had relationships with Irish women. Raja Rao's first wife was French.
47. Although *Untouchable* (Harmondsworth: Penguin, 1935) was Anand's first novel, *The Bubble* (Delhi: Arnold-Heinemann, 1984) details his early experiences in London. It fictionalizes much of the material in Anand, *Conversations in Bloomsbury* and was probably written in draft diary form during the period of the 1930s. It highlights particularly his sense of alienation in Britain, the significance of Ireland as a model and Anand's friendship with Maud Gonne, James Joyce's lover.
48. Whilst Anand focuses particularly on the Bloomsbury circle in his critique of British intellectual life, he does not examine the works of a substantial number of other English writers who were similarly marginalized and who were much more sympathetic to his stance. For example: Storm Jameson and Naomi Mitchison.
49. Anand cites this comment in 'The Story of My Experiment with a White Lie', in *Critical Essays on Indian Writing in English* (Bombay: Macmillan, 1972), pp. 2–18.
50. Anand, 'The Story of My Experiment with a White Lie', p. 16.
51. Gun Orgun, 'Definitions of Expatriation and Immigration in Bharati Mukherjee's Writing', in *Daskhat*, 2, 1993, p. 24. See also *Modernism and Empire*.
52. Fokkema Aleid, 'On the (False) Idea of Exile', in *Cross Cultures 30* (Amsterdam: Rodopi, 1997), p. 101.
53. Andrew Gurr, *Writers in Exile: The Idenitity of Home in Modern Literature* (Brighton: Harvester, 1981), pp. 18–19.
54. Aamer Hussein, 'The Echoing of Quiet Voices', in *Asian Voices in English*, ed. Mimi Chan and Roy Harris (Hong Kong: Hong Kong University Press, 1991), pp. 5–6.
55. Rosemary Marangoly George, *The Politics of Home: Postcolonial Relocations and Twentieth Century Fiction* (Cambridge: Cambridge University Press, 1996), pp. 2–3.
56. Raymond Williams, *The Politics of Modernism: Against the New Conformists*, ed. Tony Pinkney (London: Verso, 1989), p. 45.
57. I am indebted here to Patrick Williams's impressive argument in '"Simultaneous Uncontemporaneities": Theorising Modernism and Empire', in *Modernism and Empire*, pp. 13–38. Williams cites Edward Said

and Kumkum Sangari's comments which are drawn from Edward Said, 'Representing the Colonised', *Critical Inquiry*, 15, 1989, pp. 222–3, and Kumkum Sangari's well-known essay, 'The Politics of the Possible', *Cultural Critique*, 1987, p. 182.

58. Sarojini Naidu was once described by W. B. Yeats as the 'little Indian princess'. This phrase is cited in Maud Gonne, *A Servant of the Queen* (London: Gollancz, 1938), p. 331. She published widely in anthologies and collections of poetry. See: Edmund Gosse, 'Introduction', in Naidu, *The Birds of Time: Songs of Life, Death and the Spring* (London: Heinemann, 1912); also Elleke Boehmer, 'East is East and South is South: The Cases of Sarojini Naidu and Arundhati Roy', *Women: A Cultural Review,* 11, Nos 1–2, 2000, pp. 61–71.
59. There had been earlier vernacular versions of the tale of Partition and Independence. See, for example, Ishmat Chugtai, *The Crooked Line* (1944) or Qurratulain Heyder, *River of Fire* (1957)). Hosain was a contemporary of Chugtai's and attended college with her.
60. I am using the term 'internationality' here to describe the broad cosmopolitanism of this group. However, Homi Bhabha's coining of the idea of 'The Vernacular Cosmopolitan' as a title to his recent essay which appears in *Voices of the Crossing*, pp. 133–42 is also suggestive. Bhabha uses this term as a means of demonstrating the ways in which writers who translate between cultures renegotiate from a position of 'locality' which enters into larger national and social discourses. Whilst he is referring particularly to the 'double life' of British minorities in the late twentieth century, the term is also suggestive in relation to the acts of cultural translation which were the life of the *Progressive Writers Association* and earlier Indian writers in Britain where translation as he puts it is an 'act of survival'.
61. Attia Hosain, 'Deep Roots', in *Voices of the Crossing*, p. 20.
62. Hosain, 'Deep Roots', pp. 22–3.
63. Hosain, 'Deep Roots', p. 23.
64. Zia Jaffrey, 'Beyond the Veil', *The Nation*, 25 December 1989, pp. 800–1.
65. Attia Hosain, *Sunlight on a Broken Column* ([1961]; London: Virago, 1988), p. 138. All further references are to this edition and are included in the text.
66. Attia Hosain, *Phoenix Fled* ([1953]; London: Virago, 1988).
67. Hosain, *Sunlight on a Broken Column*, p. 234.
68. See R. K. Dhawan, ed., *Indian Women Novelists*, Set 111, Vol. 2 (New Delhi: Prestige Books, 1995); Iyengar, *Indian Writing in English*, p. 4612.
69. Anuradha Dingwaney Needham, 'Multiple Forms of (National) Belonging: Attia Hosain's *Sunlight on a Broken Column*', in *Modern Fiction Studies*, 39, 1, 1993, p. 105.
70. Meenakshi Mukherjee, *The Twice-Born Fiction* (New Delhi: Heinemann, 1971).
71. I am grateful for this observation to Laura Bondi's unpublished thesis entitled, 'An Image of India by an Indian Woman: Attia Hosain's Life and Fiction' (Venice: Universita Degli Studi di Venezia, 1992), p. 105.
72. Needham, 'Multiple Forms of (National) Belonging', p. 99.
73. Aubrey Menen, *The Space Within The Heart* (London: Hamilton, 1970), p. 88.

74. V. S. Naipaul, 'Taluqdars', in *New Statesman,* 7 July 1961, p. 19.
75. Attia Hosain made this point at a conference held in 1995 at Queen Mary College, University of London, on the Literatures of the Diaspora, organized by Susheila Nasta. This reference is to a taped recording of the proceedings.
76. Unpublished interview conducted by Nilufer Bharucha, 'In Conversation with Attia Hosain', June 1997, pp. 3–5.
77. Amit Chaudhuri, in 'Lure of the Hybrid: What the Post-Colonial Novel Means to the West', *TLS*, 3 September 1999, p. 6.
78. Interview with Lakshmi Holmstrom, 'Sunlight and Shadows', *Indian Review of Books*, 1, 12, 1992, p. 24.
79. Menen, *The Space Within The Heart*, p. 38.
80. Aubrey Menen, *Ramayana* (New York: Scribner's, 1954); published in England as *Rama Retold* (London: Chatto & Windus, 1954).
81. Menen, *The Space Within the Heart*, p. 14.
82. Menen, *Dead Man in the Silver Market,* p. 30.
83. Menen, *Dead Man in the Silver Market*, p. 117. Interestingly, the use of Italy and particularly Venice as a liminal space is developed in Anita Desai's diasporic novel *Baumgartner's Bombay* (London: Heinemann, 1988), which focuses on a German Jew, Hugo Baumgartner, as its central character who migrates from Germany to Bombay shortly after the start of the Second World War. As Desai describes Baumgartner's sojourn in Venice:

    [H]e stood there, as entranced as he was alarmed. Venice *was* the East, and yet it was Europe too; it was the magic boundary where the two met and blended, and for those seven days Hugo had been part of their union. He realised it only now: that during his constant wanderings, his ceaseless walking, he had been drawing closer and closer to this discovery of that bewitched point where they became one land of which he felt himself the natural citizen (Desai, p. 63).

84. Like Attia Hosain, Mulk Raj Anand and G. V. Desani, Aubrey Menen was well known in Britain both amongst what has been called the 'beautiful people of Bloomsbury' as well as in the wider literary and theatre world. A close friend of the Indian politician Krishna Menon (whose similar surname resulted in Menen changing his to avoid confusion), Menen was a regular visitor to India House and provided live coverage, like Salman Rushdie's fictional character, Saleem Sinai in *Midnights Children*, on the eve of India's Independence on All India Radio in 1947.
85. Mary Jane Hurst, 'Reintroducing Aubrey Menen: A Satiric Post-Colonial Author', in *World Literature Written in English*, 33–4, 1993–4, p. 130. This article contains a full bibliography of Menen's published works.
86. Hurst, 'Reintroducing Aubrey Menen', p. 132.
87. Cited in Mohamed Elias, *Aubrey Menen*, Vol. 7 (Madras: Macmillan, 1985), p. 5. The reference is taken from Tearsheets held in the Aubrey Menen collection, Boston University.
88. Aubrey Menen, *The Prevalence of Witches* (London: Chatto & Windus, 1947).
89. Early editions of the novel used 'gesture' as a subtitle.
90. Gillian Beer, 'Narrative Swerves: Grand Narratives and the Disciplines', in *Women: A Cultural Review*, 11, 12, pp. 4–7.

91. G. V. Desani, 'Liars, Hypocrites, Imperialists and Sages', in *Voices of the Crossing*, p. 122.
92. Desani, 'Liars, Hypocrites, Imperialists and Sages', pp. 123, 130.
93. Peter Russell and Khushwant Singh, eds, *A Note on 'All About H. Hatterr' and Hali* (London and Amsterdam: Karel Szeben, 1952), pp. 23–5. This is a very useful series of notes on Desani summarizing reviews by major critics when the book was first published and including Desani's editorial notes written for his publishers.
94. Contemporary readings include: Gerhard Stilz, ' "Truth? Hell, you will get contrast, and no mistake!": Sanitizing the Intercultural Polylemma in G. V. Desani's *All About H. Hatterr* (1948/72)', in *Hybridity and Postcolonialism: Twentieth Century Indian Literature*, ed. Monika Fludernik (Tubingen: ZAA Studies, 1998); Hadyn Williams, 'Hatterr and Bazza: Post-Colonial Picaros', in *Commonwealth Review*, 2, 1990–1, pp. 205–11. Salman Rushdie and Elizabeth West, eds, 'Introduction', in *The Vintage Book of Indian Writing* (London: Vintage, 1997), p. xviii.
95. Beer, 'Narrative Swerves', p. 5.
96. Jacqueline Bardolph, 'Language Madness in G. V. Desani's *All About H. Hatterr*', in *Commonwealth*, 8, 1, 1985, p. 10.
97. It might be useful to read Desani's experimentations with language and form in the light of recent translation theory. See Maria Tymoczko, 'Post-Colonial Writing and Literary Translation', in *Post-Colonial Translation: Theory and Practice*, ed. Susan Bassnett and Harish Trivedi (London: Routledge, 1999).

CHAPTER 2

1. George Lamming, 'Introduction' to 1983 edition of *In the Castle of My Skin* ([1953]; New York: Schocken, 1983), p. xii.
2. Derek Walcott, 'The Muse of History', in *What the Twilight Says: Essays* (London: Faber, 1998), p. 36; this essay was first published in 1974.
3. Cecil Gray's poem, 'Your Island, Your World' (in memory of Sam Selvon), in *Tiger's Triumph: Celebrating Sam Selvon*, ed. Susheila Nasta and Anna Rutherford (Dangaroo: Hebden Bridge, 1995), p. 146.
4. Stuart Hall, 'Minimal Selves', in *Identity*, ed. Lisa Appignanesi (London: Institute for Contemporary Arts, Document 6, 1987), pp. 25–34.
5. Henry Swanzy, 'The Exiled Imagination', *BBC Broadcast*, 21 May 1965.
6. Selvon frequently referred to himself as such in interviews and discussions.
7. Sam Selvon, *The Lonely Londoners* ([1956]; London: Longman, 1985); *Moses Ascending* (London: Davis-Poynter, 1975); *Moses Migrating* ([1983]; Washington: Three Continents Press, 1992), introduced by Susheila Nasta; all further references are to these editions and are included in the text.
8. Stuart Hall, 'Old and New Identities, Old and New Ethnicities', in *Culture, Globalization and the World-System*, ed. A. D. King (London: Macmillan – now Palgrave, 1991), p. 49.
9. Cited in 'Ignatius Sancho', in *Extravagant Strangers: A Literature of Belonging*, ed. Caryl Phillips (London: Faber, 1997), p. 6.

10. Simon Gikandi, *Maps of Englishness: Writing Identity in the Culture of Colonialism* (New York: Columbia University Press, 1996), p. xii.
11. George Lamming, 'The Coldest Spring in Fifty Years', *Kunapipi*, XX, 1, 1998, pp. 4–10.
12. Anne Walmsley, *The Caribbean Artists Movement* (London: New Beacon, 1992), p. xviii. George Lamming, along with Wilson Harris, Kamau Brathwaite, Andrew Salkey, Aubrey Williams (the painter) and many others were members of the 'Caribbean Artists Movement'.
13. Roy Porter, *London: A Social History* (London: Hamilton, 1994), p. 354.
14. See H. Tajfel and J. Dawson, eds, *Disappointed Guests: Essays by African, Asian and West Indian Students* (London: Oxford University Press, 1965).
15. A large number of books were published in 1998 to celebrate this moment of immigrant history. See, particularly, Mike Phillips and Trevor Phillips, *Windrush: The Irresistible Rise of Multi-Racial Britain* (London: Harper Collins, 1998); Onyekachi Wambu, ed., *Empire Windrush* (London: Gollancz, 1998); also James Procter, ed., *Writing Black Britain* (Manchester: Manchester University Press, 2000).
16. Procter, *Writing Black Britain*, p. 30.
17. I am grateful here to Elizabeth Maslen's observations in an unpublished paper entitled 'The Miasma of Englishness at Home and Abroad in the 1950s'.
18. Gikandi, *Maps of Englishness*, p. 86.
19. David Dabydeen, cited in Gifford Zerbanoo, *The Golden Thread: Asian Experiences of Post-Raj Britain* (London: Pandora, 1990), pp. 179–80; see also Michael Ragussis, *Figures of Conversion: 'The Jewish Question and English National Identity'* (London: Duke University Press, 1995).
20. Interestingly, in both Sam Selvon's short stories *Ways of Sunlight* (London: MacGibbon & Kee, 1957) and V. S. Naipaul's *The Mimic Men*, there are several references to the narrative of Jewishness in Britain, a narrative that paralleled that of the Caribbean immigrants. See the opening of *The Mimic Men*, where Naipaul describes Ralph Singh's first boarding-house run by a Jewish landlord, Shylock.
21. Sam Selvon, 'Finding West Indian Identity in London', in *Tiger's Triumph*, p. 59; this essay was first published in 1988.
22. Sam Selvon, 'Three Into One Can't Go – East Indian, Trinidadian, West Indian', in *Foreday Morning: Selected Prose 1946–86,* ed. Kenneth Ramchand and Susheila Nasta (London: Longman, 1989), p. 217.
23. Sam Selvon, *The Housing Lark* ([1965]; Washington: Three Continents Press, 1990), all further references are to this edition and are included in the text.
24. On several occasions, Selvon has referred to Moses and the 'boys' in his stories as 'Anancy' figures: see 'Interview with Reed Dasenbrock and Feroza Jussawalla', in *Tiger's Triumph*; also Selvon's Preface to *Moses Migrating*, p. ix; interestingly, this figure has frequently been taken up in recent critical debates as a trope for the postcolonial experience. As Gillian Beer argues in her essay 'Narrative Swerves', *Women: A Cultural Review*, 11, Nos 1–2, 2000, pp. 2–8, Anancy is 'not simply a con-man but a figure elusive, comedic; a Tiresias without guilt, transformative, performative, a

survivor who pays no deference to class or sex because tricks defy categories'.

25. Seamus Heaney, 'Englands of the Mind', in *Preoccupations: Selected Prose, 1968–78* (London: Faber, 1980), pp. 150–69.
26. Simon Gikandi describes Selvon's Trinidadian works in these terms in *Writing in Limbo: Modernism and Caribbean Literature* (New York: Cornell University Press, 1992), p. 28.
27. George Lamming, *The Emigrants* (London: Joseph, 1954); *Water With Berries* (London: Longman, 1971); Andrew Salkey, *Escape to an Autumn Pavement* (London: Hutchinson, 1960); E. R. Braithwaite, *To Sir With Love* (London: Bodley Head, 1959); Louise Bennett, *Jamaica Labrish* (Kingston: Sangster's, 1966); during this 20-year period over 137 novels by Caribbean writers were published in London.
28. Beryl Gilroy's fictional work has been late in gaining recognition in Britain and whilst her novel on immigrant life, *In Praise of Love and Children* (Leeds: Peepal Tree, 1996), has only recently been published, it was submitted to several publishers during the 1960s.
29. Jean Rhys, *Voyage in the Dark* ([1934]; Harmondsworth: Penguin, 1975), p. 7.
30. Philip Mason, 'Foreword', in David Lowenthal, *West Indian Societies* (Oxford: Oxford University Press, 1972), p. ix.
31. Donald Hinds, *Journey to an Illusion: A Study of West Indian Migration* (London: Heinemann, 1966), p. 4.
32. V. S. Naipaul, *The Mimic Men* ([1967]; Harmondsworth: Penguin, 1969), pp. 18–19.
33. Andrew Salkey, *Escape to an Autumn Pavement* (London: Hutchinson, 1960), p. 46.
34. V. S. Naipaul, 'Jasmine', in *The Overcrowded Barracoon* ([1972]; Harmondsworth: Penguin, 1976), p. 27.
35. Gikandi, *Writing in Limbo*, p. 34.
36. Caryl Phillips, 'Echoes of Columbus: George Lamming talks to Caryl Phillips', in *Wasafiri*, 26, 1997, p. 15.
37. See Edward Said, 'Introduction', to *Culture and Imperialism* (London: Chatto & Windus, 1993). pp. xi–xxxii.
38. George Lamming, *The Pleasures of Exile* (London: Joseph, 1960), p. 158.
39. Lamming, *The Pleasures of Exile*, p. 159.
40. Lamming, *The Pleasures of Exile*, p. 15.
41. The reference here is to Paul Gilroy's influential study, *The Black Atlantic: Modernity and Double Consciousness* (London: Verso, 1993); it is worth also noting here that Paul Gilroy is the son of the writer, Beryl Gilroy.
42. Jan Carew, *Fulcrums of Change* (New Jersey: Africa World Press, 1988), p. 113.
43. I am indebted to Simon Gikandi's argument here in *Writing in Limbo*, p. 5; see also Michael Dash, 'Introduction' to Edouard Glissant, *Caribbean Discourse: Selected Essays* (Charlottesville, VA: University Press of Virginia, 1989), pp. xi–xiv.
44. Carew, *Fulcrums of Change*, p. 91.
45. Carew, *Fulcrums of Change*, p. 108.

46. Wilson Harris, *Tradition, the Writer and Society* (London: New Beacon, 1967); see also Helen Tiffin's argument in 'Post-Colonial Literatures and Counter-Discourse', *Kunapipi*, 9, 3, 1987, pp. 17–35, to which I am indebted here.
47. The notion of counter-discourse and Selvon may be further explored in John Thieme's useful essay, 'Pre-Text and Con-Text: Rewriting the Caribbean', in *Cross Cultures 30* (Amsterdam: Rodopi, 1997), where he argues that writers attempting to 'unseat the hegemonic authority' of European colonial discourse often fail to do so because their works constitute themselves in a 'derivative relationship', which perpetuates an 'anxiety of influence', p. 82.
48. Lamming, *The Pleasures of Exile*, p. 157.
49. Michael de Certeau makes this point at a colloquium on cultural diversity cited by Winnifred Woodhall in *Transfigurations of the Mahgreb: Feminism, Decolonization and Literature* (Minneapolis, MN: University of Minnesota Press, 1996), p. 102. The argument which de Certeau advances here is interesting for he stresses that the 'modern' condition creates a situation in which we are all 'sociocultural voyagers caught in situations of transit' but the 'real' immigrants are the first 'victims . . . the pioneers of a civilization founded on the mixing of cultures'.
50. De Certeau, cited in *Transfigurations of the Magreb*, pp. 102–4.
51. Homi Bhahba, *the location of culture* (London: Routledge, 1994), p. 11.
52. Claire Alexander, 'Rivers to Cross', in *Writing Across Worlds: Literature and Migration*, ed. R. King, R. Connell and P. White (London: Routledge, 1995), pp. 58–9. It is important to distinguish the experience of these writers and the polarized racial grammar that surrounded them after arrival in Britain from that signalled by the use of 'migrant' now common in postcolonial criticism which more appropriately, in some senses, fits the later generation of diasporic writers born after Independence, for the shift from 'immigrant' to 'migrant' in critical terminologies is a complex one. This will be dealt with in more detail in Chapter 4, which focuses on the migrant sensibility as it has defined itself in Salman Rushdie's work.
53. Maya Angelou in conversation with Susheila Nasta and Sam Selvon; this comment occurred at a literary prizegiving for Selvon in 1988.
54. David Dabydeen, 'West Indian Writers in Britain', in *Voices of the Crossing*, ed. Naseem Khan and Ferdinand Dennis (London: Serpents Tail, 2000), pp. 71–4.
55. Kenneth Ramchand, 'Introduction' to *The Lonely Londoners* (London: Longman, 1985), p. 3.
56. Caryl Phillips, 'Following On', *Wasafiri*, 29, 1999, p. 36.
57. Michel Fabre, 'Samuel Selvon: Interviews and Conversations', in *Critical Perspectives on Sam Selvon*, ed. Susheila Nasta (Washington: Three Continents Press, 1988), p. 64.
58. Gerald Moore, 'The English Novel Abroad', Sam Selvon Interviewed, *BBC Radio Broadcast*, 4 January 1974.
59. Selvon, 'Three Into One Can't Go', pp. 212–17.
60. Edward (Kamau) Brathwaite, 'Caribbean Man', in *Carifesta Forum*, ed. John Hearne (Kingston: Institute of Jamaica, 1976), p. 199.
61. See Gikandi, *Writing in Limbo*, p. 16.

62. Selvon, *Ways of Sunlight* ([1957]; London: Longman, 1985), pp. 132–9. All further references are to this edition.
63. Bruce Woodcock, 'Post-Colonial Translations of the Streets of London', *Kunapipi,* XX1, 2, 1999, pp. 57–65. Woodcock makes the astute observation, adapting the title of Paul Gilroy's book *Small Acts* (London: Serpents Tail, 1993), that Selvon's story represents 'creative translation in action' (p. 60).
64. Selvon, *Tiger's Triumph*, p. 60.
65. See review history in Susheila Nasta, ed., *Critical Perspectives on Sam Selvon* (Washington: Three Continents Press, 1988); also Dabydeen in *Voices of the Crossing*.
66. The name 'Reinventing Britain' was used for a conference initiated by Homi Bhabha and Stuart Hall in 1997. Supported by the Arts Council of Britain and the British Council, the proceedings are available on the internet at the British Council Site, and were published in an issue of *Wasafiri*, *Taking the Cake*, No. 29, Spring 1999.
67. Ramchand and Nasta, eds, *Foreday Morning: Selected Prose 1946–86*, p. xvii. This collection also contains an annotated bibliography of Selvon's lesser known works.
68. Ramchand and Nasta, eds, *Foreday Morning*.
69. Lloyd Brown, 'The Calypso Tradition', in *Modern Black Literature*, ed. S. O. Mezu (New York: Black Academy Press, 1971), p. 127.
70. Peter Nazareth, 'Interview with Sam Selvon', in *World Literature Written in English*, Vol. 18, No. 2, 1979, p. 421.
71. Selvon used the term 'dialect' in the days when the novel was first published.
72. Dabydeen, *Voices of the Crossing*, p. 77.
73. John Thieme, ' "The World Turn Upside Down": Carnival Patterns in *The Lonely Londoners'*, *Toronto South-Asian Review*, 5, 1, 1986, p. 194.
74. Transcribed from, 'The English Novel Abroad', Selvon interviewed by Gerald Moore, *BBC Broadcast*, 4 January 1974.
75. Gordon Rohlehr, 'The Folk in Caribbean Literature', *Tapia*, December 1972, p. 7.
76. Sam Selvon, 'Little Drops of Water', *BIM*, XI, 44, 1967, p. 246.
77. Clement Wyke, *Sam Selvon's Dialectical Style and Fictional Strategy* (Vancouver: University of British Columbia Press, 1991), p. 145.
78. V. S. Naipaul, 'The Regional Barrier', *Times Literary Supplement*, 15 August 1958, p. 37.
79. Peter Nazareth, 'Interview with Sam Selvon', *World Literature Written in English,* 18, 2, 1979, pp. 430–1.
80. Nazareth, 'Interview with Sam Selvon', p. 430.
81. Frank Birbalsingh, 'Interview with Sam Selvon', 1986 (unpublished).
82. Jill Neville, *Sunday Times*, 24 August 1975, p. 25.
83. Gabrielle Watling, 'Colonial Mimeticism and the Metropolis in V. S. Naipaul's *The Mimic Men* and Sam Selvon's *Moses Ascending*', in *Literature in North Queensland*, 20, 2, 1993, p. 72.
84. Tiffin in 'Post-Colonial Literatures and Counter-Discourse' makes a similar point about Moses's supposed mastery of English, pp. 22–4.
85. Michel Fabre, 'Sam Selvon', in *West Indian Literature*, ed. Bruce King (London: Macmillan, 1979), p. 123.

86. Helen Tiffin, ' "Under the Kiff-Kiff Laughter": Stereotype and Subversion in *Moses Ascending* and *Moses Migrating*', in *Tiger's Triumph*, p. 132.
87. Tiffin, 'Post-Colonial Literatures and Counter-Discourse', p. 24.
88. Tiffin, *Tiger's Triumph*, p. 138. Tiffin argues here that Moses resists one dimension of the diasporic narrative, a return to his roots and a marriage to Doris, favouring instead 'an ambivalent return, as a "norphan" to his "other" London home', p. 138.

PART 2 IMAGINARY HOMELANDS

CHAPTER 3

1. Alejo Carpentier: From an interview with Eclides Vazquez Candela, *Granma*, 6 April, 1969; cited by Andrew Salkey as an epigraph to *Come Home, Malcolm Heartland* (London: Hutchinson, 1976), p. 111.
2. Edward Brathwaite, 'The House in the West Indian Novel', *Tapia*, 3 July 1977, p. 5; when this piece was written, Kamau Brathwaite was publishing under the name of Edward Brathwaite.
3. V. S. Naipaul, 'Without a Place'; interview with Ian Hamilton, *TLS*, 30 July 1971, p. 897.
4. Wilson Harris, *Tradition, the Writer and Society* (London: New Beacon, 1967), p. 20.
5. Wilson Harris, *The Infinite Rehearsal* (London: Faber, 1987).
6. Michael Gorra, *After Empire* (Chicago, IL: University of Chicago Press, 1997), p. 8.
7. See bibliography for the full range and variety of Naipaul's publications.
8. Bharati Mukherjee and Robert Boyers, 'A Conversation with V. S. Naipaul', *Salmagundi*, 54 (1981), p. 5; this interview is reprinted in *Conversations With V. S. Naipaul*, ed. Feroza Jussawalla (Mississippi: University Press of Mississippi, 1997). Jussawalla makes the interesting point in her introduction that the interviews collected in her edition, which span the whole of Naipaul's writing career, are like a '*roman* . . . a story about someone who might as well be a fictional character who is growing, developing, changing and finally coming to a knowledge of who he is', p. x. Naipaul's evolution as a writer can be seen through these interviews to be intimately connected to his biography.
9. V. S. Naipaul, *The Mimic Men* ([Deutsch, 1967]; Harmondsworth: Penguin, 1969); all further references are to this edition and are included in the text.
10. Sara Suleri, *The Rhetoric of English India* (Chicago, IL: University of Chicago Press, 1992), p. 6.
11. Harris, *Tradition, the Writer and Society*. Harris argues, like Brathwaite later, that the majority of West Indian novels belong in the main to the conventional mould – as novels of 'persuasion'. He cites Naipaul's *A House for Mr Biswas* (1961) as an example of this, whereas George Lamming's *Of Age and Innocence* (1958) supposedly represents the alternative, a novel in which 'dialogue' and 'dialectic' are explored and we do not witness the

linear development or consolidation of character typical of the other genre. This was too neat a distinction, as will be seen in the course of this chapter, in which Naipaul, like Sam Selvon earlier, does not conform in his later writings to this model. Even where he does use it, arguably in *Biswas*, a tension exists between the adapted form and its new context and results in a 'creolization' of the traditional genre.

12. Naipaul, 'Without a Place', p. 897; interestingly, Simon Gikandi uses the idea of being caught in 'limbo' as the title for his book on Caribbean literature and its relationship to modernity, *Writing in Limbo* (New York: Cornell University Press, 1992).
13. Suleri, *Rhetoric*, p. 149; Suleri suggests that the peculiar 'betrayal' that Naipaul experiences with relation to the English language cannot be repeated by a later generation of West Indian writers whose 'idiom was moulded out of the area's independence in the 1960s', and the difficulties of his individual location – caught in a period of historical and cultural transition – are ultimately productive.
14. Suleri, *Rhetoric*, p. 149.
15. Naipaul, 'Without a Place', p. 897.
16. Simon Gikandi, *Maps of Englishness* (New York: Columbia University Press, 1996), p. 194. Gikandi makes the convincing argument that the writing of identity in the postwar period occurred in what he calls the 'post-imperial aporia', a space of crisis which enabled an enormous burst of literary creativity.
17. As is pointed out in the Introduction and the last chapter, London was a 'literary headquarters' for a number of writers from Africa, the Caribbean and South Asia during this period as well as many others from the ex-colonies.
18. Gorra, *After Empire*, p. 170.
19. Homi Bhabha, 'Signs Taken For Wonders: Questions of Ambivalence and Authority under a Tree Outside Delhi', *the location of culture* (London: Routledge, 1994), p. 120. I am drawing here on some illuminating observations made by Michael Gorra in his book *After Empire*.
20. V. S. Naipaul, 'London', in *The Overcrowded Barracoon* ([Deutsch, 1972]; Harmondsworth: Penguin, 1976), p. 13. All further references are to this edition.
21. Gorra, *After Empire*, p. 170.
22. See here, Rob Nixon, *London Calling: V. S. Naipaul, Postcolonial Mandarin* (Oxford: Oxford University Press, 1992); and Selwyn Cudjoe, *V. S. Naipaul: A Materialist Reading* (Amherst, MA: University of Massachusetts Press, 1988).
23. Naipaul prefers the usage of this term to 'Asian'.
24. Stephen Schiff, 'The Ultimate Exile', *The New Yorker*, 23 May 1994, pp. 60–71; reprinted in *Conversations with V. S. Naipaul*, p. 148.
25. In *An Area of Darkness* ([Deutsch, 1964], Harmondsworth: Penguin 1968), p. 27, Naipaul describes India as a 'restingplace for the imagination'. All further references are to this edition.
26. V. S. Naipaul, 'East Indian', in *The Overcrowded Barracoon* ([Deutsch, 1972]; Harmondsworth: Penguin, 1976), p. 36.

27. Satendra Nandan, 'The Diasporic Consciousness', in *Interrogating Post-Colonialism*, ed. Harish Trivedi and Meenakshi Mukherjee (Shimla: Institute of Advanced Study, 1996), p. 55.
28. Nandan, 'The Diasporic Consciousness', p. 57.
29. I am in accord with Shirley Chew's argument here in '(Post)Colonial Translations in V. S. Naipaul's *Enigma of Arrival*', in *Translating Life: Studies in Transpositional Aesthetics,* ed. Shirley Chew and Alistair Stead (Liverpool: Liverpool University Press, 1999), in which she argues that Naipaul is both linked to, and different from, writers such as Kipling and Forster, Conrad and Somerset Maugham who were familiar with writing about 'faraway places', and those metropolitan writers who came to 'adopt the city' as their country of the arts such as Joyce, Lawrence and Nabokov. Chew quotes from Malcolm Bradbury's 'The Cities of Modernism', *Modernism 1890–1930*, ed. M. Bradbury and James McFarlane (Harmondsworth: Penguin, 1976), p. 100.
30. Salman Rushdie, *Shame* (London: Cape, 1983); Rushdie's ideas on imaginary homelands and migrancy will be explored in detail in the following chapter.
31. Chew, '(Post)Colonial Translations', p. 140; this vision of translation as a creative space derives from Salman Rushdie's analysis of migration in Salman Rushdie, *Imaginary Homelands* (London: Granta, 1991), p. 15.
32. David Dabydeen's second collection of poetry is entitled *Coolie Odyssey* (London: Hansib, 1988) and reimagines the voices of this history.
33. Vijay Mishra, 'New Lamps for Old Diasporas Migrancy Border', *Interrogating Post-Colonialism*, p. 74.
34. Paul Gilroy, *The Black Atlantic: Modernity and Double Consciousness* (London: Verso, 1993), p. 16.
35. Rushdie, *Imaginary Homelands*, p. 10.
36. Mishra, 'New Lamps for Old Diasporas Migrancy Border', p. 78.
37. V. S. Naipaul, 'Writing *A House For Mr Biswas*', *New York Review*, November 1983, pp. 22–3.
38. Naipaul, 'Writing *A House For Mr Biswas*', pp. 22–3.
39. V. S. Naipaul, 'Jasmine', in *The Overcrowded Barracoon* ([Deutsch, 1972]; London: Penguin 1976), p. 26. All further references are to this edition.
40. Landeg White, *V. S. Naipaul: A Critical Introduction* (London: Macmillan, 1975), p. 8.
41. V. S. Naipaul, Foreword, in Seepersad Naipaul, *The Adventures of Gurudeva and Other Tales* (London: Deutsch, 1976), p. 18
42. Naipaul, *An Area of Darkness*, p. 43.
43. Naipaul, *An Area of Darkness*, p. 42.
44. Ashis Nandy, *The Intimate Enemy: Loss and Recovery of Self Under Colonialism* (Delhi: Oxford University Press, 1983), p. ix.
45. Lamming, *The Pleasures of Exile*, p. 159.
46. Helen Tiffin, 'Rites of Resistance: Counter-Discourse and West Indian Biography', *Journal of West Indian Literature*, 3, 1, 1989, pp. 28–9.
47. 'Conrad's Darkness', in *The New York Review of Books*, 17 October 1974; references here are taken from the reprinted version in R. D. Hamner, ed., *Critical Perspectives on V. S. Naipaul* (London: Heinemann, 1976), pp. 54–64.

48. *Conversations with V. S. Naipaul*, p. 148.
49. Anne Walmsley, *The Caribbean Artists Movement 1966–1972* (London: New Beacon, 1992). In this brilliant history of the period, Walmsley documents the powerful effect these writers and artists were to have on 'British' culture; whilst Naipaul knew many of this group, he did not participate in the formal activities, although he socialized with many of them – particularly Andrew Salkey who was responsible for getting his first novel into the hands of the publisher. Naipaul was also editor, for a brief period following Henry Swanzy, on the influential BBC programme *Caribbean Voices* reviewing the work of many Caribbean and Asian writers resident in Britain during this period, including Attia Hosain and Nirad Chaudhuri.
50. The lack of coherent critical coverage of these writers (although they were reviewed occasionally in the national press) was remarkable and still continues in studies of the English novel today. For examples of what Andrzej Gasiorek, in *Post-War British Fiction: Realism and After* (London: Arnold, 1995), calls a 'deafening silence', see: Bryan Appleyard, *The Pleasures of Peace: Art and Imagination in Post-War Britain* (London: Faber, 1989); Bernard Bergonzi, *The Situation of the Novel* (London: Macmillan, 1970); *The Contemporary English Novel*, ed. Malcom Bradbury and David Palmer (New York: Holmes and Meier, 1980); *The Novel Today: Contemporary Writers on Modern Fiction*, ed. Malcolm Bradbury (Manchester: Manchester University Press, 1977); David Gervais, *Literary England: Versions of 'Englishness' in Modern Writing* (Cambridge: Cambridge University Press, 1993); Stuart Laing, 'Novels and the Novel', *Society and Literature, 1945–70*, ed. Alan Sinfield (London: Methuen, 1983); and David Lodge, *The Novelist at the Crossroads* (London: Routledge, 1971).
51. Naipaul, 'Jasmine', p. 28.
52. Naipaul, 'Jasmine', p. 26.
53. A Sivanandan, 'The Enigma of the Colonized: Reflections on Naipaul's "Arrival" ', *Race and Class*, 32, 1, 1990, pp. 35, 43.
54. As Satendra Nandan has shown, Lamming revises this position in a 1989 essay published in *Indenture and Exile: The Indo-Caribbean Experience* (London: Hansib, 1989).
55. George Lamming, *The Pleasures of Exile* (London: Joseph, 1960), p. 225.
56. 'Interview with V. S. Naipaul' with Adrian Rowe-Evans, in *Transition*, 40, 1971, p 59.
57. 'Foreword' to *The Adventures of Gurudeva and Other Tales* (London: Deutsch, 1976), p. 10; first published in Trinidad in 1943 by the Guardian Commercial Printery and later introduced by Naipaul in an English edition.
58. Louis James, *Caribbean Literature in English* (London: Longman, 1999), p. 162, makes this point when describing Naipaul's early days in London.
59. Gabrielle Watling, 'Embarrassing Origins: Colonial Mimeticism and the Metropolis in *The Mimic Men* and *Moses Ascending*', *Literature in North Queensland*, 20, 2, 1993, p. 69.
60. Homi Bhabha, 'Signs Taken for Wonders: Questions of Ambivalence and Authority under a Tree Outside Delhi', *Critical Enquiry*, 12, 1, 1985, p. 148.
61. Suleri, *The Rhetoric of English India,* p. 158.
62. Homi Bhabha, 'Representations and the Colonial Text: A Critical

Exploration of Some Forms of Mimeticism', in *Theory of Reading,* ed. Gloversmith (Sussex: 1984), p. 116.

63. Suleri, *Rhetoric*, p. 158.
64. Mishra, 'New Lamps for Old Diasporas Migrancy Border', p. 79.
65. Watling, 'Embarrassing Origins', p. 69.
66. Watling, 'Embarrassing Origins', p. 69.
67. The allusion here to T. S. Eliot's *The Waste Land* is not gratuitous. It is typical of the educated and literary sensibility of Naipaul's narrator, who also alludes to Keats's 'The Eve of St Agnes' (1820) and Charles Dickens's *Our Mutual Friend* in the course of his writing.
68. Naipaul, in fact, wrote large parts of the English section of the novel whilst he was in India writing *An Area of Darkness.*
69. François Guillard, 'An Unspeakable (His)tory', *Yale French Studies*, 56, 1980, pp. 129–39.
70. Angus Calder, 'World's End: V. S. Naipaul's *The Mimic Men*', in *The Commonwealth Writer Overseas: Themes of Exile and Expatriation*, ed. Alastair Niven (Brussels: Revue des Lanmgue Virante, 1976), p. 274.
71. Calder, 'World's End: V. S. Naipaul's *The Mimic Men*', p. 274.
72. White, *V. S. Naipaul: A Critical Introduction*. Landeg White points out that the merging of 'identity between Naipaul and Kirpalsingh is obviously intentional. Naipaul is perfectly capable of detaching himself from a narrator when necessary', as we see in many of his other works, p. 162.
73. B. F. MacDonald, 'The Colonial Experience in the Nigerian and Trinidadian Novel', PhD thesis, University of Leeds, p. 144. I have found MacDonald's analysis particularly illuminating in the later stages of my argument here and am closely following his analysis of the first section of *The Mimic Men.*
74. Feroza Jussawalla, *Conversations With V. S. Naipaul* (Jackson, MS: University Press of Mississippi, 1997).
75. Wilson Harris, *Tradition, the Writer and Society* (London: Faber, 1965).
76. V. S. Naipaul, *The Enigma of Arrival* (Harmondsworth: Penguin, 1987). All further references are to this edition and are included in the text.
77. There have been several critical discussions of the form of the novel. Selwyn R. Cudjoe argues in *V. S. Naipaul: A Materialist Reading* (Amherst, MA: University of Massachusetts, 1988) that Naipaul is still 'hiding' in the novel by calling it a work of fiction and refuses still to confront what is the 'unblinding light of day'.
78. Timothy F. Weiss, *On the Margins: The Art of Exile in V. S. Naipaul* (Massachusetts, MA: University of Massachusetts Press, 1992), p. 199.
79. Suleri, *Rhetoric*, p. 171.
80. Weiss, *On the Margins*; this term is used throughout this very useful study to describe the 'splitting' effect of Naipaul's 'exile'.
81. Suleri, *Rhetoric*, p. 158.
82. See Gillian Tindall, *Countries of the Mind: The Meaning of Place to Writers* (London: Hogarth, 1991).
83. I am not trying to suggest here that Naipaul deliberately sets the novel in a political context. I am merely pointing to the nature of government rhetoric on race and nation prevalent when both Selvon's and Naipaul's novels were written.

84. Rushdie, *Imaginary Homelands*, p. 91. I am in agreement here with M. Griffiths who compares the country house novels of Kazuo Ishiguro and Naipaul in an interesting article 'Great English Houses/New Homes in England? Memory and Identity in Kazuo Ishiguro's *The Remains of the Day* and V. S. Naipaul's *The Enigma of Arrival*', *Span*, 1993, 36, pp. 488–503. Griffiths discusses the context of 1980s Britain and the nostalgia of the heritage industry on pp. 488–9.
85. Griffiths, 'Great English Houses/New Homes in England?', p. 489.
86. Clearly, a number of contemporary black and Asian writers who have been resident in Britain could be added to this list – including Caryl Phillips, Joan Riley, Farukh Dhondy, Atima Srivastava and Andrea Levy.
87. Griffiths, 'Great English Houses/New Homes in England?', p. 496.
88. Chew, '(Post)Colonial Translations', p. 141. I am responding to Shirley Chew's invaluable analysis of this novel throughout this section of the chapter.
89. J. Vals-Russell, 'From the Outside In: V. S. Naipaul in Rural England', *Caliban*, 27, 1990, p. 140.
90. Chew, '(Post)Colonial Translations', p. 49.
91. Chew, '(Post)Colonial Translations', p. 49.
92. Meena Alexander, *The Shock of Arrival: Reflections on Postcolonial Experience* (Boston, MA: South End Press, 1996), p. 79.
93. Vals-Russell, 'From the Outside In', p. 147.
94. I am echoing here the title of Paul Scott's Raj novel set in India which deals with those English and Anglo-Indians who remained behind after Independence and the earlier migrations of Empire.
95. Homi Bhabha, 'Hybridity', in *Afterwords*, Artforum Home Site, p. 2. In this article originally published on the internet, Bhabha discusses the resonances of a Toni Morrison poem, 'Whose House Is This', published in 1992. The poem bears an interesting relationship to Naipaul's 'enigma' concerning modes of living and survival in his novel.
96. Derek Walcott, 'The Antilles: Fragments of Epic Memory', reprinted in *Derek Walcott: What the Twilight Says* (London: Routledge, 1998), pp. 68–9. I am grateful to some of Satendra Nandan's observations, in 'The Diasporic Consciousness: From Biswas to Biswasghat', for pinpointing the relevance of this essay by Walcott to Naipaul's diasporic experience.
97. Rushdie, *Imaginary Homelands*, p. 91.
98. Rushdie, *Imaginary Homelands*, p. 91.
99. Salim says this in *A Bend in the River*, p. 184.
100. Virney Kirpal, *The Third World Novel of Expatriation* (New Delhi: Stirling, 1989), p. 73.
101. Edward Said, *After the Last Sky* (New York: Pantheon, 1986), p. 18.

CHAPTER 4

1. Salman Rushdie, 'The Courter', in *East, West* (London: Cape, 1994), p. 211. All further references are to this edition.
2. V. S. Naipaul, 'Interview with Aamer Hussein', (1994), in *Conversations with V. S. Naipaul*, ed. F. Jussawalla (Jackson, MS: University of Mississippi, 1997), pp. 154–62.

3. Wilson Harris, 'Adversarial Contexts and Creativity', in *New Left Review*, 154, Nov/Dec, 1985, p. 128.
4. Bryan Cheyette, 'Ineffable and Usable: Towards a British-Jewish Writing', in *Textual Practice*, 10, 2, 1996, p. 295; Cheyette is drawing here on a more extended discussion of the origin of the term and its Hebrew 'roots', in *Home Rules: Some Reflections of Racism and Nationalism in Everyday Life*, ed. Phil Cohen (London: University of East London New Ethnicities Unit, 1993), p. 34. The ambivalence of the term has also been discussed at length by Vijay Mishra and Stuart Hall (see bibliography).
5. Damian Grant, *Salman Rushdie* (Plymouth: Northcote House, 1999), p. 100. I am drawing here on an argument suggested by Damian Grant, who also illustrates the extent to which Rushdie deconstructs the Good Witch Glinda's suggestion in *The Wizard of Oz* that 'there is no place like home' by suggesting in his booklet on that film (for the British Film Institute in 1992) that 'there is no longer any place *as* home: except, of course, for the home we make, or the homes that are made for us, in Oz, which is anywhere and everywhere, except the place from which we began', pp. 56–7.
6. Salman Rushdie, *Imaginary Homelands: Essays and Criticism 1981–1991* (London: Granta, 1991); in this well-known collection of non-fictional essays, Rushdie describes the fictions created by writers like himself, 'exiles, or immigrants or expatriates' as 'imaginary homelands', p. 10.
7. Salman Rushdie, 'Choice Between Light and Dark', in *The Observer*, 22 January 1989; reptd in *Critical Fictions: The Politics of Imaginative Writing*, ed. Philomena Mariana (Seattle, WA: Bay Press, 1991), p. 96.
8. Salman Rushdie, 'Homelessness is Where the Art is', in *The Bookseller*, 15 July 1994, p. 49.
9. Rushdie, 'Homelessness is Where the Art is'.
10. Aijaz Ahmad, *In Theory* (London: Verso, 1992); Ahmad uses this term to distinguish between those writers descended from the modernist tradition (Eliot, Pound, Joyce, Conrad etc.) and those postcolonial writers who are literally in political exile, such as Ngugi wa Thiong'o, who were actively involved in resistance movements in their own countries, pp. 128–39.
11. Rushdie, 'In Good Faith', in *Imaginary Homelands*, p. 414.
12. There have been several books, essays and newspaper articles published on this debate; some of the most illuminating are collected in L. Appignanesi and S. Maitland, eds, *The Rushdie File* (London: Fourth Estate, 1989).
13. Salman Rushdie, 'Minority Literatures in a Multi-Cultural Society', in *Displaced Persons*, ed. Kirsten Holst Petersen and Anna Rutherford (Mundelstrup: Dangaroo, 1986), p. 34.
14. Homi Bhabha, 'How Newness Enters the World', in *the location of culture* (London: Routledge, 1994), pp. 212–36, provides a theoretical analysis of Rushdie's *The Satanic Verses* as a postcolonial text celebrating impurity and mongrelization and 'hybridity'.
15. In Ian Hamilton, 'The First Life of Salman Rushdie', in the *New Yorker*, 25 December 1995, pp. 90–7, 110–113, 112–13.
16. Vijay Mishra, 'Postcolonial Differend: Diasporic Narratives of Salman Rushdie', in *Ariel*, 26, 3 July 1995, p. 8.
17. Bhabha, *the location of culture*, p. 224.

18. avtar brah, *Cartographies of Diaspora: Contesting Identities* (London: Routledge, 1996), p. 209.
19. Stuart Hall, David Held and Tony McGrew, eds, *Modernity and Its Futures* (Cambridge: Polity Press/Open University, 1992), p. 310.
20. Rushdie uses this phrase several times in *The Satanic Verses* (London: Viking, 1989), pp. 129, 538.
21. Vijay Mishra, 'New Lamps For Old: Diasporas Migrancy Border', in *Interrogating Post-Colonialism: Theory, Text and Context*, ed. H. Trivedi and M. Mukerjee (Shimla: Institute of Advanced Study, 1996), p. 81. Mishra discusses the challenge of the new Indian diaspora in relation to Bharati Mukherjee's novel, *Jasmine* (New York: Weidenfeld, 1989).
22. brah, *Cartographies of Diaspora: Contesting Identities,* p. 196.
23. I am indebted here to Bryan Cheyette's reading of R. B. Kitaj's, *First Diasporist Manifesto* (London: Thames & Hudson, 1989) from which he quotes: see Cheyette, pp. 36–7.
24. brah, *Cartographies of Diaspora: Contesting Identities,* p. 193.
25. Bharati Mukherjee, 'Introduction' to *Darkness* (Harmondsworth: Penguin, 1985), p. 3; Mukherjee and Rushdie have been compared in their position as 'third world cosmopolitans' by Timothy Brennan in his study *Salman Rushdie and the Third World: Myths of the Nation* (London: Macmillan, 1989). Although Mukherjee's position on the potentiality of the 'immigrant' voice differs from Rushdie's, due to the American context in which she is writing, her celebration of what she calls 'fluid identities' is similar as is her public persona as a spokesperson created by the literary and critical publishing industry for the 'third world' Indian intellectual/writer living abroad.
26. Salman Rushdie, *Shame* ([Cape, 1983]; London: Picador, 1994); all further references are to this edition.
27. Ahmad, *In Theory*, pp. 134–7; Timothy Brennan in *Salman Rushdie and the Third World* argues a similar case, and suggests that Rushdie, like other third world cosmopolitans such as Bharati Mukherjee and Derek Walcott, has set himself up as a spokesperson for the ills of the 'Third World', but bears little relationship to it in terms of active resistance.
28. Cheyette, 'Ineffable and Usable', p. 295. An interesting comparison with Rushdie's location is implied in this article's exploration of British-Jewish writing, and the dangers of the ahistorical allegorization of the Jew by postmodern theorists such as Jean-François Lyotard.
29. Amit Chaudhuri, 'Lure of the Hybrid', in *TLS*, 3 September 1999, pp. 5–6.
30. Salman Rushdie, 'The Indian Writer in England' in *The Eye of the Beholder: Indian Writing in English*, ed. Maggie Butcher (London: Commonwealth Institute, 1983), p. 77.
31. Rushdie, 'The Indian Writer in England', p. 79.
32. Rushdie, 'The Indian Writer in England', p. 80.
33. Satendra Nandan, 'The Diasporic Consciousness', in *Interrogating Post-Colonialism: Theory, Text and Context*, p. 54.
34. Salman Rushdie, in ' "Errata": or, Unreliable Narration in *Midnight's Children*', in *Imaginary Homelands*, pp. 22, 26; makes it clear that Saleem's writing of himself through his various stories is only one of many possible versions: the significant point here is the difference between 'literal and

remembered truth' (p. 24); initially, the object of the writing was to see beyond the filter of time and migration; it became through the process of writing, a project concerned with the 'process of filtration itself', the shifting truths of 'memory' (p. 25).

35. Grant, *Salman Rushdie.* I am drawing on an argument suggested by Damian Grant here (p. 24), where he quotes from *Midnight's Children* (London: Cape, 1981), p. 100.
36. Grant, *Salman Rushdie,* p. 24; Grant quotes from *Imaginary Homelands*, pp. 12, 278.
37. Rukmini Bhaya Nair and Rimi Bhattacharya, 'Salman Rushdie: The Migrant in the Metropolis', in *Third Text*, Summer 1990, p. 23.
38. Mikhail Bahktin, *The Dialogic Imagination,* trans. Caryl Emerson and Michael Holquist (Austin, TX: University of Texas Press, 1981).
39. Sourayan Mookerjea, 'Irradiations of History: The Author, Cosmopolitanism and *The Satanic Verses*', in *World Literature Written in English*, Vol. 32, 2 & Vol. 33, 1, 1992–3, pp. 107–21. Mookerjea uses this phrase in summarizing Bakhtin's arguments concerning the novel as a parodic and dialogic form, p. 109.
40. Revathi Krishnaswamy, 'Mythologies of Migrancy: Postcolonialism, Postmodernism and the Politics of Dislocation', in *Ariel*, 26, 1, 1995, p. 135.
41. Many of these writers were resident in Britain in the prewar period, well before Indian Independence and the birth of Rushdie himself; Marath is still resident in Britain.
42. Nirad Chaudhuri, who died in August 1999 at the age of 101, lived in Britain for nearly 50 years; Sankharan Menon Marath has lived in Britian since 1934 and is now 92.
43. It is worth noting here that there is a great deal of intertextuality between the theoretical writings of Homi Bhabha and the fictions of Salman Rushdie, which perhaps makes it worth reading Rushdie's fiction in the light of some of Bhabha's theories.
44. Rushdie, 'The Indian Writer in England', p. 80.
45. Salman Rushdie, 'Introduction' to *The Vintage Book of Indian Writing* (1947–97), ed. Salman Rushdie and Elizabeth West, p. xviii.
46. Daniel and Jonathan Boyarin 'Diaspora: Generation and Ground of Jewish Identity', in *Critical Inquiry*, 19, 1993, p. 721. I am grateful to Bryan Cheyette for drawing my attention to this.
47. Rushdie, 'The Indian Writer in England', pp. 83–4.
48. Cheyette, 'Ineffable and Usable', p. 303.
49. Rushdie, 'Minority Literatures in a Multi-Cultural Society', pp. 33–7.
50. This term is deliberately used by Feroza Jussawalla in contradistinction to 'hybridity', which has been current in contemporary postcolonial theory and particularly in the works of Homi Bhabha. Jussawalla argues in 'Of *The Satanic Verses*: Mohajirs and Migrants', in *Third Text*, 32, 1995, that, unlike the notion of hybridity which engenders a sense of loss, syncretism is a 'joyous recreation' which has long been indigenous to local Indian cultures, pp. 85–7.
51. Rushdie, 'Minority Literatures in a Multi-Cultural Society', pp. 34–5.
52. Rushdie, 'The Indian Writer in England', p. 82; Rushdie voices similar

sentiments in later more overtly political essays such as 'Outside the Whale', 'The New Empire Within Britain', both reptd in *Imaginary Homelands*, and 'Minority Literatures in a Multi-Cultural Society', in *Displaced Persons*, pp. 33–43.

53. Rushdie, 'The Indian Writer in England', p. 79.
54. Ben Okri, *New Statesman*, cited in T. Brennan, 'Writing From Black Britain', *The Literary Review*, 34, 1990, p. 7. Interestingly, as Lyn Innes has shown in an essay on two early migrant voices in Britain – Ignatius Sancho and Sake Dean Mahomet – these kinds of positionings were also common in review histories in the late eighteenth and nineteenth centuries. This comment by Okri could, of course, be turned around to: if you're published because you're white, you're not read because of it, and we have perhaps an explanation of why literature is little read!
55. Rushdie, 'The Indian Writer in England', p. 79.
56. I am borrowing this term from Robert Lee's usage in *Other Britain, Other British* (London: Pluto, 1995), pp. 69–90.
57. Rushdie, 'The Indian Writer in England', p. 75; Rushdie describes himself in these terms in 1982.
58. Rushdie uses this as the title for his most recent novel *The Ground Beneath Her Feet* (London: Cape, 1999).
59. Rushdie, 'The Indian Writer in England', p. 78.
60. Tim Brennan, 'Writing from Black Britain', *Literary Review*, 34, 1, 1990, p. 7.
61. Movements, such as The Progressive Writers Association which held its first meeting in Britain in 1936 led by figures such as Mulk Raj Anand, dictated the agenda for Indian nationalism. Anand's *The Bubble* (London: Arnold-Heinemann, 1984), provides a fictionalized account of his early life in Britain, and Anand's letters reveal his involvement with writers of the Bloomsbury Group as well as the Hogarth Press. The Progressive Writers Association was concerned both with the movement for Indian Independence and with the presentation of a sustained critique of colonialism.
62. See Introduction and Chapter 1.
63. George Lamming, *The Pleasures of Exile*, p. 44.
64. See Simon Gikandi, *Writing In Limbo: Modernism and Caribbean Literature* (New York: Cornell University Press, 1992); also Stuart Hall, Paul Gilroy et al. in bibliography.
65. Raja Rao, *Kanthapura* ([1938]; New York: New Directions, 1963), p. vii; I am drawing here on examples from Feroza Jussawalla's interesting essay on 'syncretism' rather than 'hybridity' as a way of describing the indigenous aesthetics of Rushdie's fiction. Jussawalla, amongst other Asian critics, argues forcefully that the roots of Rushdie's aesthetic were already present in Indian culture and has been appropriated by metropolitan Western theories deriving from poststructuralism: 'of *The Satanic Verses'* Mohajirs and Migrants: Hybridity and Syncretism and Indigenous Aesthetics in Postcoloniality', in *Third Text*, 32, Autumn 1995, p. 86.
66. Jussawalla, 'of *The Satanic Verses*' Mohajirs and Migrants', p. 88.
67. Brennan, 'Writing from Black Britain', p. 24.
68. I am drawing on Cheyette's observation here when referring to Zygmunt Bauman's *Modernity and Ambivalence* (Oxford: Polity, 1991), p. 298.

69. Rushdie, 'The Indian Writer in England', p. 78.
70. Homi Bhabha, in 'Reinventing Britain: A Forum', in *Wasafiri*, 29, Spring 1999, p. 40.
71. Edward Said, 'Intellectuals in the Post-Colonial World', in *Salmagundi*, 70/71, 1986, p. 50.
72. Perry Anderson, *English Questions* (London: Verso, 1992), pp. 14–16.
73. The remarkable absence of the significance of these works, which Timothy Brennan has called 'invisible modernities', is analysed in Brennan's critique of the parochialism of several critical studies of the postwar novel which included the themes of exile and colonialism. He refers particularly to: Jeffrey Meyers, *Fiction and the Colonial Experience* (Ipswich: Boydell Press, 1973); and Terry Eagleton, *Exiles and Emigres: Studies in Modern Literature* (London: Chatto & Windus, 1970).
74. Rushdie, *Imaginary Homelands* (Harmondsworth: Penguin, 1991), pp. 132–8.
75. Rushdie, 'Minority Literatures in a Multi-Cultural Society', p.129.
76. Rushdie, 'Minority Literatures in a Multi-Cultural Society', p. 33.
77. Rushdie, 'Minority Literatures in a Multi-Cultural Society', p. 41.
78. Brennan, *Salman Rushdie and the Third World*, p. viii.
79. Rushdie was also involved practically in a number of political activities in the 1970s and 1980s to improve the living conditions of the Bangladeshi community in London.
80. Brennan, *Salman Rushdie and the Third World*, p. 38.
81. Rushdie, 'The Indian Writer in England', p. 81.
82. In *Finding the Centre: Two Narratives* (London: Deutsch, 1984), Naipaul describes his experience of India in Trinidad as a 'dream', p. 61.
83. See particularly V. S. Naipaul's non-fictional works on India: *An Area of Darkness* (1964), *India: A Wounded Civilization* ([New York: Knopf, 1977]; Harmondsworth: Penguin, 1979), *India: A Million Mutinies Now* (London: Viking, 1990). The extent to which India figured in Naipaul's family life is also very evident in the letters: *V. S. Naipaul: Letters Between a Father and a Son,* ed. G. Aitken (London: Little, Brown, 1999).
84. Sam Selvon, *A Brighter Sun* (London: Wingate, 1952) and *Turn Again Tiger* (London: MacGibbon and Kee, 1958) deal with East Indian families and the process of creolization in modern Trinidad, as do several of his short stories collected in *Ways of Sunlight* (London: MacGibbon and Kee, 1957); these editions have all been reprinted by Longman.
85. See V. S. Naipaul, *Letters Between a Father and a Son*; in these letters, which are introduced by Gillon Aitken, Naipaul's correspondence with his father and sister Kamala reveal the financial hardship the family suffered during Naipaul's period as a student at Oxford; also his sense of responsibility to 'home' and his younger siblings. Naipaul was the first son from a large and struggling island family to leave and attend university abroad, a departure made possible by his winning of one of the few and highly competitive island scholarships.
86. Michael Gorra, *After Empire: Scott, Naipaul, Rushdie* (London: University of Chicago Press, 1997), pp. 170–1.
87. Hamilton, 'The First Life of Salman Rushdie', p. 94.

88. Like many writers before and after him, including Naipaul, Selvon and Hanif Kureishi, Rushdie did not want to represent only the voice of the Asian or black in Britain. His aim was to create three-dimensional characters whether black, white, good, bad or a mixture of both. See Rushdie, 'Minority Literatures in a Multi-Cultural Society', pp. 33–43.
89. Catherine Bush, 'Salman Rushdie: An Interview', in *Conjunctions*, 14, 1989, p. 8.
90. We can benefit here from Paul Gilroy's *The Black Atlantic: Modernity and Double Consciousness* (London: Verso, 1993), which problematizes both the essentializing rhetoric of Afrocentrism as well as a postmodernist anti-essentialism which is ultimately reductive and refigures black history within an iconography of otherness and alterity. Stuart Hall in 'Cultural Identity and Diaspora', in *Identity: Community, Culture, Difference*, ed. J. Rutherford (London: Lawrence & Wishart, 1990), pp. 222–37, also stresses the heterogeneity of diasporic experience whether old or new.
91. See M. D. Fletcher, ed., *Reading Rushdie: Perspectives on the Fiction of Salman Rushdie* (Amsterdam: Rodopi, 1994) for a number of essays which take this approach.
92. Appignanesi and Maitland, eds, *The Rushdie File.*
93. Krishnaswamy, 'Mythologies of Migrancy', p. 128.
94. Bharati Mukherjee, 'Prophet and Loss: Salman Rushdie's Migration of Souls', *Village Voice Literary Supplement*, 72, March 1989, pp. 9–12.
95. Abdul R. JanMohamed, 'Wordliness-Without-World, Homelessness-as-Home: Towards a Definition of the Specular Border Intellectual', in *Edward Said: A Critical Reader*, ed. M. Spinkler (Oxford: Blackwell, 1992), pp. 96–116.
96. Brennan, *Salman Rushdie and the Third World*, p. 25. Brennan makes the important observation here that Terry Eagleton's *Exiles and Emigres* (London: Chatto & Windus, 1970), despite its Marxist focus, fails to open out the insularity of the Englishness it critiques and stops short of including the writing of colonial subjects, 'despite their screaming relevance to his theme'.
97. Simon Gikandi, *Maps of Englishness* (New York: Colombia University Press, 1996), pp. 196–7; Gikandi is elaborating on Linda Hutcheon's description of such novels as historiographic metafiction. For Linda Hutcheon, see *A Politics of Postmodernism* (New York: Routledge, 1989).
98. Gikandi, *Maps of Englishness,* p. 199.
99. See notes to epigraphs.
100. brah, *Cartographies of Diaspora*, p. 189.
101. Rushdie, *Satanic Verses* (London: Viking, 1988), p. 537. All further references are to this edition and are included in the text.
102. Salman Rushdie, 'The Novel is Not Dead. It's Just Buried', *The Observer*, 18 August 1996, p. 15.
103. Rushdie, 'The Indian Writer in England', p. 78.
104. Rushdie, 'Is Nothing Sacred', in *Imaginary Homelands*, pp. 420, 422–3.
105. Bhabha, *the location of culture*, p. 225.
106. Mishra, 'Postcolonial Differend', p. 25.
107. Rushdie, *The Observer*, 22 January 1989; reptd in *The Politics of Imaginative Writing*, p. 96.

108. Salman Rushdie, *The Satanic Verses*.
109. Bush, 'Salman Rushdie: An Interview', p. 13.
110. Rushdie, 'Outside the Whale', in *Imaginary Homelands*, pp. 87–102. This essay was first published in 1984.
111. Bryan Appleyard, 'Portrait of the Novelist as a Hot Property', in *The Sunday Times Magazine*, 11 September 1988, p. 32.
112. Rushdie, 'In Good Faith', in *Imaginary Homelands*, p. 394.
113. Bald, Suresh Renjen, 'Images of South Asian Migrants in Literature: Differing Perspectives', in *New Community*, 17, 3, 1991, pp. 413–31. In a thorough survey of postwar Anglo-British fiction, Bald illustrates the extent to which the South Asian Briton has been invisible.
114. Bush, 'Salman Rushdie: An Interview', p. 8.
115. Sara Suleri, *The Rhetoric of English India* (Chicago, IL: University of Chicago Press, 1992), p. 174.
116. Kelly Hewson, 'Opening up the Universe a Little More: Salman Rushdie and the Migrant as Storyteller', in *Span*, 29, 1989, p. 85.
117. Kenneth Ramchand, 'The Colour Problem at the University: A West Indian's Changing Attitudes', in *Disappointed Guests* (London: Oxford University Press, 1968), p. 36.
118. Catherine Cundy, *Salman Rushdie* (Manchester: Manchester University Press, 1996), p. 69.
119. Bhabha, *the location of culture*, pp. 212–32.
120. Gorra, *After Empire*, p. 122.
121. Rushdie, *Imaginary Homelands*, p. 394
122. Mishra, 'Postcolonial Differend', p. 26
123. Grant, *Salman Rushdie*, p. 74. I am grateful to Grant's observations here on the structuring of the novel.
124. Cundy, *Salman Rushdie*, p. 83.
125. Interview with David Brooks in *Helix*, 19, 1984, p. 56.
126. Catharine Cundy provides a detailed comparison between *The Enigma of Arrival* and *The Satanic Verses*, pp. 68–74. Rushdie's novel clearly also takes off from G. V. Desani's, *All About H. Hatterr* (London: Aldor, 1948), where the main character, named after the Mad Hatter in Lewis Carroll's *Alice in Wonderland*, also jumps through the *looking-glass* of the previous Western usages of the English language.
127. Mishra, 'Postcolonial Differend', p. 16.
128. Gikandi, *Maps of Englishness*, p. 206.
129. Bush, 'Salman Rushdie: An Interview', p. 9.
130. 'An Interview with Blake Morrison', *Granta*, 31, Spring 1990, p. 121.
131. Appignanesi and Maitland, eds, *The Rushdie File*, p. 8.
132. Gikandi, *Maps of Englishness*, p. 223.
133. Gikandi, *Maps of Englishness*, p. 231.
134. Salman Rushdie, *Haroun and the Sea of Stories* (London: Granta, 1990), p. 72. Rushdie is clearly replying directly here to Macaulay's infamous Minutes of Education 1835, where he arrogantly dismissed the value of any of the indigenous literatures of India, in his efforts to colonize the minds and the imaginations of the 'natives' by imposing 'British' literature on their education curriculum. But his words here also interestingly echo those of

Mulk Raj Anand who, in one of his *Conversations in Bloomsbury* (London: Wildwood House, 1981), conversations which took place in the 1920s–1930s, discusses the eclectic range of both the Indian epic and the eighteenth-century tradition of the novel in England as an 'ocean of stor[ies]', p. 140.

CHAPTER 5

1. Hanif Kureishi, *My Beautiful Launderette and The Rainbow Sign* (London: Faber, 1986), p. 38.
2. Robert Young, 'Writing Race: Ethnicity as Otherness', in *On Writing (and) Race in Contemporary Britain*, ed. F. Galvan and M. Bengoechea (Universidad de Alcala: Servicio de Publicaciones, 1999), p. 22.
3. Meera Syal, *The Guardian Weekend*, 6 April 1996, p. 14.
4. Salman Rushdie, *Imaginary Homelands* (London: Granta, 1991), p. 17.
5. Hanif Kureishi, 'Bradford', *Granta*, 20, Winter 1986, pp. 149–69; all further references to this essay will be to 'Bradford'.
6. Sarah Lawson Welsh '(Un)belonging Citizens, Unmapped Territory: Black Immigration and British Identity in the Post-1945 Period', in *Not On Any Map: Essays on Postcoloniality and Cultural Nationalism*, ed. Stuart Murray (Exeter: University of Exeter Press, 1997), p. 47.
7. Suresh Renjen Bald, 'Images of South Asian Migrants in Literature: Differing Perspectives', *new community*, 17, 3, p. 414.
8. Stuart Hall, 'New Ethnicities', in *Race, Culture and Difference*, ed. J. Donald and A. Rattansi (London: Sage, 1992), pp. 252–9.
9. See also Hanif Kureishi, *The Rainbow Sign*, pp. 36–7.
10. 'Bradford', p. 168.
11. For a full discussion of this concept and its revisioning in the context of British culture in the 1990s, see Barbara Korte and Klaus Peter Miller, eds, *Unity in Diversity Revisited?* (Tubingen: Gunter Narr Verlag, 1998). Eliot and Orwell's visions quoted above were of course exclusive ones, not ever embracing the working classes in Britain.
12. 'Bradford', p. 169.
13. Hanif Kureishi, *The Late Show*, BBC2, April 1990.
14. Caryl Phillips, *The European Tribe* (London: Faber, 1987), p. 2.
15. Rushdie, *Imaginary Homelands*, p. 134.
16. Some of Kureishi's more recently published works, such as some of the short stories in *Love in a Blue Time* (London: Faber, 1997), or his recent novel, *Intimacy* (London: Faber, 1998), do not focus explicitly on the Asian experience in Britain. This has at times provoked a good deal of critical controversy. See Bart Moore-Gilbert's forthcoming monograph of Kureishi, to be published by Manchester University Press, which discusses Kureishi as an 'English' writer. This was also a subject of some debate at a recent conference held at the Festival Hall in London on diasporic writing in Britain and the USA, entitled 'Continental Drift'.
17. Hanif Kureishi, *The Buddha of Suburbia* (London: Faber, 1990); all further references are to this edition and are included in the text.

18. I am echoing here, of course, the title of Paul Scott's Raj fiction, *Staying On* (London: Heinemann, 1977).
19. Marcia Palley 'Kureishi like a fox', *Film Comment*, 22, 1986, pp. 50–5, esp. p. 53.
20. Stuart Hall, 'Cultural Identity and Diaspora', in *Identity, Community, Culture, Difference*, ed. J. Rutherford (London: Lawrence & Wishart, 1990), pp. 222–37.
21. The parallels between Kureishi's own background and the composition of this first novel are examined in full in Kenneth Kaleta, *Hanif Kureishi: Post-Colonial Storyteller* (Texas: University of Texas Press, 1998), pp. 1–38.
22. Robert Lee, ed., *Other Britain: Other British* (London: Pluto, 1995), p. 74.
23. Kobena Mercer, *Welcome to the Jungle* (London: Routledge, 1994), p. 2.
24. Rushdie reviews these films in *Imaginary Homelands*, pp. 102–6.
25. Mercer, *Welcome to the Jungle*, pp. 1–7.
26. Hanif Kureishi, *Borderline* (London: Methuen, 1981), p. 43.
27. Paul Gilroy, *There Ain't No Black in the Union Jack* (London: Routledge, 1987).
28. Ravinder Randhawa, *A Wicked Old Woman* (London: Women's Press, 1987), p. 29; all further references are to this edition. Interestingly, Randhawa's point here about colour as the visible signifier of racial difference echoes Sam Selvon's Galahad who, as early as 1956 in *The Lonely Londoners*, had articulated the pressing need to discover an alternative language to resolve his dawning consciousness of the colour problem. As Galahad puts it in *The Lonely Londoners*: 'Colour is you that causing all this, you know. Why the hell you can't be blue, or red or green, if you can't be white. You know is you that cause a lot of misery in the world. Is not me, you know is you! . . . Look at you so black and innocent, and this time so you causing misery all over the world' pp. 88–9.
29. Homi Bhabha, *the location of culture* (London: Routledge, 1994), pp. 38–9.
30. Hall, 'New Ethnicities', pp. 252–9.
31. Stuart Hall, 'Minimal Selves', in *Black British Cultural Studies: A Reader*, ed. Houston Baker, Jr., Mantha Diawara and Ruth Lindeborg (Chicago, IL, and London: University of Chicago Press, 1996), p. 119; see also intro. to this collection for a useful summary of the debates, pp. 1–14.
32. Hall, 'Cultural Identity and Diaspora', p. 222.
33. I am following Martina Michel's argument here in 'Un(der) Cover: Ravinder Randhawa's *A Wicked Old Woman*', *Anglistik und Englischunternicht*, 60, 1997, p. 147; this observation clearly stems from Gayatri Spivak's work on representation as a negotiation between portraying (*Darstellung*) and speaking for (*Vertretung*); see Gayatri Spivak, 'Can the Subaltern Speak', in *In Other Worlds: Essays in Cultural Politics* (London: Routledge, 1988), pp. 271–313.
34. Lee, *Other Britain, Other British*, p. 76.
35. Interestingly, G. V. Desani made a similar observation regarding the role of the writer of mixed race in *All About H. Hatterr* ([Aldor, 1948]; Harmondsworth: Penguin, 1972), p. 31.
36. I am using the term 'black' here as a political label which incorporates Asian 'immigrants' in Britain.

37. Robert Young, *Colonial Desire*: *Hybridity in Theory, Culture and Race* (London: Routledge, 1995), p. 148.
38. Said, *Culture and Imperialism*.
39. Bart Moore-Gilbert provides a detailed discussion of this in his essay, 'Hanif Kureishi's *The Buddha of Suburbia*: Hybridity in Contemporary Cultural Theory and Artistic Practice', *Q/W/E/R/T/Y*, 7, October 1997, pp. 191–207.
40. It is important to recognize, as Amit Chaudhuri has pointed out in 'The Lure of the Hybrid', *TLS*, 3 September 1999, pp. 5–7, that hybridity has a long history in Indian writing in English and the vernacular languages. Hybridity does not only need to be read as a preoccupation of migrant writers living in Western centres.
41. Aamer Hussein, 'Changing Seasons: Post-Colonial or "other" writing in Britain today', *Wasafiri*, 20, 1995, pp. 16–17.
42. Paul Gilroy, *The Black Atlantic: Modernity and Double Consciousness* (London: Verso, 1993).
43. Phil Cohen, *Home Rules: Some Reflections on Racism and Nationalism in Everyday Life* (London: New Ethnicities Unit, 1993), p. 33.
44. Much interesting work is beginning to be published making such comparisons. See: Mark Stein, 'The Black British *Bildungsroman* and the Transformation of Britain: Connectedness across Difference', in *Unity in Diversity Revisited: British Literature and Culture in the 1990s*, ed. Korte and Muller (Tubingen: Narr, 1998), pp. 89–105; Sarah Lawson Welsh, '(Un)belonging Citizens, Unmapped Territory: Black Immigration and British Identity in the Post-1945 Period', in *Not on Any Map: Essays on Postcoloniality and Cultural Nationalism*, pp. 43–65.
45. Lee, *Other Britain: Other British*, p. 75.
46. This observation is cited in Anna Rutherford, ed., *From Commonwealth to Post-Colonial* (Hebden Bridge: Dangaroo, 1992), p. i.
47. This point has been made by several critics, including Ranjana Ash and Aamer Hussein at a conference on the history of Asian writing in Britain held at the University of London, Queen Mary & Westfield College, in 1995. Randhawa's novel was important for its explicit confrontation with issues of Asian British identities. Although, as I have suggested elsewhere in this book, many earlier works provide a genealogy for the development of a continuum of Asian writing in Britain.
48. Mirian Ticktin, 'Contemporary British Asian Women's Writing: Social Movement or Literary Tradition?', *Women: A Cultural Review*, 7, 1, 1996, p. 66.
49. Prafulla Mohanti, *Through Brown Eyes* (Oxford: Oxford University Press, 1985).
50. In fact, the prescriptions/formulae/expectations for such 'ethnic' novels were so 'set' that a male English vicar, the Reverend Toby Forward, caused a scandal in the literary world by managing to pose as an 'Asian' woman writer (Rahila Khan), getting his first novel published by Virago: Rahila Khan, *Down the Road Worlds Away* (London: Virago, 1987). See Lakshmi Holmstrom, 'Travellers Tales', *Bazaar*, 19, 1991, p. 10.
51. Berthold Schoene, 'Herald of Hybridity: The Emancipation of Difference in Hanif Kureishi's *The Buddha of Suburbia*', *International Journal of Cultural Studies*, 1, 1, 1988, pp. 109–28.

52. As Schoene observes, referring to Alan Sinfield's essay 'Diaspora and Hybridity: Queer Identities and the Ethnicity Model', *Textual Practice,* 10, 2, 1996, 'political systems are highly accommodatable of counterdiscursive subversion, which is why "hybridity may or may not disconcert the system" ', p. 118.
53. Comparisons have been made by Paul Gilroy, Kobena Mercer et al to the ways in which the discourse of left-wing critics such as Raymond Williams concerning 'race' and 'ethnicity' can surprisingly be aligned in some ways with the ideological roots of right-wing politicians such as Enoch Powell; see 'Representing Blackness/Representing Britain', in *Black British Cultural Studies*, pp. 1–15.
54. During this period a number of works by Asian women writers were published by The Women's Press and Virago. These included: Rukshana Smith, *Sumitra's Story* (London: Bodley Head, 1982); Sharon-Jeet Shan, *In My Own Name* (London: Women's Press, 1985); Leena Dhingra, *Amritvela* (London; Women's Press, 1988); as well as a number of anthologies such as *Watchers and Seekers*, ed. R. Cobham and Merle Collins (London: Women's Press, 1987). Lauretta Ngcobo describes the meetings of women of this period in *Let It Be Told: Black Women Writers in Britain* (London: Virago, 1987).
55. Norman Stone, 'Sick Scenes from English Life' and 'Through a Lens Darkly', *Sunday Times,* 10 January 1988.
56. Kureishi, *My Beautiful Launderette and The Rainbow Sign*, pp. 25–38.
57. Nahem Yousaf, 'Hanif Kureishi and "the brown man's burden" ', *Critical Survey*, 8, 1, 1996, pp. 14–26.
58. Salman Rushdie, 'Minority Literatures in a Multi-Cultural Society', in *Displaced Persons,* ed. Anna Rutherford and Kirsten Holst Petersen (Mundelstrup: Dangaroo, 1988), p. 41.
59. Suniti Namjoshi, like Kureishi, examines heterosexuality as one of her major themes in many of her works. She differs from Leena Dhingra and Meena Syal in that she writes as a fabulist rather than a realist.
60. Suniti Namjoshi, *The Blue Donkey Fables* (London: Women's Press, 1988), pp. 1–3; her other works include: *Feminist Fables* (London: Women's Press, 1983), *The Conversations of Cow* (London: Women's Press, 1985), *Saint Suniti and the Dragon* (London: Women's Press, 1994), as well as a number of collections of poetry and works for children.
61. Leena Dhingra, 'Breaking Out of the Labels', in *Watchers and Seekers*, ed. R. Cobham and Merle Collins (London: Women's Press, 1987), p. 103.
62. Namjoshi's work is, of course, well known for its exploration of the magical and the fabular through the medium of fable and fairy story.
63. Gayatri Spivak, 'Can the Subaltern Speak', pp. 271–313.
64. bell hooks, *Yearning: Race, Gender and Cultural Politics* (London: Turnaround, 1991), p. 25.
65. George Orwell, *A Collection of Essays* (New York: Doubleday, 1954), p. 192; cited also in Bald, Suresh Renjen, 'Images of South Asian Migrants in Literature: Differing Perspectives', *new community*, 17, 3, 1991, p. 418.
66. Robert Lee uses the term 'post-immigrant' in *Other Britain, Other British* to describe this generation of writers; Schoene in 'Herald of Hybridity' describes Kureishi's work as part of an 'ethno-English' group, p. 111.

67. R. Radhakrishnan, *Diasporic Mediations: Between Home and Location* (Minneapolis, MN: University of Minnesota, 1996).
68. Suresh Renjen Bald, 'Images of South Asian Migrants in Literature', p. 1. See also Stevie Smith, *The Holiday* (London: Chapman Hall, 1949).
69. Immigration Acts designed to keep out Britain's black and Asian population were passed in 1962 (Commonwealth Immigrants Act), 1968 (Kenyan Asians Act), 1971 (Immigration Act), 1981 (British Nationality Act) and 1988 (Immigration Act); for a full account of this history, see Peter Fryer, *Staying Power* (London: Pluto, 1984); also Ron Ramdin, *Reimaging Britain* (London: Pluto, 1999).
70. Kureishi, *The Rainbow Sign*, p. 12.
71. Kureishi, *The Rainbow Sign*, p. 35.
72. Meera Syal, *Anita and Me* (London: Flamingo, 1996), p. 10.
73. Dabydeen has written extensively on this subject both in his critical and his creative works. These include: *Slave Song* (Mundelstrup: Dangaroo, 1984), *Coolie Odyssey* (London: Hansib and Mundelstrup: Dangaroo, 1988), *The Black Presence in English Literature* (Wolverhampton: Manchester University Press, 1983), *Hogarth's Blacks*: *Images of Blacks in Eighteenth Century English Art* (Mundelstrup: Dangaroo, 1985), *Turner* (London: Cape, 1994).
74. David Dabydeen, 'A Voyage Around Myself', *Bazaar,* Summer 1991, p. 9.
75. David Dabydeen, *The Intended* (London: Secker & Warburg, 1991), p. 196.
76. *Disappearance* (London: Secker & Warburg, 1993) is, of course, the title of Dabydeen's next novel, which bears a close relationship intertextually to V. S. Naipaul's *The Enigma of Arrival.*
77. Said, *Culture and Imperialism*, p. 386. See also Moore-Gilbert cited above.
78. John Clement Ball, 'The Semi-Detached Metropolis: Hanif Kureishi's London', *Ariel*, 27, 4, 1996, pp. 21–3.
79. Randhawa has used this terminology both in personal interviews as well as in the novel itself; see p. 41.
80. Unpublished interview with Tobias During, p. 4.
81. Kureishi, *The Rainbow Sign*, p. 35.
82. I am grateful here to Bart Moore-Gilbert, who makes a similar argument in his essay, cited above, concerning Kureishi's role as a spokesman for the 'Asian' community. As Moore-Gilbert suggests, it is worth comparing the 'Author's note' to *Borderline* (1981), p. 4, with Salman Rushdie's articulation of his position in *Imaginary Homelands*, p. 394. Whilst Kureishi and Rushdie often cite each other in their works, they have taken up very different positions on this question.
83. Hanif Kureishi, 'Dirty Washing', *Time Out*, 14–20 November 1985.
84. Mark Stein, 'The Black British *Bildungsroman* and the Transformation of Britain', pp. 90–4.
85. Schoene, 'Herald of Hybridity', pp. 118–19.
86. Schoene, 'Herald of Hybridity', p. 119.
87. Bart Moore-Gilbert argues the case for Kureishi as predominantly an 'English' writer in the article cited above, pp. 196–7.
88. Randhawa has identified with this problem in an unpublished talk delivered to my students at the University of Portsmouth in 1987.

89. Jamel Oubechou, '"The Barbarians and Philistines" in *The Buddha of Suburbia*: Dis/Locating Culture', *Commonwealth: Essays and Studies*, 4, 1997, p. 106.
90. Steven Connor, *The English Novel in History 1950–95* (London: Routledge, 1996), pp. 94–8.
91. Hanif Kureishi, *The Late Show*.
92. Ball, 'The Semi-Detached Metropolis', pp. 9–10.
93. Judie Newman, *The Ballistic Bard: Postcolonial Fictions* (London: Arnold, 1995), p. 11.
94. Connor, *The English Novel in History*, p. 95.
95. As Bart Moore-Gilbert, amongst others, has suggested, it is possible to read Rushdie and Kureishi intertextually, in terms both of explicit cross-referencing and their usage of a mixture of hybrid forms stemming both from popular culture and canonical works. Rushdie is also clearly influenced by Kureishi's exploration of the world of rock music and culture in his recent novel, *The Ground Beneath Her Feet* (London: Cape, 1999).
96. Homi Bhabha, 'The Vernacular Cosmopolitan', in *Voices of the Crossing*, ed. Naseem Khan and Ferdinand Denis (London: Serpent's Tail, 2000), pp. 133–42.
97. Alamgir Hashmi, 'Hanif Kureishi and the Tradition of the Novel', *International Fiction Review*, 19, 1992, pp. 89–90.
98. Bart Moore-Gilbert, p. 201; a similar argument is made in Jamal Obechou's essay cited earlier.
99. Sara Suleri, *The Rhetoric of English India* (Chicago, IL, and London: University of Chicago Press, 1992), pp. 4, 13.
100. Connor, *The English Novel in History*, p. 95.
101. Sam Selvon, 'My Girl and the City', *Ways of Sunlight* (London: MacGibbon and Kee, 1957); the reference here is to the Longman paperback edn, 1985, pp. 181–8.
102. Inderpal Grewal, *Home and Harem: Nation, Gender, Empire and the Culture of Travel* (Colombia, NC: Duke University Press, 1996); pp. 1–10; Grewal is also suggesting here a revisioning of Mary Louise Pratt's notion of 'contact zones' proposed in *Imperial Eyes: Travel Writing and Transculturation* (London: Routledge, 1992).
103. Sharon Montieth, 'On the Streets and in the Tower Blocks: Ravinder Randhawa's *A Wicked Old Woman* (1987) and Livi Michael's *Under a Thin Moon* (1992)', *Critical Survey,* 8, 1, 1996, pp. 33, 91.
104. Montieth, 'On the Streets and in the Tower Blocks', p. 31.
105. Randhawa described the diaspora within Britain in terms of a 'net' in a conference paper delivered at Queen Mary & Westfield College in 1995, the first conference to be held on the Asian Diaspora in Britain.
106. C. L. Innes, 'Wintering: Making a Home in Britain', in *Other Britain, Other British*, pp. 30–1.
107. Innes, 'Wintering: Making a Home in Britain', p. 31.
108. Michel, 'Un(der) Cover', for a fuller discussion of this element of the novel.
109. Patricia Duncker, *Sisters and Strangers: An Introduction to Contemporary Feminist Fiction* (Oxford: Blackwell, 1992), p. 237; I am grateful here to Duncker's observations on the number of texts that are being written within the novel by the various characters.

110. Montieth, 'On the Streets and in the Tower Blocks', p. 32.
111. Michel, 'Un(der) Cover', p. 155.
112. See Schoene above for a full discussion of this.
113. bell hooks, 'Choosing the Margin', in *Yearning: Race, Gender and Cultural Politics* (Boston, MA: South End Press, 1990), p. 148.

CHAPTER 6

1. *The New Testament*, John, 14, verse 2.
2. V. S. Naipaul, *Reading and Writing: A Personal Account* (New York: New York Review of Books, 2000), p. 62.
3. Edward Said, *Culture and Imperialism* (London: Chatto & Windus, 1993), p. 408.
4. Gillian Beer, 'The Island and the Aeroplane', in *Nation and Narration*, ed. Homi Bhabha (London: Routledge, 1990), p. 271.
5. Paul Gilroy, *Between Camps* (London: Allen Lane, 2000).
6. Sunetra Gupta made these points in an unpublished panel presentation during a conference held at Queen Mary & Westfield College, University of London, 1994. This was the first conference on the literatures of the South Asian diaspora in Britain to be held since 'The Eye of the Beholder' conference held at the Commonwealth Institute in 1981. Interestingly, at the later conference writers came from a range of different subcontinental and British backgrounds.
7. Meena Alexander, *Fault Lines* (Boston, MA: South End Press, 1993). In this memoir as Sandra Ponzanesi has argued, Alexander describes her migration to the USA and her writing as a means of making 'up my memory', p. 29. This process enables her to construct 'a space for the ideal form of migrancy: that within the self'; see Sandra Ponzanesi, *Paradoxes of Postcolonial Culture: Feminism and Diaspora in South-Asian and Afro-Italian Women's Narratives* (PhD thesis: University of Utrecht, 2000), p. 74.
8. Demetrio Yocum, 'Some troubled homecomings', in *The Post-Colonial Question*, ed. Iain Chambers and Lidia Curti (London: Routledge, 1996), p. 222.
9. Aamer Hussein, 'Changing Seasons: Other Britains', in *Wasafiri*, No. 20, 1994, pp. 16–19.
10. Amit Chaudhuri in discussion with Aamer Hussein and Susheila Nasta, Inter-University Post-Colonial Seminar, Institute of English Studies, University of London, October, 2000. Chaudhuri has developed this argument in 'Lure of the hybrid: What the post-colonial Indian novel means to the West', in *Times Literary Supplement*, 3 September 1999, pp. 5–6.
11. Romesh Gunesekera, *Reef* (London: Granta, 1994), p. 190; all further references are to this edition.
12. Iain Chambers, *Migrancy, Culture, Identity* (London: Routledge, 1993), p. 5.
13. T. S. Eliot, 'Burnt Norton', *Four Quartets*, in *The Complete Poems and Plays of T. S. Eliot* (London: Faber, 1969), p. 175. The four sections of the poem were first published between 1935 and 1942.

14. Rosemary Marangoly George, *The Politics of Home: Postcolonial Relocations and Twentieth Century Fiction* (Cambridge: Cambridge University Press, 1996), p. 11.
15. Romesh Gunesekera, in *The Bookseller*, 9 January 1998, p. 30.
16. Rocio G. Davis, ' "We are all Artist's Living Our Own Lives": A Conversation with Romesh Gunesekera', in *Miscellanea*, Vol. 18, 1997, p. 45.
17. Gunesekera, 'We are all Artist's Living Our Own Lives', p. 47.
18. Meena Alexander, 'Piecemeal Shelters', in *The Shock Of Arrival: Reflections on Postcolonial Experience* (Boston, MA: South End Press, 1996), p. 3.
19. R. Radhakrishnan, *Diasporic Mediations: Between Home and Location* (Minneapolis, MN: University of Minnesota Press, 1996), p. xv.
20. This phrase refers to Benedict Anderson, *Imagined Communities: Reflections on the Origin and Spread of Nationalism* (London: Verso, 1983).
21. Gillian Beer, 'The Island and the Aeroplane', pp. 269–72. Beer also makes illuminating comparisons between the construction of Shakespeare's famous 'sceptred isle' in *Richard III* and the growth of the national myth of Britain as an impervious 'island'. The historic notion of Britain as 'sceptred isle' is thus 'a fiction'; a mythical construct which has consistently repressed the realities of those other regional and colonial histories situated both within and outside its seabound borders. I am grateful here to the lectures and papers delivered at a conference held at the University of Mauritius in 1998, entitled 'Islands and Continents', in which many of the participants, and particularly Shirley Chew, cited Beer's essay as a way into reading Gunesekera.
22. See James Clifford, 'Diasporas', in *Cultural Anthropology*, 9, 3, 1994, pp. 302–38; also 'Foreword' by Han Suyin to Aamer Hussein, *Mirror to the Sun* (London: Mantra, 1993), p. 2, in which she refers to the modes in which literature as a 'caravan' of 'tales' has always travelled, citing the Tang dynasty of China as an example.
23. Interestingly, as Ganesh Devy notes, 'Chaucer was himself involved in translating the style of Boccacio into English when he created his *Canterbury Tales*'; see Susan Bassnett and Harish Trivedi, eds, *Post-Colonial Translation* (London: Routledge, 1999), p. 182.
24. An extensive discussion of such postcolonial transformations is included in the 'Introduction' to Anuradha Dingwaney Needham, *Using the Master's Tools: Resistance and Literature of the African and South Asian Diasporas* (New York: St Martin's Press – now Palgrave, 2000), pp. 1–23. However, I am also grateful here to Robert Fraser for his perceptive reading of Enoch Powell's 'Rivers of Blood' speech, and the narratology of migration in 'Is There a Gibbon in the House?: Migration, Postnationality, and the Fall and Rise of Europe', an unpublished address to the Open University at a conference entitled The Discourses of Migration held on 22 November 2000. As Fraser argues, Enoch Powell's 'Rivers of Blood' speech, delivered in Birmingham in 1968, is a powerful contemporary example of narrative's potential for reconfiguration being turned unashamedly into a tool for political invective. In addition, Powell's wilful appropriation of Virgil's classical

poem *The Aeneid* as his literary intertext involved deliberate misreadings which had serious political and cultural consequences. Powell's notorious reference in his speech to himself as a 'Roman of old' (inciting in his post-war white audience the memory of an age-old and respectable classical tradition of civility being threatened by *barbaric* forces from outside) and as one 'who sees the river Tiber foaming with much blood' (the violent consequences, we are led to believe, of immigration) bears little relation to the intention of his original source since, as he himself admitted later, he had offered a misreading of Book 6 of *The Aeneid.* For, as Fraser shows, there was in the Latin epic, 'no Roman, no river, and no carnage': instead, one discovers a 'passage in which the Sybil of Cumae, a Greek prophetess, welcomes Aeneas – a Trojan prince – to Italy. Journey on, she exhorts him, settle in Latium and there you will found a great city with the *tribute* [my italics] of your foreign blood'.

25. Said, *Culture and Imperialism*, p. 408. A similar point was, of course, made by Salman Rushdie in his passionate 1990 essay, 'Is Nothing Sacred', *Imaginary Homelands* (London: Granta, 1991), in which he pointed, following the Ayatollah Khomeni's *fatwa* in 1988, to the dangers of the writer's imagination becoming increasingly circumscribed by the dogged pursuit of political 'truths', whatever the colour of their cultural or religious derivation.
26. See Linda Hutcheon, *The Politics of Postmodernism* (London: Routledge, 1989); also Robert Young, *White Mythologies: Writing History and the West* (London: Routledge, 1990); Jean-François Lyotard, *The Postmodern Condition* (Minneapolis, MN: University of Minnesota Press, 1984); Peter Middleton and Tim Woods, eds, *Literatures of Memory*: *History, Time and Space in Postwar Writing* (Manchester: Manchester University Press, 2000).
27. See also David Dabydeen's novel, *Disappearance* (London: Secker & Warburg, 1993).
28. This painting was exhibited in 1840 at the Royal Academy and was greatly admired by Ruskin.
29. David Dabydeen, 'Preface' to *Turner* (London: Cape, 1994), pp. ix–x.
30. *Turner*, p. 33. Also quoted in Gautnam Premnath, 'Remembering Fanon, Decolonizing Diaspora', in *Postcolonial Criticism and Theory*, ed. Benita Parry and Laura Chrisman (Cambridge: Boydell & Brewer, 2000), pp. 57–74. Premnath makes the perceptive observation that Dabydeen's choice of name for the magician figure Manu avoids the easy romanticization of an African past for Manu, and also signifies the 'legendary giver of Brahminical, patriarchal laws in ancient India', p. 70.
31. Meena Alexander uses this as the title for her fictional memoir, *Fault Lines*. For other late twentieth-century diasporic narratives exploring such a strategy, see: Caryl Phillips, *Cambridge* (London: Bloomsbury, 1991), *Crossing the River* (London: Bloomsbury, 1993), *The Nature of Blood* (London: Faber, 1997) and *The Atlantic Sound* (London: Faber, 2000); Bharati Mukherjee, *The Holder of the World* (London: Chatto & Windus, 1993); Moyez Vassanji, *The Book of Secrets* (Toronto: McClelland & Stuart, 1995); Fred D'Aguiar, *Feeding the Ghosts* (London: Chatto & Windus, 1997); Michael Ondaatje, *Anil's Ghost* (London: Bloomsbury, 2000). These writers come from a variety of different cultural and national locations.

32. Bharati Mukherjee, 'The World According to Hsu', in *Darkness* (Harmondsworth: Penguin, 1985), p. 56. This point is elaborated on in an essay by Susan Spearey entitled, 'Spatial Odysseys in Diaspora Writing', in *Shifting Continents, Colliding Cultures*, ed. R. Crane and R. Mohanran (Amsterdam: Rodopi, 2000), pp. 151–69. The notion of 'continental drift' was also used as a title for a recent conference on international diasporic writing from the subcontinent held at the South Bank, Festival Hall, London, in June 1999. Writers who participated included: Sara Suleri (Pakistan and USA), Vikram Chandra (India and USA), Aamer Hussein (Pakistan and Britain), Meera Syal (Britain), Sunetra Gupta (Bengal and Britain).
33. I am grateful for this term to Ato Quayson, in *Postcolonialism, Theory, Practice or Process* (Oxford: Polity, 1999).
34. 'Skies', in *This Other Salt* (London: Saqi, 1999), p. 127. All further references are to this edition. Hussein also read this passage in a non-fictional presentation on the migrant writer at a conference held at the Gothenburg Book Fair in Sweden in 1997.
35. Chambers, *Migrancy, Culture and Identity*, p. 7.
36. Middleton and Woods, *Literatures of Memory,* p. 5.
37. Roger Bromley, *Narratives for a New Belonging*, p. 123. A similar point is made by Peter Middleton and Tim Woods in *Literatures of Memory.*
38. Middleton and Woods, *Literatures of Memory*, p. 5.
39. Chambers, *Migrancy, Culture and Identity*, p. 5.
40. Romesh Gunesekera, *The Sandglass* (London: Granta, 1998); all further references are to this edition and are included in the text.
41. Sunetra Gupta, *The Glassblower's Breath* (London: Orion, 1993); all further references are to this edition.
42. Bromley, *Narratives for a New Belonging*, p. 16.
43. Aamer Hussein, *Mirror to the Sun* (London: Mantra, 1993); all further references are to this edition and are included in the text.
44. One is reminded here, of course, as Demetrio Yocum observes in 'Some Troubled Homecomings', of voyages made by earlier migrants, such as Aimé Césaire in *Cahier D'Un Retour du Pays Natal* or the Jewish poet Paul Celan, whose early excavations into the poetics of migrancy were driven by a similar desire to 'trace the phenomenological capacity of the subject to constitute itself in writing', whilst simultaneously attempting to bring the 'mutilated fragments' of a diasporic past within 'textual boundaries' that may always remain just out of reach (p. 222). Yocum also cites the observations of Martin Heidegger in *Saggi sulla poesia di Holderlin* (Milan: Adelphi, 1981), who argues that there is in poetic writing 'no primary original home', p. 221.
45. Anthony Appiah sets up the idea of 'rooted cosmopolitanism' as a model of reading in his book, *In My Fathers House* (London: Methuen, 1992).
46. This is not to suggest that there has not been a significant shift in emphasis in V. S. Naipaul's later works, such as *A Way in the World* (London: Heinemann, 1994).
47. Hussein has often referred to himself as a writer who is 'ambidextrous'. The idea of 'cultural ambidexterity' is also used by Sen Gupta who reviewed *This Other Salt*, in *Biblio*, July–August, 2000, p. 22.

48. M. Asaduddin, *Book Review*, October 2000, pp. 63–5.
49. Aamer Hussein, 'Mirror to the Sun', in *Mirror to the Sun*, p. 223.
50. Firdous Azim, 'This Other Salt', in *Wasafiri*, No. 30, 1999, p. 63.
51. This is a specific reference to Caryl Phillips's work entitled *Higher Ground* (London: Viking, 1989); it also links Hussein with a group of black writers of the diaspora who were publishing in Britain at this time, namely Joan Riley, one of the editors, along with the New Zealand poet Briar Wood, of *Leave to Stay* (London: Virago, 1996), as well as Merle Collins, Fred D'Aguiar, David Dabydeen.
52. This is a term Hussein himself coins for his narrator in 'Skies', p. 105.
53. Kalpana Chauhan, 'More Sri Lankan Colour in the great English tradition', in *The Asian Age*, 26 February 1998, p. 15, citing Gunesekera who talks of writing as a means of keeping his 'world in balance'.
54. Sunetra Gupta, *Memories of Rain* (London: Orion, 1992).
55. Debjani Ganguly, 'Of Dreams, Digressions and Dislocations: The Surreal Fiction of Sunetra Gupta', in *The Postmodern Indian English Novel,* ed. Viney Kirpal (Bombay: Allied, 1996), pp. 112, 315.
56. Sunetra Gupta, 'Why I Write', in *Into the Nineties: Post-Colonial Women's Writing,* ed. Anna Rutherford (Hebden Bridge: Dangaroo Press, 1994), p. 289.
57. Ali Smith, 'Day in the Life of a Family of Outsiders', in *The Scotsman*, 7 February 1998, p. 12.
58. John Thieme, 'Are We all Migrants', in *Literary Review*, February 1998, p. 24.
59. Chauchan, 'More Sri Lankan Colour in the Great English Tradition', p. 15.
60. Smith, 'Day in the Life of a Family of Outsiders', p. 15.
61. Sunetra Gupta, *Moonlight Into Marzipan* (London: Phoenix, 1995), p. 47.
62. I am grateful to Paula Marchionni for this observation in her unpublished MA thesis 'Writing Home' (presented as part of the MA in Literature, Culture and Modernity at Queen Mary & Westfield College, 1996), p. 20.
63. Alexander, *Faultlines*, p. 29.
64. Ponzanesi, *Paradoxes of Postcolonial Culture: Feminism and Diaspora in South-Asian and Afro-Italian Women's Narratives*, p. 74.
65. Sunetra Gupta, *The Glassblower's Breath* (London: Orion, 1993); all further references are to this edition and are included in the text.
66. I am grateful to Debjani Ganguly for this information.
67. Debjani Ganguly, 'Of Dreams, Digressions and Dislocations: The Surreal Fiction of Sunetra Gupta', p. 320.
68. Monika Fludernik, 'Colonial vs. Cosmopolitan Hybridity', in *Hybridity and Postcolonialism: Twentieth Century Indian Literature*, ed. Monika Fludernik (Tübingen: Zaa Studies, 1998), pp. 280–1.
69. Sunetra Gupta, in 'Strangers and Other Ghosts', in *Into the Nineties*, p. 290.
70. Ganguly, 'Of Dreams, Digressions and Dislocations', p. 321.
71. Ganguly makes this connection on p. 318, for which I am grateful here.
72. Paola Marchionni, *Writing Home,* p. 24. Marchionni is citing a debate that Judie Newman takes up in her book, *The Ballistic Bard: Postcolonial Fictions* (London: Arnold, 1995), pp. 151–3.
73. Gupta pursues a similar literary quest in her subsequent novel, *Moonlight Into Marzipan*, which also dramatizes the difficulties of establishing a singular

narration. In this novel, the focus is on several versions of an attempted (auto)biography of an Indian scientist, Promothesh, which never come to fruition. Interestingly here, Gupta reverses the emphasis given to the male voyeurism in *The Glassblower's Breath* as the scientist is constructed in different ways by his wife, Esha, as well as in the words of his original biographer and lover, Alexandra Vorobyova, who disappears half-way through the narrative. Alexandra's story is then taken up by her abandoned daughter, Anya, who pieces together her own and her mother's life by attempting to complete the task she began so many years before. The story of Promothesh, who attempts to turn 'gold into grass', invokes the Prometheus myth which is rewritten and subverted; similarly the novel's focus on the agency of women in constructing Promothesh's identity suggests, as some have noted, a postcolonial reconstruction of Mary Shelley's *Frankenstein.*

74. Rushdie, *Imaginary Homelands*, p. 429.

EPILOGUE

1. Satendra Nandan, 'Migration, Dispossession, Exile and the Diasporic Consciousness', in *Shifting Continents/Colliding Cultures,* ed. Ralph J. Crane and Radhika Mohanran (Amsterdam: Rodopi, 2000), pp. 35–54. In this essay Nandan cites Amitav Ghosh's famous essay on the diaspora as an 'epic without a text'. See note below.
2. Amitav Ghosh, 'The Diaspora in Indian Culture', *Public Culture*, 2, 1, 1989, pp. 75–7.
3. Work has begun on this in Emmanuel S. Nelson, *Reworlding: The Literature of the Indian Diaspora* (Westport, CT: Greenwood, 1992) and *Writers of the Indian Diaspora* (Westport, CT: Greenwood, 1993). Also see: Crane and Mohanran, *Shifting Continents/Colliding Cultures*; and Anuradha Dingwaney Needham, *Using the Master's Tools: Resistance and the Literature of the African and South Asian Diasporas* (New York: St Martin's Press – now Palgrave, 2000).
4. A wide range of poetry and drama has also of course been published by writers of the South Asian diaspora.
5. avtar brah, *Cartographies of Diaspora* (London: Routledge, 1996), p. 16.
6. Homi Bhabha, *Nation and Narration* (London: Routledge, 1990), p. 45.
7. Homi Bhabha, 'The Vernacular Cosmopolitan', in *Voices of the Crossing*, ed. Naseem Khan and Ferdinand Dennis (London: Serpent's Tail, 2000), pp. 139–41.
8. V. S. Naipaul, *A Way in the World* (London: Heinemann, 1994), pp. 8–9. This passage is also quoted in Satendra Nandan's essay.
9. Even in Farhana Sheikh's novel, *The Red Box* (London: Women's Press, 1991), which has often been set up for comparison with Randhawa's story of female Asian identities in Britain, the subject matter suggests a substantial difference of emphasis.
10. David Dabydeen, 'West Indian Writers in Britain', in *Voices of the Crossing.* In this essay Dabydeen stresses that Naipaul is a 'revered and despised father

figure'; Selvon and Wilson Harris, on the other hand, represent 'the terror of the genius of ancestral voices', pp. 60–2.

11. See Bhabha, 'The Vernacular Cosmopolitan', in which he describes the 'double life of British minorities' in these terms. As 'vernacular cosmopolitans', they translate, he suggests, between cultures, 'renegotiating traditions from a position where "locality" insists on its own terms, while entering into larger national and societal conversations', p. 139.
12. Romesh Gunesekera, *The Sandglass* (London: Granta, 1998), p. 87.
13. Phil Cohen, ed., *new ethnicities, old racisms* (London: Zed Books, 1999).
14. Ghosh, 'The Diaspora in Indian Culture', p. 77.
15. Gunesekera, *The Sandglass*, p. 112.

Select Bibliography

Note: References refer to the first date of publication.

PRIMARY SOURCES

Alexander, M. *Fault Lines*. Boston, MA: South End Press, 1993.

——. *The Shock of Arrival: Reflections on Postcolonial Experience*. Boston, MA: South End Press, 1996.

Ahmad, R. *The Hope Chest*. London: Virago, 1996.

Ahmad, R. and R. Gupta, eds, *Flaming Spirit*. London: Virago, 1994.

Anand, M. R. *Across the Black Waters*. London: Cape, 1940.

——. *Coolie*. London: Lawrence & Wishart, 1936.

——. *Conversations in Bloomsbury*. London: Wildwood House, 1981.

——. *Untouchable*. Harmondsworth: Penguin 1935.

——. *he Bubble*. New Delhi: Arnold-Heinemann, 1984.

Baijnath, L. *England and India: Being Impressions of Persons, Things, English and Indian and Brief Notes of Visits to France, Switzerland, Italy and Ceylon*. Bombay: 1893.

Bennett, L. *Jamaica Labrish*. Kingston: Sangster's, 1966.

Braithwaite, E. R. *To Sir With Love*. London: Bodley Head, 1959.

Chaudhuri, N. *A Passage to England*. London: Macmillan, 1959.

——. *The Autobiography of an Unknown Indian*. London: Macmillan, 1951.

Cobham, R. and M. Collins, eds, *Watchers and Seekers*. London: Women's Press, 1987.

Dabydeen, D. *Slave Song*. Mundelstrup: Dangaroo Press, 1984.

——. *Coolie Odyssey*. London: Hansib, 1988.

——. *The Intended*. London: Secker & Warburg, 1991.

——. *Turner*. London: Cape, 1994.

——. *The Counting House*. Cape, 1996.

——. *Disappearance*. London: Secker & Warburg, 1993.

——. *A Harlot's Progress*. London: Cape, 1999.

D'Aguiar, F. *Feeding the Ghosts*. London: Chatto & Windus, 1997.

Desai, A. *Bye-Bye Blackbird*. Harmondsworth: Penguin, 1965.

——. *Baumgartner's Bombay*. London: Heinemann, 1988.

Desani, G. V. *All About H. Hatterr*. London: Aldor Press, 1948.

Dhingra, L. *Amritvela*. London: Women's Press, 1988.

Dhondy, F. *East End At Your Feet*. London: Macmillan, 1976.

——. *Bombay Duck*. London: Picador, 1991.

——. *Black Swan*. London: Gollancz, 1992.

Dover, C. *Half-Caste*. London: Secker & Warburg, 1937.

Eliot, T. S. *The Complete Poems and Plays of T. S. Eliot*. New York: Harcourt, Brace & Co, 1960.

——. *The Wasteland*. New York: Boni and Liverlight, 1922.
Forster, E. M. *A Passage to India*. London: Arnold, 1924.
——. *Howards End*. London: Arnold, 1910.
Gilroy, B. *In Praise of Love and Children*. Leeds: Peepal Tree, 1996.
——. *Leaves in the Wind: Collected Writings*, ed. J. Amin-Aiddo. London: Margo Publishing, 1998.
Gonne, M. *A Servant of the Queen*. London: Gollancz, 1938.
Grewal, S. J., Kay, L. Landor, G. Lewis, and P. Parmar, eds. *Charting the Journey: Writings by Black and Third World Women*. London: Sheba, 1988.
Gunesekera, R. *Monkfish Moon*. London: Granta, 1992.
——. *Reef*. London: Granta, 1994.
——. *The Sandglass*. London: Granta, 1998.
Gupta, S. *Memories of Rain*. London: Orion, 1992.
——. *The Glassblower's Breath*. London: Orion, 1993.
——. *Moonlight Into Marzipan*. London: Phoenix, 1995.
——. *A Sin of Colour*. Harmondsworth: Penguin, 1999.
Hiro, D. *A Triangular View*. Delhi: Hind, 1973.
Hosain, A. *Phoenix Fled*. London: Chatto & Windus, 1953.
——. *Sunlight on a Broken Column*. London: Chatto & Windus, 1961.
Hussein, A. *Mirror to the Sun*. London: Mantra, 1993.
——. *This Other Salt*. London: Saqi, 1999.
James, C. L. R. *The Black Jacobins*. London: Secker & Warburg, 1938.
——. *Beyond a Boundary*. London: Stanley Paul, 1963.
——. *Spheres of Existence*. London: Allison Busby, 1980.
Karaka, D. F. *The Pulse of Oxford*. London: Dent, 1933.
——. *Oh! You English*. London: Muller, 1935.
——. *I Go West*. London: Joseph, 1938.
——. *All My Yesterdays*. Bombay: Thacker & Co, 1944.
Kureishi, H. *Borderline*. London: Methuen, 1981.
——. *Birds of Passage*. Oxford: Amber Lane, 1983.
——. *Outskirts*. London: Calder, 1983.
——. *My Beautiful Launderette and The Rainbow Sign*. London: Faber, 1986.
——. 'Bradford', *Granta*, 20 (Winter 1986).
——. *Sammy & Rosie Get Laid*. London: Faber, 1988.
——. *The Buddha of Suburbia*. London: Faber, 1990
——. *London Kills Me*. London: Faber, 1991.
——. *The Black Album*. London: Faber 1995.
——. *Love in a Blue Time*. London: Faber, 1997.
——. *My Son the Fanatic*. London: Faber, 1997.
——. *Intimacy*. London: Faber, 1998.
——. *Sleep With Me*. London: Faber, 1999.
——. *Midnight All Day*. London: Faber, 2000.
——. *Gabriel's Gift*. London: Faber, 2001.
Ishiguro, K. *The Remains of the Day*. London: Faber, 1989.
Lamming, G. *In the Castle of my Skin*. London: Joseph, 1953.
——. *The Emigrants*. London: Joseph, 1954.
——. *Of Age and Innocence*. London: Joseph, 1958.
——. *Season of Adventure*. London: Joseph, 1960.

——. *Water With Berries*. London: Longman, 1971.
——. *Natives Of My Person*. London: Longman, 1972.
Malabari, B. *The Indian Eye on English Life; Or, Rambles of a Pilgrim Reformer*. London: Constable, 1893.
Marath, S. M. *The Wound of Spring*. London: Dobson, 1960.
——. *The Sale of an Island*. London: Dobson, 1968.
Markandaya, K. *The Nowhere Man*. London: Allen Lane, 1972.
Menen, A. *The Prevalence of Witches*. London: Chatto & Windus, 1947.
——. *The Backward Bride*. London: Chatto & Windus, 1950.
——. *The Duke of Gallodora*. London: Chatto & Windus, 1952.
——. *The Fig Tree*. London: Chatto & Windus, 1959.
——. *Cities in the Sand*. London: Thames & Hudson, 1972.
——. *Dead Man in the Silver Market: An Autobiographical Essay on National Pride*. London: Chatto & Windus, 1954.
——. *Ramayana*. New York: Scribner's, 1954. as *Rama Retold*. London: Chatto & Windus, 1954.
——. *The Space Within The Heart*. London: Hamilton, 1970.
Mahomed, S. D. *Shampooing, or Benefits Resulting from the use of the Indian Medicated Bath: as introduced into this country by S. D. Mahomed . . . containing a brief but Comprehensive view of the effects produced by the use of the warm bath, in comparison with steam or vapour bathing*. Brighton, 1822, 1826, 1838.
Mohanti, P. *Through Brown Eyes*. Oxford: Oxford University Press, 1985.
Mukharji, T. N. *A Visit to Europe*. Calcutta: Newman, 1899.
Mukherjee, B. *Darkness*. Harmondsworth: Penguin, 1985.
——. *Jasmine*. New York: Weidenfeld, 1989.
——. *The Holder of the World*. London: Chatto & Windus, 1993.
Naidu, S. *The Birds of Time: Songs of Life, Death and the Spring*. With an introduction by Sir E. Gosse. London: Heinemann, 1912.
Naipaul, S. *The Adventures of Gurudeva and Other Tales*. London: Deutsch, 1976.
Naipaul, V. S. *The Mystic Masseur*. London: Deutsch, 1957.
——. *The Suffrage of Elvira*. London: Deutsch, 1958.
——. *Miguel Street*. London: Deutsch, 1959.
——. *A House for Mr Biswas*. London: Deutsch, 1961.
——. *The Middle Passage*. London: Deutsch, 1962.
——. *Mr Stone and the Knights Companion*. London: Deutsch, 1963.
——. *An Area of Darkness*. London: Deutsch, 1964.
——. *A Flag on the Island*. London: Deutsch, 1967.
——. *The Mimic Men*. London: Deutsch, 1967.
——. *In a Free State*. London: Deutsch, 1971.
——. *Guerrillas*. London: Deutsch, 1975.
——. *India: A Wounded Civilisation*. London: Deutsch, 1977.
——. *A Bend in the River*. London: Deutsch, 1979.
——. *The Return of Eva Peron*. London: Deutsch, 1980.
——. *Among the Believers: An Islamic Journey*. London: Deutsch, 1981.
——. *Finding the Centre: Two Narratives*. London: Deutsch, 1984.
——. *The Enigma of Arrival*. Harmondsworth: Penguin, 1987.
——. *A Turn in the South*. London: Penguin, 1989.

——. *India: A Million Mutinies Now*. London: Heinemann, 1990.
——. *A Way in the World*. London: Heinemann, 1994.
——. *Beyond Belief: Islamic Excursions Among the Converted Peoples*. London: Little, Brown, 1998.
——. *Letters Between a Father and Son*. London: Little, Brown, 1999.
——. *Reading and Writing: A Personal Account*. New York: New York Review of Books, 2000.
Namjoshi, S. *Feminist Fables*. London: Women's Press, 1983.
——. *The Conversations of Cow*. London: Women's Press, 1985.
——. *The Blue Donkey Fables*. London: Women's Press, 1988.
——. *Saint Suniti and the Dragon*. London: Virago, 1994.
Ondaatje, M. *Anil's Ghost*. London: Bloomsbury, 2000.
Pandian, T. B. *England to an Indian Eye*. London: Elliot Stock, 1897.
Phillips, C. *The European Tribe*. London: Faber, 1987.
——. *Higher Ground*. London: Viking, 1989.
——. *Cambridge*. London: Bloomsbury, 1991.
——. *Crossing the River*. London: Bloomsbury, 1993.
——. *The Nature of Blood*. London: Faber, 1997.
——. *Extravagant Strangers: A Literature of Belonging*. London: Faber, 1997.
——. *The Atlantic Sound*. London: Faber, 2000.
Randhawa, R. *A Wicked Old Woman*. London: Women's Press, 1987.
——. *HariJan*. London: Women's Press, 1987.
——. *The Coral Strand*. London: House of Stratus, 2001.
Randhawa, R. ed. *Right of Way*. London: Women's Press, 1988.
Rao, R. *Kanthapura*. London: Allen & Unwin, 1938.
——. *The Serpent and the Rope*. London: Murray, 1960.
Rhys, J. *Voyage in the Dark*. London: Constable, 1934.
——. *Wide Sargasso Sea*. London: Deutsch, 1966.
Riley, J. and B. Wood, eds, *Leave to Stay: Stories of Exile and Belonging*. London: Virago, 1996.
Rushdie, S. *Grimus*. London: Gollancz, 1975.
——. *Midnight's Children*. London: Cape, 1981.
——. *Shame*. London: Cape, 1983.
——. *The Jaguar Smile*. London: Pan, 1987.
——. *The Satanic Verses*. London: Viking, 1988.
——. *Haroun and the Sea of Stories*. London: Granta, 1990.
——. *East, West*. London: Cape, 1994.
——. *The Moor's Last Sigh*. London: Cape, 1995.
——. *The Ground Beneath Her Feet*. London: Cape, 1999.
——. *Fury*. London: Cape, 2001.
Salkey, A. *Escape to an Autumn Pavement*. London: Hutchinson, 1960.
——. *Anancy's Score*. London: Bogle L'Overture, 1973.
Salkey, A. *Come Home, Malcolm Heartland*. London: Hutchinson, 1976.
Scott, P. *Staying On*. London: Heinemann, 1977.
Selvon, S. *A Brighter Sun*. London: Wingate, 1952.
——. *An Island is a World*. London: Wingate, 1955.
——. *The Lonely Londoners*. London: Wingate, 1956.
——. *Ways of Sunlight*. London: MacGibbon and Kee, 1957.

——. *Turn Again Tiger*. London: MacGibbon and Kee, 1958.
——. *I Hear Thunder*. London: MacGibbon and Kee, 1963.
——. *The Housing Lark*. London: MacGibbon and Kee, 1965.
——. *The Plains of Caroni*. London: MacGibbon and Kee, 1970.
——. *Those Who Eat the Cascadura*. London: Davies-Poynter, 1972.
——. *Moses Ascending*. London: Davis-Poynter, 1975.
——. *Moses Migrating*. London: Longman, 1983.
——. *El Dorado West One*. Leeds: Peepal Tree Press, 1988.
——. *Highway in the Sun and Other Plays*. Leeds: Peepal Tree Press, 1991.
Shan, S. *In My Own Name*. London: Women's Press, 1985.
Sheikh, F. *The Red Box*. London: Women's Press, 1991.
Shelley, M. *Frankenstein*. London: Lackington Hughes Harding, 1818.
Sidwha, B. *Cracking India*. Minneapolis, MN: Milkweed, 1991.
Smith, S. *The Holiday*. London: Chapman Hall, 1949.
Smith, R. *Sumitra's Story*. London: Bodley Head, 1982.
Srivastava, A. *Transmission*. London: Serpent's Tail, 1992.
——. *Looking for Maya*. London: Quartet, 1999.
Syal, M. *Anita and Me*. London: Flamingo, 1996.
Vassanji, M. *The Book of Secrets*. Toronto: McClelland & Stuart, 1995.
Walcott, D. *Omeros*. London: Faber, 1990.
Woolf, L. *Diaries in Ceylon 1908–1911: Records of a Colonial Administrator and Stories of the East*. London: Hogarth Press, 1963.

SECONDARY SOURCES

Ahmad, A. *In Theory*. London: Verso, 1992.
Aitken G. ed. *V. S. Naipaul: Letters Between a Father and a Son*. London: Little, Brown, 1999.
Allen, R. and H. Trivedi, eds, *Literature and Nation*. Routledge: London, 2000.
Anand, M. R. *Critical Essays on Indian Writing in English*. Bombay: Macmillan, 1972.
——. *The Letters of Mulk Raj Anand*, ed. and intro. by S. Cowasjee. Calcutta: Writers Workshop, 1974.
Anderson, B. *Imagined Communities: Reflections on the Origin and Spread of Nationalism*. London: Verso, 1983.
Appiah A. *In My Fathers House*. London: Methuen, 1992.
Appignanesi, L. and S. Maitland, eds, *The Rushdie File*. London: Fourth Estate, 1989.
Appignanesi, L. ed. *Identity*. London: Institute for Contemporary Arts, Document 6, 1987.
Appleyard, B. *The Pleasures of Peace: Art and Imagination in Post-War Britain*. London: Faber, 1989.
Ashcroft, B., G. Griffiths and H. Tiffin, eds, *The Empire Writes Back*. London: Routledge, 1989.
Bahktin, M. *The Dialogic Imagination*, trans. Caryl Emerson and Michael Holquist. Austin, TX: University of Texas Press, 1981.
Baker, H. A., M. Diawara and R. Lindeborg, eds, *Black British Cultural Studies*. London and Chicago, IL: University of Chicago Press, 1996.

Bassnett, S. and H. Trivedi, eds, *Post-Colonial Translation: Theory and Practice*. London: Routledge, 1999.

Bauman, Z. *Modernity and Ambivalence*. Oxford: Polity, 1991.

Bengoechea, M. and F. Galvan, eds, *On Writing (and) Race in Contemporary Britain*. Universidad de Alcala: Servicio de Publicaciones, 1999.

Bergonzi, B. *The Situation of the Novel*. London: Macmillan, 1970.

Bhabha, H. ed. *Nation and Narration*. London: Routledge, 1990.

——. *the location of culture*. London: Routledge, 1994.

Bharucha, N. A. and V. Sarang, eds, *Indian-English Fiction*. Delhi: B. R. Publishing Corporation, 1994.

Birbalsingh, F. ed. *Indenture and Exile: The Indo-Caribbean Experience*. Toronto: TSAR, 1989.

Boehmer, E. *Colonial and Postcolonial Literature: Migrant Metaphors*. Oxford: Oxford University Press, 1995.

Booth, H. J. and N. Rigby, eds, *Modernism and Empire*. Manchester: Manchester University Press, 2000.

Bradbury, M. and J. McFarlane, *Modernism 1890–1930*. Harmondsworth: Penguin, 1976.

Bradbury, M. ed. *The Novel Today: Contemporary Writers on Modern Fiction*. Manchester: Manchester University Press, 1977.

Bradbury, M. *The Contemporary English Novel*. London: Arnold, 1979.

brah, a. *Cartographies of Diaspora: Contesting Identities*. London: Routledge, 1996.

Brennan, T. *Salman Rushdie and the Third World: Myths of the Nation*. London: Macmillan, 1989.

——. *At Home in the World: Cosmopolitanism Now*. London and Cambridge, MA: Harvard University Press, 1997.

Brinker-Gabler, G. and S. Smith, eds, *Writing New Identities: Gender, Nation and Immigration in Contemporary Europe*. London and Minneapolis, MN: University of Minnesota Press, 1997.

Bromley, R. *Narratives for a New Belonging*. Edinburgh: Edinburgh University Press, 2000.

Butcher, M. ed. *The Eye of the Beholder: Indian Writing in English*. London: Commonwealth Institute, 1983.

Burton, A. *At the Heart of Empire: Indians and the Colonial Encounter in Late Victorian Britain*. Berkeley, CA: University of California Press, 1998.

Carew, J. *Fulcrums of Change*. New Jersey: Africa World Press, 1988.

Chambers, I. and L. Curti, eds, *Post-Colonial Question: Common Skies, Divided Horizons*. London: Routledge, 1995.

Chambers, I. *Migrancy, Culture, Identity*. London: Routledge, 1993.

Chambers, R. *Room for Maneuver: Reading (the) Oppositional (in) Literature*. London and Chicago, IL: University of Chicago Press, 1991.

Chan, M. and R. Harris, eds, *Asian Voices in English*. Hong Kong: Hong Kong University Press, 1991.

Cheyette, B. and L. Marcus, eds, *Modernity, Culture and the 'Jew'*. Stanford, CA: Stanford University Press, 1998.

Chew, S. and A. Stead, eds, *Translating Life: Studies in Transpositional Aesthetics*. Liverpool: Liverpool University Press, 1999.

Chow, R. *Writing Diaspora*. Bloomington, IN: Indiana University Press, 1993.
Chrisman, L. and B. Parry, eds, *Postcolonial Criticism and Theory*. Cambridge: Boydell & Brewer, 2000.
Cohen, P. *Home Rules: Some Reflections on Racism and Nationalism in Everyday Life*. London: New Ethnicities Unit, 1993.
Cohen, P. ed. *new ethnicities, old racisms*. London: Zed Books, 1999.
Cohen, R. *Frontiers of Identity: The British and the Others*. London: Longman, 1994.
——. *Global Diasporas: An Introduction*. Seattle, WA: University of Washington Press, 1997.
Colley, L. *Britons: Forging the Nation 1700–1837*. New Haven, CT: Yale University Press, 1992.
Collings, R. ed. *Reflections of a Statesman: The Writings and Speeches of Enoch Powell*. London: Bellew Publishing, 1991.
Connor, S. *The English Novel in History 1950–95*. London: Routledge, 1996.
Crane, R. J. *Inventing India: A History of India in English-Language Fiction*. Basingstoke: Macmillan – now Palgrave, 1992.
Crane, R. and R. Mohanran, eds, *Shifting Continents/Colliding Cultures*. Amsterdam: Rodopi, 2000.
Cronin, R. *Imagining India*. Basingstoke: Macmillan – now Palgrave, 1989.
Cudjoe, S. *V. S. Naipaul*. Amherst, MA: University of Massachusetts, 1988.
Cundy, C. *Salman Rushdie*. Manchester: Manchester University Press, 1996.
Dabydeen, D. *The Black Presence in English Literature*. Wolverhampton: Manchester University Press, 1983.
——. *Hogarth's Blacks: Images of Blacks in Eighteenth Century English Art*. Mundelstrup: Dangaroo Press, 1985.
Dabydeen, D. and N. Wilson-Tagoe, eds, *A Reader's Guide to West Indian and Black British Literature*. London: Hansib, 1988.
Davies, C. B. *Black Women, Writing and Identity: Migrations of the Subject*. London: Routledge, 1994.
Dennis, F. and N. Khan, eds, *Voices of the Crossing: The Impact on Britain of Writers From Asia, the Caribbean and Africa*. London: Serpent's Tail, 2000.
Dhawan, R. K. ed. *Indian Women Novelists*. Set III, Vol. 2. New Delhi: Prestige Books, 1995.
Dijk, T. A. van, *Racism and the Press*. London: Routledge, 1991.
Donald, J. and A. Rattansi, eds, *'Race', Culture and Difference*. London: Sage, 1992.
Dover, C. *Feathers in the Arrow: An Approach for Coloured Writers and Readers*. Bombay: Padma Publications, 1947.
Doyle, B. *English and Englishness*. London: Routledge, 1989.
Duncker, P. *Sisters and Strangers: An Introduction to Contemporary Feminist Fiction*. Oxford: Blackwells, 1992.
Eagleton, T. *Ideology*. London: Verso, 1991.
——. *Exiles and Emigres: Studies in Modern Literature*. London: Chatto & Windus, 1970.
Edwards, P. and D. Dabydeen, eds, *Black Writers in Britain 1760–1890*. Edinburgh: Edinburgh University Press, 1991.
Elias, M. *Aubrey Menen*. Madras: Macmillan, 1985.

Fanon, F. *Black Skin, White Masks*. New York: Grove, 1967.
Firth, K. and F. Hand, eds, *India: Fifty Years After Independence*. Leeds: Peepal Tree Press, 2001
Fisher, M. H. ed. *The Travels of Dean Mahomet: An Eighteenth Century Journey Through India*. [First published Cork, 1794]. Berkeley, CA: University of California Press, 1997.
Fisher, M. H. ed. *The First India Author in English: Dean Mahomed (1759–1857) in India, Ireland, and England*. New Delhi: Oxford University Press, 1996.
Fletcher, M. D. ed. *Reading Rushdie: Perspectives on the Fiction of Salman Rushdie*. Amsterdam: Rodopi, 1994.
Fludernik, M. ed. *Hybridity and Postcolonialism: Twentieth Century Indian Literature*. Tubingen: ZAA Studies, 1998.
Fraser, R. *Lifting the Sentence: The Poetics of Postcolonial Fiction*. Manchester: Manchester University Press, 2000.
Fryer, P. *Staying Power: The History of Black People in Britain*. London: Pluto, 1984.
Gasiorek, A. *Post-War British Fiction: Realism and After*. London: Arnold, 1995.
George, R. M. *The Politics of Home: Postcolonial Relocations and Twentieth-Century Fiction*. Cambridge: Cambridge University Press, 1996.
Gervais, D. *Literary Englands: Versions of 'Englishness' in Modern Writing*. Cambridge: Cambridge University Press, 1993.
Gerzina, G. *Black England: Life Before Emancipation*. London: Murray, 1995.
Gikandi, S. *Maps of Englishness: Writing Identity in the Culture of Colonialism*. New York: Columbia University Press, 1996.
——. *Writing in Limbo: Modernism and Caribbean Literature*. New York: Cornell University Press, 1992.
Gilroy, P. *Small Acts*. London: Serpent's Tail, 1993.
——. *The Black Atlantic: Modernity and Double Consciousness*. London: Verso, 1993.
——. *There Ain't No Black in the Union Jack*. London: Routledge, 1987.
——. *Between Camps: Race Identity and Nationalism at the End of the Colour Line*. London: Allen Lane, 2000.
Glissant, E. *Caribbean Discourse: Selected Essays*. Charlottesville, VA: University Press of Virginia, 1989.
Gloversmith, F. ed. *The Theory of Reading*. Brighton: Harvester, 1984.
Goonetilleke, D. C. R. A. *Salman Rushdie*. Basingstoke: Macmillan – now Palgrave, 1998.
Gorra, M. *After Empire: Scott, Naipaul, Rushdie*. London and Chicago, IL: University of Chicago Press, 1997.
Grant, D. *Salman Rushdie*. Plymouth: Northcote House, 1999.
Grewal, I. *Home and Harem: Nation, Gender, Empire and the Culture of Travel*. Colombia, NC: Duke University Press, 1996.
Gupta, S. *V. S. Naipaul*. Plymouth: Northcote House, 1999.
Guptara, P. *Black British Literature: An Annotated Bibliography*. Mundelstrup: Dangaroo Press, 1986.
Gurr, A. *Writers in Exile: The Identity of Home in Modern Literature*. Brighton: Harvester, 1981.
Hall, S. and P. du Gay, eds, *Questions of Cultural Identity*. London: Sage, 1996.

Hall, S., D. Held, and T. McGrew, eds, *Modernity and Its Futures*. Cambridge: Polity Press/Open University, 1992.
Hamner, R. D. ed. *Critical Perspectives on V. S. Naipaul*. London: Heinemann, 1976.
Harris, W. *Tradition, the Writer and Society*. London: New Beacon, 1967.
——. *The Womb of Space: The Cross-Cultural Imagination*. Westport, CT: Greenwood, 1983.
Heaney, S. *Preoccupations: Selected Prose, 1968–78*. London: Faber, 1980.
Hearne, J. ed. *Carifesta Forum*. Kingston: Institute of Jamaica, 1976.
Hinds, D. *Journey to an Illusion: The Study of West Indian in Britain*. London: Heinemann, 1966.
Hiro, D. *Black British, White British*. Harmondsworth: Penguin, 1973.
Holst Petersen, K. and A. Rutherford, eds, *Displaced Persons*. Mundelstrup: Dangaroo Press, 1988.
hooks, b. *Yearning: Race, Gender and Cultural Politics*. Boston, CT: South End Press, 1990.
Hutcheon, L. *The Politics of Postmodernism*. London: Routledge, 1989.
Iyengar, K. R. S. *Indian Writing in English*. London and Bombay: Asia Publishing, 1962.
James, L. *Caribbean Literature in English*. London: Longman, 1999.
Jussawalla, F. ed. *Conversations With V. S. Naipaul*. Jackson, MS: University of Mississippi, 1997.
Kabbani, R. *Europe's Myths of Orient*. London: Macmillan, 1986.
Kain, G. *Ideas of Home: Literature of Asian Migration*. Michigan, MI: Michigan State University Press, 1997.
Kaleta, K. *Hanif Kureishi: Postcolonial Storyteller*. Austin, TX: University of Texas Press, 1998.
Kaminsky, A. K. *After Exile: Writing the Latin American Diaspora*. Minneapolis, MN: University of Minnesota Press, 1991.
Kanneh. K. *African Identities*. London: Routledge, 1998.
King, A. D. ed. *Culture, Globalization and the World-System*. Basingstoke: Macmillan – now Palgrave, 1991.
King, B. *V. S. Naipaul*. Basingstoke: Macmillan – now Palgrave, 1993.
King, B. ed. *West Indian Literature*. London: Macmillan, 1979.
King, B. ed. *New National and Post-Colonial Literatures*. Oxford: Clarendon, 1996.
King, R. Connell, R. and P. White, eds, *Writing Across Worlds: Literature and Migration*. London: Routledge, 1995.
King, R. S. Sandhu, J. Walvin, J. Girdham, *Ignatius Sancho*. London: National Portrait Gallery, 1997.
Kitaj, R. B. *First Diasporist Manifesto*. London: Thames & Hudson, 1989.
Kirpal, V. *The Third World Novel of Expatriation*. New Delhi: Sterling, 1989.
Kirpal, V. ed. *The Postmodern Indian English Novel*. New Delhi: Allied Publishers, 1996.
Korte, B. and K. P. Muller, eds, *Unity in Diversity Revisited?: British Literature and Culture in the 1990s*. Tubingen: Narr, 1998.
Lamming, G. *The Pleasures of Exile*. London: Joseph, 1960.
Lee, A. R. ed. *Other Britain: Other British*. London: Pluto, 1995.

Lodge, D. *The Novelist at the Crossroads: And Other Essays on Fiction and Criticism*. London: Routledge, 1971.
Looker, M. *Atlantic Passages: History, Community and Language in the Fiction of Sam Selvon*. New York: Peter Lang, 1996.
Lowenthal, D. *West Indian Societies*. Oxford: Oxford University Press, 1972.
Lyotard, J. *The Postmodern Condition*. Manchester: Manchester University Press, 1984.
Majeed, J. *Ungoverned Imaginings: James Mill's The History of British India and Orientalism*. Oxford: Clarendon, 1992.
Mariana, P. ed. *Critical Fictions: The Politics of Imaginative Writing*. Seattle, WA: Bay Press, 1991.
McLeod, J. *Beginning Postcolonialism*. Manchester: Manchester University Press, 2000.
Mercer, K. *Welcome to the Jungle: New Positions in Black Cultural Studies*. London: Routledge, 1994.
Meyers, J. *Fiction and the Colonial Experience*. Ipswich: Boydell Press, 1973.
Mezu, S. O. ed. *Modern Black Literature*. New York: Black Academy Press, 1971.
Middleton, P. and T. Woods, eds, *Literatures of Memory: History, Time and Space in Postwar Writing*. Manchester: Manchester University Press, 2000.
Mirza, H. S. ed. *Black British Feminism*. London: Routledge, 1997.
Moore-Gilbert, B. *Postcolonial Theory: Contexts, Practices, Politics*. London: Verso, 1997.
Moore-Gilbert, B. *Hanif Kureishi*. Manchester: Manchester University Press, 2001.
Morey, P. *Fictions of India: Narrative and Power*. Edinburgh: Edinburgh University Press, 2000.
Morley, D. and K.-H. Chen, eds, *Stuart Hall Critical Dialogues in Cultural Studies*. London: Routledge, 1996.
Morrison, T. *Playing in the Dark: Whiteness and the Literary Imagination*. London and Massachusetts: Harvard University Press, 1992.
Mukherjee, M. *The Twice Born Fiction: Themes and Techniques of the Indian Novel in English*. London and New Delhi: Heinemann, 1971.
Murray, S. ed. *Not On Any Map: Essays on Postcoloniality and Cultural Nationalism*. Exeter: University of Exeter Press, 1997.
Mustafa, F. *V. S. Naipaul*. Cambridge: Cambridge University Press, 1995.
Naipaul, V. S. *The Overcrowded Barracoon*. London: Deutsch, 1972.
Nabar, V. and N. Bharucha, eds. *Postcolonial Perspectives on the Raj and Its Literature*. Bombay: Bombay University Press, 1994.
Nandy, A. *The Intimate Enemy: Loss and Recovery of Self Under Colonialism*. Delhi and Oxford: Oxford University Press, 1983.
Nasta, S. ed. *Critical Perspectives on Sam Selvon*. Washington: Three Continents Press, 1988.
Nasta, S. and A. Rutherford, eds, *Tiger's Triumph: Celebrating Sam Selvon*. Hebden Bridge: Dangaroo Press, 1995.
Nasta, S. ed. *Reading the 'New' Literatures in a Postcolonial Era*. Cambridge: Brewer, 2000.
Needham, A. D. *Using the Master's Tools: Resistance and Literature of the African and South Asian Diasporas*. New York: St Martin's Press – now Palgrave, 2000.

Nelson, E. S. ed. *Writers of the Indian Diaspora: A Bio-bibliographical Critical Sourcebook*. Westport, CT: Greenwood, 1993.

Nelson, E. S. ed. *Reworlding: The Literature of the Indian Diaspora*. Westport, CT: Greenwood, 1992.

Newman, J. *The Ballistic Bard: Postcolonial Fictions*. London: Arnold, 1995.

Ngcobo, L. *Let It Be Told: Essays by Black Women Writers in Britain*. London: Pluto, 1987.

Niven, A. *The Yoke of Pity: A Study in the Fictional Writings of Mulk Raj Anand*. New Delhi: Arnold-Heinemann, 1978.

Niven, A. ed. *The Commonwealth Writer Overseas: Themes of Exile and Expatriation*. Brussels: Didier, 1976.

Nixon, R. *London Calling: V. S. Naipaul, Postcolonial Mandarin*. Oxford: Oxford University Press, 1992.

Orwell, G. *A Collection of Essays*. New York: Doubleday, 1954.

Phillips, M. and T. Phillips, *Windrush: The Irresistible Rise of Multi-Racial Britain*. London: Harper Collins, 1998.

Ponzanesi, S. *Paradoxes of Postcolonial Culture: Feminism and Diaspora in South-Asian and Afro-Italian Women's Narratives*. PhD thesis: University of Utrecht, 2000.

Porter, R. *London: A Social History*. London: Hamilton, 1994.

Pratt, M. L. *Studies in Imperial Eyes: Travel Writing and Transculturation*. London: Routledge, 1992.

Procter, J. ed. *Writing Black Britain*. Manchester: Manchester University Press, 2000.

Quayson, A. *Postcolonialism, Theory, Practice or Process?* Oxford: Polity, 1999.

Radhakrishnan, R. *Diasporic Mediations: Between Home and Location*. London and Minneapolis, MN: University of Minnesota, 1996.

Ragussis, M. *Figures of Conversion: 'The Jewish Question' and English National Identity*. London: Duke University Press, 1995.

Ramanujan, M. *G. V. Desani: Writer and Worldview*. London and New Delhi: Arnold-Heinemann,1984.

Ramchand, K. and S. Nasta, eds, *Foreday Morning: Selected Prose 1946–86*. London: Longman, 1989.

Ramdin, R. *Reimaging Britain: 500 Years of Black and Asian History*. London: Pluto, 1999.

Reder, M. ed. *Conversations with Salman Rushdie*. Jackson, MS: University of Mississippi, 2000.

Robertson, G. et al, eds, *Travellers' Tales: Narratives of Home and Displacement*. London: Routledge, 1994.

Rose, J. *States of Fantasy*. Oxford: Clarendon, 1996.

Rushdie, S. *Imaginary Homelands: Essays and Criticism, 1981–1991*. London: Granta, 1991.

Russell, P. and K. Singh, eds, *A Note on All About H. Hatterr and Hali*. London and Amsterdam: Karel Szeben, 1952.

Rutherford, A. ed. *From Commonwealth to Post-Colonial*. Mundelstrup: Dangaroo Press, 1992.

Rutherford, A., L. Jensen and S. Chew, eds, *Into the Nineties: Post-Colonial Women's Writing*. Hebden Bridge: Dangaroo Press, 1994.

Rutherford, J. ed. *Identity, Community, Culture, Difference*. London: Lawrence & Wishart, 1990.

Said, E. *Orientalism*. New York: Pantheon, 1978.

——. *After the Last Sky: Palestinian Lives*. London: Faber, 1986.

——. *Culture and Imperialism*. London: Chatto & Windus, 1993.

Samuel, R. ed. *Patriotism: The Making and Unmaking of British National Identity. Vol. 1: History and Politics*. London: Routledge, 1989.

Sayers, D. *Unpopular Opinions*. London: Gollancz, 1946.

Scafe, S. *Teaching Black Literature*. London: Virago, 1989.

Segal, R. *The Black Diaspora*. London: Faber, 1995.

Sinfield, A. ed. *Society and Literature, 1945–70*. London: Methuen, 1983.

Slemon. S. and H. Tiffin, eds, *After Europe*. Mundelstrup: Dangaroo Press, 1989.

Spinkler; M. ed. *Edward Said: A Critical Reader*. Oxford: Blackwell, 1992.

Spivak, G. *In Other Worlds: Essays in Cultural Politics*. London: Routledge, 1987.

——. *A Critique of Postcolonial Reason: Toward a History of the Vanishing Present*. London and Cambridge, MA: Harvard University Press, 1999.

Suleri, S. *The Rhetoric of English India*. London and Chicago, IL: University of Chicago Press, 1992.

Tajfel, H. and J. L. Dawson, eds, *Disappointed Guests: Essays by African, Asian and West Indian Students*. London: Oxford University Press, 1965.

Thieme, J. *The Web of Tradition: Uses of Allusion in V. S. Naipaul's Fiction*. London: Hansib, 1987.

Tindall, G. *Countries of the Mind: The Meaning of Place to Writers*. London: Hogarth, 1991.

Tinker, H. *A New System of Slavery*. London: Oxford University Press, 1974.

Trivedi, H. and M. Mukherjee, eds, *Interrogating Post-Colonialism: Theory, Text and Context*. Shimla: Institute of Advanced Study, 1996.

Vidler, A. *The Architectural Uncanny: Essays in the Modern Unhomely*. Cambridge, MA: Massachusetts University Press, 1992.

Viswanathan, G. *Masks of Conquest: Literary Study and British Rule in India*. London: Faber, 1990.

Visram, R. *Ayahs, Lascars and Princes*. London: Pluto, 1986.

——. *Asians in Britain: Four Hundred Years of History*. London: Pluto (forthcoming).

Walder, D. *Post-Colonial Literatures in English*. Oxford: Blackwell, 1998.

Walmsley, A. *The Caribbean Artists Movement 1966–1972*. London: New Beacon, 1992.

Walvin, J. *Passage to Britain*. Harmondsworth: Pelican, 1984.

Wambu, O. ed. *Empire Windrush*. London: Gollancz, 1998.

Weiss, T. F. *On the Margins: The Art of Exile in V. S. Naipaul*. Amherst, MA: University of Massachusetts, 1992.

Wisker, G. ed. *Black Womens Writing*. Basingstoke: Macmillan – now Palgrave, 1993.

White, L. *V. S. Naipaul: A Critical Introduction*. London: Macmillan, 1975.

Williams, R. *The Long Revolution*. London: Chatto & Windus, 1961.

Williams, R. introduced and ed. by T. Pinkney, *The Politics of Modernism: Against the New Conformists*. London: Verso, 1989.

Woodhall, W. *Transfigurations of the Mahgreb: Feminism, Decolonization and Literature*. Minneapolis, MN: University of Minnesota Press, 1996.

Wyke, C. *Sam Selvon's Dialectical Style and Fictional Strategy*. Vancouver: University of British Columbia Press, 1991.

Young, R. *Colonial Desire: Hybridity in Theory, Culture and Race*. London: Routledge, 1995.

——. *White Mythologies: Writing History and the West*. London: Routledge, 1990.

Zerbanoo, G. *The Golden Thread: Asian Experiences of Post-Raj Britain*. London: Pandora, 1990.

Index